HERB GUNDELL'S
COMPLETE GUIDE TO
ROCKY MOUNTAIN GARDENING

HERB GUNDELL'S
COMPLETE GUIDE TO
ROCKY MOUNTAIN GARDENING

TAYLOR PUBLISHING COMPANY
DALLAS, TEXAS

Library of Congress Cataloging in publication Data

Gundell, Herb.
    Herb Gundell's Complete guide to Rocky Mountain gardening.

Includes index.
    1. Gardening — Rocky Mountains Region. I. Title.
II. Title: Complete guide to Rocky Mountain gardening.
SB453.2.R63G85   1984   635.9'0978   84-14054
ISBN 0-87833-781-4

Printed in the United States of America

10 9 8 7 6 5 4 3 2 1

To my dear wife
NAOMI
who helped me in many ways
and typed every page of this book.

ACKNOWLEDGEMENT

No matter how much knowledge a person acquires, it is never enough; hardly a day passes when I don't learn something new and helpful. I am greatly indebted to Dr. Jack Butler, Professor and Turf Grass Extension specialist at Colorado State University, Fort Collins, for his counsel and advice in Chapter Three.

TABLE OF CONTENTS

PREFACE

As a gardener I am reminded on a daily basis of the incredible order and precision in Nature. I witness the worker bee, nearly blind, finding its way to the blossoms and returning to the hive with its tiny cargo of sweetness, so many times over. I am puzzled by the female aphid, which produces her brood of young — every 10 to 14 days throughout the summer — without a male aphid nearby. Or, perhaps most humbling, I stand in awe before a large cottonwood, which may move as much as 500 gallons of water per day from the soil, transporting it to the very outer reaches of its branches with a pressure system no more powerful than that of a Kleenex. All my life I have studied plants and the biological sciences with great enthusiasm and wonder, and as a result of that study, I am now convinced that the infinite complexity and interrelatedness in the plant kingdom is not purely the result of evolution: It has most certainly made me believe in God, participate in Nature and become a gardener.

Most likely, my deep interest in gardening has its roots in the rich memories I have carried with me over the years. I grew up in the long shadows of the Alps, and I remember well my family's summer vacations in the higher altitudes when I was startled by the beauty of the mountain flora. I loved the gentians and wild rhododendrons, and I can still visualize the huge astilbe plants along rushing creeks. Oddly enough, I never saw an Edelweiss on these outings, except pressed and displayed in a shop or perhaps carefully orchestrated on a rock climber's hat. I also recollect when my dad bought some fragrant violets and I was envious because I could never find them growing wild. Somewhere in these experiences I must have developed an urge to participate in Nature and become a gardener.

My first garden was in partial shade — the best unused spot in a half-acre wooded lot near the Switzerland of my childhood. My earliest success crops were radishes, sweet peas, and strawberries (at the age of six it need not matter that they were a bit unrelated). Every child has his or her own great moments and mine happens to be the first small plate of homegrown strawberries from this first garden. The sweet peas that graced this plot of soil were colorful and fragrant, but the radishes all went to tops, likely as a result of mediocre soils. That is why I have had such good luck all these years with the poor soils of the Rockies. I learned with handicaps. (Most of the soils in the Rocky Mountain foothills and Great Basin regions are so poor that we *have* to be organic gardeners to succeed. I most certainly believe in generous use of organic materials to improve our garden soils. But I am also ready to use chemistry to achieve my garden goals. Some arguments have been voiced against the use of chemical pesticides. Some are believable; others are not. But until mechanical or other safer ways are found to control insects, weeds, and diseases we have to use the safest products that are now available.)

The United States Army brought me to Colorado in 1942. I had been selected to be a member of America's Ski Troops on the recommendation of the National Ski Patrol. My initial impression of the Rocky Mountains was of their awe-inspiring beauty. And although the tall peaks were not as close together as the Alps, they were every bit as magnificent to my eyes. I trained at Camp Hale, Colorado, not far from Leadville, where I became a United States citizen in 1943. This is where I met my wife, Naomi, who has shared in my enthusiasm for gardening all these years.

I have enjoyed gardening in the Rockies for many reasons. Perhaps the unexpected occurs frequently enough to cause excitement for an old hand like me. A 16-ounce tomato silences even the most cynical critic for a few days. And the complaints about too many gooseberries to nip or cherries to pit are long forgotten when the pies come steaming out of the oven with a fragrance that can soften bricks and stones. There is the brilliance of the sun and the cool of the shade, the orange colors at sunrise and sunset. I like to mow my own lawn — to me it is no drudgery at all. I guess I like the scent of the freshly cut bluegrass? Yes, after all these years as a professional horticulturist I still get a great sensation from the first colorful rose in the garden and I can say without hesitation that fresh raspberries on ice cream are just worth it all — the scratches, the bugs, and some disappointments. I have learned not to count on the unexpected, rather to enjoy it when it happens along.

It has been my great privilege and challenge for 35 years to make gardening interesting and adventurous to thousands through the media of radio, television, and the press. Naomi's and my garden of 20 years has become a quiet place to relax, to regain a level of sanity, to pull a few weeds or trim a branch that doesn't quite belong. My hope is that this book will provide you with the good, solid information that will assist you in experiencing the sense of peace and satisfaction with the world that only gardening can bring.

Herb Gundell
January 1985

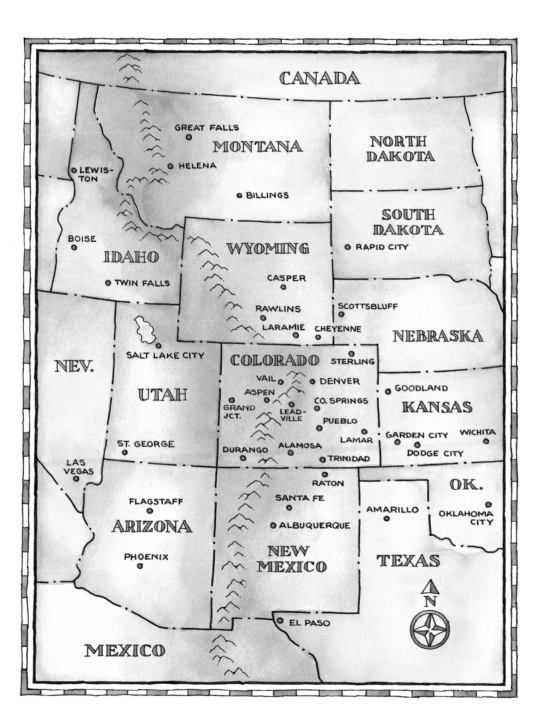

GETTING STARTED IN THE ROCKY MOUNTAINS

CHANCES are you have gardened in other places before or you have just recently moved here. If so, it is imperative to keep in mind that this area is not comparable to Michigan, Iowa, or Arkansas, to the Eastern Seaboard, or the West Coast. Our environment is very different from the nearby states of Kansas and Nebraska. Nor is it in any way similar to most of Texas and Oklahoma. What you may have learned elsewhere can be useful, certainly, but techniques will have to be modified before you try to apply them here. Methods of gardening in this moderate Western region are a strange mixture of gardening practices at best. (Mysticism and luck, at worst.) Mostly, you will have to use what I call "common-sense gardening." We cannot depend very much on the weather, on the seasons or on the soils of the Rocky Mountain territory, so don't let any weather changes take you by surprise. All have to be treated with savvy and a measure of suspicion.

In this chapter, you will be introduced to the phenomenon of unpredictable weather and varying climates and growing seasons that Rocky Mountain gardeners have learned to cope with. You will learn how to improve the poor-quality soil that is common throughout the region. And because water is one of the most precious resources in the region, the best ways and how often to water what you plant will also be carefully explained.

Natives will insist that gardening in the Rocky Mountain region, in spite of its complicated nature, is an unusual and rewarding challenge. If you are a newcomer or rank beginner, welcome. If you are a seasoned veteran, sit for a spell before we move on to more particular matters.

> **Rocky Mountain Tip:**
>
> If you don't like today's weather, just wait and it will change. A shift in the jet stream is all it takes. Be prepared for the worst, but be happy when it does not happen.

ROCKY MOUNTAIN CLIMATES

We have many different climates in the Rocky Mountain West. We have deserts, sub-alpine localities, foothills on both sides of the peaks and inhabited places that are nearly two miles above sea level. We have plateaus such as the High Plains and the Intermountain region that stretch all the way to the Cascades. We also have canyons along major streams, and we have a few sheltered areas warm enough to be called "banana belts." Each of these provides a different challenge for gardeners.

Desert Areas

The true desert areas in our region are mostly in New Mexico, Utah, and Arizona. Certain areas in Idaho also have a desert-like character. These usually are very dry and hot and have poor, alkaline soil. Occasionally, however, the rains come and then the desert areas unfold their full spectacle of short-lived flowers. Winds are also common in the deserts. But you can achieve a lot with a garden in one of these areas . . . if you have enough water.

Yucca

The High Plains and Great Basin (Intermountain)

In many ways, gardening in the High Plains and Great Basin resembles desert gardening. The soils are a little better, but still quite alkaline in reaction. Winters, however, are much meaner here, and the blizzards are very cold. Spring arrives later as you move further north, and fall may happen quite suddenly, with a snowstorm or a hard freeze in September.

The Foothills

The Foothills (Wyoming, Colorado, New Mexico, Eastern Montana, and Utah) have better soil quality, but growing seasons are much shorter than in the High Plains or the Great Basin. Late freezes are a hazard, but careful container gardening is the best way to succeed.

The Canyons

In the canyons, you often can find quite favorable gardening conditions, but you may have to

Question: Summer sun can warm us up to 100 degrees or more. What plants can take this heat?
Answer: Not many, really, without some partial shade. Roses in bloom simply burn up in a day. Marigolds, zinnias, goldenrod, rudbeckia and moss rose handle the heat well.

Question: Winds are often high in the desert plains. How can one protect against them?
Answer: Choose plants that have lacy foliage. The wind does blow through the leaves easily. Thornless Honeylocust is a good example. Low-growing shrubs are less subject to wind than taller ones.

contend with flooding streams in a big snow-melt year. Most of the canyon soils have been washed in by floods and are some of the best in the entire Rocky Mountain region. They are well-drained and nearly neutral in pH (reaction). Canyons often are sheltered from high winds. In the Grand Junction area, Chinooks can warm up higher mesas quite early. But when colder nights follow these warmups, fruit crops can be devastated in a few hours.

The Banana Belts

The so-called "banana belts" of the Rocky Mountains are a few exceptional spots that are much warmer than nearby areas, because of their sheltered locations. St. George, sheltered by mountains in southern Utah, is one of the areas. Grand Junction in western Colorado is another such location. And Lewiston, in northern Idaho, certainly qualifies. These towns usually are near a large lake or river which modifies and moderates the climate enough so that plants can be grown which might otherwise be too tender.

The High Elevations

The Rockies' highest elevations have such short growing seasons that only the native trees and shrubs and a few temperature-tolerant perennials survive. So gardening here can be very difficult — but not impossible. Plastic, tent-like structures for protection from the cold may allow tomatoes to produce and mature up to 10,000 feet elevation. For the most part, however, only the cabbage family, peas, spinach, radishes, and leaf lettuce can contribute to

Question: At elevations of 8,500 to 10,000 feet, freezing night temperatures can happen suddenly. What vegetables and flowers can survive?
Answer: Cabbage, cauliflower, Brussels sprouts, peas, radishes, carrots, beets, turnips, spinach, leaf lettuce, snapdragons and petunias.

Petunias

FOUR WAYS TO PROTECT PLANTS FROM INJURY
Plants must harden for winter to avoid unexpected injuries.

Avoid reflected heat for sensitive evergreens.

Discontinue watering in October but water before hard freezes in late November and again during mid-winter warmups.

Mulch with compost, bark, or leaves to minimize soil temperature changes and to conserve soil moisture.

Shelter cold-sensitive plants from winter winds and the hot daytime sun.

the family table from a high-elevation garden. A few flowers such as petunias also can be grown in large pots and planters, transported inside during nights when the weather suddenly turns adverse.

Weather and Growing Seasons

You can't outguess the weather in the Rockies even if you have the experience of an old-timer and a stack of almanacs. Temperature averages, granted, can be a helpful form of guidance; but they really are only means of extremes. And in the Rockies the extremes of cold and hot temperatures can be *quite* extreme.

Denver, the Eastern Front Range (those cities located east of the foothills), Salt Lake City and Billings have several climatic factors in common. But the lengths of their growing seasons can vary significantly, and this has a distorting effect on whatever their similarities. Denver, for instance, has an average growing season of 171 days. Salt Lake City's growing season, meanwhile, averages 192 days. But to the north in Billings, growing seasons average only 133 days.

These figures, like the temperature averages, can serve as rough guides, but they are no guarantees. In the Rockies, even a few miles can make a big difference. For example, in Castle Rock, Colorado, 30 miles south of Denver, the average growing season drops off to 131 days. In Pueblo, a city at the south end of Colorado's Front Range, the growing season typically lasts 174 days. But again, just 30 miles away, Colorado Springs averages only 138 days.

The growing season you can expect in any given year is certainly unpredictable. However, when you cast your bet each year, you are much better off if you bank only on the shorter of the reported yearly figures. You will then know, at least, what you are gambling with on your prized exotics.

The amount of rainfall also differs from the Colorado Front Range area to Salt Lake City to Billings, but this really does not matter. You have to water regularly in most of the region, unless you choose to maintain only a dryland flora (e.g., cactus, yucca, Pinyon pine). But keep in mind that there aren't many things that will survive in this area without some form of irrigation.

The High Plains area is windy, very cold in winter and hot in the summer. The High Plains area, virtually unshielded by mountains or bodies of water or forests, extends wide open to the north into Canada, clear to the Arctic Circle. Not surprisingly, the prevailing winds are from the north, and they can be quite a bear in winter. And the Chinooks come out of the mountains to unduly warm the area on occasion. (Salt Lake City, in contrast, is a little more protected — by the Great Salt Lake and by the mountains to the city's north.) Consequently in windy Wyoming and elsewhere in the High Plains, temperature averages often fluctuate widely.

> **Rocky Mountain Tip:**
> Wind is an ever-present factor in Wyoming and much of the whole region. We cannot prevent it, so we have to learn to live with it. Low-growing plants are less affected by wind than tall plants and trees and are strongly recommended in these areas.

The growing seasons average 133 and 141 days respectively in Casper and Cheyenne, two High Plains cities, but Cheyenne's average is taken from a varying range of 95 to 181 days, quite a large difference. A 95-day growing season isn't much at all for a gardener. Scottsbluff, in the Nebraska Panhandle, averages 138 days of growing season — but this is a mean of 100 to 169 days. Meanwhile, Lamar, in eastern Colorado, has about the same growing season average as Pueblo — 167 days.

In the foothills areas and mountain communities on both sides of the Rockies, the average length of the growing season is no less diverse. Gardeners who

Question: How valuable is snow moisture compared to rain? Are they about the same?
Answer: Because our humidity is often very low and our winds are high in the Rocky Mountain and Great West Basin areas, we usually retain only a fraction of snowfall moisture for benefit to the soil. Snow moisture usually is less than 50 percent efficient — sometimes much less.

Question: What kind of weather is the most difficult for many plants to survive?
Answer: A very rapid change in temperature is very tough on plants. A 60-degree afternoon followed by a whiff of snow and a minus 3-degree reading the next morning will kill many plants and make others suffer.

live and ski in Aspen, Vail, and Eagle can count on no more than 70 to 80 days. Dillon, Frisco, and Breckenridge average only around 30 days each year that are continuously frost-free. By comparison, Cripple Creek and the Utah mountain resorts — Park City, Snowbird, and Alta — can count on about 100 balmy days. Laramie, Wyoming, near the Medicine Bow range, averages only about 40 days of dependable weather each year, while Trinidad and Raton, on either side of Raton Pass, average 167 and 146 days respectively of dependable growing weather.

The Rocky Mountain West has a few other special places that deserve comment. Leadville is Colorado's two-mile-high town which has an average growing season of about 80 days. I have judged flower shows in Leadville where lilac, iris, and roses were on display at the same time. Durango in Southwestern Colorado averages a respectable growing season of 121 days. Yet Silverton, only a short excursion away by narrow-gauge railway, can count on only 44 days. Alamosa in the St. Louis Valley has 100 days of frost-free season, but Santa Fe, a little more than 100 miles to the south, has 178 good growing days — and they are warm enough to grow chili peppers. Two other cities of the Great Basin Region, Twin Falls and Reno, average around 155 days of dependable weather.

ROCKY MOUNTAIN SOIL

The soil in the Rocky Mountain region contains a variety of minerals, in amounts ranging from mere traces to adequate quantities for gardening. Most of these minerals are important, because they relate to soil quality. Mineral matter, in fact, makes up most of our soils. It consists primarily of weathered rock — rock broken down by freezing or thawing or by movement in a stream — that has been washed in by floods or actually was there to begin with. Limestone, or calcium, is another part of our soils. Where it is inadequate, we must add lime to the soils. But Western soils usually have more than plentiful amounts of limestone.

Organic matter, or humus, is another very important part of soil content. Humus contains the micro-organisms that carry on the breakdown of plant or animal refuse in our soils. Unfortunately, Western soils are very low in organic matter. So you must add some to your vegetable gardens or flowerbeds on an annual basis to get the results you expect.

Certain gases in the soil are also vital. Oxygen

and carbon dioxide are the major ones. Plants obtain more than 80 percent of their oxygen through their roots. Through their leaves, meanwhile, they assimilate only a minor amount of oxygen but most of their carbon dioxide. The carbon is needed for plant energy production. Air pollution has a benefit — it provides the carbon.

Acidity vs. Alkalinity

Soil reaction, also referred to as pH, is a technical measurement of the level of soil acidity, neutrality, or alkalinity. It is expressed in a logarithmic figure that ranges from 1.0 to 13.99. Actually, the extremes of the scale never occur. A level of 7.0 is accepted as the neutral point. Above that level is an alkaline or basic reaction, and below it is acid. In a practical sense, 9.0 is considered so heavily alkaline that most plants could not grow in that soil. When you add water to a soil at 9.0, all you get is a brine solution. On the acid side, some soils in the United States are close to 4.5, which is considered extremely acid.

Soils in the Rocky Mountains and the West are in relatively low rainfall areas, so they generally are alkaline due to salt accumulation. I know of only a few locations in this region where the soils are neutral (7.0) or acid. One of the penalties of alkaline soil is the poor availability of nutrient elements. So in our region we must feed plants a lot more, since the soils have little to contribute on their own.

Fortunately, there are some ways to reduce soil alkalinity. One way is by adding organic matter to the soil. As the humus is decomposed by microbes in

> **Rocky Mountain Tip:**
>
> Sulfur and organic matter are the two best materials to reduce alkalinity (soil pH) of your garden soil. Well-aged organic wastes are helpful.

the soil, better drainage is created, and this helps dispose of excess salts during watering. This reduces the pH appreciably. Another way to reduce soil pH is to add sulfur. Sulfur is an element that deflocculates soils (loosens them) and reduces pH with each application. With either method, however, do not expect dramatic reductions in the alkalinity level. Since the pH scale involves logarithmic figures, a seemingly small reduction actually is quite an achievement.

A good soil test done by an agricultural college or university can reveal your soil's pH, if it is unknown. If one of your neighbors already has such information, it should apply to your soil, as well. And once you know what level you have started with, and what level you have changed the soil to, you don't have to repeat the test, because it changes very little over the years.

Most soil tests done by Agricultural Stations are no longer free. Around $10 is now the basic charge. (You can buy a lot of organic matter or bagged fertilizer for the price of a test.) Before you take soil to be tested, however, get instructions from your University Extension Agent on how to prepare the sample properly. Otherwise, your soil test could mean very little.

Physical Properties of Soils

The term "texture of soil" is important to gardeners. It refers to a soil's makeup and proportions of sand, loam, clay, and silt. Most Western soils are very sandy or heavy in clay. Loamy soils generally are found only in or near stream beds where they were washed in by floods.

Structure of the soil, meanwhile, refers to its columnar building block makeup (like a brick wall) or its tendency to aggregate. Cohesion is the soil property that holds the particles together. Porosity is the percentage of air spaces in a soil, and this is important for moisture penetration. Absorption relates to how well and how much water the soil can hold. And tilth (crumbliness or looseness) is a nice way to describe the condition of the soil relative to plant growth.

A good garden soil has good tilth, and it has good texture. Three less important soil properties are weight, color and temperature.

I have known many good gardeners who think a good, rich soil must be dark in color. This is incorrect. I have seen dark soils that were highly unproductive, and I have observed light-colored soils that had good tilth and texture.

Rocky Mountain Tip:

Moisture drainage depends on tilth and soil structure. Soils with good structure drain excess moisture easily. Poorly structured soils often have a hard pan that stops moisture percolation.

Organic Matter

Organic matter, or humus, is the living portion of a soil. In areas of high rainfall, the soils teem with microbes, and there is a constant decay of vegetative wastes, leaves, and other plant parts. In our Western region, rainfall is scarce. As a result, natural vegetation is sparse, and decomposition of the organic matter takes years.

Virgin soils in the High Plains and Great Basin areas have less than half a percent of organic matter in the topsoil layer (to about eight inches deep). In many places, I would be hard pressed to find any surface soil that remotely could be called topsoil. So we have to add enough organic material every year in vegetable and flower beds to raise the percentage to about four to five percent.

This is not easy, nor is it inexpensive. Perhaps the most economical and practical way to produce humus material for a garden is composting, which is explained below.

Compost (decayed organic matter) is one of numerous organic materials in general that can be used in gardening. Others include: poultry waste; sheep, steer, and dairy manure; horse manure; cottonseed meal; guano; leafmold; and wood by-products.

Question: In the past I have rototilled manure into our 90'x20' garden. Because of the presence of salts, I have not used any manure for three years. What do you suggest?
Answer: In spite of salts, some organic matter needs to be added to gardens every year. You can use peat moss if you like, but it is expensive. It contains no alkaline salts. I would add some ammonium sulfate when rototilling organic matter in the fall season.

Composting

Composting can produce the finest organic material for your garden. The technique can be accomplished with a compost pile, or with a pit or special manufactured bins. The compost pit is the best answer in this region. Only in a pit can we control moisture as we should. Without moisture, nothing happens.

An excavated compost pit suitable for the average gardener's needs should be about three feet by four feet, and three feet deep. When filled to the rim with organic wastes (grass clippings, weeds, excess plant materials, faded flower prunings from perennials or vegetables, manure, peat moss), such a pit produces about 1⅓ cubic yards of compost. The more finely ground the wastes are, the easier they pack into the pit and the faster they break down. If nothing else is available to reduce the size of waste (such as, for example, corn stalks) use a rotary lawn mower and place it over a pile of garden residue. It will grind it to a smaller size.

Question: I want to make some compost of grass clippings and leaves. What do I add to aid decay?
Answer: You need two ingredients to accelerate decay, water and nitrogen. Both are needed to obtain increase of the micro-flora. Water every two to three weeks. Add ammonium sulfate or nitrate at one pound for every six bushels of residue for composting.

Now make a layer of plant or vegetable waste about six inches deep in the pit. Over this, place an inch of any manure and an inch of garden soil or excavation from the pit. Now broadcast several handfuls of ammonium sulfate or nitrate over the soil and water thoroughly. Repeat this process until the pit is full. A pit built in November should be fully decomposed by late March. The weather in the Rockies is very dry during fall and winter, so be prepared to replenish moisture several times during the winter. The use of compost bacteria available commercially from several suppliers is optional; however, the added nitrogen fertilizers from the ammonium sulfate or nitrate are usually sufficient to get the microbes going.

SOIL PREPARATION

In our region, soil preparation is the most important factor in gardening. Without good soil preparation, you may have difficulty producing anything more than a healthy crop of weeds. It matters not what you want to plant. To succeed, you must take the time to prepare the soil.

The first step is to remove debris and other undesirable inert materials, such as rocks. Don't just collect them at the edge of your lot or garden. Haul what you don't want to a sanitary landfill. And you may have to dig up the root systems of unwanted shrubs, trees, and evergreens. Just cutting these plants off at the soil level leaves a root that could sprout again or turn into a slowly decaying mass that may invite troublesome Fairy Ring fungi, which could cause other problems.

Now add compost or other organic material. Most Western soils need two cubic yards or more of organic material for each 1,000 square feet. (If you

DEPTH: HOW IT AFFECTS PLANT GROWTH

Soil acts as a reservoir to hold moisture and nutrients. To a large degree, your plants' success depends on the depth of their soil. Most ornamental trees do best with a minimum of two to four feet of good loam topsoil. Shrubs will need one to three feet of prepared top soil, depending on the size of the plant. Vines, ground covers and perennial flowers will need at least 12 inches of good, prepared soil. Turf grasses require 4 to 6 inches of topsoil or prepared seed bed.

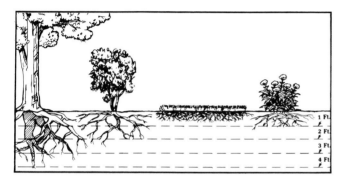

Each plant in your landscape or garden needs prepared soil so it can grow vigorously and establish readily.

can afford twice as much, your soil will be nearly twice as good.) Spread the organic material evenly over the soil and turn it under with a spade, a spading fork, or a rototiller. Leave the tilled soil uneven and, if necessary, with clods, and begin to water. In about three weeks, your soil will have settled enough for you to commence planting or establishing a new lawn. Even for ground covers which grow in virtually any difficult soil, the above preparation is recommended.

Vegetable and flowerbed soils need this preparatory treatment every year. It is best to prepare them in late fall or early winter, so they will be mellow and rich by spring.

Soil Nutrients

Nutrient elements are divided into three categories: major elements; minor elements; and trace elements. Major elements are nitrogen (N), phosphorus (P), and potassium (K). Minor elements that have a direct influence on plants include

Rocky Mountain Tip:

Good soil tests will tell a lot about your soil if they are performed by a soil testing laboratory at your state university. Watch for the readings on pH (soil reaction) and the soluble salts.

calcium (Ca), magnesium (Mg), sulfur (S), iron (Fe), and sodium (Na). Additionally, there are many trace elements in naturally occurring chemical forms. They are called trace elements because only minute amounts of them are ever used by plants. The most important trace elements are copper (Cu), zinc (Zn), manganese (Mn), and boron (B). You should at least know how the major elements perform in your garden.

Nitrogen is a very important nutrient element. It produces the solid green color of the foliage in most garden plants. It is water soluble and probably not available very long in the upper six inches of soil or lawn after two irrigations, unless it has been especially treated for timed release. Nitrogen produces the succulence we desire in such vegetables as lettuce, spinach, and radishes. Excesses of nitrogen may occur only if the nutrient is grossly over-applied or spilled. Excesses may delay maturity of fruits, lowering fruit production and decreasing disease resistance. Most lawns, however, flourish with a little excess nitrogen.

> **Rocky Mountain Tip:**
> A severe shortage of nitrogen causes a light green foliage color and stunted growth. A smaller deficiency may retard new growth. Water-soluble nitrogen is easily applied.

Ammonium sulfate and nitrate are among the least expensive forms of nitrogen you can buy. Other organic nitrogen forms have been devised to control their release and allow them to become available over a longer time period. In much of the West, where we must irrigate frequently, these organic forms of nitrogen are most cost-effective.

Phosphorus is used by plants in much smaller amounts than nitrogen. But phosphorus has a very important influence on root growth and development. It also aids in balancing out excess nitrogen. And it encourages seed formation as well as flowering and fruiting. Phosphorus even hastens maturity, which is particularly important in colder climates where the growing season is short. Phosphorus also helps transplants establish more quickly and respond with new root growth. In short, it is a very helpful nutrient in landscaping and gardening.

The effects of potassium, the third major

Rocky Mountain Tip:

Two important minor elements, sulfur and iron, relate to soil health and quality, plus a plant's lack of green color. Iron must be replenished frequently in Western soils.

nutrient element, are not quite so clear or noticeable. Potassium, however, increases plant vigor and helps the plant's metabolism by translocating sugars. Potassium also increases the yield of potatoes and helps promote tuber formation on dahlias and cannas. It is somewhat interchangeable with sodium, but in alkaline soils, sodium sometimes forms salts that interfere with normal water intake by roots.

Among the minor nutrient elements, sulfur and iron are the most important. Sulfur is removed from the soil by plants and trees at a rate of about two pounds per 1,000 square feet annually. Adding sulfur to the soil lowers its pH somewhat with each application. And sulfur also helps loosen the surface soil and allows moisture to penetrate a little easier. Some sulfur is replaced naturally each year by rainfall, but this replenishment is far less than what is actually used. An application of two to three pounds of sulfur annually for each 1,000 square feet of garden area can have appreciable benefits. Sulfur also has a sanitizing effect on garden soil: It neutralizes disease spores and bacteria.

Iron is more critical to Western soils than to the soils of any other area of the United States. Because our soils mostly have medium to high alkalinity, all the iron in them is in a totally insoluble form. This water-insoluble iron is just like iron filings from a machine shop — worthless. To be available to plants as a nutrient, iron must be in the ferrous form, such as ferrous iron sulfate and ferrous ammonium sulfate. When we apply iron in these forms it is only useful to plants for a few days — until its form changes from ferrous to ferric iron.

In recent years, however, the chemical industry has provided us with a new form of iron known as chelates. These iron chelates act in slow-release fashion and may be available for up to 60 days. But iron chelates also are expensive. Lack of iron, however, causes chlorosis, a yellowing of the green of leaves between veins. In severe cases, chlorosis causes browning. Some lawn and garden fertilizers sold in the Rocky Mountain West now contain added

WAYS FERTILIZERS ARE SOLD

Fertilizers are offered in a variety of ways for many garden uses. Each offers advantages and practical uses. An almost endless selection of analyses is available. There is a fertilizer for most any plant you may want to grow in your garden.

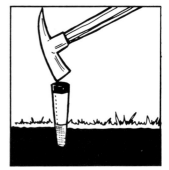

Bag
Least expensive. Easy to distribute with a spreader over large areas like a lawn. Depending on nutrients it can provide quick or timed release. Available with special additives (insecticides, weed killers, and fungicides).

Water Soluble (Crystal or Liquid)
Quickly available for use by plants, as it is highly soluble. Generally used for indoor plants and outdoor or patio containers.

Spikes
Balanced plant foods are placed in locations around dripline of garden plants. Available for trees, shrubs, fruit trees, and roses.

Cartridges
Allow application with water fertilizer solution. Useful on slopes where surface watering runs off. Do not insert too deeply . . . 8 to 12 inches is recommended.

Encapsulated
Time-release fertilizers. Good for flowers and houseplants. Used with container plants. Generally safe even in hot or cool weather.

iron; some even have it as chelates. Those are the ones you want to use.

Another element, calcium (Ca), is widely available in our Western soils. In fact, I expect no shortages in the next 100 years. Alkaline soils are caused either by too much calcium or sodium (Na). Extreme salt accumulation in low drainage areas may result in a white alkali deposit at the soil surface. The deposit is caused by calcium salts forming or surfacing in a low area. In certain soils of the West, such as in the San Luis Valley of Colorado, you may find a

> **Rocky Mountain Tip:**
>
> Soils in the Rocky Mountain and Great Basin regions do not remain improved very long. They must be prepared every year to yield beautiful flowers and bountiful crops.

black alkali condition caused by excess sodium salt accumulation. Fortunately, this condition is rare.

It is unlikely that any soil conditions will turn up where magnesium (Mg) is in short supply. If so, Epsom salts are the accepted standby remedy.

I have seen a few isolated instances where manganese (Mn), zinc (Zn), or boron (B) deficiencies were blamed for crop symptoms. I have not observed this in a garden situation. Copper (Cu), if it is ever needed, is contained in some lawn and garden fungicides.

Some recent products that stimulate rooting of transplants or cuttings contain a synthetic hormone called indolebutyric acid or Vitamin B1. I use the indolebutyric acid products every time I plant or transplant. It is hard to say what part of success is based on it, however. But anything that reduces transplanting shock is a worthwhile product to use in our region.

Plants such as blueberries, azaleas, and rhododendrons prefer an acid soil and usually fail in alkaline soils unless we make special provisions for them. In a small planting area, we can modify our soils by using large quantities of very acid peat moss from Canada or the Great Lakes area. I have successfully grown rhododendrons in full shade for twelve years. The plants don't become huge, but they bloom almost every year. I keep adding peat moss over the roots every fall.

> **Rocky Mountain Tip:**
>
> If anyone tries to sell you topsoil, don't believe it. No one in the West can afford to sell their best soils. I have found a lot of excavations of dark-colored soil sold as topsoil. Buyer beware.

Chlorosis: The Garden's Caution Signal

As we often discover in the garden, chlorosis is a disease condition of a plant caused by a reduction in the amount of its chlorophyll or green color. This

Chlorosis on shrub rose

results in the paling of a plant's normal green color to light green, yellow and, in some instances, even white or brown at the edges or margins of leaves. In any case, chlorosis is an alarming situation. Its cause must be assessed, so you can obtain correction or enough improvement that the plant regains its attractiveness and contributes color and beauty to a garden. There are, of course, certain variegated plants that have leaf margins or speckles that range from light green to nearly white. These variegations could be genetic in character, and some of these plants are highly prized for this different appearance. But even variegations could become diseased because of soil conditions such as alkalinity and extremely heavy clay.

Chlorosis can be caused by a variety of conditions. Some are related to soil, some to nutrients or a lack of them; some are linked to excess water and others to virus attacks or severe winter weather. I will describe some of these and outline ways by which you can obtain correction or change. In rare instances, the only corrective measure is to remove the plant from the garden and replace it with one of greater tolerance.

Lack of iron available to a plant is one of the most frequent causes of chlorosis. And "available" is the key word. Iron may be abundantly present within the root zone of a given plant. But the plant cannot retrieve much of it unless a chemical means can be found to change the iron from its ferric sulfate form to ferrous sulfate. Ferrous sulfate is the only chemical state where inorganic iron is water-soluble. And plants can only absorb chemicals in water solution.

Let me assume that you apply ferrous iron sulfate or copperas, as it is sometimes called, to a plant in dry or liquid form. The chlorotic plant will enjoy this benefit only for a few days — until the soil chemistry, which is alkaline in the West, brings about a change from ferrous to ferric. As soon as this happens, the iron you applied joins all the other iron molecules in the soil since the beginning of time and becomes unavailable to plants, seemingly forever.

Chemical science, however, has provided us with a better way in recent years. Chelated iron is released slowly and therefore remains available, that is, water soluble, much longer, usually six weeks or more. The advantage is obvious. Now the corrective benefit can really influence the diseased plant's condition and help return normal new growth and healthful appearance. Chelated iron is sold under several names. It is most often Sequestrene 330 Fe. If you read the labels carefully on liquid iron products, you will find some that contain Sequestrene or chelated iron instead of ferrous iron sulfate. The cost of chelates is higher but worth the benefits to be derived.

Chlorosis also can be caused by a severe lack of nitrogen, but this is far less common. I have seen lawns in very heavy clay soils that were so short of nitrogen that the grass yellowed noticeably. This was easily corrected by using a high-nitrogen fertilizer. The green color was restored in about five to eight days.

The diseased chlorotic condition could also be caused by deficiencies of one or more minor and trace elements. Magnesium sometimes is partially blamed. If you have a chlorosis condition, and you already have tried supplemental iron and nitrogen without success, you could give Epsom salts or magnesium sulfate a try. In some instances, aluminum sulfate in small quantities will give you a correction.

Excess chemicals also can cause chlorosis in sensitive plants. High calcium or sodium could be responsible. One sign of high calcium is white alkali spots in rural fields. This sometimes occurs, too, in gardens, in soils below a reservoir or lake, and especially in exposed soil galleries where land cuts were made by a developer to correct the grade for home construction. Excess sodium is rare, but not uncommon on the western slope of the Rockies and in some high mountain valleys. Excess calcium can be corrected by applying commercial sulfur. Excess sodium can be corrected only by using gypsum (calcium sulfate.)

Improper soil reaction or pH can cause chlorosis. Some soils in the Western region have a reaction as high as pH 8.5 to 8.8. According to scientists, hardly any desirable plant can tolerate such excessively alkaline conditions. Plants that normally are acid-loving have difficulty surviving under such stress. That is why I cannot recommend blueberries, azaleas and rhododendrons very strongly in our region. Most soils are just too alkaline for these plants. But you could prepare an area of acid soil for such plants to get good results for several years. Even certain trees that prefer acid soils in a pH range of 5.0 to 6.5 have a tough time in our region. I have seen pin oaks that constantly have yellow foliage and stunted growth, because the soil reaction is too high for them.

In our very heavy clay soils, we also experience compaction, and that often causes plant damage and chlorosis. The lack of air in a plant's root zone can create an anemic appearance that closely resembles chlorosis. Aeration is the best answer, but chemical surfactants applied to the soil often partially correct the problem.

Excessive waterlogging in a heavy soil likewise can create a condition that resembles chlorosis. The remedies are more careful watering and aeration to improve the drainage. Under severe conditions, agricultural drainage tile may need to be installed. In isolated spots, sod removal or plant removal followed by soil conditioning is recommended.

Chemical spray damage and virus disease also can cause chlorosis. Once spraying damage has occurred, no remedial action can be taken. Just try to avoid a similar situation. And virus controls still are too rudimentary to be counted on by the gardener.

Finally, severe winter damage also can cause yellowing of surviving stems and foliage of such hardy plants as tea roses, climbing roses, clematis and euonymus. The affected stems and foliage usually die as the heat of summer prevails. When new growth emerges and develops a normal color, however, the old stalks can be pruned away to eliminate unsightly portions.

Where soils are alkaline, heavy with clay and poorly drained, you should not set out plants that normally require an organically fertile and acid soil. If your heart is set on trying certain plants anyhow, you must prepare the soil adequately with lots of peat moss.

Ferrous iron sulfate, ferrous ammonium sulfate and chelated iron usually are the best controls for iron chlorosis. Chelated iron is more expensive, but it lasts longer in the soil.

Iron filings from machine shops are worthless in the garden. They will solve no iron-shortage problems.

How Water Is Absorbed By Plants

WATERING

You should understand one important relationship between soil and moisture. Western gardeners generally classify soil water into three technical groupings, according to how it affects plants.

The uppermost portion of the total water supply, usually above the soil saturation level, is called gravitational water. It either runs off at the surface or percolates through the soil and eventually reaches the water table. This water rarely benefits plants. Rather, it is easy come, easy go. Much of the water from thundershowers we get in the summer is lost to gravitation. Field capacity is the term agronomists apply to soils that are saturated with water. Gravitational water is in excess of field capacity.

The next grouping of soil moisture is called capillary moisture. This is the only moisture plants actually can utilize through their roots. Capillary moisture can move about in a soil freely, sideways and up or down, within limitations of three or four feet. In Western soils the natural capillarity is less than 15 percent. So we have to add organic material or humus to the soil to increase capillary retention. The bottom point of capillary water availability is called the wilting point. Below the wilting point, no water can be utilized by plants.

The third grouping of water, which exists below the wilting point, is called hygroscopic moisture. It causes soil to look wet and feel wet, but plants cannot realize any of it. It is too tightly held by the soil particles. The very low pressure that plants can apply to the soil through their roots can only help them

Rocky Mountain Tip:

A rain gauge can tell you how much precipitation you have obtained. If it pours, the moisture may run off before it penetrates your soil and lawn areas. Western clay soils absorb only ½ inch per hour.

GRAVITATIONAL WATER (RUN-OFF)

Gravitational Water
(Run-off)

Field Capacity

Capillary Water

Water
Plants
Can
Use

Wilting Point

Organic Matter
Additions
For Capillarity

Lowered
Wilting Point

Water
Plants
Cannot
Use

Hygroscopic
Water

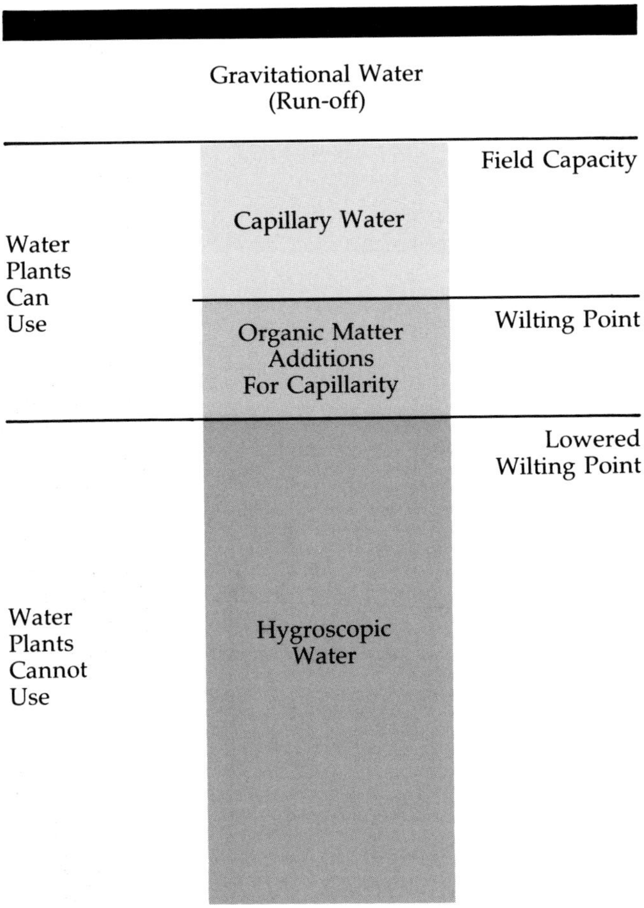

use capillary moisture. Now, if I have confused you, look at the drawing and perhaps you will understand more readily.

Garden Hoses

The inside diameter (I.D.) of a garden hose determines the amount of water the hose can deliver. For instance, a ½-inch I.D. hose delivers, with good pressure, about nine gallons per minute, a ⅝-inch hose delivers 16 gallons, and a ¾-inch hose about 26 gallons. The ⅝-inch hose is the most suitable size for home gardens; the pressure in water systems is rarely enough for the ¾-inch size.

Spongy rubber hoses are the most durable ones now being marketed, followed by reinforced rubber, then reinforced plastic. Plastic hoses, however, are not very pliable when they are cold. Sprinkler hoses that have perforations on one side can be used upside down for watering vegetable gardens and flowerbeds. The water-delivery rate of sprinkler hoses is about ⅛-inch per hour. You can run them almost all day to add an inch of water to the soil.

Sprinklers

Sprinklers differ greatly in their efficiency and service. But the delivery of water often is reduced by whatever mechanical action the water pressure must produce. Some of the most effective sprinklers are the pulsating models. They have a low arch and a large pattern of delivery. They rarely apply more water than a soil can absorb. Some water in a full circle; others are adjustable to whatever pattern you need.

Pulsating type sprinkler

Some people love oscillators, but these sprinklers are the least efficient. The trouble is, they throw the water up so high that a little wind will alter the delivery pattern materially.

One of the oldest and best sprinkler types is the Thompson Twin. This sprinkler is inexpensive and has a very flat pattern of water application. To handle lawn edges, there are half and quarter circle sprinklers available for use along sidewalks and in corners. These sprinklers do the best work where there is a changing water pressure.

Thompson Twin or "Frog-eyes"

Crawler types of sprinklers are usable but are quite expensive. And you must have the right type of hose to let them function properly.

There are also square sprinklers that handle a square area most efficiently.

The following summary can help you pick the right sprinklers for your needs:

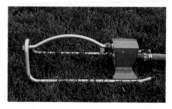

Oscillating sprinkler

1. Automatic sprinkler systems use different heads for varied water delivery patterns. They must be kept clean. They are available in brass and plastic. The heads must overlap to ensure adequate coverage.
2. Garden hoses are available in several types with different inside diameters. For average home garden uses, a ⅝-inch I.D. hose is best; it delivers nearly twice as much water as a ½-inch I.D. hose. A ¾-inch I.D. hose, however, is a little heavy and harder to handle. Flexible rubber hose is most durable even at below-freezing temperatures. Nylon-reinforced plastic hose also is useful and durable.

Water timer

Water bubbler

Drip irrigation components

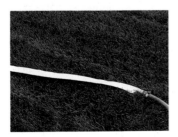

Soaker hose

3. Water timers are handy when you cannot stay home to turn the water off. After a preset delivery, the timer shuts itself off automatically.

4. Many different hose nozzles are available including a water breaker that works like a shower head. At full volume, you may have to move it frequently.

5. Water bubblers work well in flowerbeds and vegetable garden rows. They deliver more volume without eroding the garden soil. They are usable in newly planted beds and areas.

6. Drip irrigation is efficient and dependable. It lets you get by without water waste. A drip irrigation system can be installed so its emitters are near trees, shrubs, and other permanent plantings. Units are available for vegetable and flower gardens. Drip system emitters save water from being lost to evaporation and runoff.

7. Soaker hoses such as Leaky Pipe are excellent devices to lay in large flower gardens. They are very durable, more so than canvas soakers and plastic sprinkler hoses.

8. Oscillating sprinklers may be attractive to observe, but their efficiency is poor whenever wind is a factor.

9. Pulsating sprinklers generally are reliable. Some are adjustable to partial circles. And their droplets are large enough so that wind has only a minor influence on the efficiency of their water delivery.

10. Traveling sprinklers must move along a garden hose that has been carefully lined up. They are rather expensive and subject to theft. They cover larger lawn areas but can be a little wasteful.

11. Plastic sprinkler hoses are useful in narrow lawn sections and in sloped lawn areas. Their delivery is only about 0.15 inch per hour, and even in heavy clay soils, they help prevent runoff. Sprinkler hoses are excellent for watering repaired lawn areas and reseeded spots. They can be inverted and used as a soaker hose in a flower bed.

12. The Thompson Twin spray is the least expensive, but ever so effective, lawn sprinkler. It emits a flat pattern of water. With good water pressure, it easily covers a 30-foot-diameter circle. Its drops are large, so wind is not usually a problem.

Water Quality

Water quality is very important in gardening. In our Western locations, municipal water usually is at a medium alkali level — a pH of about 7.5 to 7.7. Well water may be much more alkaline and harder, however. If the well water is fairly high in sodium, it is not the best for plants that prefer a slightly acid surrounding. Most commercial water softeners have a sodium base. This rules out commercially softened water for use with indoor gardens and houseplants. If your water is very hard, simply repot your plants in fresh soil mixes more frequently.

Commercial wetting agents generally are useful. They make the water wetter. When used outdoors, they lower the surface tension of water particles and reduce their molecular size for easier soil penetration. With houseplants, wetting agents let the water percolate easier to wet the soil. Some soil mixes high in peat moss are difficult to wet. Wetting agents overcome this problem easily.

Water Conservation

Water conservation is a very important aspect of lawn watering. No matter where you live in the Rocky Mountain West, rainfall is inadequate and water is precious. Most of this region depends on moisture from the annual snow-melt runoff. This water is stored in large reservoirs, ground water supplies, or aquifers.

No discussion on watering would be complete without the subject of trickle irrigation. It also is

Homemade irrigation system for vegetables

referred to as drip or ooze watering. The major principle involved is making a little water go a long way. What we have learned mostly from countries in the Middle East is that when only a portion of the root system of a plant gets watered, the plant will actually thrive. Through capillary action, moisture will move over to the dry areas on its own. The trickle or drip irrigation systems are quite simple and do not require much expertise to install. With drip irrigation, the term I favor for all systems that use this concept, we apply a little water over a long time either by emitters or spaghetti tubes. The gentle action of the water will not disturb the soil surface (by washing), nor will it distrub the soil structure (by puddling). As a result, no aeration deficiency is created because of a temporary oversupply of water. With emitters, only about half of a tree's or shrub's roots are wetted, compared to nearly 100 percent in sprinkler irrigation. Good emitters are set up so only a little water is applied — perhaps daily or on alternate days. Component parts of a drip system are main leader, PVC laterals, emitters and/or spaghetti tubes and nozzles. The water in a drip system must be very pure and clean. Any soil particles or impurities may clog the system quite easily.

Easier to install yet are soaker hoses. These ooze water droplets along their entire lengths. A soaker hose may be up to 400 feet long. But 100-foot sections are the most efficient with average domestic water pressure.

Winter Watering

Winter watering probably is the most important garden activity of the entire season. Many home gardeners feel that once they turn off and drain their sprinkling systems and put away their hoses for the winter, nothing more needs to be done until the following April.

How often should you water in winter? Older, well-established home gardens with relatively good soil should have a half-hour watering approximately every four to six weeks — temperatures and weather permitting. Areas that have been established 15-25 years could be well served by a half-hour watering every three to four weeks, weather permitting. Naturally, if the ground has six inches of frost, it would make little sense to water. Fortunately, frost of that depth does not occur every year, and, if so, not usually until January.

Developments of new homes are the locations

> **Rocky Mountain Tip:**
>
> Winter watering of evergreen trees and shrubs is very important. If the climate is dry, one irrigation a month for spruces is not too much. Broadleafed evergreen shrubs also need a fair amount of winter watering.

for which I have the most concern. Some of these have heavy clay soils which hold very little water. Others have sandy soils that let water through so fast that it doesn't make much of an impression. For people in these areas of newer homes, I advise winter watering every two to three weeks, whether your yard looks like it needs it or not. It is costly in time and money to have to plant a new lawn. You can save yourself this possible discouragement by doing a bit of extra winter watering. Water may be valuable and expensive, but if you use it wisely, it will rescue your yard in a dry winter.

I do not suggest using underground sprinkling systems for wintertime watering. A good 50- to 75-foot length of a soft-rubber garden hose is all you need in most cases to do the watering. To keep your hoses serviceable during winter, don't store them on the patio or outdoors but move them to a garage or basement room when they are not in use. That way, they will not be frozen up when you need them again. Thawing a hose for several hours can be a frustrating experience.

In winter watering, it makes little difference what type of sprinkler you prefer to use. From the standpoint of simplicity and easy manipulation, I prefer the Thompson Twin spray, which is always serviceable. And as for hoses I have found the Gates soft hose and similar products, such as Swan, to be fully dependable.

It doesn't take a long time to ensure the survival of your plants. The basic cause of 95 out of 100 plant losses every winter can be attributed directly to dehydration. We live in a High Plains desert, and

> **Rocky Mountain Tip:**
>
> Most perennials including roses should have two or three good irrigations every winter unless the snow cover is exceptional. Alkaline clay soils just don't have a good moisture reservoir.

Roses in full bloom

during the winter — especially October through January — the emphasis truly can be put on "desert."

Water your trees and shrubs in winter with a Greenie or Ross root feeder and pay special heed to moisture-oriented trees such as birches, willows, and Redosier dogwood shrubs.

Your rose garden will benefit from a monthly deep soaking, as will your raspberries, strawberries, and grapes. And — if you want your clematis plants to be beautiful again — water them deeply along with your roses and exposed rock garden areas.

A FAMILY PROJECT

Gardening Is for Children, Too

Children are great learners if you give them the opportunity. The experience they may gain from gardening will give them the start of a lifetime. Gardening methods don't change all that much over the years, in spite of innovations. Mechanical tools and gadgets come and go. But the adventure of a plantlet emerging from a seed is an experience that is hard to forget.

Try to remember if you can who taught you the first steps in gardening. I remember mine very clearly. My family owned (with two other families) a small wood lot where we kids could play many active games. There was a small, sunny spot. And I wanted to grow something. Next door were the Schreber gardeners who grew nearly everything. One of them gave me, at age eight, two dozen excess strawberry plants and some seed of sweet peas and mignonette. I can still remember the pride I felt when I brought the first little plate of strawberries to my mother. Well, I was hooked for life!

Remember, please, that children have very short spans of attention. Do all the hard work first, but include them at the climax. Sowing seed is something they like to do. But don't keep them too busy picking weeds! A few moments of your life will bring a lifetime of pleasure and excitement to them. Plants are still fascinating and exciting to me now many years later. I became a horticulturist because of the early encouragement I got from neighbors.

We all need to start somewhere. Your kids or your grandchildren deserve to experience the rudiments of gardening with you. This is your golden opportunity. Just get the kids started. They'll be back for more. Let them harvest and teach them the care and patience of gardening.

Always give your youngsters a prominent spot to garden. They need recognition. Even if your landscape plan is a little disturbed, their garden must be fully visible. Behind the ash pit is no place for a kid's garden. You can plant your own garden there if space is a problem. Your children will remember you more for the help you gave them in gardening than for most other activities.

LANDSCAPING

GOOD landscaping is not simply an afterthought. It is the result of careful planning. With proper landscaping, a home and its property complement each other and create a good quality of life.

Landscaping can provide an orderly arrangement of plants and a nice decor to surround what is likely the most important investment in a lifetime — your home. Landscaping can develop privacy and screen out unpleasant views. And it can be used to frame and emphasize a desirable mountain view, a stream, or a nearby lake.

With proper landscaping, you can create a protective buffer against prevailing winds, and, in time, that buffer can also help your home's energy efficiency. It can let the rays of the sun warm your home in winter when you need the heat or shade your house in summer to reduce cooling costs.

Good landscaping pays, and will add dependable value to your property year after year. It can be as expensive as you can afford. Or it can be less expensive, if you can afford to wait a few years for small plants to grow to decorative sizes.

LANDSCAPING ON A BUDGET

Anything can be done on a budget, whether it is a very generous budget or a very tight one. Nothing is free, but generally you can get what you are willing to pay for. And when you realize that landscaping is more than just plants, you can fully appreciate that it is not too much to spend an amount equal to 12 to 15 percent of the initial investment in your house — on landscaping. This figure should include fences, sprinkler systems, lawns, rocks for a rock garden, and whatever else you would like to include in your total plan.

A colorful balcony

That plan is step one. It is a blend of what all members of your family want in their (and your) garden. Young children need a place to play and exercise. Older people need a place to sit and relax. There are certain basics you'll need in any event: A fence to keep pets in or other people's pets out; a lawn to play on; or a patio to sit on or eat on. All of these have a price tag, and they are basics in your landscaping budget. There are some corners you can cut. But let's face it: Quality is quality, and it deserves a fair price.

Believe it or not, 90 percent of all home landscapes are installed on a budget over a period of years, depending on what a family can afford. It is not excessive to budget 12 percent of a home's basic cost for landscape improvements. And that won't include a swimming pool or a hot tub.

Who will do the work has an important influence on the total cost. Labor costs often consume a major portion of a project. But with patience you can do a lot of it yourself.

There are three ways you can achieve landscaping. One is to hire a landscape contractor to do the work. He bids the entire job at a price. You should get several bids and compare. The lowest bid is not always the best, and certain costs can be negotiated. You may want a certain contractor because you have confidence in him and his performance, but he may charge more than you expected. Sometimes a minor modification of a plan may save you hundreds of dollars. And the completion date and price should be in writing.

The second way is to be the contractor yourself

and hire various jobs to be done. In that case, you must supervise and make sure that you get what you are paying for. This ties you down more because you'll have to check up on the subcontractors you hire. Your presence on the job is not required full-time, but at least part-time. You may get some work done better if you know and trust certain craftsmen to do their job. Naturally, weather can interfere. But you must keep things moving or the work will never get done. Pay only when you are completely satisfied. But be careful. Some workmen can put a lien on your property if you don't pay them when the agreement calls for payment.

The third way is to do it yourself. You, however, must be fully honest about your abilities and physical energy. It takes more than wishful thinking to build a good, solid fence or to install an underground watering system. These are the jobs I would get bids on and proceed with a written agreement on completion date, price, and specific description of what you are contracting to have done. You can do a lawn by yourself if you follow the instructions given in Chapter 3. You can install many shrubs and trees yourself. You may even install a rock garden or a drywall yourself. For this you may have to rent some equipment. And buy the rocks from a dealer, unless you have a good-sized truck, so you can have them delivered. Family automobiles are not ideally suited for transporting rocks or large trees.

If you cannot afford to pay for your whole landscaping program at once, you can determine what you can get along without for the moment. You also

may put your whole landscape program on a three-year plan or even a five-year plan for completion. You must, however, establish priorities and get the basic work done first.

You may encounter most of your problems in the selection and purchase of plants. There really are no true bargains. I have nothing against large grocery chains, and I most certainly buy our groceries there. But nursery plants should be bought from someone who understands how to handle the plants properly and how to care for them. Go out of your way a little and find a nurseryman or a garden center that has proper facilities for plants. I used to watch a national-chain department store bring in truckloads of evergreens in March, April, and May and offer them at a very opportune price. Then, if a snowstorm followed, the plants would soon lose their vitality, because the facilities on a paved parking lot were not really favorable for plants. You could get excellent stock as the plants were unloaded. But you had to be prepared and ready for them.

Good landscaping may be fairly inexpensive if you can afford to wait a few years longer for your trees to reach noticeable size. Smaller plants often transplant more readily.

It also pays to obtain recommended plant lists or to follow this book's selections. After 35 years in the horticultural profession, I feel qualified to give you honest and dependable answers. If a plant is not frequently found in your locality, it may be, at best, a borderline choice. I would not put too much of my landscape on a gamble. You can try a few plants that are "exotic," but you also have to be prepared to replace them if unusual weather strikes and jeopardizes them. If you are ordering plants from a mailorder house, read the guarantees and the fine print on the delivery policies. This may save you a lot of grief later.

Planning Is Important

If you choose to do the landscaping yourself, you should draw up a sound development plan. Make a drawing on your lot plan, which should be available from the builder or the previous owner. Priorities must be established — financial as well as plant selections (trees, shrubs, evergreens, etc.) — to get the project underway.

Help Is Available

Many sources of help are available to you if you are resourceful and patient and know where to look.

To begin with, several free services may be able to answer specific questions or help you solve clearly defined problems. The State University Cooperative Extension Services can answer many technical questions and supply a variety of publications from which you can make wise choices and selections.

If you want to use a particular plant or technique that is not described in the literature, you can consult a horticulture specialist on a university staff. Believe it or not, these people are hired to assist you very impartially. I served in such a capacity for more than 29 years, and organized many free classes to help homeowners become good gardeners.

Local nurserymen can also be very helpful. They know what plants will grow in your locality and which ones have the best chances for survival. Some of the larger nurseries have a landscape designer who can create a landscape program to fit your

DO-IT-YOURSELF LANDSCAPING

needs. The charge for such a plan usually is quite reasonable and often is absorbed by the nursery if you purchase the plants that are recommended in the plan.

A more expensive option is to hire a professional landscape architect to draw a landscape plan tailored to your family's needs. He will also prepare your landscape plan for bids and supervise installation for an agreed-upon fee or on a basis of hourly or daily charges.

Enjoying Landscaping

The art of landscaping dates back thousands of years. Some graphic examples are the Biblical Gardens of Babylon, the Taj Mahal, the gardens of Egypt, and many others. In previous centuries, only emperors and kings usually had the privilege of such luxuries. Today, good landscaping can be enjoyed by anyone who has the time, energy, and desire to install and maintain it.

Landscaping in early times was a cumbersome task. No machinery was available — only the brawn of men and animals. There were no nurseries, but there were people who designed with plants. These people are now called landscape architects, landscape contractors, and landscape gardeners. They are available to you if you need them. But I hope that I can get you involved in, and excited about, every aspect of landscaping. Whether you live in an old home or a new one, or even reside in a modular-mobile home, you can enjoy do-it-yourself landscaping.

Where to Begin

The first important step in landscaping is an assessment of what you have to work with. That includes sizing up your land, its contours, its existing plants, and the amount of preparation your soil needs. Also, you must decide if you can afford an underground watering system now or if one will be added at a later date.

Some Rocky Mountain soils not only are poor in composition and reaction but they also are rich in bentonite clays. Bentonite causes a soil to swell excessively with moisture. Homes built on bentonite clay soils usually are situated on caissons to stabilize them. If you own such a home, the most important precaution to take in landscaping is that you should not install any plants nearer than six feet from the home's foundation. Ten feet is even safer. The idea is to avoid watering near the foundation. In order to do this, you will be obliged to use inanimate materials (such as crushed rock, flagstone, gravel, and lava rock) to cover the ground next to the home.

In your landscape plan, you must carefully consider the climate you live in. Are you in a sheltered location, or is your property quite windy and exposed? What can be done with plants to modify the existing surroundings and create a more sheltered microclimate in your backyard? Can walls, hedges, and fences be used both for privacy and climate control?

What is the orientation of your home? The foundation plantings should be different depending on whether your home faces south or north. East and west facings can use similar plants. The matter of energy conservation has become a very important point. A maximum of solar exposure from the south can save you up to 25 percent on your utility bills during the winter. A properly situated tree can also shelter your home in the summer and cool it. When the leaves have dropped, it will let the rays of the sun through to warm you. Solar energy can be collected by an active system which transfers heated water to a storage tank or a passive system which allows warmth from the sun to warm interiors of the home.

If you are a relative newcomer to the West, you may not know what trees, shrubs and evergreens are most useful to achieve good landscaping effects. You may want to visit a botanical garden (if one is nearby) or browse at local nurseries to become acquainted with the plants they stock. Even local parks may have a good selection of shrubs and trees of interest. They may not be labeled, but at most nurseries, they are.

You should answer as many questions as possible before you begin your landscaping efforts. Do you intend to install some special garden features? Where do you want to locate your flower beds? Does your dream include a rose garden, a pergola to sit in, or a rock garden? Does your home have a patio, or do you want to design and create one for your garden? Are you a bird enthusiast and wish to create a feeder station and erect a bird bath? All of these special features should be planned early, before actual installation of plants begins. It is difficult to move 500 pounds of rock, for instance, through a 27-inch gate. Do you plan to add a room to your home in the future? You certainly don't want to plant a tree in the

Question: Last fall, we built a solar greenhouse across the south-facing side of our home. Its purpose was to save energy. There is no cooling or heating in the greenhouse, not an ideal environment for plants. The temperature range in winter was 35 to 40 degrees F at night, 90 to 95 degrees F with full sun in the daytime. Only alyssum survive. Any suggestions?
Answer: Your experience is interesting. Is there no way to cool the house during the day? Only hardy cacti or yucca can take 90-95 degrees day after day. Root crops just cannot stand that much heat. I suggest New Zealand variety spinach, broccoli, and petunias. There is a solar-energized ventilation opener on the market that you may want to consider.

Petunias

same spot. In five years you may have to cut it down to open the ground for construction.

If you place your shade trees somewhat in relationship with others on your block, it may help your garden blend in better with the atmosphere of your street or neighborhood.

Your garden can be a family project. It may have a sandbox for the children to play in — one that can be eliminated when they grow up. If your lawn is neat and you have a large enough open area, you can even play croquet and other active games there. You may want to raise a few vegetables to teach your kids how it is done. This has to be planned, too, because vegetables don't compete well with tree roots or thrive in shade.

Privacy is another objective of landscaping. It is a very necessary consideration in our fast-moving existence. Peace and quiet are priceless.

Good landscaping also secures your investment in your home. It has been pretty well established that good landscaping, well-maintained, may add as much as 15 percent or more to your investment value. Few of us create a home to sell it. Most of us enjoy permanence. But there are times when economic considerations force us to relocate. Then, the landscape value adds to the home's selling price and desirability. Some realtors maintain that any sound improvement, such as a patio or a sprinkler system, is an investment that you can enjoy yourself, then cash in on and let the buyer enjoy it after you.

Landscaping should be a well-planned activity. It should combine the best plants in desirable locations. It should be ornamentally attractive and secure privacy when it is needed.

Landscape Renovation

A nice home garden landscaped 15 or 20 years ago may need a little renovating after all that time. Even if the initial plants were properly chosen, family needs change over time. In our homes, renovating is easy. We simply redecorate, buy some new furniture, or perhaps even remodel the kitchen. But outdoors presents a different story. Many homeowners feel that a plant is a good plant as long as it is green and growing. Who hangs on to a three-legged chair? A "three-legged" shrub or an overgrown Pfitzer juniper is just as expendable. In fact, a few new evergreens and other shrubs will give your home a facelift and add some new interest to your garden. Think about it: The old shrubs will never look better,

A colorful flower bed

but some new plants can really make your place
sparkle. And that sparkle might be contagious
enough to get your neighbors feeling the same way
about their yards.

How to Purchase Nursery Plants

There are no true bargains in nursery plants.
There are no model years and no stripped-down versions. But there is distress merchandise. Large
nursery-producing firms often decide to clear a field
in May. Then, you sometimes can get two trees for

Question: We are moving into a new house with a very small backyard on the west side. We would like to plant a tree that will grow full enough to provide shade for the rear windows but not too tall. What do you suggest?

Answer: If only one tree is to be selected, this is difficult. Most trees do not have exceptionally short branch development with a lot of width. Russian-olive and flowering crabapples can be pruned so as not to get too large. You might also consider two or three dwarf fruit trees at 10-foot spacings and at least six feet from the property line. Delcon apple is semi-dwarf. Red Delicious apple on dwarf is blight-resistant. Sour cherry Montmorency and Kansas Sweet will not exceed 15 feet. Meteor and North Star cherries are even shorter.

the price of one. But you should have planted the trees six weeks earlier for a good start. And these bargains often are not guaranteed. A normal guarantee on nursery plants is for one year (at planting time) or for six months with canned or growing nursery stock. Fall-planted trees and shrubs should be guaranteed to be alive the following spring. It may well be worth paying a little more for a good guarantee.

Every spring, I observe dealers selling nursery plants from trucks at vacant areas along major streets. The plants may be beautiful when you see them. Arborvitae, for instance, often are offered at bargain prices. But be sure that arborvitae grow well in your locality. Otherwise, your beautiful evergreens soon will be "nevergreens." And remember: guarantees from such dealers are worthless.

Instead, buy your plants from a reputable local dealer if you can. He will offer you free advice and other assistance along with your purchase. You might even sleep better especially if you don't know too much about nursery plants.

Guarantees on nursery plants are important. They establish a nursery's confidence in its stock and ensure a replacement should the plant fail to perform at promised standards or fail to survive altogether.

Before you go shopping, you should do a little reading. Familiarize yourself with the ultimate size of the plants you want to buy. A tree that matures at 50 feet cannot be pruned back forever to 20 feet. Also, you should know the natural shape of a tree or shrub. If you need a narrow, upright tree or shrub, you cannot reshape a round, canopy-forming tree to a narrow, upright form.

Using Mail-Order Nurseries

Researching plants is especially important if you use mail-order nurseries. There are quite a few of them now, and they really send you what you order. They have cleaned their acts over the last 20 years. If there are trees you want that you cannot buy locally, you will have to order them by mail. Be sure of your dealer, however. The best of them have excelled in business for many years. Some reputable companies include: Stark Nursery in Louisiana, Missouri; Wayside Gardens Nurseries in South Carolina; and Inter-State Nurseries in Hamburg, Iowa. I get some of my best rose plants every year from Armstrong

Nurseries in Ontario, California, and from Jackson and Perkins in Medford, Oregon. But when you order by mail, always put the expected delivery date on your order form. When the mail-order nursery accepts your money, they also accept the delivery condition. And you can hold them to that. Remember, however, that the U.S. Postal Service does not handle anything but small, bare-rooted trees and shrubs.

Whether you buy from a local nursery or a mail-order firm, get their guarantee in printed or written form. Some dealers are very good about this; with others, you may have to ask for it. If you have local nursery sources, it is to your advantage to buy from them. They are local businessmen, and they often can do the planting for you (especially of larger trees) at a prearranged price.

How to Create a Landscape Plan

DESIGNING YOUR LANDSCAPE

Landscaping — designing garden areas around your home — is not beyond your capabilities. It is a matter of logic, and does not actually require creative talent. Most plants will be placed in the garden for a purpose, which you can easily identify.

Paper and pencil are the only tools you need. You also can use some nursery catalogues and University Extension printed guides on plants and their growth habits and usefulness.

Before you get too far along on your efforts, however, you must identify what kind of landscape your family really needs. It will help if you follow these steps:

1. Assess your land: The lot on which your home was built may have slopes or other irregularities. Some residential lots are pie-shaped, usually along cul-de-sacs. These often have a wide front area of irregular shape that can be used for such things as vegetable or flower gardens. Fruit trees and brambles also can be designed into such an area.

2. Prepare an "as-is" sketch: Draw the outline of your property on a sheet of graph paper. You can use a scale of one inch equals 5 feet or 10 feet or whatever you wish. The scale of one inch equals 10 feet may be easier for others to read. If you have a sidewalk and/or a driveway, draw them on the graph sheet along with the outline dimensions of your home. Also pinpoint utility poles and all existing outside features that are already there. You probably won't change these. If there is a desirable view from portions of your home, mark the direction on your paper.

3. Sketch in the landscaping features: Almost all residential landscapes consist of three basic parts: the public portion (front yard), the private portion (back yard), and the work or service area. Each responds to specific needs.

Establish the boundaries of the three parts of your landscape before you start planting or developing. The first, the public area, is what the general public sees when they pass by your home. It is usually street-side. Next there is the private area, which includes your garden and backyard areas — landscaped space that's reserved for your family. And, finally, there is the service area, which is a utility area. This is where the compost pile, clothesline, trash cans, and storage building are located. This area must be screened from public and private areas and from street view.

You can start your landscaping program any time the desired plants are available at nurseries or sod can be secured and laid. If starting your lawn from seed, April to mid-May and late August to September are the best times for germination.

Deciding What Plants to Use

Picking the right plants to match your landscape plan may be the process that takes the longest. You will have to study the resources you have available, such as catalogues, and you may have to visit several nurseries. You should know what you can expect and depend on from each plant that will become a part of your landscape. And here is a little well-meant ad-

Use graph paper and draw your plan to scale. You won't need to be artistic. Place existing improvements in their respective place on the graph. 1" usually represents 10 feet.

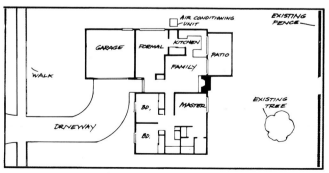

Measure the landscape's dimensions carefully. Locate all permanent features (such as walks, drive, patio, windows, entries, and utilities).

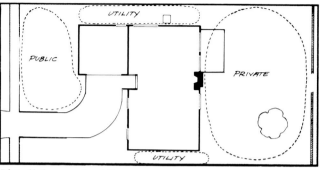

List the prime objectives you want to include in your landscaping . . . the things you want it to accomplish or your family needs.

Plot all three parts of the landscape (public, private and service) in a rough plan of your grounds.

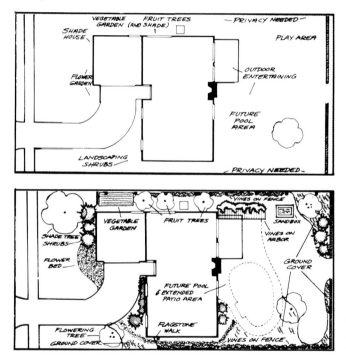

Mark each of your goals into the appropriate area.

Using those goals and the precise measurements, fill in the plants you want for shade, screening, separation, privacy, family activities, etc.

vice: Don't get carried away. The plants that attract you at the nursery are quite small now. Be sure you don't overload your land. You won't need a forest.

Planning for Active Areas

Your drawing should make provisions for the special outdoor activities you and your family enjoy. These might include vegetable and flower gardens, a patio, an herb or kitchen garden, a bird bath, or an outdoor barbecue. Even a small greenhouse, if you hope to have one in the future, should be located on the drawing, to protect that spot against too much planting or shade. Even if you don't realize your greenhouse dream, you always can fill the spot later, either temporarily or permanently, with another, more affordable feature.

Keep It Simple

Keep your plan simple, because you probably will have to maintain what you design. And if you get carried away, you won't have much time to enjoy what you create.

Before you make final decisions on your landscape plan, you should look at the neighbors' gardens — if you have neighbors next door. If one of them has planted a shade tree five feet from your property line, you don't need another tree there. In any case, it is not a good idea to plant a tree so close to your neighbor's property line. Some major limbs eventually will encroach across the fence and may become a problem.

Formal or Informal Landscaping?

You probably will have to answer this question only if your home is designed symmetrically. Some Eastern designs of homes are formal or symmetrical. Most family homes in the West, however, are not. Ranch-style designs largely are informal or asymmetrical.

Formal landscaping attempts to maintain equal sight values in the placement of trees, shrubs, evergreens. Among other things, it utilizes clipped hedges of equal height and width. It may go well with a plantation-type residence or Georgian-style architecture. If you travel in Europe, you can observe beautiful formal gardens in such places as Versailles and Villandry in France and Mainau Island in southern Germany. There also are some excellent examples of formal gardens in the United States and Canada, such as Mount Vernon outside Washington, D.C., and Butchart Gardens in Victoria, B.C.

In an informal landscape, visual values complement each other to produce an attractive total design. We attempt a visual balance, but we don't feel bad if, by necessity, total balance cannot be achieved. Also, it is difficult to make Mother Nature behave exactly as we want.

Formal landscaping is lovely if you are creating a show garden, but impractical for family needs. In-

Flowers at Versailles

Formal gardens
Villandry Castle, France

Villandry Castle

formal planting is practical to achieve shade, shelter, separation, and land-use division.

FENCES **Choosing the Right Fence**

Unless your home is in the countryside or in a mountain area, you may want to fence in your garden area — all of it or at least part of it. Front areas of property normally are not fenced unless you choose to do so for security reasons or if a fence or wall is designed as part of a formal landscape.

Fences come in many forms and descriptions. Some are more ornate, others more functional, and many are primitive. In the past 35 years, I have used several different types. All have advantages, but some also have drawbacks.

For instance, there is nothing natural or decorative about a chain-link fence. It creates a definite separation, but it could hardly be called attractive. It can be modified by using some wooden — instead of steel — supports or by inserting plastic strips into the chain-link fence to help it blend with a garden or to increase your privacy. In spite of its otherwise unattractive appearance, chain-link fence is galvanized and requires no maintenance. That is why it is so widely used for industrial and construction-safety purposes.

On the other hand, ornate steel or ironwork fences are very formal, impressive, and quite beautiful. They usually involve masonry or brick pillars.

Some of the less formal fences are of wooden construction. The picket fence was one of the earliest

Redwood

Rustic wood

Split rail

Cedar

Wrought iron

Picket

Wrought iron with masonry pillars

fences of wood materials, but in our Western region it has largely given way to fences of redwood or cedar. Both woods are used in tongue-and-groove panels. Some wooden fences are made more ornate by adding decorative, inlaid crosses near the top. Cape Cod basketweave fences are still in use, but grapestake (cedar) is less formal and a bit more seclusive. Cedar stockade is also popular. And many split-rail fences are found, especially in suburbia, where horses and other farm animals may be kept.

Fences are expensive, and therefore should be soundly installed. There are several ways to secure fences and keep them free of pests and other problems. Most wooden fence posts are set in concrete. Termites are a very minor problem in the Rockies, since our soils really are much too dry for them to survive. Pentachlorophenol is still in use and approved to treat fence posts where needed.

Cedar fencing need not be painted and will assume a rather rustic, greyish appearance after it has weathered for several years. Redwood, on the other hand, must be stained about every two to three years to preserve its color.

In the West, informal fences are very practical and relatively cost-effective. Cedar fencing requires practically no upkeep and blends well as a background with other garden features.

An unusual garden gate is certainly a special asset to a lovely garden. If it is a wooden gate, it can be decorated or carved to suit your taste. Make sure that your gate is wide enough to allow lawnmowers and other maintenance equipment easy access to your backyard.

A very important point about fences must be considered before you install one. When a fence is set exactly on a property line, it becomes common property with your neighbor after seven years. (The time period may vary from jurisdiction to jurisdiction.) You can reduce the cost of your fence by inviting your neighbor to participate in the cost of that portion that is adjacent to his lot. If you cannot obtain his participation, the only way you can keep the fence your sole property is by installing it at least three inches inside your property line.

Sometimes, to engage a neighbor's cooperation, the fence you select must be attractive on both sides. Some fences, unfortunately, are strictly one-sided in their beauty. Fences perform some of the same roles as the walls of your house — privacy, security, and

overall appearance. Plan a fence that blends well and adds to your landscape.

Rocks and Plants in the Landscape

ROCK GARDENS

Rock gardens are very popular landscaping features in the West. These pleasing combinations of stones and plants work best on ground that has a slope or in an otherwise elevated area of the garden.

Rock gardens don't happen by accident, of course. They are planned, then executed with some degree of perfection. I have created several, and each was distinctly different from the other. A lot depends on how much ground you wish to devote to a rock garden. And such gardens should not be viewed as an easy way to get out of maintenance work. They must be kept up to be beautiful.

How to Build a Rock Garden

The attractiveness of a rock garden is judged by its design qualities. It must have a good composition of plants; it also must have balance, although the parts in it may not be symmetrical. Good design balance can be achieved by unequal values of size, color, and dimension of the rocks. A rock garden needs a focal point such as a large, interesting rock, plants, or character pine for emphasis, plus some continuity in repetition. To be sure of repetition and unity, use the same type of rock with much the same color. The rocks should be unequal in size and shape, however, to create unique character.

Arrange the stones or rocks in a dramatic manner, then select a few plants that will grow tall, but will not be overpowering. I suggest some native evergreens and aspen to achieve this. Fine specimen plants of Pinyon pine, Concolor fir and Foxtail pine are not too explosive in growth and will not get out of scale very soon. Mugho pine and dwarf Alberta spruce also are very dependable and have useful forms.

A rock garden is a well-thought-out design that uses different shapes of rocks from the same origin. Lichen-covered rock is dramatically beautiful and creates unity most plants cannot achieve.

Once the stones and larger plants have been installed, you can give thought to what flowering plants and ground covers you may want to use. Below is a listing of the plants I recommend for decorative use in rock gardens:

Sedum (2-15") — **Stonecrop** — At least eight

Question: A few years ago, a friend gave me a start of Bouncing Betty. It is taking over a big part of my terraced rock garden. I don't know what to do to get rid of it. Also, a coarse type of grass started growing in my yard a few years ago. I have dug it, but it continues to spread. How can I get rid of them?

Answer: For both the grass and the Bouncing Betty, a single new product should be helpful. It is Ortho Kleen-up. It should be diluted — one ounce to 16 ounces of water. Use a plastic trigger sprayer and apply it only to the Betty and the grass. It is absorbed through the leaves and translocated to the roots. It will kill the grass in about 10 to 12 days and the Bouncing Betty a little more slowly. You can replant the area with a more desirable plant as soon as the weeds are gone.

good varieties available, including Sedum acre and Dragon blood.

Armeria (6-8″) — Thrift — A light pink flower.

Alyssum saxatile — Goldentuft — Early mass of yellow flowers; gray-green foliage all summer.

Arabis (6″) — Rockcress — White flowers; a dense ground cover.

Arenaria (1-3″) — Sandwort — Whitish to lavender.

Campanula (8-12″) — Carpathian Harebell — Blue/white

Cerastium (4-6″) — Snow-in-Summer — Gray foliage, very dense; delicate white flowers in early summer.

Heuchera (6-16″) — Coralbell — Coral color, dainty flowers on 12-inch stems.

Phlox subulata (6-8″) — Creeping Phlox — Pink, white, lavender.

Primula (4-8″) — Primrose — Many colors.

Viola cornuta (6-8″) — Tufted Pansy — Various colors.

Potentilla verna and aurea (4-6″) — Green and gold.

Ajuga (9″) — Genevensis and Curly Bugle — Blue flowers.

Leontopodium (8″) — Edelweiss — Velvety white flower.

Sempervivum (2-4″) — Houseleeks

Select plants for rock gardens that have interesting foliage, color, and texture, and lovely or dainty flowers in spring or summer. Also keep in mind that the faster these plants spread, the more often you may have to divide and regroup them.

A few evergreens also stay short and compact. Some can be purchased at nurseries or even collected in the mountain areas:

Kinnikinnick or Bearberry (6-8″) — Red berry.

Iberis (12″) — Candytuft — White.

Mahonia repens (6-8″) — Creeping Holly grape — Yellow flowers followed by edible blue berries.

Creeping Junipers (6-12″) — Andorra, Bar Harbor, Wilton

Some bulbs that flower in April or earlier are also very dependable in rock gardens. Among them are:

Flagstone drywall

Iris reticulata (2-4") — Blue and yellow
Crocus (2-4") — Yellow, white and lavender
Red Emperor tulips (6-8") — A show of red
Muscari (4-5") — Grape hyacinths
Galanthus rivalis (3-4") — Snowdrop — White
Chionodoxa (5") — Glory of the Snow — Blue
Scilla (3-5") — Squill — Blue

You can also fill your rock garden ledges at the outset with annuals, and later the perennials will fill the spaces. The best annuals are:

Ageratum — Available in blue, white and purple
Alyssum — White, pink or lavender
Lobelia — Blue and white
Marigold dwarf — Janie, Bolero
Portulaca — Mixed or single colors
Verbena — Mixed or single colors
Zinnia dwarf — Best is the 1984 All America Selection pink called Border Beauty Rose

How to Maintain a Rock Garden

The most urgent care a rock garden needs is weed control. Weeds and grasses seem to flourish in rock gardens. They must be combatted early, or it will be too late to do much good. You can dig them, pull them or even use a sterilant such as Round Up. You have to deal with them firmly. Otherwise, they will take over.

Neatness is also necessary. A late-fall cleanup of dry stalks will improve a rock garden's lovely appearance even when it is covered with a fresh cover of snow.

GARDEN WALLS   Do You Really Need One?

Garden walls may be erected for slope control and maintenance or for privacy. And they may be a necessity in certain small-lot situations to help control moisture and prevent soil erosion. Creating a garden wall is easier said than done, and walls are not always a good garden feature. They may create an overly busy appearance or interrupt a smooth visual effect.

There are also some other limitations we cannot overlook. A wall that is less than two feet high probably should be built of used railroad ties, which blend better into a garden area than masonry materials. Any wall that exceeds four feet in height, meanwhile, is a major construction project. An

Masonry wall

Masonry entrance

amateur would do well to employ an experienced craftsman to accomplish such a program.

Although excessive rainstorms are not a common problem in the semi-arid West, a stone or brick wall needs a solid concrete footing that gets down to the frost line, so soil expansion or heaving will not affect the wall. However, if a wall is needed, several types are useful and practical. The ones most practical for an amateur to plan and execute are made of railroad ties, stone or rubble, brick, or precast cement.

Making Walls From Railroad Ties

The railroads helped pioneer developers reach the Rockies. And they continue to be important. Not surprisingly, then, used railroad ties are generally available at prices that will not unduly stretch a landscape budget. Most larger cities have at least one dealer in railroad ties. Railroad ties can be purchased at various stages: new, used, creosote-covered, or untreated.

Holes should be drilled through the ties that are large enough to allow the passage of a reinforcement rod, usually ⅜" to ½" in diameter. Pound the rod deep enough into the soil below to ensure stability. Walls built with railroad ties are most secure at heights of 36 inches or less.

Stone or Rubble Walls

In the Rockies, stone and rock are a natural resource and, for the most part, inexpensive. Rubble can be bought by the truckload. It most often consists of broken pieces of flagstone, and may be the easiest

Question: I plan to build a berme in my backyard approximately 35 feet long, eight feet wide, and three feet high for privacy instead of a fence. What is the best proportion of the following materials to be used: soil, bark mulch, peat moss, and sand? **Answer:** I would use about four parts of soil and one part each of bark mulch, peat moss, and sand. You must have enough soil to start with or your berme will gradually sink as the peat moss and bark mulch decay. Also, if you plan to plant any shrubs or trees on the berme, you need enough soil for proper anchorage of the trees and shrubs.

Rock berme

Flagstone drywall

material to handle when used at about a 75- to 85-degree grade slope. If the pieces are fashioned together carefully, there is no need to secure the wall with mortar. Such a wall is called a drywall. Masonry stone walls may also be built of flagstone. This is really the job of a craftsman or a stonemason. In the sections of drywall that are less than 10 feet wide, built-in drainage holes are not needed. If drainage holes are needed, it would be best to consult a professional stonemason.

Brick Walls

Brick is a very solid and attractive wall material, especially when matched with the color of your home. Walls of brick usually are two bricks thick, and should be laid by an expert craftsman. The weight of a brick wall also requires the use of a solid concrete footing. Capping the wall with flagstone is

very effective, especially if flagstone is used on a nearby patio. It is even possible to incorporate a small fountain in a brick wall for additional outdoor-living quality.

Precast Cement Walls

If your backyard has a rather massive slope away from your house, you can enlarge the useful play area by erecting a wall of cinder blocks. Such walls are not very attractive, but they do what is necessary very effectively. You can help the wall's appearance by planting shrubs to cover the cinder blocks.

The precast cement industry also makes several patterns of blocks that have a design of voids where plants can be grown. These blocks lay easily to create a privacy separation that is intermittent or solid. A cement or concrete footing must be properly plumbed to erect a five-foot wall upon it. A capping at the top is also recommended. Such walls can be covered with a light-colored concrete paint to help them blend with other garden features.

Some precast companies also manufacture a lightweight concrete wall in curved sections that can be filled with soil and planted with annuals every summer.

Adding a Patio to Your Garden

PATIOS

There are good reasons for having shaded patios in the Rocky Mountains. In the higher mountain elevations, the sun can be very intense and warm. A tree can provide the shade you need on the patio, but it takes several years to achieve enough of a canopy to furnish protection. A roof over the patio is a quicker solution.

The most dependable patio roofs in the Rockies are permanent wood constructions with shingles or cedar shakes on top. Corrugated fiberglass or aluminum patio covers do not seem to fare as well in hard winds and heavy, wet snows. Canvas covers are stylish and elegant, but they have to be removed and stored over winter to avoid fading and fabric deterioration.

Patio floors are most commonly made of poured concrete. But on bentonite soils, that means the floors will crack sooner or later. Larger patio surfaces should have steel wire mesh worked into the concrete to avoid these problems.

Patio floors of red flagstone are also quite popular but not always quite as smooth or level as concrete. A flagstone floor is a good do-it-yourself

Brick patio

project, because you can lay the stone sections on sand, then simply use cement between the cracks.

Brick is a very elegant way to pave a patio; however, it can be quite expensive. A hard-fired brick is needed to resist deterioration. The bricks should be laid on an undersurface of sand. In recent years, a new interlocking brick known as I-brick or M-brick has become popular. It makes a very solid surface over which fine sand can be sifted. This is one of the best solid surfaces in the trade and is rapidly gaining in popularity.

Wooden decks usually are applied over uneven soil surfaces. They often are built with tongue-and-groove boards to secure a good fit. And they are relatively secure for a number of years, since termite populations are rare in the West.

Indoor-Outdoor Carpeting

Concrete patio surfaces can be softened and made less slippery with indoor-outdoor carpeting, sometimes referred to as Astro-turf. This carpeting is available in green and a few other colors. I find some of the green shades do not blend well with natural outdoor grasses and ground covers. Some of the browns, however, are less noticeable and are preferable for this reason. A sound installation of the carpeting is imperative, as it will have to withstand wind, sun, snow, and rain.

Patio Planters and Tubs

Patio planters and tubs are an extra touch that can add pleasure to your outdoor living area and make it part of your garden. The larger of these containers are often constructed of redwood. Others are made of plastic, earthenware, or clay. Whiskey barrels cut in half create a rustic decor for the patio. All these tubs and planters can be filled with the best of potting soil, and flowers will provide a very colorful and charming note to your patio.

The Best Plants for Patios

For a sunny patio, the best annual flowers are geraniums, marigolds, petunias, fibrous-rooted begonias and ageratum.

For a shaded location, I heartily recommend impatiens, vinca, fuchsia, lobelia, Dusty Millers, and coleus.

If you wish, you can use a qualified number of perennials, even some ornamental trees and shrubs. However, dry winters are very hard on dwarf Alberta spruce and Tammy junipers. Perennials — with the exception of roses — have only short bloom cycles, hardly worth their choice over annuals that flower consistently throughout summer and fall. I have found that miniature roses are more suitable for patio tubs and easier to transplant to the garden in October or November.

You can also grow a few vegetables in containers on the patio. My first choice would be one of several tomato varieties. One called Patio is of intermediate size and has velvety foliage. Two other varieties you may select are Burpee's Basket King Hybrid and Pixie Hybrid, which matures very early for a lengthy production season.

Some people even grow strawberries on the patio in ceramic planters. Our generally dry conditions, however, are not too favorable for success. Also, Bonanza peach bushes that are severely dwarfed are promoted for the patio by some West Coast nurseries.

In the mountains, the seasons are a bit shorter. There, patio planters and tubs will do well with petunias. Petunias can take a chilly night much better than many other annuals. Dwarf snapdragons can also stand cold temperatures with little or no damage. White or lavender alyssum also survives a chilly night better than ageratum or lobelia.

Question: What are the best plants for patio tubs?
Answer: Growing evergreen shrubs and trees on a patio in containers involves a calculated risk. The best plants for patio tubs are small, spreading or upright junipers, small specimen Pinyon pine, and small Ponderosa or Mugho pine. You can also try floribunda or miniature roses.

Barbecue Grills

If you plan a large patio that is free-standing, you can construct a stone barbeque grill outdoors. Speciality books are available for the construction of outdoor grills. You should use the grill frequently to justify its cost. Portable grills have been perfected in recent years and are much more controllable than an open fire. Also, bottled gas has replaced charcoal in many units.

Patio Furniture

Patio furniture made of redwood has the Western qualities of comfort and informality. Oh, I love the elegance of ornate cast-iron seats and tables, but they really belong on a formal patio. The choice, however, is yours. Plastic and aluminum are often too light to bear occasional windstorms or hail damage.

Pools and Fountains

Since our summers generally are very warm and dry, an outdoor pool or a fountain may add a cooling, comfortable quality to your garden. Water is not abundant, and cannot be wasted, but a few drips and splashes have a quieting effect. (I am sure one of the reasons oscillating sprinklers are so popular is the soothing effect they have on people. An oscillator sprays fine streams of water back and forth into the air and lets the drops cascade down.)

The easiest way to add a small pool to your garden is to purchase a pool or fountain kit from a garden distributor or from a mail-order catalogue. It is not difficult to dig an excavation large enough to accommodate the pool's dimension, nor to line it with the kit's presized plastic. Clean sand and washed rock or stone can be used to hold the plastic securely in place. A recirculating pump usually is included in the kit. Such a pump delivers 1/50 horsepower or more and is fully capable of recirculating between 100 and 150 gallons per hour (depending on how the water is forced through the pipes or hoses) to create a splash, drip, or fine spray.

A plastic or pre-cast concrete bird bath will also provide a welcome water trickle into your garden. All you must supply is a few gallons of water and a small amount of electrical power to run the pump. Often, a 100-foot, waterproof electrical extension cord is adequate to bring power to the pump from an indoor or outdoor outlet. It is also interesting to let water cascade over rocks into a small pool. To complete such a project, you need a strong back and some patience to achieve the effect you want. The evaporative moisture can be a great asset to your garden. You can even try to raise a few plants that like wet feet and high humidity, such as Japanese iris and Calla lilies. The latter are not fully hardy and must be stored over winter.

NIGHTSCAPING THE GARDEN

A garden is a place for restful enjoyment. If it is lit at night it can extend its useful qualities beyond the hours of daylight when we usually are working.

Subdued lighting can contribute a form of magic to a garden. Here, we deal with shadows and silhouettes, not with color combinations and balances. Lighting up a garden can be functional and even slightly mysterious. With a slight air movement or a breeze, the magic qualities become even more attractive and challenging.

Night lighting is very popular in the West, where outdoor living often begins at dusk as daytime temperatures cool to a more comfortable level. Many types of lighting can be utilized.

There are different ways to install and utilize night lighting. It can be done with spotlighting if you have a large backyard and enjoy entertaining and playing outdoors. With spots, you can also put special emphasis on statuary, a large flowerbed, or even a special rose garden. A 150-watt bulb usually is quite enough for illuminating an average backyard.

If shadows intrigue you, you certainly can create them with a spot placed behind the garden feature you want to highlight. The placement of such a fixture can be tried and moved until the full effect is realized. You actually can use a garage utility light on a 50-foot or 75-foot cord and place it in likely places to obtain the desired effect. After you have found the exact placement by trial and error, you then can determine how strong a bulb is needed to achieve the qualities you want.

Using Outdoor Lights Safely

Anytime you use electricity outdoors, you must select cables or extension cords that are waterproof. Your outdoor light installation also must be secure from lawnmowers, edgers and other mechanical maintenance tools. Dark-colored extension cords can be laid above the ground along lawn edges but should be stored securely when summer's outdoor season is over. And all fittings that are used must be grounded for safety reasons.

Also, for safety reasons, you likely will elect to use a low-voltage system in your outdoor lighting. Most of these are pre-manufactured 12-volt systems that come complete with transformer and an even spacing of the outdoor lights. These sets are offered in mail-order catalogues if they cannot be found locally. Many electrical suppliers now routinely stock several versions of these outdoor lighting sets.

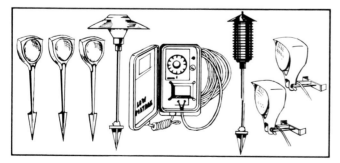

Outdoor lighting accessories may include time clock, low-voltage transformer, lights, mounting fixtures, low-voltage line. It can also be manually operated.

You can also use single-colored strings of Christmas lights very effectively on outdoor evergreens and deciduous trees. Tiny white lights in strings can be attached to tree branches to supply a special holiday effect outdoors. And these strings can be removed before new leaves emerge. Their effect is fascinating.

It is also quite fashionable to use Tiki lights in the garden for outdoor barbeques and other garden activities. Kerosene flames do not attract insects. Patio lightbulbs should be orange to discourage bugs from participating in your family's outdoor activities.

FREE PLANTS **Adding Collected Specimens to Your Landscape**

In some parts of the Rockies, you may elect to collect some of the plants you need from the natives in the forest. This can be an arduous task, but a welcome challenge, too, especially for rock gardens and natural-habitat portions of your garden. You must secure a collector's permit from the U.S. Forest Service and pay the necessary fees to validate your right of collection and ownership. Some states do not allow any plants to be removed from their forests. Others have more lenient policies. It is your obligation to collect your plants legally. If you own mountain property and aim to transplant specimens to your home, you must give yourself written permission to have the plants in your possession. I know this sounds a little ridiculous, but any law officer can stop you and make you prove your right to possession.

Incidentally, the best time of the year to move aspen trees is as soon as their leaves have turned a golden color. Look for single trees, not the end of a

large clump, that usually have only rudimentary
roots. All evergreens should be transplanted as soon
as the soil thaws.

It is a challenging task to collect plants from the
wild. You have to know precisely what you are looking for. Dormant plants must be identified, and there
are no labels out there.

Other Sources of Free Plants

There are times when older plants become expendable, such as when an older home is being torn
down or moved out, or has been destroyed by a fire.
These old shrubs usually are deemed surplus and can
be had free of charge. They are not worth much,
however. I consider them a waste of energy unless
they are otherwise extinct specimens or specimens
that for sentimental reasons should be preserved.
This is a decision only you can make. But I urge you
to be realistic and reasonable. Old lilacs that you
have to trim to the ground and root-prune severely
will take years to be attractive again. The time you
spend might be invested more prudently in some
other activity.

Growing Your Own Landscaping Plants

Growing your own plants for landscaping purposes is a project that makes good sense if you are
several years away from actual need. Offsets can be
cut from shrubs by first separating them from the
mother plant. Allow them to grow on their own for
one season before moving them permanently to
another location. Small, selected seedling trees will
grow as well under your good care as they would in a
commercial nursery; however, you cannot make
seedling plants grow faster than at their own inclina-
tion. Growing your own may help you understand
why nursery-grown plants can be expensive. Your
time and labor may be free, but a nurseryman grows
these plants for a living.

You cannot achieve a maintenance-free landscape unless you automate everything you can and
hire services for everything else. That's the way
many condominiums and apartments deal with the
problem of landscape maintenance. If your free time
is very limited, you can hire a number of established
lawn service firms that will fertilize your yard when
it needs it and control weeds, insects, diseases, and
even compaction of the soil. Lawn mowing may be
done by smaller individual firms, usually on a

**MAINTAINING
YOUR LANDSCAPE**

Question: We are purchasing a home with 2½ acres on top of a hill. There are no trees or bushes, only cacti and weeds. We are looking for a ground cover that requires minimum maintenance and water, no formal lawn. The land should remain in its natural state.
Answer: The only ground cover that answers your need is Crested wheatgrass (Fairway strain). Once established, it requires no watering. It may require mowing once or twice a year. Buffalo grass requires about 10 to 12 inches of irrigation each year. The trees or shrubs you need also must be drought tolerant and able to stand wind, poor soil, and weather. The only trees that answer to that must have small foliage and short stature. Siberian elms have been successful. Hackberries also can survive. Pinyon pines and Juniper scopulorum can take minimum care and watering. Even native Ponderosa pine should be successful. Among shrubs, we have a few natives from the mountains. They have to be tried in similar locations to test their survival. Certain sumacs, snowberries, cinquefoils, and native plums can succeed with little watering.

street-by-street basis. A dependable neighborhood boy or girl may be your best mowing bargain, because he or she will listen to you and do your lawn as you expect it — your way. Tree services also are well established. They will do the needed trimming and repair work. They also will control tree insects with powerful spray equipment and follow state and Environmental Protection Agency regulations that govern the use of pesticides. If you have several arborists in your area to choose from, you may want to get bids before you decide. Underground watering systems also should be serviced at least once every year. The dealer who installed the system often is the best one to maintain it.

There are many ways to create a landscape that requires a minimum of maintenance. The process starts when you first install your lawn and select the plants for your garden. Many new homes are now limited to less than 3,000 square feet of lawn area. This conserves a lot of water, but it also forces you to diversify with the remaining portions of your lot. In lawn area design, you should avoid square corners, have edging on the outside of a lawn to reduce hand trimming, and avoid placing trees and shrubs in the middle of an area. Otherwise, you will have to do extra work in order to mow around them. Furthermore, avoid planting trees and shrubs in spots with difficult access or steep slopes.

Ground covers are touted in Chapter 6 as a way to solve many problems; however, they are no panacea. Few of them are attractive year around, and none of them can tolerate any foot traffic. Some ground covers also are very dense and low, but they take years to fill an area solidly. In the meantime, you will have weeds to pull and blown-in debris to collect.

Rock and gravel are now widely used with new homes in areas where lawns are restricted in size. But just imagine how long it takes to cool all that rock after sunset on a day that has been 95 degrees. Try to sit comfortably on a patio among all this "molten lava." Crushed rock and gravel should be used in certain service areas where you don't spend your free evenings.

You can save a lot of time by using shrubs in informal hedges that don't need to be trimmed four or five times a year. A solid fence will also give you needed separation and privacy without needing watering, insect control, and trimming. If you choose cedar, you won't even have to paint or stain the fence.

You can reduce the time of maintaining a garden by reducing turfgrass areas and replacing some of them with shrub masses, inanimates such as stone or gravel, or ground covers that need little upkeep.

Choose and locate your trees carefully. Select trees that require little raking in the fall and trees that naturally establish a good form and will need little trimming. Another consideration: Some trees have fewer insect and disease problems to worry about.

Dwarf and semi-dwarf fruit trees reduce your pruning chores and are safer trees to maintain because most of their fruit can be picked while standing on solid ground.

In the mountain communities, you can simplify your landscape maintenance by sowing native grasses, such as the gramas, or industry-prepared seed mixes for wildflower meadows that will naturalize and survive with little maintenance. These will help your garden blend with the native environment of your locality. The Rocky Mountains region now has several suppliers of wildflower seed and plants. Among them are Applewood Seed Company of Golden, Colorado, whose seed packets are widely available in the retail garden trade.

Protect Your Investment

If you are a home owner in the Front Range or the Western areas, you already may have first-hand knowledge of the damage that swelling or expansive soils can do to your most prized investment — your house.

But if you follow some simple and economical procedures, you can minimize the problems and the losses.

PRECAUTIONS FOR BENTONITE CLAY SOILS

To correctly combat the expansive soils problem, you first must know exactly what you are fighting. To boil it down to the basics, the clay mineral bentonite (a hydrophilic compound) found in soils and rocks reacts to water by expanding. As more water is introduced, bentonite molecules take on the water, followed by a proportionate increase in size. Pure bentonite molecules may increase between 10 to 15 times their original volume. Research tells us that most soils will not expand over 35 to 50 percent. However, this increase or expansion of colloidal volume is enough to cause damaging pressures and movements that can affect building foundations. Bentonite clay soils are quite common in the West, so water must be used sparingly near foundation walls in affected areas. Find out if you are in such an area by either obtaining qualified soil tests or by inquiring locally.

Clay-based soils are not the only ones that swell. Soils which have 15 to 20 percent gypsum or white alkali content may also swell and cause damage to various underground metal pipes and certain types of concrete.

Because of soil expansion, foundations and slabs are now required to withstand pressures of 20,000 pounds per square foot or more.

Swelling soils, one of the most prevalent causes of building and construction damage, annually create losses totaling $2 billion nationwide. Swelling soils create cracks in sidewalks, driveways, and basements, do serious structural damage, and interrupt the operation of underground sprinklers.

There is no predictable direction the forces may take. Damage may result from horizontal or vertical movements — or, in some cases, it may come from both directions.

You can control expansive soils with proper drainage and grading, creative landscaping, and effective watering methods in bentonite soils. When you are landscaping in bentonite soils, be sure that the lawn areas surrounding your home slope away from the foundation. Familiarize yourself with shade trees and low-moisture evergreen shrubs and trees that are compatible with bentonite soils. Plant shrubs and trees a proper distance from the foundation of your home, and investigate the feasibility of using ground covers — such as bark chunks or plants which require very little watering — particularly in areas close to the foundation.

If you have bentonite clay soil, some plants are

listed below that have the ability to sustain some drought conditions and still maintain desirable appearance.

Among shade trees, these are the best choices:

Hackberry	Cottonwood
Russian-olive	Aspen
Green ash	

Numerous evergreen shrubs and trees do well despite limited moisture. Among them are the following:

Pinyon pine	Juniper scopulorum
Ponderosa pine	Tammy juniper
One-seed juniper	Yucca

And there are numerous low-moisture shrubs. These are the best:

Peking cotoneaster	Mountain mahogany
Alpine currant	Apache plume
Potentilla	Wayfaring bush viburnum
Persian lilac	Caragana peashrub
Bush sumac	Tartarian honeysuckle

LANDSCAPING IN THE MOUNTAINS

Landscaping at these heights can be just as great an experience as anywhere else; however, there are some critical points you must observe to avoid disappointments. For instance, there are soils of different composition and quality between hillsides and stream or creek bed locations. You probably have a better view from a ridge, but the soils there are poorer and your climatic limitations are more acute. On the other hand, the soils along a stream or creek are alluvial: they have been washed in by floods over the centuries. They are sandy, but they are also organically rich soils. If the climate in your area is somewhat sheltered, you can expand the choices of available plants from the bare essentials to a much wider variety.

You must also carefully assess the natural flora indigenous to your location. The plants already growing there are what Ma Nature came up with under conditions of natural rainfall and climate. Many plants cannot survive long in areas with a 70-day or 80-day growing season. Evergreens are likely your safest choice. You can have a host of annual flowers from a greenhouse, such as petunias, snapdragons and geraniums every summer. But marigolds, ageratum and zinnias cannot stand below-32 degrees Fahrenheit or zero Centigrade. If you have a local nurseryman or garden center dealer, take your business to him. He can get many plants for you that are suitable for higher elevations and give you guarantees that are meaningful and realistic.

Successful Gardening at High Altitudes

Summer rainfall in some mountain communities is significantly greater than in others. I encourage you to use a rain gauge so you can tell what you have received from the showers.

Once snow covers the ground, it will act as insulation for the roots of many plants. It is good strategy to water thoroughly before the snow cover commences. This will give your plants a little extra staying power through a tough winter season.

You should also observe the winds you are exposed to and from what direction they approach your garden. Some plants do better if they are a little sheltered from wind.

Trees, shrubs and evergreens that are to be planted in a mountain area should, if at all possible, be grown at a nursery in a Northern state. I realize that it is often difficult to find out where a plant supply originates from, but Iowa, Kansas, Nebraska, the Dakotas, Colorado, Montana, and Utah invariably are better sources than California, Oklahoma, or Texas. If the nurserymen cannot help you, try to locate a different supplier. A tree or shrub from a Southern source may have lower hardiness than the same species from a more northern nursery.

Since the vast majority of nursery plants are sold leafed-out and growing, you have a choice to make as to when to accept delivery of shrubs or trees. If you obtain them early enough so that they are still dormant, you can bring them to your mountain property and keep them dormant until natural climatic conditions force them to leaf out. However, you should plant them as soon as the soil is workable. The plants that already have leafed out are more difficult to handle. The soft growth on these trees and shrubs may be subject to freezing during a cold night. You will have to condition them to the outdoors gradually, over a period of two weeks or more, by taking them in and out of your garage. For best results, do not bring growing plants to a mountain location until the weather has become frost-free and settled. In higher mountain elevations, you cannot set out new potted and growing plants until the climate has settled well enough so that these transplants can adjust to their new environments and grow happily.

When you can safely set out your plants, you can help them become established by using mulch. Several materials can be used for this purpose, but they should be closely related to what you would naturally find near your situation. Well-decomposed pine or spruce needles or compost of aspen leaves would be ideal if handy. A good quality sphagnum peat moss or bagged bark mulch are the best you can get for similar appearance and character. The mulching will keep the soil cooler in the spring and warmer in early fall. Cooler soil temperature assures more satisfactory rooting of the new plants and less transplanting shock. After all, plants sometimes have to make several transitions, and the last one to your garden is probably the most demanding.

If your new leafed-out plants are exposed to full sun, they will benefit from some temporary shade. You can erect a wooden frame with a burlap or dark plastic covering that will create shadows during the midday to afternoon exposure.

The intensity of sunlight increases steadily with higher elevations. And plants that are not used to the light can suffer from sunburn just like we can.

Don't be surprised if a shrub that normally blooms in late May at 4,000 to 5,000 feet decides to wait until the end of June to bloom at 8,500 feet. The bloom cycle of most shrubs is delayed 10 days for every 1,000 feet of elevation. If fruit never quite matures on shrubs or trees, it is because the season is really too short. When we garden in high elevations, we are thankful for a normal season, but we should never be too surprised if we get shortchanged. That is the price we pay for what we have in scenery and wildlife.

Speaking of wildlife, I should mention that deer are very fond of a variety of shrubs. If you want your shrubs and trees to develop as well as they can, you may have to provide some protection. A new product in the market place is called Hinder. It is a nontoxic spray that seems to be less than palatable to wild-forage feeders, such as deer. It is generally available

> **Rocky Mountain Tip:**
>
> For every 1,000 feet of elevation you move upward from 5,000 feet, the emergence of flowers on shrubs will be delayed by 10 days. For example, at 8,000 feet, you will achieve bloom a month later than you would at 5,000 feet.

now. And most Western states now have wildlife conservation officers who can assist you with special problems.

Shrubs for High Altitudes

Here are some shrubs that can be expected to succeed at elevations that reach up to 8,500 feet:

Mountain mahogany

Siberian peashrub — *Caragana arborescens*
Mountain mahogany — *Cercocarpus montanus*
Peking cotoneaster — *Cotoneaster acutifolia*
Bearberry honeysuckle — *Lonicera involucrata*
Zabel honeysuckle — *Lonicera korolkowii*
Creeping holly grape — *Mahonia repens*
Shrubby cinquefoil — *Potentilla fruticosa*
Gooseberry — *Ribes species*
Currant — *Ribes species*
Mountain willow — *Salix monticola*
Red-berried elder — *Sambucus pubens*
Persian lilac — *Syringa persica*
Common lilac — *Syringa vulgaris*
European cranberry bush — *Viburnum opulus*
Water birch — *Betula fontinalis*
Redosier dogwood — *Cornus stolonifera*
Tammy juniper — *Juniperus sabina tamariscifolia*
Chokecherry — *Prunus melanocarpa*
Raspberry — *Rubus species*
Amur maple — *Acer ginnala*
Pfitzer juniper — *Juniperus chinensis*
Common mountain juniper — *Juniperus communis*
Common privet — *Ligustrum vulgare*
Skunkbush sumac — *Rhus trilobata*
Boulder raspberry — *Rubus deliciosus*
Spirea Froebel — *Spiraea bumalda*
Spirea bridal wreath — *Spiraea thunbergii*
Spirea Vanhoutte — *Spiraea vanhouttei*
Wayfaringbush viburnum — *Viburnum lantana*

High-Altitude Trees

Some trees are adaptable to the highest elevations. These are mostly native stands of evergreens. From elevations of 8,500 to 9,500 feet, the following trees have been found and should be useable in good soils:

Thin-leaf alder — *Alnus tenuifolia*
Rocky Mountain juniper — *Juniperus scopulorum*
Engelmann spruce — *Picea engelmannii*
Colorado spruce (blue or green) — *Picea pungens*
Bristlecone (Foxtail) pine — *Pinus aristata*
Lodgepole pine — *Pinus contorta latifolia*
Limber pine — *Pinus flexilis*
Ponderosa pine — *Pinus ponderosa*
Narrowleaf cottonwood — *Populus angustifolia*
Balsam poplar — *Populus balsamifera*

Pfitzer juniper   *Sumac*

White Poplar — *Populus candicans*
Quaking aspen — *Populus tremuloides*

Trees relatively dependable in good soils at elevations from 7,000 to 8,500 feet are:

Concolor fir — *Abies concolor*
Boxelder — *Acer negundo*
Norway maple — *Acer platanoides*
Silver maple — *Acer saccharinum*
White birch — *Betula pendula*
Downy hawthorn — *Crataegus mollis*

Concolor fir   *Boxelder*

Russian-olive — *Elaeagnus angustifolia*
Green ash — *Fraxinus pennsylvanica lanceolata*
Thornless honeylocust — *Gleditsia triacanthos*
Pinyon pine — *Pinus edulis*
Lombardy poplar — *Populus nigra*
Newport plum — *Prunus Newport*
Shubert chokecherry — *Prunus virginiana*
Staghorn sumac — *Rhus typhina*
Black locust — *Robinia pseudoacacia*
European mountainash — *Sorbus aucuparia*
Siberian (Chinese) elm — *Ulmus pumila*

Some of the native trees and shrubs listed above may not be available commercially. You may have to obtain a permit to collect these in their native forest and transplant them to your garden. It should be safe to collect these plants in late September for immediate transplanting to your garden location.

NATIVE LANDSCAPES   In the Rocky Mountains and the West, water is a precious natural resource. Our mountains store moisture in the form of snow and yield it at melting time to reservoirs and streams. The collected water is channeled to cities, where people maintain lawns and gardens. In the 1970's, I heard many optimistic outcries for "going native," thereby conserving the precious water for domestic needs but not for lawns and garden plants. This is but a wishful thought. There are practically no plants that can exist with only the natural precipitation in a given area. (The few we have are a few native grasses, Rabbit bush, sage and mesquite in the Great Basin region and, at best, yucca, cacti, *Juniperus monosperma*, or *utahensis*, and

Rabbit bush (native plant)

Native hardy cacti (Opuntia)

Pinyon pine. If you can build a landscape from these, I am all for it. However, large rocks weighing a ton or more won't give your desert garden much variety or character.)

You can choose to supplement what few plants are there naturally; yet without consistent watering, the hot sun soon will take away all but the toughest plants. Just look at what are considered drought-tolerant plants and you will understand what I am saying. Take mesquite, for example. It has practically no foliage from which to lose moisture. Notice also that most other plants that can withstand drought have thin foliage with hairy or villous leaf surfaces, which reduce their direct exposure to the sun.

Fleshy plants such as sedums and sempervivums can store more water than a thin-leafed plant can. So they need to replenish moisture less often, and they can survive adversity longer.

Some plants have a root system that is more extensive than other plants of similar size. Since their moisture collection area is larger, they, too, can resist dehydration longer. Crested wheatgrass is a good example. It is bunchy and virtually never covers the ground, because its roots extend out further than with other grass plants of similar size.

Researchers in Colorado, Nebraska and Utah have tested Buffalograss for drought tolerance. Like Crested Wheatgrass, it goes dormant in midsummer when rainfall is absent. It also is a warm-season grass and does not green-up until mid-June, and it browns with the first killing frost.

Native scrub oak (Gambel oak) grows and

Gambel oak (native tree)

spreads slowly under natural rainfall conditions near the foothills of the Eastern Rockies and in northern New Mexico; however, successful transplanting of these oaks is not easy. And nursery-grown seedlings take many years before they contribute visually to a landscape.

We can also supplement our landscapes with inanimates such as stone, gravel, and crushed rock, but the qualities of life we sacrifice are in addition to the near pavement-like appearance we create. Only along a stream or a lake are sand and stone attractive.

In the mountains, native landscaping is a natural. Bluegrass survives well with only afternoon showers. Bluegrass will adjust to foot traffic much better than other grasses or ground covers. Wildflower mixes will create a delightful meadow with legumes and grasses and will blend in well with the natural surroundings. And they usually re-seed well over the years.

XERISCAPE LANDSCAPES

A new concept known as xeriscape landscapes has evolved in recent years. Its purpose is to provide sound landscape practices for water conservation. It utilizes plants and other materials that require minimal watering. One need not go xeriscape totally. A partial acceptance of xeriscape practices is quite adequate to achieve a level of drought tolerance in a garden.

Xeriscape is of particular importance in heavily populated areas such as the Front Range of Colorado, Salt Lake City, and Albuquerque, where water will continue to be a precious resource. Xeriscape sug-

gests limiting turf area to conserve water. It also suggests the use of ground covers that are adaptable to seasonal drought conditions. Instead of fence-to-fence Kentucky bluegrass turf, we can, in selected areas, use Fairway Crested wheatgrass or even Blue Grama grass in higher mountain locations. Even a mixture of coarser, deep-rooted grasses that need only occasional mowing maintenance, like Kentucky 31 or Alta fescue grasses known as utility turf, may be adaptable.

Xeriscape encourages the planting of dwarf fruit trees. Sour cherries, apples, pears, and plums in mulched sections of the garden can be used where water can be provided by trickle irrigation during sizing and maturing of fruit.

Xeriscape includes placing foundation plants farther apart to avoid crowding, using two or three plants where five to six might otherwise be placed. Each plant is then able to develop a better root system and increase moisture intake from subsoil layers.

Some gravel, rock and/or bark can be used in sections for low maintenance. Some of the new woven plastics such as Mirafi, Terrabond, or Typar are used under the bark or rock to let moisture, rain, and air go through the plastic layer, yet control weed growth. Wood shavings and chipper chips from tree or shrub prunings may be applied to a soil surface to conserve soil moisture and create an attractive appearance.

The plants designated in the tree and shrub chapters as drought tolerant should be used in a xeriscape plan.

3

LAWNS

A LAWN is as basic to a family home as a stove is to the kitchen. A landscape without a lawn is impractical and unrealistic. Children cannot play many games on gravel or ground covers. A lawn has to be tended to and watered frequently, of course. But most of us live within the boundaries of well-managed municipal water systems, utilities fully capable of supplying our domestic needs, and enough water to maintain green lawns in our immediate environment.

What we really don't need today, however, are lawns that cover our entire lots. Nobody needs that much lawn, especially since the costs of treated municipal water keep going up, and future supplies of water will be more limited.

Recently I was involved in the landscaping of a conservation demonstration home at Sanford's Governor's Ranch in southwest Denver. The lot is approximately 18,000 square feet. The house, garage, and driveway occupy about 4,000 square feet. On the remaining 14,000 square feet, we installed 5,800 square feet of quality turf, watered by an automatic underground sprinkler system. What was done with the other 8,200 square feet? Some of it now is under plastic and large chunk bark with Pinyon pine trees that will need no watering after an initial year's establishment. Part of the landscape that might have been lawn now is a small fruit orchard with wood shavings covering an underground trickle irrigation system. And the balance of the ground is occupied by a family-size garden complete with raspberries, currants, gooseberries, and grapes and watered with a surface drip watering system.

We had water conservation in mind when we created the new landscape. And you should, too,

Rocky Mountain Tip:

Because there is only a limited amount of water for all people in a given area, we must try to confine lawns to not more than 6,000 square feet on large lots and as little as 3,000 square feet on smaller lots.

when you install a lawn. I feel that any new home can be attractive and easier to care for with about half of its ground planted to lawn and the other half under a selection of other covers, such as shavings, chunk bark, gravel, and ground cover plants. Recent information discloses that more than one in three new homes in the Rocky Mountain states have automatic lawn watering systems. Such systems are not a necessity, but they are a nice, practical convenience.

Today's family patterns often do not mesh well with the time required to care for a lawn. In many families, both adults hold career positions. For them, and many others, an underground watering system that is automated may be fully justified.

How much time you have to spend on yard work may dictate what kind of new lawn you will install. Or, if you want to improve an established lawn and learn some shortcuts to easier and better lawn

Well-maintained lawn

care, you can find plenty of helpful tips in this chapter. Planting, fertilizing, watering, and mowing a lawn all can take many hours and much effort. With careful preparations and planning, however, you can reduce the amount of work and increase the pleasures you derive from your lawn.

Preparing the Soil

THE NEW LAWN

Good soil preparation is mandatory in this region. Our soils are so poor that if you fail to prepare them properly, you will get mediocre turf at best. Such a lawn ultimately will cost you much more for water than one that thrives from good soil preparation.

For years, landscapers and contractors have only applied a token amount of soil preparation to new homes. Unfortunately, innocent home owners have paid an exorbitant price for more water to keep a poorly installed lawn alive. Good soil preparation is expensive, but it is worth every penny you pay for it. Its cost can be retrieved very likely in two years with reduced water needs.

At a new house, good soil preparation for a new lawn begins with removal of rocks and other building debris still on the site. Once the rocks and building debris are removed, you must improve the soil by adding organic matter. This is very important. You really will have but one chance to achieve a good soil seed bed. Once a lawn is fully established, it is too late to do it over or add manure as a top dressing. Such a late application could never end up where it is most needed.

You must spread enough organic matter on the existing soil to increase the percentage in the top six inches from 0.25 percent to about 4.0 percent. You will need a minimum of three to four cubic yards of organic matter, such as manure, compost, or peat moss per 1,000 square feet. What organic matter you choose makes little difference as long as the price is

Rocky Mountain Tip:

Sound soil preparation for a lawn and garden requires a general debris cleanup, followed by three to four cubic yards of humus-forming organic matter per 1,000 square feet of area. The organic matter should be tilled under 3 to 5 inches to establish a sound basis for a lawn.

right. Organic material should be spread over the rough-graded surface and rototilled into the soil three to five inches deep. Heavy-duty rototillers will do a much better job of improving our poor clay soils than the smaller, walk-behind units.

Now you must establish a grade so rainwater and irrigations will drain away from your house and then manually sift the soil to establish a smooth bed for planting grass seed or laying sod. The grade should slope away from the house in all directions and be one to two inches below sidewalks and driveways to reduce hand maintenance, such as edging. The sifting of the soil cannot be done as well with a machine as by hand. The back side of a rake is suitable for sifting until the grade is perfect. Sometimes we have to remove soil, sometimes add more. Now use a roller with about 40 to 60 pounds of water added to reveal the soft places where more soil is needed.

It is also important that you find the spots where piped services such as water and sewer cross your lawn. These locations must be puddled with lots of water, so they won't sink six months or a year after the lawn is established. A Ross root feeder or a Greenie is a good tool to settle the soil and prevent later disappointment and extra work.

If you have decided to install an underground lawn irrigation system, it should follow next, before the seed is planted or the sod is put down. Settle the soil in the trenches around irrigation pipes and heads by soaking. The advantages and disadvantages of underground systems are discussed later in this chapter.

The total costs involved in starting a new lawn vary according to the amount of work you are willing to do yourself, what you choose to have done by a contractor and whether you seed or sod. Soil preparation costs depend on how much you have to pay for manure or other organic materials in your locality. Even hauling the organic matter yourself

Rocky Mountain Tip:

Soil preparation for a new lawn must be an exacting activity. Floating and rolling for a smooth grade are essential unless an even grade and level is not a fair expectation. The grade must be away from the home to prevent damage to the footing walls by water.

will reduce your costs substantially. You may even have a free source nearby, such as a dairy, horse stable, or sewage disposal plant.

Should You Seed or Sod?

With a fully automatic underground irrigation system, you can easily establish a new lawn from seed or sod. It is a bit more work with above-ground lawn sprinklers and garden hoses, but that is the way most people do it. The major difference between using seed or sod is that sod is nearly functional from the day it is installed. A seeded lawn, meanwhile, is cheaper but takes at least 60 days or more to be well-enough established for family play. And a heavy downpour could wash away the seeds in 30 minutes under unfortunate circumstances. High winds also could blow away many seeds from a newly seeded lawn.

Sod may be the easiest way to do your garden's wall-to-wall carpeting, but the cost in some places may be too high depending on how far the sod has to be hauled. In some cities, such as Denver, Colorado Springs, Salt Lake City, and others, there is healthy competition among sod sellers, so the prices can be reasonable.

If you invest in a sprinkler system, you can recover some of the initial cost by seeding. You can obtain a superior blend of Kentucky bluegrasses that will save you money through less watering and less maintenance. So the scale weighs slightly in favor of seeding if you have the time, patience and a little gardening confidence. The only real gambles with seeding are wash-outs and blow-outs. Wash-outs are rare in April or May, but high winds may be quite common in your locality. If so, a good sod blend may be your surest road to success.

How to Sod

Sodding eliminates nearly all of nature's hazards. In many localities with favorable climates, you can lay sod up to eight or nine months out of the year — almost any time the ground is not frozen.

The cost and quality of sod, however, can vary a good deal, depending on the locality and distance to a sod grower. Sod may be purchased by single rolls or many rolls on pallets. There can be massive differences in sod costs from one time to another, depending on supply and demand.

Before you contract for a shipment of sod, check out the grower's reputation carefully. Look at sod he has provided for others and talk to home gardeners for a candid evaluation.

You can lay all the sod yourself, or you can organize a spring or summer sod-laying party. This can be a fun activity for you, your family, and your friends.

Begin by staking out flowerbed areas and other spots that will not need a grass cover. Try to lay the sod rolls with the same mowed direction if possible and as tightly fitted as practical. Then lightly water each lawn portion that has been completed. Apply a granular "Starter" fertilizer with high phosphorus before watering again. If you cannot secure that type of fertilizer, apply any common lawn food. It is not advisable to roll freshly laid sod. If the sod turns yellow to brown in a few days, it probably needs more frequent water. However, it will take almost 30 days for it to green-up.

How to Seed a New Lawn

Seeded lawns should be started only in late March, April, or toward mid-May and again from late August until early October. Summer is too hot except in mountain locations, and requires an excessive amount of watering.

Though a seeded lawn is less expensive than a sodded one, planting the seed involves greater risks and more work. However, it does allow you a wider selection of newer Kentucky bluegrass varieties than sod growers can supply, as well as other grasses recommended in this chapter. Still, without an automated sprinkler system, you will have to "babysit" the new germinating lawn for the first two weeks or longer, watering three or four times each day to keep sudden high winds or the warm, drying sun from jeopardizing the growth.

Seeding should be done mechanically on a wind free morning. A well-adjusted drop spreader, which may be rented at a dealer or rental agency, is an excellent and accurate tool for sowing. Divide your seed in half, and apply the first half while wheeling your spreader north and south. Then spread the

Rocky Mountain Tip:

Seeding of grass seed should be done with a mechanical spreader or seeder. Apply half the amount traveling north and south, the other half going east and west.

other half of the seed while going east and west. Before you use a spreader, test it thoroughly on a clean garage floor or patio. If it does not work properly, take it back. It's cheaper in the long run to apply the seed very evenly. As soon as an area is seeded, go over it lightly with a flexible fan-type rake. This will bury some of the seed a little deeper than others and will ensure better germination of the seed.

It also is worth the extra time and effort to roll the seed bed after seeding, to ensure the best seed/soil contact. Now apply peat moss with a scoop or a wide-open mechanical spreader over the seed and water for the first time, just lightly moistening the peat moss. (Sow only what one circuit of your sprinkler system will cover to avoid walking on wet ground.) Incidentally, seeding should be done only under wind-free conditions. You may have to wait a while until the weather cooperates.

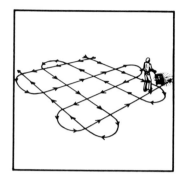

It is best to sow seed (or apply granular fertilizers) half going one direction, the other half at right angles. Test the spreader on a driveway or garage floor before use for accurate delivery.

The Best Bluegrasses and Blends

Cool-season grasses predominate on lawns in the Rocky Mountains region and the Great Basin area. Cool-season grasses include the Kentucky bluegrasses, fescue grasses, ryegrasses and bent grasses. Fine-quality home lawns in our region generally are Kentucky bluegrasses or blends. A blend is two or more Kentucky bluegrass varieties without fescues or ryegrasses added. Certain grasses also work well for utility lawns or athletic fields; I will discuss these under another heading. Kentucky bluegrass varieties were all developed by selection or breeding from Common Kentucky bluegrass. Since the late 1940's, more than 100 new Kentucky bluegrasses have been introduced and named. Most are patented to protect the originator from un-licensed production.

The first high quality turf-type bluegrass was **Merion** bluegrass, a strain collected from a golf course fairway at Merion Golf Club, Ardmore, Pennsylvania. It is a dark-green variety with a broad leaf. Its density fights off weeds. It has fair drought tolerance and is resistant to melting out or leafspot disease but susceptible to mildew, rust, and stripe smut. Merion permits close mowing but thatches heavily and will not thrive in shade. However, it holds up well with hard use and in heat.

One of the next Kentucky bluegrasses intro-duced was **Windsor,** which for years was an O.M. Scott and Sons' exclusive. Windsor largely has been

LAWN GRASSES

Kentucky bluegrass

replaced by newer varieties such as Victa and Bristol.

Since about 1965, many new Kentucky bluegrass varieties have been introduced from Holland, Denmark and many American universities and commercial seed companies. Many land-grant universities in the Western states have developed testing programs to demonstrate which bluegrasses are best in their areas. I will acquaint you with some varieties and strains that are generally preferred in these states.

Fylking Kentucky bluegrass has excellent resistance to the major diseases, such as leaf spot, stripe smut, rust and fusarium blight. It grows slower than some other Kentucky bluegrasses but maintains good color and density. Alone, it is a little fine for me, but in blends I like it. (Warning: it may become chlorotic.)

Baron Kentucky bluegrass also needs less cutting, since it grows dense and low. It is disease-resistant but tolerates traffic well. It, too, is available in several blends.

Ram I also has excellent disease resistance and excellent color even in problem soils. Its turf becomes very dense and withstands close mowing, even in hot weather.

Touchdown is another newer Kentucky bluegrass variety that has nearly everything going for it. It establishes a turf quickly, one that is disease resistant, has a low-growth quality, and stays green with close mowing. Touchdown also has excellent drought and summer-stress tolerance in spite of its early green-up.

Victa and **Bristol** followed Windsor from the research plots of O.M. Scott and Sons. This company has an impressive program of lawn research. When Scott's release a new product or variety of seed, it will be dependable. Both Victa and Bristol are rather good in shade and have good disease resistance.

America Kentucky bluegrass also is low-growing, dense and of good color. It greens early and stays green late, and is drought tolerant.

Glade is given excellent ratings for shade tolerance and resistance to mildew under trees or in dense shade. It also has excellent resistance to other major turf diseases. It establishes well and easily and forms a thick, low-growing turf of medium green.

Parade and **Bonnieblue** have good early-season performance. They tolerate short mowing and develop a dense, disease-resistant turf. Their growth is quite vigorous, and their color is bright green.

Any new lawn started from seed should be a blend of several Kentucky bluegrass varieties. Usually, a blend of three varieties is a good choice. Each variety has different resistance qualities to diseases. Some green-up earlier than others. A seed dealer can blend any number of them whose qualities are attractive to you. I would select at least one or more varieties for their qualities of resistance to disease and drought. If you anticipate having a lawn with quite a lot of shade, you should blend in a variety or strain that will persist in partial shade. In our region, the light intensity is quite good even if a spot is never directly exposed to the sun.

Some national seed companies, such as Scott's, Northrup King and others, sell blends of high-quality bluegrass seed under their own names. Almost every sod grower has recognized the advantages of blended varieties. Some have their own names for blends, while others tell you what is in their blend. Warren's A34 and A20 are frequently a major constituent of blends found in sod. Some of the above may be in commercial blends.

Rocky Mountain Tip:

New lawns should be established from Kentucky bluegrass blends of two, three, or more varieties. Each has its particular qualities of density, disease resistance, mowing quality, and water needs.

The Best Ryegrasses

Although Kentucky bluegrasses are the basic lawn grasses of the Rocky Mountains and Great Basin region, several fescues and ryegrasses have been developed for lawn-seed mixtures that offer greater resilience to wear and, in a few cases, lower moisture needs. They are also tolerant of high salt conditions. Appearance-wise, ryegrasses often are difficult to distinguish from Kentucky bluegrass. Only upon close observation can you see that ryegrass has a glossier blade underside than bluegrass. Ryegrasses do not form a sod like Kentucky bluegrass. In mixtures, this usually is difficult to observe, since bluegrasses will form a sod-like mat around the more bunchy ryegrass. Avoid annual ryegrasses (Italian types).

The main advantage of ryegrasses in a mixture is their fast germination and initial growth. If a lawn is needed in a hurry, and bluegrasses establish too slowly to be satisfactory, then ryegrasses are what the doctor ordered — but ryegrasses have some disadvantages. The most important is that they are subject to winterkill, particularly in short summer-season areas. Many times, the loss of ryegrass from a mixture is not critical, because the bluegrasses frequently fill the void in a few months to a year.

Among the newer perennial ryegrasses now popular in lawn seed mixtures are:

Citation Perennial — A fine-bladed ryegrass. Germinates very quickly and is attractive at low mowing. Has excellent summer performance, is relatively disease-resistant and performs well in partial shade.

Manhattan — Also fine-bladed. Germinates visibly in five days if there is good moisture and daytime warmth. Mows clean and remains dark green even in problem soils. Also resistant to most turf grass diseases. Dense growth.

Regal — Likely the best of all ryegrasses at the present time. Quite dark in color and blends well

> **Rocky Mountain Tip:**
>
> Some of the newer fine-bladed ryegrasses are excellent for overseeding in lawn sections under trees where heavy shade causes a thinning of the grass each summer. These ryegrasses germinate in five to eight days and establish well in 30 days in places where bluegrass would take much longer to succeed.

Perennial ryegrass

with the better Kentucky bluegrasses. This is the variety most often used in a mixed sod. Excellent heat tolerance and good resistance to major turf grass diseases.

Pennant — Will let you see a lawn in 10 to 14 days. An economical grass for over-seeding in lawn areas of heavy shade or places lost to dry winter conditions. Drought resistant. High resistance to brown patch and dollar spot diseases.

A host of even newer perennial ryegrass varieties likely will be marketed in the next few years. Experiment stations and seed development organizations are continually testing a number of new strains in Oregon and other Western states. Some very new names recently developed include Manhattan II, Yorktown II, and Prelude.

The Best Fescues

Fescues are very durable, generally coarse grasses that are useful for athletic fields and areas of frequent use. Fescue's appearance is rated below Kentucky bluegrass.

The best fescues for lawns in our region include:

Rebel Tall — A new, improved, fine-leafed fescue that can provide a very uniform turf of fine texture. Quite drought-tolerant and withstands traffic at low maintenance. Can be seeded at a rate of eight pounds per 1,000 square feet.

Falcon Tall — Another recently introduced

Rebel fescue

Crested wheatgrass

Metal edging of galvanized corrugated steel must be 6 inches deep to keep most of the grass out of flowerbeds. Plastic is also useable but not often available in 6" wide. Galvanization protects edging from corrosion.

turf-type fescue. Can be mowed selectively at two to three inches, where it maintains medium-green color. Stands heavy wear, heat, and drought. Resists many turf grass diseases quite well. Finer than several pasture-type fescue grasses.

Houndog Turf — Type Tall —A good choice where durability is needed and limited maintenance anticipated. Stands up well in heat and drought, two major climatic features of the West. Due to the size of the seed, most turf-type tall fescues must be seeded at 8 to 10 pounds per 1,000 square feet. Houndog can be mowed from 2 to 3 inches, depending on use.

Fescues are bunch grasses, not sod formers. They are not the same as bluegrass in total appearance.

Helpful Pasture Grasses

If your home site is larger than 15,000 square feet, you may find that certain pasture grasses can be helpful and economical. Pasture grasses have two very useful qualities: they tend to withstand the stress of drought, and they have lower moisture requirements.

Fairway crested wheatgrass has been used successfully in situations where there has been 14 inches or less of annual precipitation. It will not sod over, because of its exceptional root development. It may brown-out temporarily in summer heat, but it often greens well after a few showers. It is, in my judgement, the only grass that can persist with low rainfall year after year. It is widely used for these qualities along interstate highways.

> **Rocky Mountain Tip:**
>
> Crested wheatgrass (Fairway strain) is the only acceptable grass that is completely drought tolerant in localities with 14 inches or less precipitation. Its roots fan out much farther than other grasses.

Under dryland situations, Crested wheatgrass should be sown before spring rains occur to take advantage of what Mother Nature provides. In a dry spring, you may have to supplement Mother Nature with hoses. Buffalo grass is not comparable to Crested wheatgrass. It is a warm season grass and has a relatively short green season, but it is a good conservation ground cover. It requires about twice as much water as Fairway wheatgrass. You'll have to water it every 10 to 12 days, especially in hot weather. Tall fescue grasses such as Kentucky 31 or

Buffalo grass

Alta are quite coarse, but fairly deep-rooted. When they are used they may give the appearance of an athletic field.

Bromegrasses also can be used for a permanent ground cover, but the semblance of a lawn will not result.

How Much Seed to Use

How much seed you will need for your new lawn can depend on whom you talk to. Naturally, some people who sell seed may try to sell you a little more than you need. There is also quite a variation in the number of seed per pound of different types and varieties of grasses. The following table, however, contains averages that you can depend on:

Type	Number of seed per pound	Pounds needed per 1,000 square feet
Kentucky bluegrass	1,500,000	1½ to 2
Ryegrasses	250,000	4 to 5
Fine fescue grasses	500,000	3 to 5
Tall fescue grasses	250,000	4 to 5
Buffalo grass	45,000	2 to 4
Fairway crested wheatgrass	300,000	4 to 5
Smooth bromegrass	140,000	4 to 5
Blue grama grasses	700,000	1 to 2
Mountain mixtures	varies	2 to 4

Even with low seeding rates, you can get many seeds per square foot. A prominent sod grower once established excellent turf in 10 months with a seeding rate of only six pounds per acre. The majority of seed you plant will die from seedling blight or other environmental causes. In the final analysis, you may not get more than 30 to 40 Kentucky bluegrass plants per square foot of lawn, but that is adequate cover. It is simply a matter of survival of the fittest.

WATERING   **A Schedule for New Lawns**

Lawn watering is quite different from watering trees and shrubs or vegetables. Although horticulturists have long insisted on deep, thorough watering on an infrequent basis, recent tests indicate that this method is less effective than more frequent water applications. More on this later.

Newly spring-seeded lawns need careful watering from the start, generally as follows:

A. Germination period (10 to 18 days)	Lightly water 3 to 4 times each day
B. Next 2 weeks	Mornings and late afternoons about 1½ to 2 inches per week
C. Next 4 weeks	Daily
D. July and August	Every 2 to 3 days about 2½ inches per week
E. September and October	Every 3 to 4 days about 1½ inches per week
F. November to March	Every 3 to 4 weeks as weather permits

Lawns seeded in late summer should follow A, B, and C, then F as above.

> **Rocky Mountain Tip:**
> Experience has demonstrated that it takes a year or more to establish a new lawn from seed. A sound but not excessive watering and fertilizing program is essential for best results.

Newly sodded lawns are much easier to care for. They should be watered as follows:

A. First 10 days	Daily, about .4 inches (twice daily with summer sod)
B. Next 21 days	Every 1 to 2 days, .25 inch
C. Summer	Every 2 days, .5 inch
D. Fall	Every 3 to 5 days, .75 inch

E. Winter   Every 3 to 4 weeks
                                   as weather permits

Watering Established Lawns

Kentucky bluegrass is the principle cool-season turf used for lawns in the Rocky Mountains and the West. It thrives on warm days and cool nights. Numerous attempts have been made in the Rockies to switch to a more drought-tolerant grass; however, no satisfactory substitute has been found so far. Kentucky bluegrass is very attractive and forms a good sod — if it is watered properly.

Feeding, mowing, and watering are the basics in lawn maintenance. In the Rockies, the annual lawn maintenance season generally begins in April and goes through October, but the dates can vary largely by location. Furthermore, annual rainfall varies, and the degree of variation is unpredictable.

> **Rocky Mountain Tip:**
> It is not necessary to use only tap water on lawns and gardens. Well water may be satisfactory and less expensive.

A Kentucky bluegrass lawn usually requires an inch of water per week, except in the extreme heat of July and August. Then, an inch-and-a-half is a dependable amount. Every home water system has different pressure levels that influence water delivery, and there are variable factors involved in determining how much and how often you can or must water.

A newly seeded or sodded lawn needs much more water than a well-established turf. The seasons also influence lawn watering needs. Daylight is shorter in April and September than in June and July. The longer the day, the more photosynthesizing action takes place, which in turn requires more water. The prevailing weather certainly matters. Much more moisture is lost by plants on a windy, hot day than on a cool, humid one. And the nature of your soil dictates different water needs. A sandy soil loses moisture to percolation much faster than a heavy clay soil.

Measuring the Water You Apply

To have some idea what your water system can deliver, try this simple test. Locate four cans of equal size, such as coffee cans. Space them evenly from the sprinkler you are testing to the outside area of water delivery. Now run your sprinkler exactly 30 minutes. To get a reading, pour the water from all four cans into one and measure the result with a ruler. Divide the result by the number of cans. This figure is the actual amount of water — in inches or fractions of an inch — that you have applied in 30 minutes. If you have applied a full inch of water and only want half-an-inch, you simply water for 15 minutes. Using this method, you can test every sprinkler you have, so you will know exactly how long to run each one to obtain the amount of water desired.

Using Sprinkler Systems

There was a time when almost everybody did their own watering. Not by hand, I mean, but with hoses and sprinklers. Today, we are a computerized society. Only a small minority of us now water manually. A sprinkler system is not a must item, at least not when you have just moved into a new home and are overwhelmed with major expenditures. A sprinkler system can be added later. Some sprinkler system engineers actually prefer designing a system after the major trees and garden features have been located and placed where they should be.

An underground sprinkler system for a lawn is no longer pure luxury. Competition among dealers has made them more affordable for many. Although the perfect system has not yet been created, today's underground lawn sprinkling systems have become very reliable and efficient. Many well-established manufacturers now offer systems that are easily installed and trouble-free. Most municipal water systems still require that a licensed craftsman make the connection to the home's water service.

If you have adequate ground water at a reasonable depth, it may be less costly to install a pump and use a well for lawn watering. Although most ground water is hard and alkaline, Kentucky bluegrass tolerates it very well.

If you are considering the installation of an underground watering system, you should let an engineer design it or work with a sprinkler system company that has a qualified designer-draftsman.

The cost of installing most underground watering systems is about 40 percent parts and 60 percent labor. Unless you know what you are doing, you should depend on someone responsible to help you install yours.

Sprinkler systems are activated by circuits. Each

zone or section has only as many sprinkler heads as your water pressure allows. The layout of the spray heads has to overlap some, or you will experience coverage problems if the water pressure is down at certain times.

Most modern underground irrigation systems are made of polyvinylchloride (PVC) plastic. The actual outlets or heads often are copper or brass, but many now are made of a very durable plastic, too.

A clock controls when and how long each zone is turned on. In recent years, fully automated systems have appeared, using computerized circuitry that can be activated, deactivated, or changed by the home owner or gardener as needed.

The latest helpful devices to become available are moisture monitors. These collect data from several lawn areas on the amount of moisture a few inches below the grass and relay the information to a control board that hooks on to the computerized clock. The clock then opens a given circuit or two when moisture availability falls below a given level or percentage. This is really the ultimate in water conservation. You avoid watering a lawn section that does not really need it.

I am not an engineer, so there are certain points related to sprinkler systems that are beyond my knowledge, and certain factors can vary wherever these sprinklers are used. For instance, the moisture absorption capacity in clay soils is, in many cases, only a quarter to half-inch per hour. To avoid wasting water, apply it no longer than eight to ten minutes perhaps three times in a day to obtain sound saturation. Sandy soils, on the other hand, take water very quickly but do not hold it too well. So here, too, you must be careful not to over-apply. Sandy soils should be watered frequently (perhaps every other day), but for only ten minutes or so.

One very important feature of any underground sprinkler system is line drainage. Draining avoids costly repairs due to freezing.

Underground installations using perforated tubes to supply the needed water below the surface rely on the capillarity of the soil. I am a bit apprehensive about these systems, because it is difficult for them to circumvent trees and other permanent installations. Gravitational water loss is also substantial. With bentonite clay soils, we have to be careful to keep water away from dwellings, in order to prevent swelling of the soil and damage to the structures.

**CARING FOR
A NEW LAWN**

Weed Control and Early Mowing

In a newly sodded lawn, there should be no weeds at all or only a few during the first 60 days. Many sod growers guarantee their products to be weed free. Although cut sod has only about a fourth of its normal roots, it will grow new ones with favorable weather and care. Try to avoid mowing newly installed sod for about 10 days. Then mow it to about 1¼ inches before watering. The grass may appear to be slightly off-color. This will correct itself in about two weeks of regular mowing. In about 30 days, the new turf should be a lovely, emerald green. At this point, it should be given a normal lawn fertilizer application.

A seeded lawn — no matter what you may have been told — will be a great weed patch as soon as the green fuzz is visible. With all that careful watering and fertility from the organic matter, weeds will thrive. Do not let this get you down, because these very weeds actually will help your lawn get a better start. The weeds will shade and protect your seedling lawn grasses. When the weeds get but two inches high, you can begin to mow them to about ½ inch. Any attempt to pull them will only weaken your new turf and expose more weed seed to light and growing opportunities. Weeds are undesirable, but make the most of them. After you have mowed three times, some of the weeds will die naturally while your lawn grasses get stronger, developing more roots and beginning to thicken. Try to use a hand mower the first few times you mow. It is much lighter and will not make wheel marks on the soil. After your newly seeded lawn is in watering schedule C (page 86), you can switch to a mechanical mower.

Chemical weed controls on a newly seeded lawn should not be used for 10 weeks after sowing — and then only if the weather is warm enough (65 degrees F. or above) to obtain good results. Siduron can be used at time of seeding of several grasses to reduce annual grasses and broadleafed weeds. Bromoxynil

---

Rocky Mountain Tip:

Don't be concerned about weeds in a new lawn. They will come up in large numbers in spite of (or perhaps because of) the excellent care you provide. Mow them as soon as a hand push-mower can cut them — and do it often.

may be used on young lawns to control broadleafed weeds. In a sodded lawn, some weeds such as bindweed may be noticed after several weeks. As soon as weather permits, this difficult perennial weed must be fought vigorously by using recommended chemical weed controls.

When and How to Fertilize

Some years ago, a well-respected person bragged to me that he never fertilized his lawn. He lived on a piece of bottomland near a stream, and his soil was of above-average quality. I saw that lawn a few weeks later, but it left me unimpressed. It was little more than a utility ground cover, uneven in color and texture. It reminded me of a dirty floor, nothing to be pleased about or proud of. If you want a lawn that you can be proud of, you must find the time and the means to promote your objective. Since that day, I have counted lawn fertilization as one of three basic operations in sound lawn care. The other two are mowing and watering.

Lawn fertilization is the most important health and beauty treatment a lawn can receive, and should be applied four or five times each year. Lawn fertilizers are purposely designed to provide sound nutrition to a lawn. Most of them contain the three basic major nutrients: nitrogen, phosphorus, and potassium. Some of the better lawn foods also have adequate amounts of sulfur and iron. All of these elements can be mighty important if they are unavailable in adequate amounts. The entire analysis of lawn fertilizer hinges on availability. Any blend or mixture of fertilizers should contain at least 20 percent or more quickly available nutrients. And in many states, the area coverage must be enough to provide one pound of available nitrogen (actual) for each 1,000 square feet of lawn to be covered. Thus, if a fertilizer has 20 percent nitrogen, five pounds of it would yield a pound of nitrogen.

Nitrogen is the element most directly associated with leafy growth. Since leaf development usually provides attractive green color, nitrogen is the nutrient most needed to achieve the best turf appearance. The percentage of nitrogen is always the first figure in a fertilizer analysis.

Phosphoric Acid (P_2O_5), the second percentage in a fertilizer analysis, is more directly associated with healthy development of roots and rhizomes, the underground runners that allow individual plants to spread into a healthy sod. Phosphorus is

FERTILIZING

Question: How should a new lawn be fertilized?
Answer: There are special starter fertilizers that are for new lawns. They have less nitrogen, but more phosphate so the roots get early emphasis. A leftover bag of Winterizer fertilizer would be equally useable. Apply it about 30 days after sowing and immediately after sodding.

also associated with seed formation, which really is not desirable in an otherwise neat lawn. For this reason, some of the newer lawn fertilizers have less phosphate in their total analysis.

The third number in a fertilizer analysis is potassium. It is essential for photosynthesis, the energy production process of the plant. Potassium also aids in the cellular structure and development of the grass plant.

A 20-10-5 analysis on a fertilizer bag would guarantee 20 percent available nitrogen, 10 percent available phosphoric acid, and five percent available potash (K_2O).

The fertilizer's source of nitrogen is important and it can vary from one fertilizer product to the next. If the nitrogen is in the nitrate or ammoniated form, it is almost immediately water soluble. This can be helpful if you need a lot of nitrogen at once. With rain or normal watering, it can also leach the nitrate below the roots of bluegrass. This is why the fertilizer industry has developed forms of nitrogen known as synthetic-organic products. Urea formaldehyde is only slowly water-soluable. Its nitrogen release must be assisted with millions of microorganisms in the soil. In our alkaline Western clay soils, the microflora is rather limited and synthetic. Synthetic urea products convert slowly to the nitrate form, the only formula that can be assimilated and used by plants. There are different synthetic organics that can be represented in a lawn fertilizer, 45-percent urea or 38-percent urea formaldehyde. The latter is compounded to slow the release of nitrogen even further; it destroys some of the microflora that would assist in releasing nitrogen. Urea may burn a lawn if it is not quickly watered. Another form of urea is sulfur-coated. It is used mostly by commercial lawn service companies that fertilize home lawns and apply other chemicals in an efficient, money-savng way. Natural organic lawn fertilizers are from sewage, tankage, and other plant or animal products. Most are of low analysis and non-burning.

Rocky Mountain Tip:

It is important to remember that nitrogen is nitrogen. When you purchase urea or urea formaldehyde nitrogen fertilizers, you obtain slower release and utilize your lawn food better.

HOW TO APPLY FERTILIZER

Apply in early morning or evening to reduce the chance of "burned" grass. Soil should be moist but grass blades dry. Apply about half the fertilizer with your first pass. Then, to minimize missed spots and overlap, apply the second half on a path at right angles to the first.

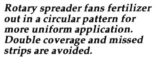

Rotary spreader fans fertilizer out in a circular pattern for more uniform application. Double coverage and missed strips are avoided.

Mark your path carefully. If the spreader wheel leaves tracks, you can use them to guide you. Otherwise, use stakes, rocks, or other landscape marks to direct you.

Water the fertilizer into the soil according to instructions on the bag. Leaving the plant foods on top of the lawn increases the chance of chemical burn to the grass.

All of this sounds complicated, but really it is not. All you need to remember is that the chemical form of your nitrogen controls the relative speed of nutrient release. If you want quick green-up, you can have it with a nitrate or ammoniated nitrogen form. But if you want gradual release over six to eight weeks, then synthetic organic products are designed to give you that response. I have used them all. I now have settled for a product that affords my home lawn a luxuriant color all season long.

Iron is the most important of minor elements in Western soils. Although our soils often contain an excess of iron, it is mostly in chemical forms unavailable to lawn grasses. Ferrous iron sulfate and ferrous ammonium sulfate, once diluted, greens up Kentucky bluegrass plants for a short time. However, it is soon changed to insoluble iron forms and becomes nearly as useless as iron filings, nails, or other bits of iron metal. Chelated iron products can be used to solve iron problems of turf and trees. But a little bit goes a long way. A lawn fertilizer that utilizes iron chelate instead of iron sulfate offers advantages because the iron in it remains available to grass plants for weeks, not just a few days.

Fertilizers can be applied to lawns in one of two forms: liquids may be sprayed on or granulars may be applied dry. Liquid lawn foods are mostly used by commercial applicators with heavy duty equipment.

The home gardener can use a drop-type or cyclone-type spreader. The drop-type is accurate in a narrow band of lawn, while the cyclone or rotary spreader services a band six to eight feet wide. Both drop and rotary spreaders are easy to use and will do an excellent job if in proper adjustment. If you don't own this equipment and must borrow it from a dealer, you should test it on the garage floor or driveway before using it on your lawn. If it does not apply an even pattern of fertilizer granules, it should not be used. Take it back and get one that works.

A good lawn fertilizer program often consists of five applications each year. A beautiful dark-green color and the velvety appearance and texture of your lawn will be sources of well-earned pride and satisfaction through the season.

> **Rocky Mountain Tip:**
> Apply most lawn fertilizers to a dry turf and water them in after application. Follow what the label on the bag directs you to do. Test the spreader every time before you use it, unless it is your own.

To assist you in timing lawn fertilizer applications, I have prepared the following schedules for five, four, and three applications. Use in each instance five pounds of a 20-10-5 fertilizer or four pounds of a 24-3-3 for every 1,000 square feet of lawn area, plus other suggested chemicals to keep your lawn healthy and beautiful. If your lawn food has a different analysis, simply follow the manufacturer's suggested rate of application. Water before or after application as suggested on the bag's instructions.

Five Application Program:

1st Application:	March to April
	Fertilizer plus insect control and/or disease control as needed.
2nd Application:	May
	Fertilizer plus crabgrass control and broadleaf weed control.
3rd Application:	Late June to July
	Fertilizer plus iron and weed control as needed.

4th Application: August to mid-September

Fertilizer with iron plus weed control and/or insect control as needed.

5th Application: October

Fertilizer plus disease control.

Four Application Program:

March to April
June
August
October

Three Application Program:

March to April
June
September

Please observe the manufacturers' recommendations closely.

How to Mow a Lawn Properly

MOWING

Mowing a lawn is part of our general urge for neatness. Some home gardeners enjoy this activity just as much as I do. Others hire professionals to do the job. I mow my lawn when it needs it. Commercial mowers usually show up every seven days or later if weather slows them down. They rarely come

Properly mowed turf area

Rotary mowers provide best all-around service, and can cut thick and tall turf. Mulching rotary mowers eliminate collection of grass clippings.

Reel mowers deliver a very smooth cut if they are sharp. They are used professionally for golf courses. Mow your lawn in different directions to keep grass from developing a "grain."

Plastic coils or paper tree wrap protect young trees against lawnmoweritis. A tree well also reduces damage potential.

> **Rocky Mountain Tip:**
> The more frequently you mow a lawn, the better it appears. Mow every time the clippings are half an inch long. This varies a lot from April until October.

more often than weekly. Lawns should be cut to 1¾" to 2¼".

The mowing machines we use vary widely. Few gardeners still use hand mowers, however. Hand mowers work well but need to be sharpened at least once a year. Until 1975, gasoline powered reel-mowers were popular but also needed annual maintenance. Since then, rotary mowers have become the only practical mower for home lawns. Park and golf course maintenance is still done mainly with mowers that have large gangs of reels.

A rotary mower which has a capacity for mulching is now available. I have used one for six years and am very pleased with its performance. The mulching mower does not require you to collect the grass clippings. It grinds them to very fine clippings. As they fall to the grass they are quickly decomposed by microbes. The only obligation that you assume is to mow every three to five days instead of weekly, and to mow the lawn only when it is dry. Wet grass clippings cake inside the mower housing. In spite of mowing more often, a mulcher saves time. And, your lawn benefits with the soil nutrients the grass clippings provide on breakdown.

All rotary mowers should have their blades sharpened every six to eight weeks. The easiest way is to have two blades for your mower. You can use one while the other is being sharpened.

All new mowers have several safety features built in, but they still cannot be made completely safe. So here are two safety rules that I recommend. Always wear closed shoes when mowing. And never try to pull any weed or other matter from a mower without turning the engine off. Believe it or not, Colorado General Hospital in Denver reports more than 600 mower accidents with injuries every year. And those are only the accidents with major injuries. Please be careful and be safe.

A properly maintained lawn mowing machine should give you 10 years or more of reliable service. A mower and its normal servicing should cost you about one hundred dollars or more each year. So if an enterprising youngster in your neighborhood is willing to mow your lawn for less than ten dollars each week with his Dad's mower, think about it. It may be a bargain.

If you catch grass clippings with a bag, you can use them for mulching in the garden and composting. When you mulch-mow, you leave them where they are.

Weeds and Their Control

WEEDS

Weeds occupy space and use nutrients and water but yield nothing of value. They not only survive against all odds, they even surprise us. They are drought-hardy and energy-efficient. Even in the most inferior soil and surroundings, weeds generate more growth in less time than any of our pampered garden plants. There are no crop failures among weeds. Once they germinate and commence to grow, neither drought nor freezing temperatures deter them from achieving a crop of seed to continue their existence. Weeds appear to have no severe disease or insect problems. They are the perfects plants — except that we don't want them.

Weed control is either dependent on hard work or perfect timing. It is best to control weeds when they are still immature. The hard work is to dig them out one by one. The perfect timing relates to a period when it is wind-free, 75 degrees Fahrenheit, and won't rain for three days.

To deal effectively with weeds, we first have to classify them into four general categories:

1. Annual broadleafed weeds — These are the common weeds that grow strong from seed. Good examples are dandelions, knotweed, kochia or fireweed, lambs quarters, pigweed, and Russian thistle or tumbleweed. These complete their cycle in a single season and carry from one year to the next by seed only.

2. Annual grassy weeds — These include crabgrass, stinkgrass, annual bluegrass, sandbur, and barnyard grass. These grassy weeds also survive only by seed from year to year. The exception is the common cheatgrass, which starts in the fall, lives over winter, and matures in early summer.

3. Perennial broadleafed weeds — These, for the most part, are tough to eliminate. Among these tougher ones are Canada thistle, bindweed, yarrow, Japanese and white Dutch clover and Mouse-ear chickweed. These weeds start out

Crabgrass

Bindweed

White Dutch clover

Canada thistle

Question: Our lawn is getting quite a bit of white clover in it. Is there anything that can be put on it to kill it but not harm the grass?
Answer: It is relatively easy to eliminate White Dutch clover in a lawn. Any chemical herbicide that contains 2, 4-D and Banvel-D (dicamba) will eliminate most clover in one or two treatments. Farm suppliers also have these chemicals. You can ensure less clover in the future by using a lawn fertilizer that contains very little phosphorus. An analysis of 23-4-4 or 25-3-3 is what you are looking for. There are several products of this type in the trade.

from their perennial roots each year, and they get larger and larger if permitted to grow.

4. Perennial grassy weeds — These are mostly native or introduced forage grasses of the livestock industry. They are not easy to eradicate. This group includes several coarse fescues, quackgrass, several wheatgrasses, orchard grass, and even such plants as creeping bent grass and Bermuda grass.

Numerous chemical weed controls are manufactured for home garden purposes. Here are some suitable ones most frequently used in lawns:

2, 4-D — This is the oldest member of the phenoxy group. It is sold in ester and amine form. Amine is less subject to drift and is most widely used. There are some low-volatility esters, but the amine is still tops. Its best effect is within 48 hours of application in warm weather without water or rain.

Banvel-D or dicamba — This is often used in conjunction with 2, 4-D. Most dry and liquid weed controls are one to three percent dicamba. This chemical is a bit more effective on perennial broadleafed weeds. In excessive applications, it can damage ornamental plants, whose roots are under the lawn. It is effective on the more difficult broadleafed weeds.

Trimec — This is a combination of several herbicides that are quite effective together. 2, 4-D is the most basic part of this blend.

Pre-Emergent Weed Control — Several chemicals are so-called pre-emergence materials. They control weeds at about the time of germination, before they start to grow. They will not control a weed that already is up and growing. Among the pre-emergent weed killers are Dacthal, Balan, Bensulide, Betasan, and others. These garden weeders are nontoxic and have no effect on growing plants.

Vegetation Killers — These products generally are referred to as sterilants. They not only kill a plant but render the treated soil sterile for three months to three years and longer in some cases. There is little use for them in a garden. But they may control weeds in a driveway or in cracks between pieces of concrete. Read their labels carefully. There are generally no antidotes for them, so you cannot reverse their chemical action once they are applied.

A chemical known as Round Up is also effective in weed control. The generic name for it is Glyphosate. It can be purchased under this name or under several brand names, such as KLEEN-UP — a more diluted form. Round Up is non-selective. It kills any green foliage, including Kentucky bluegrass. It is now sold in trigger sprayers with solutions diluted for lawn and garden use. I have used Round Up successfully on quackgrass in a rose garden several times without damaging the roses. But when the rose leaves are out, you must be extra careful. You can dab the solution with a sponge onto the foliage of weeds you wish to destroy.

How fast do chemical weed controls work? It is difficult to generalize; not as fast as a shovel, but reasonably so in warm weather. Any chemical that must be translocated to the roots from the absorbing foliage will move faster when metabolism in the plant is fairly high. Vegetation killers on the other hand work pretty fast in any weather. They may move into the soil during heavy rains, and that is why nearby plants that are desirable must be protected from vegetation killers. Most herbicides should be effective in less than 30 days. If nothing visibly happens in that time, the chemical should be applied again at the prescribed rate. When in doubt, it is best not to use sterilants.

If you use a hose or tank sprayer for weed control, use it for this purpose only. Buy another one to have handy for other uses. Sometimes, small residues of weed killers may adversely affect roses and other ornamental plants. It is difficult to rinse the sprayers well enough to ensure against any danger of contamination.

Garden weeders can be applied out of shaker cans or rotary applicators if they are in dust or granular form. They affect only weeds that are in the process of germination. A flowerbed should be cleaned up or hoed before a garden weeder is applied. I have used Dacthal in the rose garden. It works on annual weeds if I clean up all existing weeds before applying the chemical. This does not affect perennial weeds that grow from surviving roots.

Lawn fertilizer spreaders, in which fertilizer with weed controls have been applied, need only be rinsed lightly to wash out any residue of the chemicals. Since such a spreader is only used again for a lawn fertilizer application, it does not matter if particles of the weed control remain.

If you must use a weed control chemical near a flower or vegetable garden — yours or a neighbor's — it is important that you follow instructions carefully and completely. If there is even a slight breeze, weed controls should not be used. The early morning hours (5-6:30 a.m.), usually the calmest portion of a summer day, are best for weed control work. Always read and follow the label directions on pesticides.

INSECTS **Lawn Insects and Their Control**

Insect pests affect almost every plant in our environment. Some insects are noticed because of the damage they cause to emerging or mature plant foliage. Others do their damage underground or near the soil surface.

Most insects have several distinct stages in their life cycle. The normal sequence is: eggs, larva, pupa, adult. Some insects make this entire cycle only once each year, others more often, while a few insects only complete their cycle every 17 years or so (e.g., the 17-year locust).

In a home lawn, there may be several different insects. The ones that cause moderate to heavy foliage or root damage are readily noticed and should be controlled. In most instances the larva or worm stage is the part of an insect's life cycle that is most damaging to plants. Many adult forms of insects, including moths and butterflies, do not feed on anything, but instead use the energy accumulated in the larval stage to fly around and lay eggs. That is why larvae remain active longer than the adult stage of a lawn insect.

If you observe a flock of birds assembling on your lawn, it is safe to assume that you have lawn insects, in the form of larvae, feeding on your lawn. An insect's egg mass usually is very tiny, and as the larvae hatch, they increase in size gradually with their food intake. When you notice the damage to your turf, it already may be too late to obtain any good chemical control. Often, a lawn recovers on its own, the first time it has been attacked by insect larvae. But the next time may not be so simple. Most insecticides applied for lawn pests work better if the larvae are actively feeding.

A sure sign that you have problems with sod webworm is when you notice a small tan moth (about ¼ inch to ½ inch long) flying about from evergreens to your lawn in late afternoon. The moths lay their eggs on the fly as they come in for a landing, then take off again. They look like pilots of airplanes practicing landings and take-offs. Major turf grass insects in this Western region may vary from state to state, but they generally include sod webworms, grubs, pillbugs, ants and armyworms. Your local garden supply or University Extension Service agent usually can update you on lawn insects of special concern in your locality.

Sod webworm larvae

In 1972, the Environmental Protection Agency assumed complete control of the use of pesticides, including insecticides for farm and garden. Every chemical used for insect control now has to be registered with this agency, and labels giving directions for the chemicals' use must be approved by the EPA. Use of many chemicals has been restricted or entirely canceled.

The different types of turf insecticides now in use generally can be classified as contact, stomach, or systemic, depending on how they affect an insect.

Armyworm larva

Contact chemicals, such as Malathion, eliminate the insect within a few minutes through direct contact. Stomach poisons may be cumulative. The more a larva ingests, the closer to death it will be. Systemics are absorbed by the stems, foliage, and roots of plants. They render the plant toxic to the insect enemy. Gradually, as the insects feed, they accumulate enough of the chemical and perish.

How chemical pesticides affect humans and animals has been a matter of disagreement for years. The United States Department of Agriculture long ago established its LD50 measurements. Without getting very technical, the higher the LD50 number, the safer the product to warm-blooded creatures. Most of the relatively high-toxic chemicals are no longer on the shelf for home owner use. Diazinon, Dursban, and Sevin have EPA endorsement. These have been joined in some states by some newer chemicals, such as Oftanol.

You will be completely safe today while using chemicals for insect control if you:

1. Read the label carefully for instructions
2. Use the chemicals only as instructed
3. Keep the chemicals out of children's reach
4. Do not expose food or vegetables to chemicals
5. Never put chemicals in unmarked bottles or containers
6. Immediately wash any accidental spills on your skin with soap and water
7. Saturate soil spill area with buckets of water for dilution
8. Keep children and family pets indoors while you are spraying and until the spray has dried or been watered in
9. Follow other specific use statements on the label

You should not have any problem when you apply insecticides in granular form with a spreader or mixed with a lawn fertilizer. If you experience any discomfort, nausea, impaired vision, chest pains, or other abnormal symptoms, you should contact a physician immediately or call the nearest poison control center for further instructions and help.

In the Rocky Mountains region and the Western Plateau, we are plagued by night crawlers. These worms do some harm and much good. They aerate a tight clay soil, but they leave the soil surface so bumpy that you can hardly walk on it.

I have some in my lawn and I accept night crawlers as a necessary evil. No absolute chemical control has been suggested. Perhaps the best control is to use a flashlight and pick them up at night as they surface after a heavy irrigation. Then use them as fishing bait.

A good lawn can support some insects without major damage. Sometimes the help from birds is all you need to keep the bugs under control.

Turf Grass Diseases and Their Control

DISEASES

Not only are bluegrass lawns attacked and damaged by insects, but plant diseases also affect them. These diseases are caused by pathogens, which are disease organisms. Fungi, bacteria, or virus can create varying degrees of trouble for turf. Weather conditions that provide ideal moisture and temperature ranges also bring about a turf disease spread by a large increase in the fungal organisms that are parasitic to turf grasses, including, of course, Kentucky bluegrass varieties or selections. Some of the older varieties, such as common Kentucky bluegrass, Park, Delta, and Merion do not have much resistance to several common turf grass diseases. That is why they have been gradually replaced by newer varieties that have a high degree of resistance.

What damage may fungal diseases cause to an

Mushrooms

Question: How can I get rid of mushrooms?
Answer: Mushrooms and toadstools are the spore-bearing structures of decay fungi in the soil. Often, after rains, they become noticeable. Unless they appear in a circular pattern, I would just knock them over with a rake. The circular emergence of toadstools indicates fairy ring disease.

established lawn? Disease organisms can attack grass blades, crowns, and/or roots of plants. Some only attack one of these. Others, such as melting out, or leafspot disease, attack all three. Telltale lesions on the blades, caused by melting out, are easily detected by a trained observer. Disease also causes certain patterns of damaged or dead grass, but these can be misread. The best way to identify a disease is by culturing its microscopic-size organisms in a growth chamber. Only university research and test personnel have the means and experience to identify the culprit organisms that are causing the problem.

The secret of Kentucky bluegrass disease control is prevention, not cure. The old ounce-of-prevention dogma could not be more real. In my observation, it is already too late for a fungicide treatment for many diseases when the damage to the turf is obvious, because the environment of a turf grass disease pathogen is a very limited temperature, humidity and moisture situation only at certain times of the year. Once that environment has changed, the organism no longer causes further damage.

Rocky Mountain Tip:

The secret of Kentucky bluegrass disease control is prevention, not cure. Most chemicals work far better at prevention. Once the disease has broken out, good watering and mowing management helps more than fungicides.

Turf diseases that are common in our Western and Rocky Mountains region include:

(1) Leaf spot or melting out (Helminthosporium sp.) — Circular to elongated purple spots with tan centers form on leaf blades. Turf browns and thins out crowns of plants. Roots may be attacked in severe situations. Hot weather following a moist, humid period enhances the disease. Survives in spores.

(2) **Dollar spot (Sclerotinia homeocarpa)** — Lesions on blades are tan with reddish edges. Dead bleached spots in the turf are the size of a silver dollar. As disease progresses, spots overlap, producing irregular areas of dead turf.

(3) **Rhizoctonia brown patch (Rh. solani)** — Occurs in small to larger circular spots. Affected leaves turn dark and water-soaked, then light brown as blade tissue dies. Sclerotia are the

Leaf spot disease

Snow mold disease   *Dollar spot disease*

black, minute seed-like forms in which fungus survives.

(4) **Gray snow mold** *(Typhula sp.)* — Appears as snow melts. Affected areas are circular to ovoid, four to twelve inches in diameter and light yellow in color. A ring of gray mycelium (thread-like growth) may appear over each spot.

(5) **Pink snow mold** *(Fusarium nivale)* — Occurs at about the same time as gray snow mold and is more common in the West. Irregular circular spots blend together to affect larger lawn areas. The light pink color occurs at the outside

Question: How can I treat fairy ring?
Answer: Fairy ring disease relates to soil compaction. It appears to exist best under matted-tight clay soil conditions. It spreads by spores that are borne on toadstools. It is possible that a lawn mower could spread the disease. To contain fairy ring you must aerate the circles of dark green from four to six inches inside to six inches outside with a water or step-on aerator plugger. Then, after the soil is opened, prepare a drench with one ounce of a surfactant (such as Revive) plus one ounce of a fungicide (Daconil 2787, Zineb, or Captan) in a 2½ gallon bucket of water. Drench the liquid over the aerated lawn portion. If no change is visible in 30 days, repeat the treatment. I have found this drench about 50 percent successful.

rim. Inside turns yellow. Pathogen survives in dormant mycelium on debris of affected plants.

(6) **Fusarium blight *(Fusarium roseum)*** — Known as "frog-eye" disease, because it forms irregular to round circles or crescents, usually 2 to 18 inches in size. The larger circles have a green tuft of grass in the center.

(7) **Stripe smut *(Ustilago sp.)*** — Black streaks on blades start yellow-green, then become gray. Turf becomes thin and gray in color. When diseased lawn is mowed, a cloud of disease spores rises from the agitation. Pathogen survives in infested plants. Merion and Windsor Kentucky bluegrass are highly susceptible.

(8) **Powdery mildew *(Erysiphe graminis)*** — A disease that hits bluegrass mostly in shade during spring and early fall. Light gray color is followed by blades turning tan, then brown.

(9) **Fairy ring** (Many different fungi) — Appears in circles or crescents that are perfectly round. Disease grows outward from a center infection. Often, undigested organic matter and heavy clay soils create good conditions for this disease. Circles get larger each year. Outer edges are dark green in an underfed turf. In severe drought stress cases, grass in the circle dies. Aeration, followed by drenches of one ounce each of a liquid surfactant and a turf fungicide in 2½ gallons of water, usually will be satisfactory. Repeat later on the survivors. Small toadstools will form around the rings after warm, rainy weather.

The fungicides I am listing here were available in 1984. Other effective chemicals no doubt will be registered in the future. Take a sample of the diseased grass to a garden center or a county extension office of your university for proper diagnosis.

	Leaf Spot	Dollar Spot	Brown Patch	Gray Snow Mold	Pink Snow Mold	Fusarium Blight	Stripe Smut	Powdery Mildew	Fairy Ring
ACTI-DIONE R Z	X	X	X			X		X	X
ACTI-DIONE -THIRAM	X	X	X	X	X			X	X
DACONIL 2787	X	X	X						X
DYRENE	X	X	X	X	X	X			X
FORE	X	X	X		X				X
TERSAN 1991		X	X			X	X	X	
TERSAN LSR	X		X						
TERRACLOR (PCNB)	X	X	X		X	X	X		X

Fairy ring

Changes in temperatures will give you about the same recovery rate as a chemical treatment. Fungicides have become very expensive and may need to be used several times. Some commercial fertilizer-fungicide product combinations are less expensive to apply in early spring and late fall than some of the chemicals named above.

Compaction, Thatch, Mat, and Aeration

Several conditions can influence the quality of a mature, established turf. Compaction (hardening of the soil) is a problem caused by the soil, while thatch and mat relate to the grass itself. Aeration is an aid for an ailing lawn.

Thatch is an accumulation of dead and live organic material that is inadvertently deposited above the soil surface. If soil is mixed with the thatch by topdressing, earthworms, mulch, etc. it is called mat. Air and water have great difficulty penetrating through thatch. This affects lawn roots. Thatch provides protection for insects and a source of inoculum for disease spread. Thatch can be reduced by using aerators and dethatching machines.

The need for dethatching, raking and/or aeration can be determined by a very simple test. You must determine the thickness or density of the thatch deposits. The best information on thatch accumulation can be obtained in April or May by removing a lawn section 6 to 8 inches square with a spade or shovel to measure the thatch. If it is a half-inch or more thick, dethatching or raking is a definite advantage. If it is less that that, power-raking may not be needed, but some hand raking may be beneficial. Lawns should not be power-raked during the heat of summer.

MAINTAINING QUALITY TURF

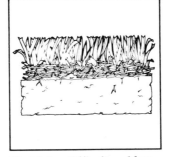

Thatch is a difficult problem with Kentucky bluegrass lawns. Unless it is removed annually when it exceeds a half-inch, it turns into a more solid mat which prevents moisture from penetrating. Aeration also works against thatch.

Dethatchers or power rakes are used to remove some of the thatch mechanically. They can be rented in most localities by the hour. The removed thatch must be vacuumed or raked.

The best available hand rake is a Cavex rake. It is a relatively inexpensive tool sold at most garden centers and hardware dealers. It not only benefits your lawn but also your physical well-being if you apply a rake to a few hundred square feet of lawn each day. Lawn edges will need less raking than portions in the center.

In a general way, aeration of a lawn will do a better service than dethatching, because aeration directly affects the soil and root structure. Most home gardeners don't realize that the lawn's roots are an important part of the grass plant. Aeration, fertilization, and proper watering are needed for healthy roots. Soil compaction is quite common in most of our clay soils and it affects roots adversely. Aeration opens the soil to air and helps with water penetration. Compacted soils can be improved with aeration. This can be accomplished with mechanical aerators or with hand tools. Both methods are effective, but hand tools are more adapted to smaller portions of a lawn than the entire turf area. Suggested hand tools would be a step-on plugger or a hose-attached Greenie. Both work well along sidewalks and driveways where water does not easily penetrate

Rocky Mountain Tip:

Aeration of a lawn will provide a better service to the well-being of the turf than any other mechanical activity, because soil compaction is a constant problem in Western clay soils.

Mechanical aerator

the soil. Aeration in heavy clay soils should be scheduled every year or two.

Important preparations of the soil must be made before aeration or raking. You must thoroughly water a lawn a day or so before aeration. Otherwise it will be too tough to penetrate. On the other hand, for raking or power-raking, the soil surface should be quite firm, and watering should follow.

The chemical industry has provided some new surfactants that contain organic humates, one of several chemicals that can be used. These increase moisture intake into tight soils that resist wetting. I have used them with success along my sidewalk and driveway where compaction causes the water to run off before it soaks in. These applications of wetting agents like Revive are usually good for 45 to 60 days, but they are not quite as effective as aeration. They are more a stop-gap when it may be too hot for aeration.

Renewing Damaged Turf   **LAWN REPAIR**

Sooner or later, even the best kept lawn needs a little repair work. The reasons why could be many. We can do injury to a lawn in several different ways. Our mowers may slip off the curb edge and cut a section so short that it may not survive. We call that scuffing or scalping. Perhaps you can borrow a small piece of your turf from a less visible spot of your lawn to repair the area. Such quick repair usually is very successful.

Perhaps the most important step in lawn repair is the proper identification of the reasonable cause why the turf failed in the first place. It could be compaction from heavy foot traffic, buried debris (that the contractor left you), or a tree stump somebody left for you just a few inches below the turf. Add a little organic matter to the soil before you replace the sod. You will not have to do the job every year if you do it right. Perhaps your fertilizer spreader balked at the turn-about and spilled more granules than the lawn could tolerate. Even though O.M. Scott's of Marysville, Ohio, found in experiments that they could fertilize four times the normal amount without burns, you can still burn a spot in your lawn. Without resodding, it may take 30 days before the grass recovers. Neighborhood dogs may have a similar effect on your lawn. This too will mend by itself in about five to six weeks. If you are not that patient or if the accident occurred in a very visible spot, you may have to do a little repair with sod.

Areas under trees that are heavily shaded may also lose the turf from lack of light and from competition for moisture. For such a need, the new turf type perennial ryegrasses are excellent because they germinate in about six days and, if seeded in spring, they can make a dense stand even before the leaves of your tree are fully extended.

Your lawn may become uneven in certain places because, somehow, the soil under a spot has shifted. You can cut the sod piece and replace or take out the needed soil to level the area. If the low spot is along your waterline, you also can add about a half-inch of sand and peat moss mixed about half-and-half in the spring and early fall to compensate and gradually re-establish a neat grade and level.

Rolling a lawn is a questionable way to obtain a

Question: What can cause small or larger brown spots in a lawn? At what time might these brown spots occur?
Answer: The most common causes for larger brown spots in July and August are lack of water, excess alkalinity of the soil, or severe soil compaction. Diseases may also affect a lawn and turn it brown almost all season long. Snow mold diseases occur in March or April, leaf spot disease usually in June, fusarium in July and stripe smut in August or September. Grubs, sod webworm and other soil insects usually damage a turf in May or September. Fertilizer or gasoline burns, dog spots, or lawn mower scuffing may occur anytime through the season. Sometimes two different causes may occur at the same time making it a challenge to correct them.

Rocky Mountain Tip:

The most important approach to lawn repair is to honestly identify the problem that caused the lawn sections to fail. Unless you make amends for the cause, you will only apply a "Band-Aid" treatment that really won't last.

better grade or level. If we have enough weight (water) in the roller, the compaction of the soil is worse than the benefits derived from rolling.

One other task I consider repair work is the first mowing each spring. Here we must attempt to cut the lawn as closely as possible to remove all the remaining stover or hay, so the new grass does not have to work its way through all the dead debris from last year. Hopefully, your lawn will show an attractive green early. If you have a grass catcher, you should remove this old grass and put it in your compost pit. If you mulch, you can let it drop to the soil level. The tiny microbes will appreciate their first good meal of the season.

TREES

TREES are man's and nature's monument to beauty and gracious living. They are a living permanence in the forests and a needed oasis in the plains. In the Rocky Mountains and the Western Plateau, trees provide us with shade and comfort and more than casual shelter from wind and weather. From an environmental viewpoint, trees are second only to lawns as important processors of carbon dioxide. They take it in and give off oxygen, the most vital element of the air we breathe. Trees provide a nesting place and food supplies for birds and other wild life. They resist pollution more successfully than numerous other garden plants, and they can cool our outdoor living areas and patios to enjoyable comfort. Some trees also provide a colorful climax of flowering and fruiting and some, in autumn, even turn to brilliant oranges, reds and yellows before they defoliate. Trees also help screen out unsightly views and frame a particularly fine exposure if we place them thoughtfully.

Well over 100 years ago, a Nebraska political leader and newspaper editor, J. Sterling Morton, launched Arbor Day as a special day for tree planting on his own birthday. In the often tree-barren West, we still observe Arbor Day every year by planting tree seedlings and larger trees on that provident man's birthday. Many families also observe the practice of planting a tree upon the birth of a child or other meaningful events.

CHOOSING TREES FOR YOUR LANDSCAPE

What many home gardeners want to know about any tree is how fast the tree will grow, how large it may be at 20 years of age (16 years after planting), what shape the tree canopy will form, and how much ground area it will eventually shade. The

How Plants Are Sold	Advantages	Disadvantages
Bare-rooted or packaged	*Least expensive but no longer a big nursery item. Fruit trees may be mail-ordered this way. Best roses are shipped from West Coast nurseries bare-rooted.*	*Must be kept moist until planting. May have to be heeled in if weather prevents quick planting. To heel in, dig a trench 12-14 inches deep and lay plants (root and top) at a slant, then cover all in the soil and keep moist.*
Balled and burlapped	*Larger plants are moved in this manner. Plants that must be moved from home can be moved B and B. It is work but preserves the plant. Use a root stimulator to help plants overcome shock.*	*Large plants may take several years before active growth is noticed. Soil balls must be kept moist or loss from dehydration may occur. May be stored too long at nursery.*
Container-grown	*All roots remain intact so plant hardly senses that it is transplanted. New environment may cause temporary shock. Can be planted safely March to October. Compact roots develop easily in larger planting hole.*	*Containerized plants are usually smaller to medium-sized. Beware of container plants that are unusually large for a 5-gallon or 10-gallon size. Their roots may have been severely pruned to make plants marketable.*

answers to these questions depend, to a degree, on location, moisture supply and soil quality. But I will attempt, in this chapter, to give you a good idea of what you can expect. If you do not intend to stay in a home for more than six years, you may have to start out with a much larger tree specimen. Naturally, the cost of bigger trees will be substantially higher, because the plants have obtained long-term, continuous care in a nursery.

The time you can invest in waiting for a full-grown tree in your landscape is a factor in what size your initial tree should be. I have planted most of my deciduous trees at a six- to eight-foot height, with a trunk caliper of about one inch. A tree's trunk caliper is a measurement of its diameter about a foot above

the ground. The availability of trunk calipers 1½ to
two inches in size has become much greater in recent
years and at quite reasonable prices. When you purchase trees exceeding two inches in diameter, the
weight of the soil ball gradually becomes heavier.
And at diameters of 3½ inches and up, we often need
the service of a mechanical tree spade. A mechanical
tree spade is usually a truck-mounted transplanting
machine that is operated hydraulically. It digs the
plant from its current nursery location and
transplants it into a similarly sized hole in the
garden. Planting a large tree is a bit too much for an
amateur gardener. And survival guarantees for the
tree often are honored only if the nurseryman
planted it for you.

Arborvitae

You now can get trees as large as 20 to 24 feet
tall, with a trunk caliper of 5½ inches. These large
trees must be pruned extensively to compensate for
loss of roots and reduce the effects of transplanting
shock. One reason I still prefer a tree ten feet tall or
smaller is that it transplants without much risk, and
you usually can plant the tree yourself. I have seen
many 12-foot to 14-foot Ponderosa pines moved and
transplanted mechanically. They may appear impressive, especially around a large commercial
building, but they often do not increase much in size
for several years while their reduced root system is
slowly regenerated. For a home landscape, I consider
an evergreen tree five to six feet tall an ideal size for
planting. They are quite visible, and there are few
transplant failures. I will discuss in detail the best
planting steps under the heading of transplanting.

Rocky Mountain Tip:

When your needs point to a more mature landscape, you can plant larger trees (up to five inches in
diameter.) It will cost substantially more to install
such trees on your property. But you buy valuable
time.

Most small to intermediate-size trees now are
sold in buckets or papier mache containers. They actually are grown that way at the nursery. These days,
fewer trees are sold "B and B" (balled and burlapped). And only a small number of trees are sold
bare-rooted. Bare-rooted plants can be sent by mail,
so mail-order nurseries handle most of their sales.
Although an offer of 50 trees and shrubs for $4.97

might sound very inviting, most of them merely are rooted cuttings. The survival rate is less than 25 percent. I advise purchase of trees and shrubs from a local nurseryman. It is even well worth a trip of 75 to 100 miles to shop for trees and shrubs. Also, if I told you that there rarely are any bargains in nursery stock, I would be telling it like it really is. There are good deals offered at the end of a season to reduce inventory and create cash flow. Also in September and October, some nurseries sell certain overstock items at 25 to 50 percent off. If you are ready, that is a good time to buy a few trees or shrubs you have wanted but placed a little lower on your priority list. You may receive mail-order clearance offers that are much reduced in price. They usually appear too late to be of value. After it gets hot outdoors, the nursery stock planting season is over. Save your money for a better deal. And when you see some advertisements in periodicals and magazines that seem unreal, they really are.

Rocky Mountain Tip:

Most intermediate sized trees 6 to 10 feet tall are now sold either in large containers or balled and burlapped (B & B). These may not be as impressive at the start, but they grow faster in the first few years than larger trees do.

Collecting Evergreens from the Wild

Not all evergreen trees are nursery-grown. Some may be collected from the wilds. Some are collected by nurserymen, others by individuals, and entrepreneurs. For instance, most Pinyon pines and Foxtail or Bristlecone pines are collected because it takes too many years to produce a five-foot tree in a nursery. Colorado spruces that appear thinly branched also may be collected. Nursery-produced Colorado spruces are more dense and attractive because they were produced in better soil and light. You should resist the temptation to purchase larger collected trees. They often have a root ball no larger than that for a four- to five-foot tree. The best chance for survival remains with collected trees about five to six feet tall.

GOOD TREES FOR SHADE   My Favorite Selections

After debating (with myself) the order to list shade trees — alphabetically or by my own preference — I

Rocky Mountain Tip:

The best size for native collected evergreen trees is around five to six feet. This includes collected spruces, Ponderosa, Foxtail and Pinyon pines, Concolor firs, and Monosperma junipers.

decided that my favorites might be more helpful to you. I really cannot give you a clear cut number-one choice, but these are the trees I like best, and some recommended varieties:

Green Ash *(Fraxinus pennsylvanica lanceolata)* -- Tolerates alkaline soil. Develops a round form with dark-green compound leaves. Makes a good street tree. Develops a sound set of scaffold branching. Needs little maintenance. Resists storm breakage well. Transplants very well. A good lawn tree. Twenty-year height: 25 to 30 feet. **Pests:** aphids, caterpillars, scale, borers.

Green Ash

> **Marshall's Seedless Green Ash** — the most dependable seedless, clean tree.
> **Summit Green Ash** — symmetrical upright variety — pyramidal shape.
> Also recommended — **Autumn Purple** and **Kimberly Blue.**

Thornless Honeylocust — The best available lawn shade tree. Creates filtered shade. Some varieties nearly seedless while others, in some years, have pods. Among the cleanest of shade trees: compound leaflets disintegrate after dropping. Tolerates dry conditions. Makes a round canopy. Twenty-year height: 25 to 30 feet. **Pests:** mites, blister beetles, borers.

Thornless Honeylocust

> **Skyline** — More pyramidal than most others, nearly podless.
> **Shademaster** — Vase-shaped; very symmetrical top; straight trunk, nearly podless.
> **Imperial** — smaller than most; matures at 30 to 35 feet.
> **Sunburst** — Foliage is golden yellow early in the season, but turns green later except for growth tips. Seedless. In very alkaline clay soil, it will be very chlorotic, which means it will turn a little more yellow than gold.
> **Moraine** — a good choice in better soils.

Linden — The most durable shade tree of all. Grows very slowly. Very few problems; almost

American Linden

Soft Maple

maintenance-free. Honeybees love the nectar. Semi-pyramidal form. Prefers well-drained soil. Twenty-year height: 15 to 25 feet. **Pests:** caterpillars, mites.

American Linden — A very durable shade tree. Young trunk needs winter protection.

Littleleaf Linden — Pyramidal shape; leaves about two to two and a half inches across. Variety Greenspire is quite upright and narrow.

Redmond — A variety of American with large, dark-green leaves.

Also recommended: June Bride, Fairview, Crimean.

Maple — The most popular tree in the Northern United States, but not #1 in our Western area. Maples sunscald badly during winter seasons. Sunscald is exposure damage to the cellular structure of the bark, usually caused by mid-winter sun. Some maples are of poor scaffold structure and break up as badly as Chinese elms under heavy, wet snow. Soft maples are quite hardy; hard maples are more subject to temperature extremes. Some transplant easier than others. Twenty-year height: 20 to 35 feet. **Pests:** leafrollers, caterpillars.

Soft Maple *(Acer saccharinum)* — Also known as silver maple. One of the fastest-growing hardy trees. Prefers good drainage but roots often rise to surface and break up sidewalks. Variety Wier cut-leaf maple is a good choice. Soft maples are susceptible to chlorosis in heavy alkaline soils. They also break easily in heavy snows.

Norway Maple *(Acer platanoides)* — A tree with sounder scaffold limbs. Turns dark green, then yellows in the fall. Resists pollution well. Creates heavy shade. Varieties Columnar Norway, Emerald Queen and Schwedler are good choices under a little protection. Schwedler unfurls its leaves purple-red in spring and turns dark green in summer.

Amur or Ginnala Maple *(Acer ginnala)* — Makes a small tree if trained to a single trunk or can be grown as a clump or a tall screen. Native to this region and excels in orange and red fall colors. Takes well to poor soils.

Boxelder *(Acer negundo)* — Once established, will survive difficult conditions. Suitable for elevations to 8,500 feet. Very gnarly bark and irregular trunk.

Wasatch Maple *(Acer grandidentatum)* — A

smaller tree native in Wyoming, Utah and New Mexico. Well-adapted. Leaves are pubescent (hairy) on the underside.

Hackberry *(Celtis occidentalis)* — A good shade tree. Adapts well to poor soils, heavy as well as sandy. Has a deep tap root. Does not heave the sidewalk or disturb a good lawn. Main problem is transplanting. A six-to-eight-foot tree will transplant easier than larger specimen. Tolerates heat and drought. Twenty-year height: 20 feet. **Pests:** nipple gall (causes swelling of leaf tissue; unsightly but does not damage growth later in summer).

Catalpa *(Catalpa speciosa)* — The Western catalpa can survive almost anywhere. Produces large, white flowers in early summer. But the long seed pods hang on until winter and have to be raked for neatness. Develops good branching and has very large, heart-shaped leaves averaging five by 12 inches. Tolerates drought, wet and dry soils, and adjusts well to a variable Western climate. Transplants well. Twenty-year height: 20 to 25 feet. **Pests:** none.

Hackberry

Burr Oak *(Quercus macrocarpa)* — A tough, hardy, drought-tolerant tree. Like other oaks, difficult to transplant, but smaller sizes (five to eight feet) can be transplanted most successfully. Most have large acorns. Foliage is six to eight inches long and lobed, with a gray cast underneath. Twenty-year height: 15 to 20 feet. **Pests:** leafrollers, aphids.

Red Oak *(Quercus rubra)* — Needs a well-drained, rich soil. Prefers neutral to acid soil reaction. Also subject to chlorosis (iron deficiency).

Gambel Oak *(Quercus gambel)* — Native to the eastern foothills, Northern New Mexico and west of the Rocky Mountains. Often found in scrubby stands. Sometimes has red fall color. Generally adapted to 8,000 feet. Twenty-year height: 10 feet. **Pests:** aphids, gall insects.

Catalpa

Russian-olive *(Elaeagnus angustifolia)* — Very tough, hardy tree with informal trunk and growth habit. Accepts any soil or location. Transplants well from seedling size on up. Silver-gray foliage creates a desirable contrast in any landscape. Can be grown as a single or multiple trunk. Will last longer as a single-trunk tree. Has fragrant flowers followed by a half-inch seed favored by many birds. Also can be used as a large shrub or tall hedge. Long, narrow foliage resists high winds well. Twenty-year height: 25 feet. **Pests:** leafrollers, gumosis.

Prunus Chokecherry *(Prunus virginiana*

Russian-olive

Newport Plum

Cottonwood

Question: Many small yellow leaves are falling off my 25-foot cottonwood trees. This has never happened before. What may be the cause?
Answer: This is the result of an on-again off-again spring. Some of the leaves emerged early and were damaged by cold before they were fully developed. Now the trees have made much new growth. The leaves are large and function properly. The little leaves contribute little to the tree's development, so they are shed·to reduce water use. Nothing needs to be done for the trees but normal care.

melanocarpa "Shubert") — Very adaptable to Rocky Mountain and Plateau region. May sunscold without winter protection. White flowers followed by fruit for jelly. Purple foliage. Transplants easily. Twenty-year height: 15 feet. **Pests:** aphids, caterpillars.

Newport Plum *(Prunus blireana)* — Grows to a small tree. Purple foliage an excellent, contrasting color for interesting landscaping. Same height and pests as Shubert Chokecherry.

Ohio Buckeye (Aesculus glabra) — A small, round tree with large, compound leaves and greenish-yellow candles of flowers. Seems to establish slowly but forms inedible seed after a few years. Start small as it forms a tap root. Twenty-year height: 15 to 18 feet. **Pests:** None.

Cottonwood *(Populus sp.)* — The genus Populus presently is the only recognized native tree of the High Plains and Great Basin. Several species may be used for landscaping, but only the male cottonless forms are recommended. With few exceptions, all grow to very large trees. Populus are dioecious, meaning male and female flowers occur on separate trees. Cottonwoods need a large area to develop in. They overshadow a whole garden. Roots go everywhere after water, even into the sewer system or leaching field. These trees must not be overused. They struggle in a dry location. Twenty-year height: 60 feet. **Pests:** cytospora canker (no control), galls, caterpillars and leafrollers. Also recommended:

Sargent Poplar *(P. sargentii)* — A Colorado native. Grows to 90 feet.

Mountain Cottonwood *(P. acuminata)* — Has dark green upper leaf color and light green undercolor. Matures at 45 feet. Good to 7,500 feet.

Narrowleaf Poplar *(P. angustifolia)* — Foliage similar to a willow. Grows to about 60 feet. Will grow at very high elevations up to 10,000 feet.

Robusta Cottonwood *(P. robusta)* — Grows up to 60 feet high with large leaves. Very rapid growth.

Siouxland Cottonwood *(P. deltoides)* — An improved form over the Sargent poplar. Golden fall color. May grow up to 90 feet.

Theves Poplar *(Populus sp.)* — Theves Upright tree used for screening instead of Bolleana and Lombardy, which are subject to disease before they are 10 years old. Twenty-year height: 30 to 40 feet. **Pests:** caterpillars, leafrollers.

Cutleaf Weeping Birch *(Betula pendula gracilis)* — A beautiful tree with white bark. Native to North Central states where soils are acid and rains are good. More are planted than succeed. Dry winters can be devastating to mature trees. Drought is the #1 enemy. But if you like a birch, you can plant this one and care for it with extra winter watering. Twenty-year height: 20 to 25 feet. **Pests:** aphids, borers.

Rocky Mountain Birch *(Betula fontinalis)* — Prefers moist, creekside, but well-drained soil. Bark is cinnamon color. Sound up to 9,000 foot elevations. Best grown as a clump. Has weeping form with age. Twenty-year height: 15 feet. **Pests:** aphids.

Quaking Aspen *(Populus tremuloides)* — Belongs to the cottonwood's genus, but there is such a difference. The leaves are smaller, as are the trees themselves. Aspen has become one of our most popular smaller trees, outselling even crabapples. Does not like dry clay soils. Aspens do well as a group in berms. Twenty-year height: 12 to 15 feet (may not live 20 years; 12 to 15 years is the average). **Pests:** cytospora blight, scales, aphids.

Black Walnut *(Juglans nigra)* — About the only nut tree that produces fruit for the squirrels. Should be in a large area by itself, far away from a vegetable garden, because the roots have a toxic effect on some garden crops. A good squirrel guard may let you harvest a few nuts every few years. Twenty-year height: 30 to 35 feet. **Pests:** aphids, mites, caterpillars.

Willow *(Salix sp.)* — Prefers a moist soil loca-

Sunburst Locust

Question: I have a Sunburst locust. The leaflets turn yellow in a spotted, irregular pattern, eventually spreading over the entire leaf, which then falls off. How can this problem be controlled?
Answer: The Sunburst locust has a natural tendency toward chlorosis. This is the result of clay soil and alkalinity, both of which are a problem in our area. Treat the soil in the root zone with chelated iron. Sequestrene 330 Fe, good for this purpose, is generally available at garden centers. Don't forget to water your locust monthly in winter.

European Weeping Birch   *Aspen*   *Black Walnut*

tion near a pond or lake. Weeping willows have graceful, procumbent branches. Not a good tree for limited home grounds, since the roots are hard on sewers and septic tanks. Some varieties are a bit smaller than others. Transplants easily.

Niobe Weeping Willow *(Salix alba)* — Has yellow bark on twigs. Very hardy. Twenty-year height: 30 feet. **Pests:** aphids, scale.

Globe Willow *(Salix umbraculifera)* — Excellent street tree in Grand Junction, Colorado; may be grown in central Idaho cities, but not as easy to grow on eastern slope of the Rockies. Twenty-year height: 25 to 30 feet. **Pests:** aphids, scale.

Corkscrew Willow *(Salix matsudana tortuosa)* — A bit more tender than other willows mentioned. Seems to grow better in clumps. Has twisted trunk and branches. Twenty-year height: 35 to 40 feet. **Pests:** aphids, scale.

Weeping Willow *(Salix pentandra)* — An old-timer found mostly in irrigated areas of the West or along larger rivers. Mainly propagated by cuttings now. Twenty-year height: 35 to 40 feet. **Pests:** aphids, scale.

THE BEST FLOWERING TREES

We would be fortunate if we had flowering trees that bloom all season long, from May to September. But we don't have them. Most of these trees flower in May and a few in June. Actually, the flowers are Mother Nature's lure to the insect world to get pollination so a large amount of fruit and seed is matured. We should gratefully accept a bountiful spring season with many colorful blossoms on our trees and no killing frosts at night.

Crabapples *(Malus sp.)* — One of the largest genera of useful plants for landscaping. Several species have been crossed to obtain such a large number of cultivars. I will list for you over 30 varieties that are sold in the Denver market. It is reasonable to assume that twice that many could be obtained in the Rocky Mountains and Western region. Most crabapples in our region will bloom from mid-April to mid-May. Some produce very small fruit, some large enough for crabapple jams and jellies. These goodies are a lot of work, but the fruits make some of the best Christmas gifts. A few of these varieties are rated resistant to fireblight, a bacterial disease. If this problem exists in your location, you should stick with the resistant varieties.

Crabapple in bloom

Variety	Bloom Color	Foliage Color	Fruit Color	Fireblight Resistant
Adams	Deep Pink	Green	Red	X
Almey	Light Red	Green	Orange-red	
American Beauty	Red	Bronze-green	Red	
Baccata	White	Green	Red	
Bechtel-Klehms	Double Pink	Green	None	
Beverly	White	Green	Red	
Candied Apple	Purplish Pink	Dark Green	Red	
Centennial	White	Green	Red	
Dolgo	White	Reddish Green	Red	
Echtermeyer	Purplish Pink	Bronze-green	Purple-red	
Eleyi	Red	Purplish Green	Purple-red	
Flame	White	Green	Red	
Floribunda	Pink-white	Green	Red	
Henry Kohankie	White	Green	Yellow-red	X
Hopa	Dark Pink	Dark Green	Orange-red	
Inglis	White	Green	Red	
Katherine	Double Pink	Green	Yellow-red	
Kelsey	Double Pink	Bronze-green		
Liset	Rose	Bronze-green	Maroon Red	X
Pink Perfection	Double Pink	Dark Green	Yellow (few)	
Pink Spire	Pink	Green	Purple-red	
Radiant	Deep Pink	Reddish to Green	Red	
Red Silver	Crimson	Purplish red w/silver hair	Deep Red	
Red Splendor	Pink	Green	Red	X
Robinson	Deep Rose	Bronze-green	Red	
Royalty	Purplish	Rich Purple	Dark Red	X
Selkirk	Pink fragrant	Dark Green	Red	X
Snowcloud	Double White	Dark Green	Yellow (sparse)	
Snowdrift	White	Green	Orange-red	
Sparkler	Rose-pink	Dark Green	Dark Red	
Spring Snow	White	Green	Sterile	
Strathmore	Pink to Red	Reddish Purple	Red	
Van Eseltine	Double Pink	Green	Yellow	
Vanguard	Rose	Reddish to Green	Red	
Zumi	White	Green	Red	

20-year height: Varies from 12 to over 30 feet
Pests: Fireblight, Caterpillars, Leafrollers, Mites

Eastern Redbud *(Cercis canadensis)* — Blooms early and often is hurt by late frosts. Best location is a sheltered north side. Flowers are purplish-pink. Twenty-year height: 20 feet. **Pests:** Aphids, Caterpillars.

Hawthorn *(Crataegus)* — Some varieties are hardy and safe in our region; some are borderline in many places.

Cockspur Hawthorn *(Crataegus crusgalli)* — Has its own protection with spurs one and a half to three inches long that are as sharp as needles. Birds love to nest in this tree. Has white flowers and red fruit that clings well all winter. Foliage is green, with brilliant fall color. Twenty-year height: 20 feet. **Pests:** leafrollers, mites.

Downy Hawthorn *(Crataegus mollis)* — White flowers followed by red fruit. Considered very hardy. Foliage green and covered by soft, whitish hair as it unfolds. Requires careful transplanting. Twenty-year height: 20 feet. **Pests:** leafrollers, aphids.

Washington Hawthorn *(Crataegus cordata)* — Needs some protection. White flowers followed by

Redbud

Goldenraintree

Hawthorn

Mountain Ash

Tree Lilac

scarlet red fruit. Dense foliage turns from green to brilliant orange in autumn. Twenty-year height: 15 to 18 feet. **Pests:** leafrollers, caterpillars. Borderline.

Paul's Scarlet Hawthorn *(Crataegus oxycatha Pauli)* — Double-red flowers turn to scarlet fruit. Small tree with round top. Needs some protection from extreme weather. Twenty-year height: 15 to 18 feet. Borderline. **Pests:** caterpillars, leafrollers.

Goldenraintree *(Koelreuteria paniculata)* — Clusters of yellow flowers in June are followed by lantern-shaped seed pods. A small tree that also can be grown as a multiple trunk. May die back early in some winters.Twenty-year height: 15 to 20 feet. **Pests:** mites.

Mountain Ash *(Sorbus aucuparia)* — Attractive white flowers are followed by orange berries. Subject to sunscald. Best planted away from afternoon winter sun. Sometimes difficult to transplant. Excellent attraction for birds: waxwings prefer the fruit. Autumn color is spectacular. Twenty-year height: 25 feet. **Pests:** fireblight, mites, cytospora canker.

Japanese tree lilac *(Syringa japonica)* — Usually a tall shrub that can be single-stemmed by pruning into a small tree. A neat plant with white flowers, but seems to get nipped in my garden on a cold night every year. Recovers and flowers dependably. Twenty-year height: 15 feet. **Pests:** leafminers.

Bradford pear *(Pyrus calleryana)* — Excellent resistance to fireblight. Thornless. Flowers white in large clusters and produces small, inedible fruit that are eaten by birds. Resists pollution well and is very hardy. Transplants easily. Good fall color. Twenty-year height: 25 feet. **Pests:** pear slug.

THE BEST TREES FOR FALL COLOR

These trees, which I already have evaluated, can produce stunning colors in their fall foliage:

Amur maple	Washington hawthorn
Staghorn sumac	Norway maple
Red oak	Aspen
Mountain ash	Cutleaf weeping birch
Bradford pear	Gambel oak

THE BEST TREES FOR MOUNTAIN LOCATIONS (6,500 to 8,500 feet)

In mountain valleys, there are many climatic extremes. So no one can guarantee that a certain tree will grow in a specific location. The following suggestions are the best I can offer. Much depends on individual location and terrain. If a certain tree you want does not succeed the first time, try again. You may be charmed on the second try. Sometimes, the second plant you purchase may be in better condition than the first one. We cannot peek under the bark or evaluate the roots. All we can do is hope and pray.

Alder (native) *(Alnus sp.)* — Small tree or large shrub, needs moist soil location, but good drainage. Suitable up to 10,000 feet for a very short season. Twenty-year height: 15 feet. **Pests:** aphids.

Also recommended:

Aspen	Crabapples — Dolgo
Rocky Mountain birch	— Hopa
Boxelder	— Kelsey
Cottonwood — Acuminata	Amur or Ginnala
— Augustifolia	maple
— Empire	Mountain ash
	Gambel oak

Pear Tree

Question: What kind of a shallow-rooted tree can I use over or near a sewer line (within five to six feet)?
Answer: You would be better off leaving well enough alone. Every year, thousands of homeowners have to use sewer repair services because they thought a certain tree would never affect their sewer line. A shrub such as cotoneaster or lilac would be a more likely choice. The loss of a shrub is not as severe as the loss of a treasured tree.

Crabapple

Ginnala Maple

HOW TO TRANSPORT A TREE FROM THE NURSERY

After you select the trees you want at the nursery you must haul them safely to your lot. Root balls or containers must be carefully anchored in your car's trunk and a plastic cover placed over the foliage to protect it. Also, secure plants that extend out of a trunk with a rope and a red marker at the end. Try to hold your speed down to avoid excess moisture loss. Secure the trunk lid, if needed.

Always carry the plant by soil ball, never lift or carry by tree's trunk.

Brace soil ball securely, then tie trunk lid in place. Drive slowly . . . wind burns leaves especially in p.m. heat.

Get extra help with heavy loads. If you cannot lift the soil ball, you may slide it on burlap, cardboard, or heavy plastic.

PLANTING AND TRANSPLANTING TREES

Do It Right

It is better to dig a $10 hole for a $5 tree than the other way around. Our soils need careful improvement before you plant or transplant a tree. For a small tree in a five-gallon container, you should dig an excavation about 24 inches wide and 18 inches deep. The soil ball will not be that large. But in our poor Western soils, we have to do all we can to provide trees with a good start in our garden. For most shrubs, the process is quite similar.

If the tree is larger than a five-gallon container, we may find that a backhoe can save us a lot of shovel work. Even a posthole digger on a tractor, with a 12-inch auger, will be very helpful. I don't believe in heroics.

Anything a machine can do, let it. You may also use a mechanical spade, which will set the tree into the planting hole but leave the soil around it unprepared.

When you dig a tree-planting hole with a shovel, try to salvage some of the topsoil, if there is any, and set it aside in a separate pile. That will become part of your planting soil. To the salvaged topsoil, add an equal amount of peat moss and mix it well.

After the excavation, you need to do some testing for drainage. The simplest way I know is to fill the excavation you have made with water all the way to the top. Do this around 5 p.m. If — by the following morning — all the water has percolated down, you have selected a spot with excellent drainage, and planting can proceed. Should there be no more than four inches of water remaining, you can dig the hole that much deeper and mix in enough sand and gravel to accommodate the tree. The purpose of this is to keep the roots out of the standing water. But if there is more than five inches of water remaining in a hole 16 to 18 inches deep, your soil drainage in that spot is too poor to ensure development of a healthy tree. If the location is an absolute must, you will just have to dig at least another 12 inches deeper and add more rock and gravel until you have drainage enough to have a healthy tree in your garden.

The tree is now removed carefully from its container. If the container is a large metal can, it should be cut for you at the nursery before you take the tree home. If the container is one of paper or cardboard, it will cut easily with a knife. Try not to break the soil ball in the process. The root system will be less shocked if the soil around it remains intact. Now you have to guess or measure how deep the hole is. The top of the soil ball should end up level with the soil surface. Otherwise, the plant will be too deep, and this may harm the root system. Add enough peat moss and soil mix so the top of the soil ball protrudes two inches above the level of the garden. Watering then will compact and contract the medium in the planting hole, and the tree will settle to the desired position.

If the tree and soil ball are heavy, and you cannot safely handle them by yourself, please get some help before you try to lift the tree and place it in the planting hole.

Rocky Mountain Tip:

A newly planted tree often requires two years of root development to regain what is lost in transplanting. It also takes time for roots to grow out of a soil ball from a container.

Now add more peat and soil mix to the hole and press down by walking around the outside of the soil ball until the planting hole is filled to within two inches of the top. At this point, add water slowly out

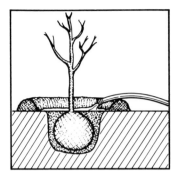

Soil berme allows more thorough watering during prolonged drought. Berme may be removed after the first year of establishment.

of an open hose. When the water level is up to the rim of the hole, turn off the water and let it soak in. The next watering, which should follow immediately or within 24 hours, should be from a bucket or sprinkler can with a root stimulator added. Follow label directions and use about four to six tablespoons of root stimulator per gallon of water.

If you are planting your tree in spring, water again every 7 to 10 days until your routine schedule of lawn watering provides the needed moisture.

The first winter is the most critical time for your new tree's survival. You should plan to water the tree every 30 days unless snow or frozen ground prevents you.

Late summer or fall planting gives your new tree only a nominal chance to grow new roots. In this case, winter watering must be provided every two weeks unless the soil freezes or is covered by a good layer of snow.

The described planting process is very similar for most evergreen trees and all shrubs, deciduous or evergreen. A good planting program often lets you be nearly 100 percent successful at landscaping.

Rocky Mountain Tip:

Fall planting is practical only with container-stock plants.No bare-rooted fall transplanting should be attempted, except for certain perennial flowers.

A CHECKLIST FOR SUCCESSFUL TRANSPLANTING

Following soil preparation, the transplanting process can start. The landscape plan (chapter 2) should direct you to stake the accurate locations of shade trees, shrubs, fruit trees, and evergreens. The success of your planting process relates to accuracy. If in doubt, double check. Planting too close to foundations, fences, or property lines is an error you cannot easily correct later on. Be sure you follow these ten steps to success:

1. Understand and write down the ultimate height, shape, and width of every plant and any other requirements of the plants you have selected. Delay the use of exotics from "back home" until you have a good start of your new landscape.

2. Dig every planting hole at least 50 percent wider and deeper than it appears necessary.

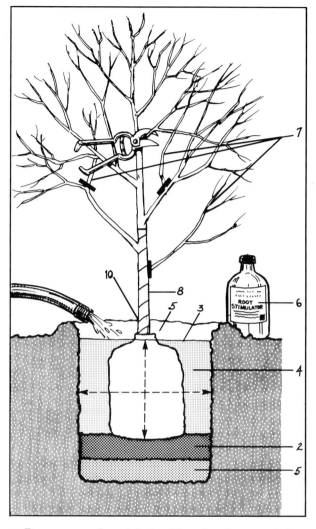

Remove rocks, debris. Use the best soil from near the top for back fill.

3. Locate the soil ball so the plant will be at the same height as the top of the ball or the soil in the container. Deeper planting is not better. It may be a hindrance. Do not remove burlap. Cut any ropes at the top or sides after the plant has been properly situated. Also remove paper-type containers. They do not disintegrate easily in Western soils. If a stake is needed at planting, insert it securely before you backfill.

4. Now use the best soil you have with equal amounts of peat (Canadian or equally acidic). Fill around the rootball until the planting hole

is about ⅔ full and water slowly from an open garden hose. Make sure that the plant remains upright and steady as the water settles the soil-peat mix.

5. Finish the backfill with the soil-peat mix and water again. Leave a one- to two-inch basin so you can water again weekly during the first growing season. If drainage is a problem, use three to four inches of sand and gravel in the bottom of the planting hole.

6. Use super-phosphate or bonemeal in the planting process. It can be placed near the top of the backfill or added during the soil-peat mix repacking. Use a handful for small plants. Trees up to one-inch trunk diameter need a half pound. Larger trees can use from one to two pounds. You can help the plant overcome shock by applying root stimulator or Up-start according to directions after the initial watering.

7. Pruning about a third of twigs and branches helps the plants establish more completely in less time. Bare-rooted plants such as privet hedging should be pruned back to three inches above the ground.

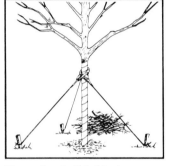

Prune about a third to compensate for roots lost during transplanting. Stake or guy tree so that wind moving the tree will not disturb the roots.

8. Use rolled paper wrap to protect the trunk of deciduous trees against sunscald. Plastic coils also perform the same task, but don't need removal for two to three years. Paper wrap should be removed the following spring.

9. Staking or guying is sensible for trees or larger plants in wind-exposed situations. Wires can be fastened around the trunk, two-thirds up, with sections of rubber garden hose.

10. Check frequently for presence of insects or spray regularly every three weeks to be sure with a combination chemical such as Isotox or anything designated as shrub or tree spray. Also protect the lower trunk of the tree against lawnmowers.

PROTECTING YOUR TREES

How to Stake or Guy a New Tree

Let's suppose you have just planted a new eight-foot tree in your backyard. Let's also assume that you followed the planting instructions to the letter, and that you have done a job to be proud of. But your backyard does not offer much shelter or protection. The north or west winds whistle by and whip that young tree unmercifully. To prevent the tree from suffering damage, we can stake it or guy it. Either system for physically supporting a new tree

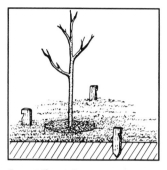

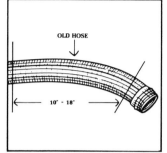

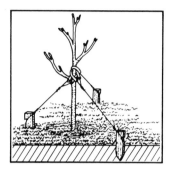

Insert the stakes around tree, with one facing north or west (prevailing wind).

Protect tree trunk with short section of old garden hose or scraps of burlap wrapped loosely around trunk.

Use rope, twine, or fine metal cable to secure tree. Do not attempt to pull tree into vertical position if it is not straight. If needed, apply plastic colored strips to guys, especially in public area (front).

can help protect the root system and the growth it has made in your garden.

There is another reason for staking or guying. Some trees grown in a commercial nursery are tall for their age. The favorable growing conditions at the nursery coupled with a little excessive feeding sometimes create tall-for-their-age specimens. This means that their trunks are a bit thinner than normal and cannot support the height as well as they should. Evergreens are particularly susceptible to this problem. Their density of growth and branching make them highly subject to twisting and vibrating in high winds. And that creates problems for their roots. It takes new roots a while to respond to their new soil environment and start active growth. But relentless twisting of a tree by high winds will break those new rootlets, and you will be back to point zero. Staking or guying will provide needed protection for your tree.

Most parks and recreation districts stake every tree they plant. They have learned through experience that staking does more than just fortify the trunk. It also protects a tree, at least on one side, from "lawn mower-itis." That is a problem caused when lawn mowers hit lower trunks and injure the bark of trees. They also add sections of used automobile tires at the lower six inches to protect the new tree from all sides. They find, too, that potential vandalism is reduced by staking. A number of different materials can be used for staking trees, including aluminum or steel rods, two-by-fours, and even bamboo. The idea is to lend support to young trees and prevent damage and breakage. You should plant your stakes at the same time you plant your trees.

Guying a tree achieves a similar result in a dif-

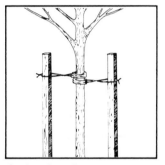

Optional method: Drive two strong stakes, one on the north side, the other south. Use rings of old rubber hose around the tree trunk and secure them to the stakes with wire.

ferent manner. It is most often accomplished with three or four pieces of sisal rope or wire affixed to a collar or to a piece of used garden hose wrapped around the trunk about two-thirds of the way up. Each rope or wire is anchored with a short wooden stake. Place the stakes in three or four spots away from the tree about 120 or 90 degrees apart respectively. Each guy rope or guy wire should have a turnbuckle so you can tighten the supports and reduce play to a minimum.

Guy ropes or guy wires can be more of a safety problem than staking a tree, since people can stumble over the wires. Only a location with no outside access will do. But guys are the only solution if you have a crooked trunk that needs straightening. Heavy snows can cause such a problem. Also, a settling of the soil in the planting hole could cause similar problems.

How long should you stake or guy a tree? That will depend to some degree on the tree's location and wind exposure. It also matters whether the tree was planted in the spring, summer or fall. With spring planting, over-winter should give us sufficient new anchorage in the soil. With summer or fall planting, you should keep this support for about a year. If a tree does not grow a lot the first season, you should keep the guy lines or stakes in place another winter.

Large trees and evergreens brought in the yard with a mechanical tree spade should always be guyed. Often, such a tree will take two full years to regrow a portion of the root system that the spade separated and left behind when it was transplanted. I strongly suggest that you guy for at least two years any collected specimen evergreen, such as a Pinyon pine, that is 6½ feet high or larger.

How to Fix Tree Breakage

In the Western states, we experience all kinds of weather — some of it good, some of it bad, such as wet snows. Wet snows are heavy, and when they pile up, they can cause considerable damage to trees. I remember a big, wet snow that hit Denver in late May of 1949. I believe it took the public works department until September to haul away all the broken limbs and branches. I have seen similar storms since then at an average of one every eight years. In 1982, Denver had its famous Christmas blizzard, the kind that is said to occur once in 100 years. Well, we had another one like it on Thanksgiving,

1983. So in spite of all predictions and almanacs, we had two 100-year storms in less than a year.

You can imagine what wet snows do to trees. Not all people can afford to have their trees trimmed regularly by a commercial tree service company. So their pruning, unfortunately, is done by heavy snows and not according to best arboricultural practices.

When tree limbs break, frayed stubs and wounds are left behind. To save the tree, these stubs and wounds must be cleaned up and treated. Professional tree service people leave about a half-inch stub when they saw off the broken remains. This ensures the wounds will heal quickly with a minimum of disease exposure. Research has shown that a stub cut will heal over more successfully than a flush cut.

Many trees do not develop a sound scaffold structure without our help. Narrow-angled crotches result. These can compound the breakage problems when we suddenly find ourselves in the middle of a heavy wet snow. We can shake small trees to lighten the load, but who is able and willing to climb a ladder in sub-freezing temperature to shake the limbs of a big tree? Narrow crotches are problem spots because as the diameter of trunk and limb increase every year, more dead bark gets caught between the two, and the structural attachment of one to the other diminishes. As the breakage occurs, we often lose half the tree. And once a limb is broken, there is no way to re-attach it to the trunk.

Using Cabling to Prevent Tree Breakage

The best way to prevent limbs from breaking under the weight of wet snow is to use cabling. This process can distribute the weight equally between both sections of a tree's fork. Trees having limb diameters of four inches or more need to be cabled. About five feet above the narrow crotch, drill a half-inch-diameter hole through both tree sections and install eye bolts in each, with the circle on the inside of the branch. Then, place a quarter-inch-diameter cable between the eye bolts. Preferably, the cable should have a turnbuckle so you can vary the tension. Do not wrap the wire or cable around the entire branch. This may girdle the upper portions of the tree and cause their eventual loss. Cabling on large shade trees should be done by a qualified arborist. You may not have adequate tools and experience to do the job right. Worse yet, you could end up in a cast for several months if you fall.

REPAIRING A SPLIT TREE TRUNK

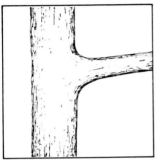

Strong branching. Limbs form at or near right angles to main trunk for good union of strong internal tissues. That occurs rarely.

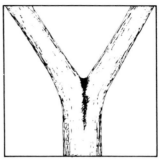

Weak branching pattern. Dead bark and debris are caught within narrow angle of branches. This branching is found on many fast-growing shade trees.

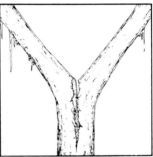

Split trunks often result from narrow limb angles. Chief causes include wind, ice, fruit load, and heavy wet snows.

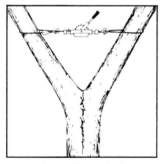

To repair a split trunk, first draw the limbs back together using clamps or a portable winch. Try to prevent drying of the tree's internal tissues. This is especially important for trees in foliage.

Assemble repair needs: a drill and ½" bit, all-thread rod (slightly smaller in diameter than the bit), large washers and nuts to fit eyebolts, a sharp knife, and pruning paint.

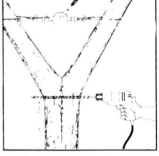

Drill completely through the trunk at right angles to the split. Support on top with eyebolts to reduce weight pressure on split.

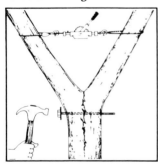

Put washer and nut on one end of all-thread rod, then install it through hole.

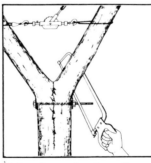

Put washer and nut on other end of all-thread, then cut to desired length.

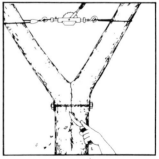

Install eyebolts and cable on both sections above split. Trim any damaged wood or loose bark. Treat exposed wood with pruning paint. Carefully remove winch. If weight of limbs is too great, prune to reduce weight.

CABLING TREES FOR SUPPORT

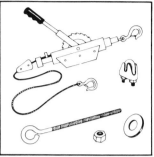

Use only heavy-duty supplies: cable, clamps, eyebolts, etc. Local hardware dealers may supply your needs.

Climb carefully . . . be sure limbs are sound before putting weight on them. Have someone secure a ladder for you.

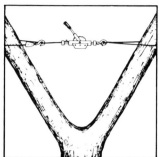

Pull limbs together slightly with portable winch. Use fabric or burlap scraps or portion of used garden hose to protect bark on limbs. Prune twigs that interfere.

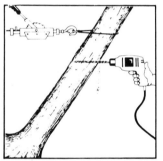

Drill level through each limb. Drill should be ½". Holes drilled should be very slightly larger than diameter of bolts. (3/8 or 7/16)

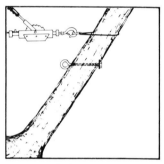

Insert eyebolts. Use large washers on both sides to keep bolts from pulling through.

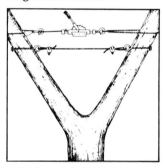

Attach cable in eyebolts using appropriate clamps. Tighten securely.

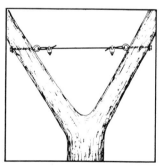

Carefully release winch. If cable does not draw tight, repeat the process and shorten the cable slightly.

PRUNING

How to Prune Trees

It would help us greatly if trees grew naturally in such a way that pruning was only a minor task. Unfortunately, very few trees have a sound natural shape and growth pattern. Also, many grow substantially taller than we require for adequate shade. And when trees exceed 20 feet, we no longer can give them the pruning care they need — without risking injury to ourselves.

Pruning Tools

The tools you need to properly prune a tree include hand pruners, long-handled loppers, and saws. Hand pruners usually come in scissor-types and anvil-types. The scissor-type generally is considered the most effective and durable: Two knives work past each other to make the cut. This action ensures a damage-free cut to the remaining branch. Anvil-type pruners, meanwhile, have only a sharp top blade which works against a narrow plate on the bottom tongue. Since only one sharp blade is involved in the cut, it takes more strength to make the anvil-type pruning tool work.

Both scissor-type and anvil-type loppers are sold through the garden trade. Most have a measurement diameter potential of an inch-and-a-half.

Question: How soon should I start pruning my ornamental and fruit trees?
Answer: As soon as the weather permits in January. Unless you have a lot of pruning work to do, wait for a warm day and enjoy the exercise. Ladder climbing means you need another adult to help you keep the ladder steady. Don't take any chances. A broken bone takes a long time to heal.

You also will need a tree saw for making cuts on limbs larger than 1½ inches in diameter. A curved saw often will help you make easier cuts. But straight saws have as many teeth and usually will perform the same service. Some straight saws have two sides with different sets of teeth. This will give you a choice of usage.

There also are special pruners and small saws mounted on extension poles. Home gardeners can use these to work higher up in a tree. Cutting branches near power lines, however, should not be attempted by an amateur. But if it is difficult to obtain professional tree service in a rural area or small town, perhaps the crew of the power company serving your area can assist in correcting the problem.

Manual or electric hedge shears also work well, not only on hedges, but on upright junipers that must be shaped several times each summer to keep them attractive.

When pruning, you should keep a jar of denatured alcohol available. Some tree diseases can be transmitted by pruning tools. Clean your pruners and saw blades with the alcohol before moving on to another tree.

CHOOSE THE RIGHT TOOL FOR THE JOB

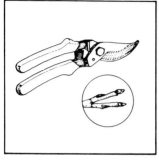

Hand shears: cuts twigs less than one-half inch in diameter.

Lopping shears: cuts branches one-half to one inch in diameter and larger.

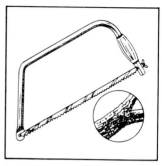

Pruning Saws: limbs over one inch in diameter.

Pole pruner: aluminum and wood models, they extend to 12 to 14 feet in height. Do not use near power or utility lines.

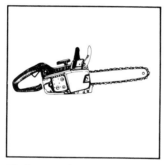

Chain saw: electric models for light pruning and gasoline models for cutting firewood.

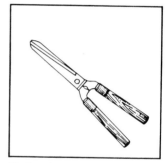

Hedge shears: for formal pruning and shaping. Also useful for cutting thistles and other woody weeds.

Electric hedge shears: be careful with cords. Best on large privet hedges or junipers.

Although no longer used by commercial arborists it is useful for the home gardener on 1½" and larger wounds.

Question: What happens when you prune?
Answer: Terminal buds . . . those buds at the ends of twigs and branches . . . produce a growth hormone (auxin) that directs most of the growth to occur at the tips. Side shoots are slower to develop as long as the terminal bud is in place,. Pruning the terminal bud suddenly frees the side shoots from their growth inhibitor, encouraging them to grow. Generally the bud nearest the cut is the one that develops most rapidly.

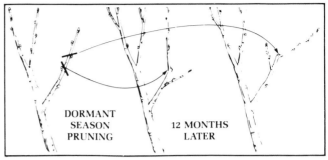

DORMANT SEASON PRUNING

12 MONTHS LATER

By choosing the position of your pruning cut carefully, you can select the future growth of the plant.

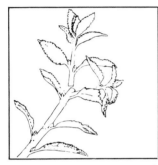

Prune directly above outward facing bud in the leaf axil to encourage more side growth. Most plants should be pruned in this manner.

Best   *Acceptable*   *Not acceptable because it may become leggy.*

Shaping a hedge

Prune directly above an inward facing bud to encourage more vertical growth. Few plants need more vertical development.

What to Prune

Sometimes in nature, a tree develops two or more leaders instead of one. A leader is the main, central, upright trunk of a tree. Extra leaders soon crowd one another. Do not wait too long (no more than three to four years) before correcting this. Prune off all but the single most desirable leader, according to its health and position. Psychologically, this is a difficult task for many people — they don't like to cut away any part of a plant they have paid for. But you simply must do it. Otherwise, a section of the tree might break off at a later date, and this would do severe injury to the rest of the tree.

You also should attempt to prune out any late-forming branches that you do not need or branches that might grow straight upward or even inward. Such branches can reduce light accessability and affect the health of the tree. It is good maintenance to keep a tree from becoming an unmanageable thicket. New side branches that form on a healthy tree almost every year should be kept pruned out unless they are a sound replacement for a damaged branch that is to be removed.

When a large limb of considerable weight has to be pruned, we secure against unwarranted damage to the bark by making an undercut with a saw about 12 inches away from the spot where the limb attaches to the trunk or larger branch. You should cut upwards about halfway through the branch to be pruned. Then, closer to the trunk, cut down all the way through the branch or until its weight breaks across to the undercut. Later we remove the remaining stub to about a half-inch.

Don't top that tree! This may develop a lot of broom-like new growth.

Using pruning paint or orange shellac after pruning is now optional. Research has shown that this treatment is not necessary if good pruning practices are followed. But I still like the appearance of the work after such a treatment. Only pruning cuts two inches in diameter or larger should be painted or shellacked.

Experience also has demonstrated that pruning should be a continuing, annual process, not a crash program every few years. Overpruning can have a detrimental effect. Some trees are stunted by such action. Others grow an undue amount of suckers at ground level or up the tree. These will have to be pruned, too.

If you must prune a branch, prune nearly flush with a remaining limb.

Commercial arborists prune any day of the year that climate and weather permit. But if you do your own work, you should prune larger trees during the dormant season, because you can better observe what needs to be done after the leaves have fallen.

Rocky Mountain Tip:

Narrow crotches between limbs on trees should be eliminated before heavy snows cause broken limbs and damage to the bark. You should prune twigs at narrow angles before they become too large to remove.

Types of Pruning

Types of pruning generally fit into four categories: (a) thinning out (b) heading back (c) shaping (d) topiary.

Thinning out involves taking out a number of small branches so more light can filter through the tree canopy. Thinning out also helps protect against unseasonal snow damage.

Heading back is performed on a large tree that has overgrown its useful height by some extent. It leaves visible stubs that sometimes sprout a hundred little branches. Most have to be pruned a year later to maintain an orderly growth pattern.

Shaping is usually work against excessive outer growth development to adhere to a desired spread and pattern. Some trees, such as Norway maples and Linden lend themselves to such a practice.

Topiary work involves creating a variety of shapes and patterns, mostly geometric squares, ovals and such that are formally maintained by tedious pruning. Topiary pruning involves plenty of hand work and is time-consuming.

Any tree that tends to grow over your roof must be managed very carefully. If substantial pruning is necessary, it should be carefully assessed, and competitive bids should be sought from tree professionals who are properly equipped and bonded.

TRAINING YOUNG TREES

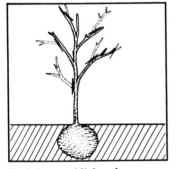

Training establishes the ultimate shape and scaffold limbs of a tree. Prune to the outside.

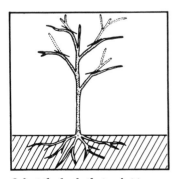

Select the buds that point to the outside to obtain width in the scaffold branching.

Getting the Proper Start

A young tree in a garden is a silent companion that soon will provide valuable shade and comfort.

One way to take care of that tree and help it grow is to "train" it with the help of proper pruning.

It is easier to correct a pruning mistake than to repair the damages of excessive overgrowth. If you accidentally overprune, new growth usually will form, and eventually it will correct your overzealousness.

You do not need many pruning tools to train a young tree. A good set of hand pruners and a pair of long-handled loppers are enough. And the loppers are used only if a branch that is to be removed is larger than a quarter of an inch in diameter.

There is a marked difference between pruning and training. The purpose of pruning is simply to thin out and broaden the canopy of a tree without letting it get too tall. Training mostly involves selecting the major scaffold branches in the first two or three years the tree exists in your garden. Scaffold branches that will become the major limbs of the tree structure must be chosen from existing side branches of the whip, which later will become the main leader. (A whip is the initial shoot of a tree, before it develops branches). And the branches — not more than four to six — must be well-spaced as they emanate from the trunk. They also should extend in the four basic directions — east, west, north and south. These wide-angled branches should help create a visual balance for the tree and avoid one-sided growth. The selection of all the side scaffold branches may have to wait until the tree has been in your garden two or three years. Some trees like to grow upward for a while without branching. You can try to put a stop to that by cutting the leader back about 12 to 15 inches. Try to cut to a dormant bud that points in the direction you want the leader to grow, usually south or west The main scaffold branches you select also should not be too close together as they originate from the trunk. Four- to five-inch spacing is desirable for a smooth bark cover later on. Otherwise, at maturity, there might be swelling at the point where the large branches emanate from the trunk.

Before any training work is done, all damaged branches must be removed. You cannot always depend on nature's healing powers. Although fireblight damage is very rare in a young tree, it is possible any time after the first bloom cycle for apples, crabapples, hawthorn and mountain ash.

After the scaffold branches have been selected in years two or three, you also must begin to thin out the interior of the young tree and encourage spread. The idea is to gain width before height.

Rocky Mountain Tip:

Young trees, especially fruit trees, must be trained by selecting three to five scaffold branches that will become limbs later on. They must be spaced at least four to six inches apart along the trunk.

You must consider the location of the tree in terms of the objects that need to be shaded or the screening the tree is expected to provide. Remember that in mid-summer, very little shade needs to be counted on until the afternoon hours. Morning shade is less important, since heat usually is not a problem until after 1 or 2 P.M.

Trees that get a proper start through training often outlive other trees by 30 or more years. You always can do some tree repair work later on. But what you can do during a tree's early years will pay major dividends later on.

Insect Control on Shade Trees

INSECTS

You cannot always avoid insect injury to shade trees. But it helps to know what kind of bug trouble to expect for specific trees in your garden. Insects are believed to have been on planet Earth much longer than man. Their existence dates back billions of years. They have survived all kinds of adversity, and

Question: What product can consumers buy and use to control elm leaf beetles? Or must this be done professionally? When is the best time to tackle this problem?
Answer: Elm leaf beetles have become a #1 pest in recent years. A new spray is sold: Pine Tree and Ornamental Spray. It contains Sevin and molasses. You can spray it yourself and reach as high as you can to obtain good control. The proper time to spray is after the new leaves are developed in early June and again in early July. Professionals use heavy-duty equipment and can cover an entire tree better than you can.

despite modern pesticides, they continue to be a severe menace to man's food production, health, and environment.

Not all bugs are bad, of course. Some beneficial insects in our gardens help hold down the numbers of damaging pests.

And despite attacks by insects, many useful varieties of shade trees have survived the eons on their own. But home gardeners wanting beautiful trees cannot depend purely on "whatever will be, will be." A tree barren of leaves does not provide much shade from the summer heat.

Inorganic chemicals such as sulfur and lead arsenate were some of the early insect controls. Then, organic chemistry opened a Pandora's box of new chemicals that are still widely in use today. The Environmental Protection Agency, established in 1972, today supervises and regulates the use of pesticides for our protection. Although all of us wish for full, non-toxic ways of insect control, such practices are at best experimental right now. There also have been encouraging results from a concept known as integrated pest management. This process uses means other than chemical pesticides for insect control in home gardens. Avoiding problem trees such as elms also can deliver you from elm-leaf and bark beetles. It also has been shown that a healthy tree will withstand insect pests much more readily than a sick, undernourished or damaged tree.

Biological controls of destructive tree insects help prevent major insect population outbreaks. Ladybugs, mantids, lacewings, aphid lions — the natural enemies of many other insects — do their job well if we don't tamper with them. And bacterial controls of moths such as Bacillus thuringensis have been moderately successful in reducing caterpillar populations. Insect pheromones (sex attractants) now are used to lure males into traps where they are sterilized. But all these newer methods do not provide enough controls. For the moment, we still have to depend at least in part on chemical insect controls.

I am a firm believer, however, in letting the good bugs have at the bad bugs in my garden. If they can handle some of the pests adequately, I will leave them alone. But if I want apples without worms, I have to do some spraying. And I'll do it at times when it has the least consequences on good predatory insects.

Encouraging the presence of birds in your

garden is another natural pest control. But I fear the insect feeders are outnumbered by other birds that are not so desirable. We live near a lake and have a lot of magpies. They seem to drive away the more desirable birds.

On page 144 is a table of controls for insects that attack ornamental trees. I am suggesting only those insecticides that I am reasonably sure will be safe and dependable enough for years to come. You should keep in touch with your local University Extension Service agent, who can give you an update every year on recommended useful pesticides. Please read the labels on each chemical carefully before you dilute and use them. If you follow these instructions to the letter, you will be safe and the effects will be noticeable. Keep these chemicals out of the reach of children and use them only when weather conditions are calm and favorable.

Controlling Tree Diseases   **DISEASES**

Our exceedingly dry climate does give us one great advantage: We have to put up with very few diseases on trees. The only one that seems to cause problems is bacterial blight, often called fireblight. Unfortunately, its control is difficult, because the timing of treatments must be very precise. Rainy or cool weather often can interfere with successful control.

Ornamental trees affected by fireblight include most flowering crabapples, plus hawthorns, mountain ash and, infrequently, plums.

The recommended controls include the antibiotics Agrimycin or Agri-strep. Both are used in sprays that must begin with about 10 percent bloom of the tree and be repeated every three to four days until petal drop is complete. The chemicals do not provide any controls before or after bloom. During a normal flowering, they are used three or four times. You must do the spraying yourself or with the help of a friend, because most professional tree sprayers cannot stop at your home three or four times in a two-week period. If they did, the cost would be excessive.

Before and after bloom and during summer, the alternate control of fireblight is to prune the affected twigs and branches. The affected areas will have an appearance of having been singed by a blowtorch. The disease spreads beyond the point of infection (blossoms) to twigs and branches. Between pruning

CHEMICAL CONTROLS FOR TREE INSECTS

Aphids:
Willow aphid   Malathion 50 EC
Misc. other aphids   Diazinon 25 EC
                                      Meta-systox — R
                                      Orthene 16 EC

Beetles:
Cottonwood leaf beetle   Malathion 50 EC
Elm leaf beetle   Sevin 50 WP
Elm bark beetle   Diazinon 25 EC
Misc. other beetles   Methoxychlor 25 EC
                                      Orthene 16 EC

Borers:
Birch borer   Methoxychlor 25 EC
Locust borer
Poplar borer
Willow borer
Ash borer
Misc. other borers

Caterpillars:
Fall webworms   Malathion 50 EC
Leafrollers   Sevin 50 WP
Elm caterpillars   Diazinon 25 EC
Inchworms   Methoxychlor 25 EC
Tent caterpillars   Orthene 16 EC
Misc. other caterpillars   Orthene 16 EC

Leafhoppers:
Misc. leafhoppers   Malathion 50 EC
                                      Diazinon 25 EC
                                      Sevin 50 WP
                                      Meta-systox — R
                                      Orthene 16 EC

Leafminers:
Cottonwood leaf miner   Malathion 50 EC
Tree Lilac leaf miner   Diazinon 25 EC
Misc. other leaf miners   Cygon 2 E
                                      Meta-systox — R
                                      Orthene 16 EC

Scales:
Cottony maple scale   Dormant Oils
Elm scale   Malathion 50 EC
Oyster shell scale   Sevin 50 WP
San Jose scale   Diazinon 25 EC
Misc. other scales   Methoxychlor 25 EC
                                      Orthene 16 EC

Mites:
Two-spotted mites   Malathion 50 EC
Misc. other mites   Diazinon 25 EC
                                      Kelthane 18 EC
                                      Meta-systox — R
                                      Cygon 2 E

EC = emulsifiable concentrate
WP = wettable powder
Note: Principal controls are underlined.

cuts, disinfect your pruners in denatured alcohol to prevent disease spread.

Bacterial blight overwinters in large, holdover cankers on major limbs and trunks of affected trees. It is spread primarily by honeybees, on which we depend for pollination. You should secure professional assistance to treat holdover cankers. Severely diseased trees should be cut down. They can make great fireplace wood.

Other tree diseases, such as anthracnose or various leaf spots, rarely are found in the Rocky Mountain and Great Basin regions.

Aspen trees have been used in large numbers for ornamental plantings. They are a member of the cottonwood family, so they are susceptible to the same diseases as poplars and cottonwoods. Ink spot disease is quite common, and looks exactly as it sounds. Hand-picking the affected leaves is the only possible control.

Elms, poplars, and willows all suffer from Cytospora canker for which no practical control exists. This causes an overgrowth on the twigs that girdles the water conductive tissues. Elms also sometimes develop Slime-Flux or wetwood disease on their trunks. It looks like a leak of moisture; a foam usually appears at the wound. All this is caused by a fermentation of the sap, and usually is cured by drilling a half-inch hole into the trunk at the lower point of the wet bark and inserting a ⅜-inch galvanized steel tube one inch deep to provide for drainage and relief of sap pressure.

Question: Last year I planted a Foxtail pine in our front area. Now all the needles are covered with white specks that look like some kind of an insect. What should we do?
Answer: Nothing at all. The white specks on your Foxtail pine are resin deposits (or exudates) that form naturally on this tree and Bristlecone pines. It is a good sign, not one of danger.

Should You Fertilize?

FERTILIZING TREES

The available nutrients found in many soils in our area are sometimes good enough to support trees. Some trees need very little fertilization. And you may not want any additional growth for the moment. With sound and proper fertilization, trees sometimes will grow more rapidly than you desire. By reducing the food, you can slow their development without having smaller, sickly leaves.

Rocky Mountain Tip:

Due to overwhelmingly dry conditions in the West, we have to cope with only a few tree diseases. Bacterial blight is a problem of the pome fruits, and several fungi attack members of the cottonwood family.

Adequate lawn fertilization often supplies trees with all the nutrients they need. But several different types of plant foods can be used to promote tree growth. Inorganic chemicals make up the bulk of these materials. Some are fertilizers with analyses such as 6-10-4 or 8-12-4. (The first number represents available nitrogen, the second, phosphoric acid and the third, potassium.) Some tree foods contain both quickly available nitrogen and slow-dissolving ureas, another nitrogen source.

Some plant foods are organic matter reinforced with chemical nutrients to boost their usefulness. And a few others are purely organic with no chemical nutrients added. The latter also may contain weed seed, which we don't really want. Cottonseed meal is a bit expensive for the feeding of trees, but it works well if you want to try it.

You also can feed trees with root feeders which use running water to dissolve fertilizer capsules. This technique is practical and useful but rather expensive if you have several larger trees to feed.

There now are tree spikes that you simply hammer into the soil. These work well but dissolve too slowly to be of any immediate benefit. The old-fashioned way of punching holes in the ground and filling them with fertilizers is a bit tedious, but it works and is relatively inexpensive.

How Much Fertilizer to Use

For each diameter inch of a tree's trunk, measured about 12 inches above the ground, you should use one pound of 6-10-4 or 8-12-4 fertilizer. It can be applied in about 12 to 15 pot holes, the size of a small shovel, dug into the ground around the tree and generally within the drip line (the farthest point out where water drips from the canopy). The older the tree is, the less plant food you will need per diameter inch.

Newly planted trees should be left without feeding, at least during their first year. If you planted well and improved the soil around the roots thoroughly, you can go for two years before you must start feeding the tree.

You can feed trees with liquid plant foods. But in a lawn area, that could be difficult, since the grass will take its share of the nutrients. Professionals feed trees with liquid fertilizer that is under fairly high pressure. The granular methods of feeding trees are a bit simpler for home gardeners.

The use of iron sulfate, ferrous ammonium

sulfate or chelated iron can be helpful with some trees. With soft maples, those chemicals can help you control leaf yellowing or chlorosis. Follow use directions for each product.

EVERGREEN TREES

Every tree that holds its foliage through winter from one year to another is an evergreen. Our Western regions offer us almost endless choices of different evergreen tree species. They are hardy and grow reasonably well even in poor, alkaline soils.

Evergreens add a quality of permanence to a home garden. They are excellent sources of shelter from the wind. And they often create a micro-climate in a backyard in which other desirable plants can thrive.

When we first moved to our present home, I installed groupings of Pinyon pines along the edge of the property to act as a windbreak of our rose garden. Twenty years later, I have to top prune those Pinyon pines every few years to keep them from reaching the utility lines under which they are situated.

Evergreen trees are relatively easy to maintain. They are subject to a few insect pests for which we have to provide controls. And their basic dark greens and blues create interesting color features, especially against the often lighter greens and the exquisite fall colors that we may enjoy.

Evergreen trees often are so dense in their growth that they create excellent shelter for many birds.

To help you select some evergreen trees for your garden I have divided the useful varieties into those that are well-adapted natives and others. Your local nurseryman may offer a few more to make your choice even a little more challenging. My order of presenting them to you is based on my own preferences. The initial group of pines, spruces and firs are native of the Rocky Mountain region.

Pines

The most popular pine is the native Ponderosa pine. Other varieties also are planted frequently.

Ponderosa Pine *(Pinus ponderosa)* — Very hardy and drought tolerant. Widely used by collectors and transplanted in sizes up to 15 feet with mechanical spades. An excellent tree in a nonirrigated part of a garden. Will survive in many Rocky Mountain and Great Basin locations with only natural rainfall and snow moisture. Four- to six-foot

Question: We have noticed many brown, dying needles on several of our Ponderosa pines. Could this be a disease or caused by an insect? How can we control it?
Answer: The browning of older needles on Ponderosa pines is quite normal. It sometimes occurs in fall; otherwise, it happens in the spring. It is a normal process for Ponderosa pines to shed their four-year-old needles. No treatment is necessary. There is no indication that the trees are under any stress.

Foxtail or Bristlecone Pine

trees can be planted safely by most home gardeners. Twenty-year height: 20 feet. Pests: beetles, aphids, scales, budworms.

Lodgepole Pine *(P. contorta)* — A tall, narrow native for higher elevations. Particularly effective above 9,000 feet. Twenty-year height: 20 to 25 feet. Pests: aphids, scales.

Foxtail or Bristlecone Pine *(P. aristata)* — A beautiful, dark-green skeleton pine with resin spots on the needles that form in autumn. My preferred tree of all evergreens. Has real character. Slow growing and useable at elevation clear up to timberline. Said to be the oldest species in North America. Must be transplanted at six feet or less. Twenty-year height: 15 feet. Pests: budworms, aphids.

Pinyon (or Piñon) Pine *(P. cembroides edulis)* — Native of southern Colorado and northern New Mexico. Very drought tolerant. Most nursery plants are collected. Best size to buy is 4½ to 5½ feet. Larger trees often have the same size root ball. Maximum height is 20 feet. More round than tall. Twenty-year height: 10 to 12 feet. Pests: pitchworm, needle miners, scales, pitch borers.

Limber Pine *(P. flexilis)* — Slow-growing native of the Rockies. Sometimes referred to as Western white pine. Irregular shape. Twenty-year height: 10-12 feet. Pests: aphids.

Spruces

There probably is no more beautiful and symmetrical tree than a Colorado spruce. Colorado's state tree can add a lot of interest to a landscaped garden. Whether you choose a grey-blue, shiner, a good blue, one of many bluish-green shades, or even a nice green specimen, you will enjoy the steady growth of this magnificent tree. This is not a plant you can crowd. It has to have open space for full development. It is a tree that ultimately may become a maintenance liability. But for 25 years, I can recommend it warmly.

Colorado Blue Spruce *(Picea pungens)* — A five-foot specimen moves easily with a good-sized, solid root ball. Initially may grow more than a foot each year. Needs moisture; not a good dryland specimen. Mature spruces have interesting cones. Does not fare well under utility lines. Twenty-year height: 18 to 25 feet. Pests: gall aphids, tussock moth, needle miners, needle scales, mites.

Engelmann Spruce *(Picea engelmanii)* — A

Colorado Blue Spruce

Colorado Blue Spruce with new buds

very tall-growing spruce suitable for elevations up to 9,500 feet. Very adapted to temperature extremes. Grows about six inches a year. Color: green to silvery-blue. Twenty-year height: 15 feet. Pests: gall aphids, needle miners, mites.

Dwarf Alberta Spruce *(Picea glauca conica)* — A small green cone of dense growth. Not well adapted to full winter sun. Needs water during winter drought, like all spruces. Very slow growing. Mine is 18 years old and a little over five feet. The best of dwarfed evergreens. 20-year height: five to six feet. Pests: aphids, mites.

Firs

I can recommend only one true fir in the Western region: the Concolor fir. In its first 15 years, it is as symmetrical as a Colorado spruce. Later, its form becomes a little less perfect.

Concolor Fir *(Abies concolor)* — A native of the Rocky Mountains, but rarely found now in large stands. Has soft needles and a good bluish-green color. A fine specimen tree, like the Colorado blue spruce. Twenty-year height: 20 to 25 feet. Pests: tussock moth, aphids.

Douglas Fir *(Pseudotsuga taxifolia)* — For many long years, the original Christmas tree. Some fancy varieties now grown at tree farms for eventual cutting. Needles are soft and only one inch long. Bluish-green in color. Performs better at elevations of 6,500 feet and higher. It is not a true fir, but a nice, fast-growing tree. Twenty-year height: 25 to 35 feet. Pests: gall aphids, tussock moths, needle scales.

Douglas Fir

Austrian Pine

Exotics

Some landscape evergreens from other parts of the United States or the world have proved useful in the Rocky Mountains. They offer some unique characteristics that make their choice practical. Certain pines and spruces especially are gaining in popularity:

Austrian Pine *(Pinus nigra)* — In many respects, a look-alike to the native Ponderosa pine. Its form is slightly more symmetrical. Foliage is almost the same length and color but a little denser. Safe to 7,500 feet. Twenty-year height: 20 to 30 feet. Pests: budworms, aphids, bark beetles, scales.

Scotch Pine *(Pinus sylvestris)* — Among the fastest-growing evergreens. Has short needles light to medium green. Useful at elevations to 7,500 feet. Twenty-year height: 30 feet. Pests: aphids, scales.

Tanyosho Pine *(Pinus densiflora umbraculifera)* — Has an umbrella-like head with dense, upright, spreading branches. Very hardy, but only recommended for protected locations. A good rock garden subject. Twenty-year height: 10 to 12 feet. Pests: aphids, needle scales.

Norway Spruce *(Picea abies)* — Dark-green needles on a fairly fast-growing tree. Branches are more pendulous than Colorado blue and Engelmann spruce, which I prefer. Twenty-year height: 15 to 20 feet. Pests: aphids, mites.

Junipers

Upright junipers are attractive and useful garden plants. They have varied forms and growth patterns. Some have high tolerance levels for drought and alkaline soils, two features our region has in excess. There are also some differences in mature height and their ability to withstand seasonal trimming to maintain a sleek appearance. Upright junipers are preferred because they can be successfully planted closer to a home or patio than spruces and pines. They also can be used for dense wind breaks. They naturally vary in their normal rate of growth. Their needles usually resemble a knotted piece of twine or rope, but newly emerging growth resembles needles temporarily each year.

Junipers are single-sexed plants. They are either male or female. They either produce clouds of yellow pollen that make hayfever sufferers swear, or bluish to green, berry-like cones that hang on to the plant for one or two seasons. The most adapted junipers in the Rocky Mountains and the West are the scopulorum species and a few other natives, such as J. monosperma and utahensis. The scopulorum species has many named varieties. Most of them are nursery selections.

Rocky Mountain Juniper *(Juniperus scopulorum)* — Has many popular varieties, such as:

Admiral — Broadly pyramidal with gray green foliage. Mature height: 15 to 20 feet.

Blue Haven — Very narrow, symmetrical. Excellent blue color all year. Height: 15 to 20 feet.

Cologreen — Compact pyramidal form with forest-green color. Height: 15 to 20 feet.

Erecta glauca — Narrow form with soft, silvery-blue foliage. Height: 15 to 20 feet.

Gray Gleam — A beautiful, slow-growing tree of columnar form. Silvery gray foliage. Height: 15 feet.

Rocky Mountain Juniper

Moffet — Blue-green foliage in a very dense, upright plant. Height: 15 to 20 feet.

Pathfinder — Densely pyramidal form, fast growing, blue-gray foliage. Height 15 to 20 feet.

Skyrocket — Excellent columnar tree for narrow space or location. Blue-green foliage. Height: 15 to 20 feet.

Sutherland — Dense, pyramidal form, fast growing, vivid green color. Height: 12 to 15 feet.

Welchi — Narrow, upright cone shaped form with dense branching. Height: up to 20 feet.

Wichita Blue — Blue color all year long, pyramidal growth. Height: 12 to 20 feet.

Eastern Red Juniper *(J. virginiana)* — Includes some popular, upright trees of a more open form. Most are not quite as hardy as the Rocky Mountain species *(scopulorum)*.

Burki — Broad, pyramidal form with blue foliage. Quite hardy. Height: 15 to 18 feet.

Canaert — Dark-green, tufted foliage in a conical-shaped tree. Remains green all winter. Has light-blue berries. Height: 20 feet.

Hillspire — Bright green foliage through the entire year. Form is narrow. Height: 15 to 20 feet.

Manhattan Blue — Blue-green foliage in compact form. Height: 12 to 15 feet.

One-seeded Juniper *(J. monosperma)* — These are tough, because they survive at 7,000 feet in poor soils with little moisture. They are a challenge to

Question: My upright junipers, which are sheared several times every year, are getting brown on the outside. Can you prescribe something to prevent this from happening?
Answer: There could be several reasons for this. Red spider mites are usually to blame, because they are so numerous on junipers. For them, I recommend a spray of Kelthane or any labeled evergreen spray to be applied every 30 days. It is also possible that the junipers are trimmed too much. In that case, only time and patience will heal. You can try some liquid fertilizer spray, such as Rapid-gro, to speed up the recovery. This should be diluted and sprayed over the entire juniper.

transplant. Not many available in the nursery trade. Their shape is vase-like. Color is greyish-green. Height: 20 feet.

Utah Juniper *(J. osteosperma utahensis)* — Scale-like needles overlap and are yellowish-green. Height: 20 feet. Pests: Aphids, scales, mites.

Transplanting Evergreen Trees: The Best Sizes

Perhaps I am more patient than many, but I firmly believe that evergreen trees transplant most successfully at sizes ranging from three feet to six feet in height. This is also the size the home gardener can handle easily by himself or with but one helper.

The larger the soil ball of the transplanted tree, the greater the chance for success. I hope that all the

---

Pests of Evergreen Trees and Their Control

Aphids

Spruce Gall aphid	Malathion 50 EC
Juniper aphid	Diazinon 25 EC
	Meta-systox — R
	Orthene 16 EC

Caterpillars:

Douglas Fir Tussock moth	Malathion 50 EC
Colorado Spruce Tussock moth	Sevin 50 WP
Saw flies	Diazinon 25 EC
Tiger moths	Methoxychlor 25 EC
	Orthene 16 EC

Leaf Miners:

Pinyon leaf miner	Malathion 50 EC
Spruce needle miner	Cygon 2 E
	Meta-systox — R
	Orthene 16 EC

Scales:

Pine needle scales	Dormant Oils
Pinyon needle scales	Malathion 50 EC
Juniper scales	Sevin 50 WP
	Diazinon 25 EC
	Methoxychlor 25 EC
	Orthene 16 EC

Spider mites:

Spruce mites	Kelthane 18 EC
Two-spotted mites	Meta-systox — R
	Cygon 2 E
	Malathion 50 EC
	Diazinon 25 EC
	Orthene 16 EC

Borers:

Pinyon pitch borer	Mechanical removal
	Reduce water

evergreens you plant in your garden will be 100-percent successful. But larger evergreen transplants should be handled by someone who knows how, has the proper equipment and is willing to assume a guarantee. Tree spades can successfully handle much larger evergreen trees, up to 15 feet in height, but the trees are not available everywhere in our Western territory. Besides, the cost involved is fairly substantial.

It also has been my observation that large transplants grow very little for several years after they are moved. Five- to six-foot evergreens frequently produce more new growth in the first two to three years than larger transplants.

Use larger trees if you cannot wait. But the smaller trees appear to catch up very well over several successive years. The evergreens in my garden were all between three and six feet when they were transplanted. They are choice plants today and my family enjoys them.

WATERING TREES

Trees are quite competitive for water. They can fend quite well for themselves even if they have to rob lawn areas or flower beds for the food and water that they need. I have discovered massive roots from an elm or a cottonwood more than 50 feet from the tree. If you want trees for shade and comfort, you must accept their invasive roots everywhere you want to grow flowers or vegetables. Even a live-and-let-live arrangement in your environment will let trees come out ahead in the contest for adequate moisture. You can act as an equalizer, and put out enough water for the trees to have a good drink and for the flowers and other plants to survive.

> **Rocky Mountain Tip:**
> Keep members of the cottonwood family of trees as far as possible from sewer lines. About 75 to 85 feet is a safe distance. If you have problems, you can use copper sulfate as a timely deterrent.

When watering trees, you should be most concerned with getting the water to a certain depth where the roots can recover the water as needed. The amounts used could be five to ten gallons a day for a small evergreen, 30 to 35 gallons for a medium shade tree or as much as 300 gallons and more a day for a mature cottonwood.

In sandy soils, it is relatively easy to get good moisture penetration down to about 24 to 30 inches. In heavy clay soils, you have to try harder and apply water longer. Here, you can use a root watering attachment connected to the garden hose. For this I can recommend a Greenie or a Ross root feeder. Both insert to a depth of 24 inches, placing the water where it is most needed.

Watering Evergreens

The watering needs of evergreen trees and shrubs vary from one type to another, and also depend on the season. These plants all need attention from January to December. Their native habitat tells us a good deal about how they must be watered.

Pines by and large take the least irrigation. Ponderosa and Pinyon pines require almost no watering at all except during the first two years after they are planted in the garden. From then on, natural precipitation of 10 inches or more each year is adequate for their well-being. Foxtail or Bristlecone pine and Austrian pine take a little more water. They should have three good irrigations each year to supplement about 15 inches of measured precipitation. Limber pine utilized in landscaping also needs two or three good waterings each year, especially in a lengthy dry period. But Limber pine would not be my choice in a lawn area that is under frequent irrigation. In such a situation, Scotch pine is a much better choice. It needs more frequent watering than the pines already mentioned. The only other useful pine for general landscaping in the Rocky Mountain region and the Great Basin area is the Mugho pine. It is not a tree but a shrub, and is used widely as a foundation plant of contrasting texture with junipers. This very handy and valuable shrub pine needs a few good irrigations in the summer and one or two during a dry winter.

Spruces prefer plenty of soil moisture. Colorado spruce deserves a lawn situation where it can thrive. A monthly deep watering with a Greenie attachment from November to March is not too much. In spring and summer, their water needs are continuous. Colorado spruces — blue, silver, or green — require the same waterings without reference to color. The very blue blues are just more expensive and equally beautiful. The Engelmann spruce is useful primarily in higher elevations. In high resort areas where snow and rain are plentiful, it grows to a fine, narrow tree. In garden situations in the Eastern Rockies, the Engelmann spruce needs watering equal to the Colorado spruce. Dwarf Alberta spruce also has a high moisture need. But since the plant is quite small, it does not need to be watered very deeply or broadly.

Douglas firs and Concolor firs also are used in landscaping. Their growth rate is almost twice that of Colorado spruce, but these trees cannot grow well in areas of standing or excess water. But they adapt well even in wind-exposed places. Their water needs are halfway between that of spruces and pines.

Junipers are somewhere between pines and spruces in water needs. Near a lawn they obtain enough from regular irrigation. Against a home they need two winter waterings.

Rocky Mountain Tip:

Winter watering is essential for most evergreens and deciduous trees and shrubs on a sustained basis unless frozen soil and adequate snow moisture make this unnecessary.

Mother Nature's Fall Show

FALL COLOR

Mother Nature's exhibit of fall colors is the most brilliant foliage display of the year. The autumn colors are fixed genetically in each plant species. All green plants have chlorophyll, which produces the carbohydrates and oxygen on which plants grow, flower and fruit. The green chlorophyll completely masks the undercolors of the anthocyanins (red) and the carotenes (yellow). When the green chlorophyll dies, triggered by cooler nights or a light frost, the undercolors emerge.

Our colors usually begin with the Aspens. Their yellows, with a little pink, are followed by the fabulous oranges and reds of the Gambel oaks. Sumac, Euonymus, wild plums and Red oaks have mostly anthocyanins and turn pink, orange and red. Poplars, birches, honeylocusts, cottonwoods and elms have mostly carotenes and turn a brilliant yellow.

There are Fall seasons when Mother Nature has ample time to develop her brilliant finery. But in some years an early hard freeze turns everything brown or black and we miss this colorful display. Enjoy it whenever you can.

ORNAMENTAL SHRUBS

WHILE trees provide shade to protect us from the heat of the sun, ornamental shrubs furnish the character of our landscapes. Shrubs serve useful functions in the landscape as they furnish screening, separation and privacy. Shrubs are very attractive in bloom — some of them bloom as early as April and others as late as August.

BUYING AND PLANTING SHRUBS

Shrubs can be purchased from nurseries in several easy-to-handle forms. The majority are marketed in containers, usually metal or pressed-paper pots. Some shrubs actually are raised in containers at the nursery. Others are potted by retailers just before they are sold. And some shrubs are sold bare-rooted. Most of these are hedging plants such as privets, or small mail-order stock which are available through catalog nurseries.

The survival rate of mail-order, bare-rooted shrubs can depend on how the plants are shipped and how long they are in transit. If you have a near-by source of canned or potted shrubs, buy them there rather than by mail. Pay a little more to get a solid start. Small, bare-rooted shrubs often may not succeed too well, especially in the Rockies where winds and weather can be quite harsh. Small shrubs also are barely visible for a year or two and often are accidentally bruised or injured before they grow sufficiently large to be noticed.

The guarantees provided by the sellers of plants are variable. Some nurseries guarantee living growing plants only at 50 percent of the purchase price. I also have found some garden centers which offer a full guarantee for one growing season and up to 12 months. The sellers' guarantees may relate to the price at which the shrubs are offered.

You also should evaluate your own expertise as a gardener. If you have experience and confidence in your green thumb, you may take certain risks that I would not recommend for a novice. Beware of roadside truck sales of shrubs and other plants. If you don't know much about plants, rely on the professional expertise of a nurseryman. But if you do know something about the plants you are buying, you can usually trust your judgment enough to make deals. Remember, though, that you don't buy shrubs like grocery items once or twice a week. You buy them more like once or twice in a lifetime. And if you make an improper choice, you may have to bear the consequences for many years — or start over again.

> **Rocky Mountain Tip:**
>
> In the West where rainfall is irregular at best, I advise paying a little more for container-grown shrubs to get a solid start. Bare-rooted shrubs often get too dry before you can plant them.

Higher elevations and mountain resorts have a shorter growing season. There, it is important that you use containerized or balled-and-burlapped (B&B) plants. B&B stock has a soil ball large enough to contain a major portion of the plant's root system. The ball is dug round or conical, then wrapped tightly with burlap, which is secured with hemp, nails or a wire basket. Bare-root plants have a difficult time succeeding in places where growing seasons are

Nurseries offer shrubs in several container sizes ranging from 1 gallon or 2 gallons to 5 gallons. These will transplant easily.

Balled-and-burlapped (B&B) plants are also preferable to bare-rooted plants where growing seasons are short.

short. By the time they get growing, the season may already be coming to an end.

The planting process for shrubs is generally the same as for setting out small trees explained in the previous chapter.

Deciduous Shrubs

To obtain a truly enchanting effect with ornamental shrubs, we must select them carefully. Some are small size, some medium and others quite large. To help you make the right shrub selections for your needs, I have divided deciduous shrubs into three size categories: small — up to four feet; medium — five to seven feet; and large — eight feet and larger. These sizes are an approximation. They could vary at least a foot higher or shorter in very fertile or very poor soil. Shrubs also differ in their natural form. We can alter their shape somewhat with pruning tools, but unless we clip them constantly, they eventually will reach their own character. Some of these shrubs may flower. And some are natives or will grow well up to 8,500 feet in mountain localities. These are marked with an asterisk (*) in front of their name. If a shrub is particularly tolerant of drought or poor soil, it has a bullet (•) by the name. In some instances, I also list the botanical name to ensure clarity. This listing should allow you to make better choices for the landscape of your home grounds and for the shelter and privacy you richly deserve.

Small Shrubs (up to 4 feet)

Flowering Almond — Double pink flowers. Shiny green foliage. No fruit. Blooms April-May.

Japanese Barberry — Varieties Green Leaf and

THE BEST ORNAMENTAL SHRUBS

※ UP TO 8500'
◦ Tolerant of
drought &
poor soil

Redleaf Barberry

Rosy Glow have red fruit and leaves in fall. Blooms in May.

Redleaf Barberry — Deep-red colored leaves all season in full sun. Berries attract birds. Blooms in May.

Chokeberry (Aronia sp.) — Glossy green leaves; good fall color. White flowers in May followed by black fruit. Blooms in May.

Cranberry Cotoneaster — Arching branches with dark-green, glossy leaves. Small, pinkish blossoms followed by red berries. Blooms in May.

American Cranberry-bush compacta — Flat-headed clusters of white flowers, followed by red berries. Good fall color. Blooms in June.

*Alpine Currant — Small, green leaves that develop early. Nice bushy round form. Good for informal hedge. Blooms May-June.

Alpine Currant

Wax Currant

Variegated Dogwood

Flowering Quince

*Yellow Flowering Currant — Bright yellow flowers in May, which develop into yellow to black fruit. Blooms May-June.

*Wax Currant — Dense, slow-growing mountain shrub with pink flowers in June. Red fruit. Blooms in June.

Kelsey's Dwarf Dogwood — A small plant with brilliant red twigs in winter. Blooms in May.

Variegated Dogwood — Green leaves with white flowers and red stems. Excellent for contrast. Blooms in May.

*Native Elder — Native to the Rockies. White flower clusters followed by red berries. Blooms in June.

Japanese Flowering Quince — Orange to pink flowers; very glossy leaves. Flowers very early and sometimes forms small quince fruit. Blooms in May.

Hydrangea Annabelle — Short stems with near-white, showy blooms. New stems form every year. Prefers north side or shade. Blooms in July.

Hydrangea

Mock-orange

Cinquefoil

• ***Lead Plant** *(Amorpha sp.)* — Ferny leaves; purple flowers in June. Very hardy. Blooms in May.

*Dwarf Korean Lilac — Blooms lavender on short stems — May-June.

Glacier Mockorange — Double white flowers. Blooms in June.

*Cinquefoil *(Potentilla sp.)* —Varieties Gold Drop, Katherine Dykes, Klondike, Mount Everest and Sutters Gold are fine selections. Most flower yellow, but Mount Everest is white. Newest color break includes: Red Ace — orange-red; Sunset — golden tangerine; and Royal Flush — rosy pink. Blooms June through August intermittently.

Lodense Privet — Can be clipped at 12 to 18 in-

Privet Hedge

Anthony Water Spirea   *Yucca*

ches for a low formal hedge or border. Foliage a good green.

• ***Dwarf Rabbitbush** — Gray to light-green foliage; narrow leaves. Clusters of yellow flowers in late summer. Blooms July-August.

• ***Black Sage *(Artemisia sp.)*** — Grayish leaves common in plains and foothills. Resists elements well with little care.

• **Southernwood *(Artemisia sp.)*** — Fine green foliage. Needs to be pruned back in spring.

• ***Rocky Mountain Smooth Sumac** — Very fine small shrub with superb fall colors. Blooms July-August.

• ***Three-Leaf Sumac** — Often called Lemonade or Skunkbush Sumac. Slow-growing, aromatic native. Good fall color. Blooms July-August.

Blue Mist Spirea *(Caryopteris incana)* — Blooms blue in July. Bees love it. Sometimes dies back partly but always recovers. Blooms in July.

Froebel Spirea — Flat clusters of pink flowers in June. A neat shrub even for shade. Blooms in June.

Anthony Waterer Spirea — Green foliage, but new growth is reddish. Deep-pink flowers in June or later. Thrives in full sun. Blooms in June.

• ***Yucca** — Several Yuccas are well adapted for very hot, dry places. Varieties most often used are glauca, baccata and filamentosa. Blooms in July.

Medium Shrubs (5 to 7 feet)

• *Apache plume *(Fallugia sp.)* — Interesting native. Rose-like flowers followed by fuzzy seed heads. Adjusts to dry, alkaline conditions. Blooms in June.

Mentor Barberry — Semi-evergreen, spiny leaves. Branches cascade naturally.

Coralberry — Gracefully arching stems. Neat foliage, oval in shape. Has red berries. Blooms in May.

Spreading Cotoneaster *(divaricata)* — Arching branches of glossy, small green leaves with reddish fall color. White-pink small blooms. Red fruit. Blooms in June.

*Peking Cotoneaster** — One of the best shrubs for us. Formal hedges. Upright, oval-shaped. Has black berries in winter for the birds. Blooms May-June.

Multiflora Cotoneaster — A wide-spreading shrub with bright red berries. Blooms May-June.

Golden Dogwood — Also called Yellow-twig Dogwood. Not quite as large or full or hardy as Red-twig Dogwood. Interesting bark color in winter. Blooms May-June.

Burningbush *(Euonymus sp.)* — Bark of mature branches has a winged appearance. Excellent fall color. Tolerates shade. Blooms in June.

Forestiera (New Mexico Privet) — Leaves similar to privet. A fair hedge plant. Blue fruit in fall. Blooms June-July.

Redtwig Dogwood

Hibiscus   *Lilac*

Hibiscus (Rose of Sharon or Shrub Althea) — Large lavender flowers in summer. May need shelter from winter winds. Blooms in August.

Lilacs *(Syringa sp.)* — Some of the best shrubs for screen and color. Bloom May-June. Recommended are:

French:	**Charles Joly** — red-purple
	Congo — red
	Edith Cavell — white
	Edward Andre — pink
	Ellen Willmott — white
	Mrs. Ed Harding — red-purple
	Pres. Grevy — lilac-blue
	Pres. Lincoln — blue
Canadian:	Very hardy, blooms a little later
	Nocturne — blue
	Pocahontas — purple
	Royalty — purple
Chinese:	Blooms second or third year
	Chinese — purple
Hungarian:	Blooms a little later
	James McFarlane — pink
	Sylvia — pink
Cheyenne:	Very hardy — purple

Mock-orange (Minnesota Snowflake) — Very fragrant. Double white flowers in June. A great shrub with good spread. Blooms in June.

• ***Mountain Mahogany** — Dull green, leathery foilage. In fall has fuzzy, twisted seed heads. Very alkali-tolerant. Blooms June-July.

Golden Ninebark — Foliage turns yellow in bright sunlight. Good shrub for contrast. Blooms in June.

*Dwarf Ninebark — Almost same size as Golden Ninebark. Clusters of pinkish flowers. Red-brown fall color. Blooms in June.

Cheyenne Privet — Small green leaves. Good for screens and hedges.

Prunus (Western Sandcherry) — White flowers early followed by edible small fruit. Variety Hansen's Bush cherry has better fruit. Tends to spread.

Purple-Leaf Plum *(Prunus cistena)* — Has small, pink flowers before foliage unfurls. Blooms in May.

Prunus Newport — More upright but otherwise similar to Prunus cistena.

Boulder Raspberry (Thimbleberry) — Very hardy native. Arches gracefully. Rose-like flowers in May and June. Thornless, attractive foliage.

Shrub-rose — Blooms May-June. Recommended varieties:

Austrian Copper — Flowers orange with yellow center, but only in May. Very hardy.

Harrison's Yellow — lovely when in bloom. Yellow single flowers.

Red-leafed — Flowers pink in late spring. Leaves are colored all season. Has nice rose hips.

Other shrub-roses in this class worthy of trial include:

Hansa — Purple-red, fragrant.

Magnifica — Repeats blooming throughout summer under favorable conditions. Flowers carmine. Fragrant.

Therese Bugnet — Double lilac-pink flowers. Repeat throughout summer.

Shrub-rose

Rocky Mountain Tip:

Shrub roses that are drought tolerant and for high altitudes up to 8,000 feet include Austrian Copper, Harrison's Yellow, Hansa, Therese Bugnet and the red-leafed rose *Rosa rubrifolia.*

*Serviceberry *(Amelanchier sp.)* — Has white flowers followed by edible black fruit.

Snowberry — A common hardy shrub. White berries stay all winter. Accepts any location; spreads from roots.

Spirea Vanhoutte (Bridalwreath) — A lovely arching shrub with small foliage. White clusters of blooms in May. Pinkish fall color.

Spirea Garland — Literally covered with white flowers in May. Should be pruned after bloom.

Viburnum Carlesi (Fragrant Snowball) — Spicy, cream-colored flowers. Slow-growing. Protect from winter winds.

Blue Arctic Willow — Slender, bluish foliage on a twiggy plant. Needs a moist location.

Tall Shrubs (8 feet and up)

*Buffaloberry — Distinctive gray-green to silver leaves. Rocky Mountain native. Separate male and female plants. Latter bear red berries. Blooms May-June.

• ***Common Buckthorn *(Rhamnus sp.)*** — Very hardy shrub. Tolerates poor soil. Black berries for birds. Blooms in May.

• ***Glossy Buckthorn** — Has shiny green foliage.

Spirea Bridalwreath

Snowball Blossoms

Tallhedge Buckthorn

Highbush Cranberry

Russian-olive

Question: Several of my shrubs have berries this year. Are they edible or useable for jams and jellies? They are honeysuckle, Highbush cranberry and cotoneaster.
Answer: No doubt these berries are edible. If they were superior in taste, the birds would have used them up as quickly as cherries. The taste quality of berries on most ornamental shrubs is on the bitter, some even on the woody side. I doubt that at current prices of sugar this is a very worthwhile project.

Spreading habit. Red berries turn black in fall. Blooms in May.

Tallhedge Buckthorn — Narrow, upright-growing shrub. Excellent for screen or tall hedge. Blooms in May.

Highbush Cranberry — Attractive foliage. Excellent fall color. Very hardy. Good for background planting. Clusters of white flowers in May. Red berries. Blooms in June.

• ***Redtwig Dogwood (Cornus sp.)** — Attractive shrub. Flowers in June. White berries. Best feature is red winter color of branches. Blooms May-June.

*American Elder — Very-fast-growing, massive shrub with white berries after clusters of white flowers. Green foliage. Blooms June-July.

*Golden Elder — Naturally yellow foliage. In alkaline soils, leaf margins turn brown. Takes full sun. Blooms June-July.

*Zabel Honeysuckle — Best of this genus. Red-flowering plant. Red berries for the birds. Good, upright shrub. Blooms May-June.

Japanese Tree Lilac — Very-early-emerging lilac, but flowers two weeks later than most. Ours get frost-curled every year, but secondary leaves are fine. Blooms in June.

• **Autumn Olive** — Silvery foliage. Has berries and upright growth development. Good for tall hedges.

• **Russian-olive** — Fragrant flowers in May. Very hardy. Drought tolerant. Silvery gray leaves. Used for large estate hedges. Blooms in June.

• **Siberian Peashrub (*Caragana sp.*)** — Has large seed for birds. Thorny. Extemely hardy and drought tolerant. Good-sized clusters of yellow flowers in June. Blooms May-June.

Honeysuckle

Golden Elder

Viburnum Snowball

Viburnum Wayfaring Tree

Staghorn Sumac — Often found growing near home foundations. Suckers extend underground. Excellent fall color. New growth covered with velvet-like skin. Blooms in July.

• **Tamarix** — Feathery foliage but thinner than junipers. Forms large plumes of pinkish flowers in mid-summer. Found native along stream beds. Blooms in July.

*****Viburnum Snowball** — Beautiful round, creamy balls of flowers in June but no fruit. Foliage turns reddish in autumn. Blooms in June.

*****Viburnum Wayfaring Tree** — Leaves are visible in winter. Buds are medium green and turn red to maroon in fall. White flower clusters. Seed turns from green to yellow-orange-red to black. Blooms in June.

*****Native Bluestem Willow** — Silver-blue branches turn out grey catkins early.

*****Yellow Mountain Willow** — Silvery catkins on yellow twigs. Twigs later turn yellow-green.

Evergreen Shrubs

Broadleafed Evergreens

Our cup does not run over in this department. We do have a few dependable broadleafed evergreen shrubs and a few others for gamblers. But we simply lack the humidity and rainfall that many of these evergreens are used to. But I have seen the firethorns in Salt Lake City, and they were magnificent with their colorful berries. I have had two rhododendrons in my back yard for 14 years. In that time, they have missed flowering only once.

Broadleafed evergreen shrubs need absolute shelter from wind and the winter sun, and they prefer shade. If we provide some sulfur twice a year, they may even act as if they are in acid soil.

Recommended Choices:

Euonymus coloratus — Leaves turn purplish during winter. Sometimes climbs on any support, such as a brick wall or trellis. Blooms June-July.

Euonymus Manhattan — Dark green, very glossy leaves. Blooms in June.

Euonymus Sarcoxie — Dark green with same winter color. Sometimes will climb a wall. Blooms June-July.

Mahonia aquifolium (Oregon Grape) — Leaves turn purple in winter. Needs some winter protection. Blooms in May.

Mahonia aquifolium compacta — This is a smaller version of the above. Blooms in May.

Pyracantha (Firethorn) — Gnome — Orange-berried. Hardy. Densely twigged variety. Blooms May-June.

Pyracantha

Rhododendron

Kasan — Orange-red berries are food for the birds. Blooms May-June.

Lalandi — A taller variety with vigorous growth. Orange berries. Blooms May-June.

Wyatti — Tolerates mediocre soils. Useful as a specimen or in hedges. Needs wind and sun protection in winter. White flowers followed by orange berries. Blooms May-June.

Rhododendron — Hybrids that have catawbiensi as one of their parents generally are the safest to select. Some of these actually are recommended for this area. But you have to be a gambler to try them. Blooms in June.

Rock Cotoneaster *(C. apiculata)* — A short, spreading shrub. Holds its foliage through most winters. Needs a little shelter. Blooms May-June.

Nandina (Heavenly Bamboo) — This white, summer-flowering shrub survives around Albuquerque and Santa Fe, New Mexico and should be safe in St. George, Utah. I have seen a few around Salt Lake City. Has bright red berries in fall. Needs an acid soil. Blooms in June.

Holly (Ilex sp.) — Some nurseries stock varieties. Try Blue Princess as far north as Denver — as a gamble. You must have male and female plants to obtain berries. Blooms in June.

Watering Broadleafed Evergreens

Broadleafed evergreen shrubs are useable in the Rocky Mountains mostly in shady places, but because of the intense winter sun, they need watering every 30 days on a year-round schedule. The hardiest include firethorn (Pyracantha), mahonia or Oregon grape and various euonymus. In a few sheltered places, yews also may be tried. They should be watered similar to broadleafed evergreens.

Coniferous Evergreen Shrubs

This group, fortunately, is much larger and less restrictive in its use than broadleaf evergreens. Coniferous shrubs are needled shrubs. For one thing, coniferous evergreen shrubs have practically no exposure limitations. But they are very attractive to spider mites. This is a problem we have to watch for and treat consistently. If you are a no-pesticide gardener, you can at least discourage the mites with a hard stream of water every 30 days. You may sometimes get more spread from a plant than promised, which then needs pruning or shaping.

Many coniferous evergreen shrubs can be purchased from nurseries in one-gallon containers. Sometimes, the containers are smaller than that. But the sizes of the plants do correspond to what the nursery trade accepts as representative. Junipers are the largest group in this class of shrubs.

Junipers (Spreading)

Junipers are, by and large, the most useful shrubs for the Rocky Mountains region. They are tolerant to mediocre or poor soils and can sustain some degree of drought.

Some recommended varieties include:

Juniperus chinensis pfitzeriana — Dark green and can become quite large in size.

Green Pfitzer — Grey-green, sharp-needled foliage. Will grow very large to 10 feet high. Can be used as a screen.

Blue Pfitzer — Large, blue, dense plant. Good in banked slopes and as tall screen.

Gold Tip Pfitzer — Grey-green foliage with gold tips. Good for full sun or partial shade. Not quite as large as Green Pfitzer.

Green Pfitzer Juniper

Blue Pfitzer Juniper

Gold Tip Pfitzer Juniper

Armstrong Juniper

Compacta Pfitzer — Grey-green foliage, but a much smaller plant: not more than six feet high.

Gold Coast Pfitzer — New growth is bright gold. Grows only up to three feet high.

J. hetzi glauca — Vase-shaped, semi-erect form. Height to 12 feet. Blue-gray color.

J. chinensis **Armstrong** — Light-green, lacy foliage. Not more than four feet high. Slightly arching branches. Often sold as a global shaped shrub.

J. chinensis **Old Gold** — Not larger than four feet. Rich, gold color. Dense branching.

J. chinensis **Sea Green** — Richer color than Pfitzer but grows only up to six feet tall.

J. sabina **Scandia** — Fine-textured spreader. Will grow to 36 inches high. Dark green color.

J. sabina tamariscifolia **(Tammy)** — One of the best. Very popular spreader that rounds off at 36 to 40 inches. A very hardy, tough plant. Grows in almost any soil. Tammy has relatively low moisture requirements. An occasional deep watering is all it needs. Blue-green color. Procumbent at the end of branches.

J. procumbens — Blue color. Grows slowly to about two feet high. Finely textured.

J. communis saxatilis — Common Juniper found native in the Rocky Mountains. Two to three feet high. Needles are further apart from each other than chinensis.

Shrubs That Attract Birds

Birds in your garden are a sign of good fortune. These lovely creatures not only can entertain you with their song and chatter, but when they nest in your trees, your garden has achieved a measure of tranquility and protection. Some of the birds we discover roosting on a high, overhead wire soon pair up and build nests to raise their young. Many of them are seed-eaters, but some will help police the insects in your garden.

Though robins usually are happy with a worm or two, they go into delirium when cherries are beginning to ripen. At our home garden, we have created a peaceful compromise. I cover part of our cherry tree with plastic netting — and leave the rest to the robins.

A number of shrubs can provide food for the birds. A few trees also can provide a bit of sustenance for them in a cold, snowy winter. You also can establish a feeder station for birds. Local garden sup-

Redleaf Barberry   *Pyracantha*

pliers keep supplies of bagged seed on hand, and this is very helpful in supplementing the birds' winter food needs. Feeder stations for birds may be homemade or obtained from garden centers or mail-order houses. It is important that they are kept well-removed from family pets and squirrels. The pleasure of watching and counting bird visitors is full payment for the small effort of charity. If good-quality bird seed is not locally available, you can secure assistance from a game warden or the National Audubon Society.

These are some of the ornamental shrubs that produce fruits and berries that birds like to eat:

Autumn Olive	**Western Sand Cherry**
Barberry	**Nanking Cherry**
Common Buckthorn	**Pyracantha** (Firethorn)
Columnar Buckthorn	**Redleaf Rose**
Buffaloberry	**Austrian Copper Rose**
Caragana	**Serviceberry**
(Siberian	**Sumac**
Peashrub)	**Wayfaring Tree**
Wax Currant	(Viburnum)
Yellow-twig Dogwood	**Nannyberry**
Redtwig Dogwood	**Viburnum Carlesi**
American Elder	**American Cranberry**
Golden Elder	**bush**
Zabel Honeysuckle	**Gooseberries**
Oregon Holly Grape	**Currants**
(Mahonia)	

Ornamental Shrubs Need Care

Ornamental shrubs in Western gardens often receive very little care — unless they are situated by accident in a favorable location where water and food are abundant. But they can display their expected potential only when they are fed and watered properly. Shrubs which hang on and show hardly any symptoms of discomfort tend to get only minimal attention or care, especially during lengthy hot spells, when conservation measures force home gardeners to be frugal in their water use. Yet ornamental shrubs are very much alive, and they need timely attention, too, just like lawns, flowers, trees and vines. At times, they can shift for themselves. But our weather usually does not provide enough precipitation to satisfy their needs.

PRUNING

Shrubs grow a little or a lot every year. And the more they grow, the more they need pruning. Yet gardeners frequently neglect to prune their shrubs.

Shrubs often have dead wood created by disease, storm damage or other injury. And this dead wood needs to be pruned. The best time to detect what work needs to be done is during winter, when deciduous shrubs are without foliage. Dead twigs or canes usually are different colors than live ones — mostly gray or black. Another excellent way to tell dead wood from live branches is with the breaking test. Dead twigs snap off and break; live branches bend and snap back easily.

Question: How do you prune a Mugho pine that is growing out of bounds? I would like to keep the plant but it is just too large for the space.
Answer: You can prune back a Mugho pine but you cannot go any further down than half of the green needles. If you prune beyond you will have not much but dry sticks. This pruning should be delayed until the new growth is stretching. Then you can also trim off half of the new candles on the plant. Re-shaping an overgrown Mugho pine takes several years of work.

Shrubs also need pruning because they do not always grow in the shape or fashion we want them to. Rounding off the top of a plant is not the best of practices, but sometimes we have to do it to keep sunlight flowing into our rooms.

Hedges must be kept in scope with their purpose to maintain their usefulness. They have little regard for property lines and will obscure a portion of a neighbor's garden if we fail to trim and reshape them every year.

Some ornamental plants such as cherries and plum bushes have a habit of suckering. A sucker is a new shoot emerging from the roots of a plant or the understock. Suckers have several causes, such as winterkill, graft incompatability, and mechanical injury. Unless this unexpected growth is terminated by pruning, we may end up with such things as a green section in a Redleaf plum. Unless you like things that are unusual, you may not want your landscape design changed by accident. You may want to preserve a few suckers, but certainly not all of them.

Mugho Pine

To continue the magnificent flowering period of ornamental shrubs, you must find the best time to prune them. It would be sad, for example, to cut away half of the flowering potential of a Forsythia because we failed to time our pruning effectively.

Here are the best times to prune several popular shrubs:

Shrub	Time to Prune	How to Prune
Flowering Almond	After bloom	Thin as needed
Barberry	March/April	Shape and thin
Cotoneaster	February to April	Thin selectively
Dogwood	April	Prune oldest branches, reduce excess height
American Cranberry-bush	March	Thin and renew
Alpine Currant	February/March	Thin for balance
Burningbush	April	Thin as needed
Forsythia	After bloom	Thin a third
Hydrangea	March/April	Prune dry stalks
Lilac	After blooms fade	Thin and prune, get suckers seed heads
Mock-orange	After flowering or March	Thin and prune some old canes
Ninebark	March/April	Thin as needed
Potentilla	November to March	Thin as needed
Privet	Anytime	Thin and trim
Prunus	March or after bloom	Shape
Sumac	March/April	Get suckers
Spirea	April or after bloom	Thin
Viburnum	March	Thin and renew

With slower-growing shrubs, annual pruning may not be necessary. But you should at least prune every other year. Some shrubs, however, may need very little pruning unless they are getting beyond expectations. Spreading evergreen shrubs may have to be contained, but not to the point of reducing their appearance. Broadleafed evergreen shrubs also grow so little that occasional thining is all they may need.

There are some shrubs that may need renewal pruning. That is a process where we replace the entire, often overgrown, plant over a period of three or four years. I realize that it may become necessary at times to cut a shrub clear back to the ground or to three-inch stubs. This upsets the balance of many plants so much that the resulting new growth is equally undesirable, because it may force tens and tens of little shoots to grow.

Renewal pruning is just what the name implies. It is a programmed revival for a shrub that may have been neglected for too many years and may present a very naked, unwholesome appearance. To begin renewal pruning, select two or three of the heaviest, oldest canes in the spring and saw them off near the ground. Leave the rest of the plant intact. A year later, repeat the process and remove another third by pruning at near soil level. The third spring, we complete the task by pruning away the final third so only young shoots of two previous seasons remain. Many old plants that fail to contribute much decor to the garden may be completely renovated or renewed by this process.

Question: I need to prune some honeysuckle bushes that are 12 years old. They are in fair condition and had sparse foliage last year. There is heavy bark on the old main branches. The soil is covered with plastic and rocks, but there are many air holes in the plastic. New sprouts are growing from the bushes. How can I improve the bushes?

Answer: This is a good situation for renewal pruning. Take out one-third of the oldest, heaviest stems as close to soil level as possible. It may take some sawing, but it will give emphasis to the newer growth at the outside of the bushes. You can also, if you wish, reduce the total height of the bushes by about 24 inches. As you remove old stalks give attention to better spacing between remaining stems.

> **Rocky Mountain Tip:**
> Renewal pruning with ornamental shrubs is a program usually spread over three years. An old, overgrown shrub is pruned of one-third of the oldest growth each year, until only new plant remains.

Occasionally, there may be a shrub in the garden that you assumed from your home's previous owner. If you decide that the plant is totally misplaced or without function, you should remove it, roots and all. And you may or may not want to replace it. If you choose to do so, be sure to make a more suitable selection. I call this activity re-landscaping. It is somewhat similar to re-decorating inside a home.

Honeysuckle

Topiary Pruning

Topiary pruning is a very formal process mostly involving geometric designs. Formal gardens or hedges require topiary work. They are constantly shaped and trimmed to preserve a specific design style. Some topiary work is round, oval, or square, and some even uses figurine forms. Topiary pruning often is the work of an aficionado who devotes the time and effort for the recognition, beauty or oddity his projects can achieve. But in an ordinary American backyard, there seldom is room for such artistic endeavor.

Feeding Shrubs

FERTILIZING

How much and how fast do you want your shrubs to grow? If the answer is fast, you should feed them a lot. But if they have grown to a desired size and form, and you need little additional growth other than some renewal, then feed the shrubs more sparingly.

In good soils, plants get some nutrition just from normal decomposition of leaves and roots. In a poor soil, this hardly happens.

The plant foods that are right for shrubs and trees are a little different than those for lawns. Shrubs as a rule need fertilizers that are higher in phosphates and lower in nitrogen. They also may need extra iron. The analysis should be something like this: one part nitrogen to two parts of phosphoric acid to one part of potash. A 5-10-5 or 10-20-10 analysis would be nearly ideal.

If you can purchase a 6-10-4 tree and shrub food, it should be used in the following manner:

Small deciduous shrubs — ½ pound
Medium deciduous shrubs — 1 to 1½ pounds
Tall or large deciduous shrubs — 2 to 2½ pounds
Small evergreen shrubs — ½ pound
Medium evergreen shrubs — 1 pound
Large evergreen shrubs — 1½ pounds

You can use several methods to apply granular commercial fertilizers. Smaller amounts my be broadcast over the root system all around the plants. Larger amounts may be applied in equally saced pot holes all around the outside of the plant. Gradually, the plant food is watered in to benefit the plant by its water-soluble nutrients.

It is also possible to feed plants with liquid

Use these granular 6-10-4 or similar fertilizers at the rate of ½ to 2½ pounds per plant depending on plant size.

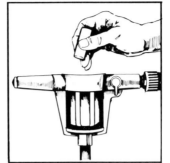

A root feeder with concentrated fertilizer capsules disperses both water and food underground. Don't insert it too deeply, only about 6 to 10 inches deep.

Plant food spikes, which dissolve slowly, are less efficient than fertilizer granules applied in pot holes around the drip line.

Question: Every year my garden is blitzed by a spider mite infestation. Two of my bushes lost most of their leaves despite my spraying. I have used Kelthane and Orthene without success. Is there any new control and is there a carryover from year to year on the foliage? Please outline the best technique for ridding my garden of this annual infestation.

Answer: There are several things you can do to add to your present control program. One is to spray shrub foliage with a hard stream of water. This will dislodge some of the mites. You can also use a dormant oil spray in late winter before the leaves emerge.

nutrients. Because the strength and analysis of liquid commercial fertilizer varies so much from brand to brand, you should carefully follow the instructions on the bottle label or bags.

The preferred time for feeding shrubs is spring, when they are making their most significant growth of the year. Most normal shrubs need feeding only once each year. If you notice a yellowing or chlorosis effect on the foliage in early summer, there probably is a shortage of iron in the soil. And in the alkaline soils of the West this could be quite detrimental to the plant. A normal iron feeding once or twice during the summer should correct this problem easily. If you fail to get results, you may have a disease organism affecting your plant. Seek the assistance of County Extension Service personnel or a specialist at a state university.

There are a few other ways to feed shrubs. One way is to pound stakes made of fertilizer into the soil around the outside of your shrubs. I have found that they dissolve slowly unless a lot of water is available. Another method is to use a root feeder with concentrated chemical capsules. The water stream dissolves the plant food, and both moisture and food are dispersed underground by the feeder's long stem.

Rocky Mountain Tip:

Ornamental shrubs need to be fed every spring according to their size, from ½ to 2½ pounds of an 8-12-4 fertilizer for each plant. This amount can be applied in pot holes around the roots of the plant.

This is a convenient method of feeding plants but a little on the expensive side. Whatever method you use is entirely optional. And if you fail to feed your shrubs in any given year, the results hardly may be noticed. But failing to provide them with plant food for a number of years in a row could result in spindly, unhealthy foliage.

INSECTS

Shrubs are victims of some of the same insects as trees. And these pests can be controlled in the same manner as described in Chapter 4's section on tree insects. Please refer to that section for specific details on how to control the following insects:

Aphids	**Leafminers**
Beetles	**Scales**
Borers	**Spider Mites**
Caterpillars	

Leafhoppers are another insect that can be damaging to shrubs. Individually, leafhoppers cause little damage. But in large numbers, they can be a problem. For leafhoppers the following controls are registered:

Malathion 50 EC	**Meta-systox — R**
Diazinon 25 EC	**Orthene 16 EC**
Sevin 50 WP	

DISEASES

Fortunately, with our overwhelmingly dry climate, plant diseases are only a minor concern with shrubs.

Pyracantha or firethorn is susceptible to fireblight when in bloom. The only acceptable prevention is by spraying with Agri-mycin or Agri-Strep every three days during the flowering periods,

Pyracantha

> **Rocky Mountain Tip:**
>
> Don't be concerned over diseases on ornamental shrubs. Very few have problems. Careful pruning is the soundest way to curb most of them in the garden. Disinfect pruning tools in a denatured alcohol between cuts.

which last about two to three weeks. Pruning diseased portions of the shrubs is the only other alternative.

Russian-olives often have a wilt which appears on one branch or another. The disease, caused by bacteria, is not controllable with any known chemical at this time. Pruning of suspected branches is recommended.

Dogwoods occasionally may display a canker caused by a fungus organism. There also is no satisfactory solution available other than careful pruning in early spring, when droplets ooze and then dry out as the season progresses.

The major problem for many ornamental shrubs is lack of watering. After they bloom, these wonderful plants often are hardly noticed or cared for. Do not forget or abandon your ornamental shrubs.

GOOD NATIVE SHRUBS

The Rocky Mountains and the West have an abundance of plants that are native or indigenous to the area. One of the first planned attempts to utilize some of these plants dates back to the beginnings of the United States Air Force Academy near Colorado Springs. The lack of funds for any project with native plants had made such an event out of the question for many years, in spite of urgings by celebrated plants men and botanists. When landscape plans were designed for the Academy's several thousand acres at an elevation of 7,000 feet, soon it was realized that ordinary ornamental shrubs would not survive without supplemental irrigations. The vastness of the project dictated the use of plants that could survive on a dryland basis.

If you have ever visited the countryside near the United States Air Force Academy, you know that there are few native plants of note nearby. Plants men had to search in the foothills to find the plants now in use. A special attempt was made to propagate the selections. Some did not respond well to accepted propagation methods; others fortunately did. A short tabulation follows, listing the more useful of

Question: What shrubs will grow and survive at elevation of 8,500 feet?
Answer: Not many. Colorado Redosier Dogwood will grow well. Willows may also make it. You can also try a few common Lilacs *(Syringa vulgaris)*. Alpine Currant might also be successful. Start with relatively small plants and let them get used to the location.

these plants. These are stock items in the nursery trade. Those already listed before will only be enumerated but not described again:

Apache plume *(Fallugia paradoxa)*

Buffaloberry *(Shepherdia argentea)*

Smithi Buckthorn *(Rhamnus Smithi)* — Very glossy leaves. Only five to six feet high.

Alpine Currant — Black-fruited

Wax Currant *(Ribes cereum)*

Redtwig Dogwood *(Cornus stolonifera coloradensis)*

Native Elder *(Sambucus pubens)* — Grows only two to four feet.

Fendlera rupicola — White flowers. Grows about six feet tall, upright habit.

Fernbush *(Chamaebatiaria millefolium)* — Has finely divided leaves. Fine white flower clusters in summer. Three to four feet.

New Mexico Privet *(Forestiera neo-mexicana)* — Bush to six feet tall. Forms dark-blue fruit.

Honeysuckle *(Lonicera involucre)* — Requires a shady location.

Jamesia *(J. americana)* — White bloom. Three to five feet. Fall colors orange and red.

Mountain Mahogany *(Cercocarpus montanus)*

Native Ninebark *(Physocarpus monogynus)* — White to pink flowers. Good fall color. Some drought tolerance. Three to four feet.

Shrubby Cinquefoil *(Potentilla fruticosa)* — Spreading branches. Two to three feet high. Very adaptable.

Chokecherry *(Prunus virginiana melanocarpa)*

Rabbit Bush *(Chrysothamnus sp.)*

Rock Spirea *(Holodiscus sp.)* — Pinkish-white flowers. Three to five feet. Full sun to partial shade.

Wild Rose *(Rosa woodsii)* — Hardy. Grows to six feet. Single pink bloom.

Rocky Mountain Tip:

A great many native shrubs are now available through the nursery trade. Not all dealers handle all plants, but you might find some of them enjoyable and well chosen. Both evergreen and deciduous shrubs can be fashioned into formal hedges. They may become a maintenance problem if you do not trim them properly three or four times each year.

Tall Western Sage *(Artemisia tridentata)* — Common in plains and foothills. Greyish foliage.

Serviceberry *(Amelanchier alnifolia)*

Cismontana Sumac *(Rhus glabra cismontana)* — Three to four feet. Dwarf. Smooth foliage, Eventually suckers.

Three-leaf Sumac *(Rhus trilobata)*

Tamarisk *(Tamarix sp.)*

Thimbleberry *(Rubus deliciosus)*

Native Bluestem Willow *(Salix sp.)*

Redstem Willow *(Salix sp.)*

Yellow Mountain Willow *(Salix sp.)*

Yucca (Yucca bacata and glauca)

Gambel Oak *(Quercus gambel)* — Eventually will grow up to be a tree.

Hedges of evergreen and deciduous ornamental shrubs and trees are excellent separations within a garden. They are equally effective as a demarcation line between properties. Hedges do require a bit more room or space to develop than a fence does. They also are warmer and more colorful than a fence but usually require more annual maintenance.

Hedges frequently are not regulated in height or width the way fences are, but they must not be on a property line, either. Many disputes between neighbors have been created by hedges over encroachment, maintenance and shade. On the other hand, fences do not always solve problems, either.

FORMAL AND INFORMAL HEDGES

Formal Hedges

Formal hedges belong mostly with formal gardens around large estates, or castles, as in Europe. The word "formal" denotes balances and symmetries, geometrical forms, and evenness of flow almost to the point of monotony. Formal hedges also must extend far enough to avoid sudden interruption. In short, they are difficult to execute, and they require more manual maintenance than any other separation or enclosure.

For relatively short formal hedges, one evergreen juniper excels in adaptation: the Tammy juniper. It grows to a certain width without much help. It is feathery enough so constant shaping and snipping won't uncover bare spots or unsightly voids. At a height of up to four feet, it is a natural.

If you want a much taller evergreen hedge, you may have to settle for Colorado spruce. Such a hedge started with six-foot trees may require ten years

Formal Gardens — Villandry, France

before it really looks like a formal hedge. You really have to want such a hedge badly to wait long enough for it.

A formal hedge also can be produced from deciduous shrubs. But it will look a little bare in winter without its leaves. For taller formal hedges, use Russian-olive or lilacs. The plants must be spotted about 30 to 36 inches apart to obtain desired density. To a hedge height of four feet, several privets can be used. Amur, English and Golden privet have lots of twigs and small leaves, two features you will need for density. Few other plants perform equally well. At heights of only 12 to 18 inches, Lodense privet is the only plant for formal hedges, unless boxwood survives well enough in your locality.

When you purchase hedge plants such as regular privets, you have to plant them about 12 to 15 inches apart, prune them almost to the ground (which hurts) and let them grow for an entire season without pruning or shaping. Lodense privet should be planted 8 to 10 inches apart and pruned within two inches of the ground to eventually obtain a solid, thick hedge. For a well-shaped formal hedge, always let the base grow wider than the top. Other-

Formal hedges require extensive manual maintenance.

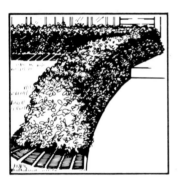

Informal hedge pruning retains natural shape. A hedge should be slightly wider at base than at the top to allow all foliage to receive equal sunlight.

wise, shade will influence the lower portions, and the hedge will become "leggy" or thin at the bottom. Failure to cut hedge plants back immediately after planting also may cause irreversible legginess.

In early spring, you can purchase privet in packages of 12 or 25 bare-root plants. Dig a trench about 12 inches wide and six inches deep to arrange the plants for a neat hedge in your garden.

Informal Hedges

Informal hedges take advantage of the natural forms and shapes of a given plant. Some shrubs are more uniform in their growth than others. What kind of informal hedge you should have depends really on how tall a separation you desire. Using evergreen plants may dictate the eventual height and width of the hedge, but without pruning the hedge may grow to five or six feet in width. For a tall separation without great width but good density, Pinyon pine, if available, is an excellent hedge. It may grow up to 12 feet without pruning, but it can be selectively headed off at 8 to 10 feet by pruning back the central leader. Pinyons also can be trimmed or the new candles broken off to contain the trees within an acceptable size or width.

Several species of upright juniper scopulorum also can be arranged into an informal hedge. Naturally, they must be quite compact, but the plants should be placed at about 36 to 42 inches center to center to facilitate the density of a tall hedge without waiting for many years. Such a hedge can be of a controlled height of between 8 and 10 feet.

Juniper chinensis Armstrong and Mahonia or Oregon grape also are excellent shrubs for evergreen informal hedging. J. Armstrong is vase-shaped but grows slowly. Mahonia also has very deliberate, slow growth and needs very little pruning over a period of years. Mahonia will do better in shade. J. Armstrong performs very well in partial to full sun.

An almost unlimited choice of shrubs can be arranged into an informal hedge. Probably most important is that you choose the same species throughout. A mixed hedge does not make a very unified impression. Besides, there is enough variation of forms within many species that you should not have to select from different species.

At a height of two to three feet, several barberries can be worked easily into an informal hedge. Most of these plants have spines — which may or may not be desirable. At three feet, potentilla or shrubby cinquefoil excels. It is one of our best and hardiest shrubs. Its side growth cascades pleasantly if given enough spacing. Golden and Alpine currants make a lovely informal hedge ranging from three to four feet in height. Several spireas are very twiggy and full of foliage and make a good hedge. Varieties Vanhoutte, Garland and Froebel are among the most qualified for this use.

My choice informal hedge plant, however, is Peking cotoneaster, *C. acutifolia*. It has small, glossy leaves, is well-branched and naturally makes an oval shape reaching a maximum height of six feet. Although its flowering is nothing dramatic, the fall colors of this plant are lovely, and the berries are a good emergency food supply for birds. Its density is quite excellent. A stray branch or two can be pruned easily. And cotoneaster will top or round off at a selected height quite easily.

Tallhedge buckthorn makes into a narrow, columnar shrub mass of a hedge at a height of about eight feet. It has become very popular for this use and purpose.

Watering Large Shrubs

WATERING

Large shrubs such as lilacs, mock-orange and snowball usually get enough watering care until after their magnificent bloom. Then they are often the most neglected garden plants. Yet, if they are watered well every month, they will bloom much better the following year. Large shrubs also benefit from timely, deep watering with a Greenie attachment or root-feeder.

Watering Medium Shrubs

Medium shrubs such as cotoneaster, forsythia and redtwig dogwood often get adequate moisture in or near a lawn area. But where they are located away from frequent water sources, they must have a good drink every three weeks during the summer. The amount depends on how isolated they are. 10 to 15 gallons, however, would not be too much.

Watering Small Shrubs

Small shrubs such as Vanhoutte or Froebel spirea, Bush cinquefoil *(Potentilla)* or Japanese barberry must have a good water supply of five gallons for each plant, or water approximately every two or three weeks from May through September.

Forsythia

VINES, CLIMBERS AND GROUND COVERS

L ANDSCAPE plants that are largely decorative include vines and climbers. Some of these are evergreen and mostly suitable for exposures that are sheltered from the intense winter sun. Others like Clematis excel in lovely bloom through a good part of the summer season. Most vines and climbers are perfectly hardy and well accustomed to the alkaline clay soils of the West. Insects are not a serious threat to most of them.

There are numerous ground covers that are well adapted to the Rocky Mountain area, the High Plains and the Great West Basin. Ground covers are not always a practical departure from lawn maintenance. Many need at least some irrigation and frequently require manual maintenance and weeding.

Vines and climbing plants can make us think of the legendary vine-covered cottages of the past. Vines do have a tendency to cover buildings, fences and walls, but at the same time, they soften architectural features and add a quality of hominess that suggests simple, good living.

VINES AND CLIMBING PLANTS

Only a limited number of vines are hardy in the Rockies; however, the ones that are hardy can be attractive and useful. Which are right for your garden depends to a degree on the exposures the plants must face, the amount of support you can provide for them to grow on, the shelter they will receive in our garden's microclimate, and the quality of the soil they will grow in.

A few vining plants can sustain our hot summer sun on the south and west sides of a house. But these plants must also survive the freezes and thaws of our unpredictable winters. There they do less well. On the other sides of the house, where plants face north and east, other climatic challenges of wind and cold temperatures must be met.

Some vining plants are able to adjust to every condition found in the Rockies. Their numbers, however, are small indeed. Often, trial and error is the only way you can gain precise answers about whether a plant will, or will not, work in your locality. The vines that survive in our gardens are the ones we can depend on. But which ones actually will survive is a matter that can change from one side of town to another.

East exposures are likely the safest overall. They get good light, a fair amount of sun and warm-up and shade when it gets very hot. The problem is, we don't often need vines on the east side of a house. Evergreen vines often adapt to an east exposure, since the sun does not warm up early on a winter day.

North-facing exposures are always safe for evergreen vines. There, English Ivy and Euonymus Wintercreeper usually will succeed. But making these climbing vines work their way up a brick wall is a challenge. Even with various supports, our coaxing will not always be effective. For instance, after 15 years of trial, my English Ivy still performs better as a ground cover near the north brick wall of our garage. It has started up the wall several times, but winds and environment have put the damper on it almost as often.

A few vines will grow anywhere. The Virginia Creepers, often called Woodbine, belong to this

English Ivy

Rocky Mountain Tip:

Climbing plants and vines are usually most dependable along an east wall or a bright north exposure. Woodbine or Virginia Creeper and Silverlace
Vine are among the hardiest.

group. If you are tired of trying to get results with
different plants, you may find this one to be your
final successful choice. If Virginia Creeper cannot
survive in your location, I would try for some other
type of wall decorations.

Using Fences As Supports

Fences are a ready-made support for climbing
plants and vines. Among the best is chain-link.
Plants that have no tendrils of their own may wind
their way through this steel fabric and cover much of
it in good time. But I like the effect of Clematis on a
weather-seasoned cedar or grape-stake fence. The
lovely qualities of Silverlace Vine on these fences is a
treat, especially in late summer. The effect and appearance of an old-fashioned white picket fence,
meanwhile, can be greatly enhanced with annual
climbing vines such as Scarlet Runner Bean or Morning Glory. Mature tree trunks and large shrubs may

Morning Glory

Boston Ivy

permit vines to scale their way up to better sunlight. There is a special use for almost every vine. Vines add character to any garden, and you should choose the ones that you like. Some of the following may fit your needs:

RECOMMENDED VINES AND CLIMBERS

Boston Ivy *(Parthenocissus tricuspidata)* — Clings to masonry; may reach 50 feet without pruning. Will even work its way up utility poles, which should be discouraged. Has blue-black berries in fall. Brilliant orange-scarlet leaves in fall sun or part shade.

Bittersweet *(Celastrus scandens)* — Aggressive vine in full sun to part shade. Two plants needed for berries; male and female sexes are separate. Fall color: yellow. Prune in March or April.

Clematis *(Clematis sp.)* — Numerous small-and large-flowered varieties and species. Requires rich

Clematis

and preferably near-neutral soil and winter mulching with peat moss over roots. Must have trellis or other support to climb. Will grow on fences and in a northern exposure, with good light. Large-flowered varieties of note are: Jackman, purple; Ramona, light blue; Markham, red; Countess Bouchard, pink; Nelly Moser, pink on rose; and Henry's white. Sweet Autumn is small-flowered and white. All make attractive, fuzzy seed heads.

Climbing Roses (*Rosa sp.*) — Only the hardiest climbing roses are dependable in the Rockies, except in places far south, such as Santa Fe, Albuquerque, Reno and St. George. The really hardy climbing roses include: Paul's Scarlet, red; Improved Blaze, red; New Dawn, light pink; White Dawn, white; and Don Juan, red. Climbing hybrid tea roses, which bloom on second-year canes, are dependable only where winters are on the warmer side and where there is adequate shelter.

Dutchman's Pipe (*Aristolochia durior*) — Vigorous vine; often starts slow. Large leaves. Small flowers look like pipes.

Gourds (*Cucurbita sp.*) — Fast-growing vines yield fascinating fruit for drying. Annual, so must be planted every year. Need full sun.

Grape (*Vitis sp.*) — If it can be found, Beta grape is the hardiest. Others that are sound are: Concord, blue; Niagara, white; and Fredonia, blue. Excellent for arbors. For fruit, prune annually (February or March).

Hall's Honeysuckle (*Lonicera japonica*) — Semi-evergreen foliage. Must be controlled by pruning. Sun or shade tolerant. Fragrant white flowers fade to yellow. Layers (roots) easily.

Honeysuckle Vine

Morning Glory (Ipomoea sp.) — Provides some shade and lovely flowers on supports. Heavenly Blue and Early Call Rose are popular varieties. Annual.

English Ivy (Hedera helix) — Evergreen, three-lobed leaves. In shade, tendrils will attach to mortar or stucco. With help may grow up a wall slowly.

Scarlet Runner Bean (Phaseolus sp.) — Dark green foliage. Works well on wire fences or other support. Very prolific and fast-developing. Beans edible when young. Scarlet seed. Annual.

Silverlace Vine (Polygonum aubertii) — Sun exposure and good soil needed. Sprays of small, white flowers in profusion in late summer. Clings to any support. Very hardy.

Trumpet Vine (Bignonia) — Orange and red flowers available. Excellent for screening. Will climb on supports only. Works well on trellis.

Question: I am wondering why my Trumpet Vine does not bloom? It is three years old, healthy and grows lots of new vines, but no flowers. Perhaps it is not getting the right mixture of fertilizers?
Answer: Trumpet Vines often take their time before they start to bloom. I don't believe the age of three is very old. Probably you are on the threshold of success. If you want to help the plant, you can feed it with Super-phosphate or Bonemeal. Both will support early and good flowering.

Question: My Boston Ivy and Concord grapes are growing new shoots so fast I cannot believe it. What can I do to slow things down?
Answer: Don't water too often. Also hold fertilizers off these vines if you can. Prune off what you don't want. I know it means frequent pruning, but at least you can keep the plants in control.

English Ivy

Silverlace Vine

Trumpet Vine

Engelmann Virginia Creeper *(Parthenocissus sp.)* — Green, five-parted foliage in summertime; brilliant red in autumn. Has adhesive tendrils which attach to brick, mortar, etc. Climbs fast; must be contained. Very tough. St. Paul variety grows slower than Engelmann and not as aggressive. Best on north walls or in shaded places. Brilliant fall color.

Wintercreeper *(Euonymus fortunei)* — Produces roots on stems. Evergreen foliage. Shade only. Foliage turns purple in winter sun. Size of leaves depends on variety. Vigorous after slow start. Available varieties include Baby Wintercreeper, Big Leaf Wintercreeper and Purple-Leaf Wintercreeper.

Wisteria *(Wisteria frutescens)* — Too tender for some places. In protection or shelter, can be a large plant. Lavender flowers. Needs sunny location. Prune in April.

Virginia Creeper

Wisteria

Wintercreeper

Controlling Vines in Limited Spaces

Vines generally are fast-growing plants. Annual vines such as Scarlet Runner Bean, gourds and Morning Glory develop an entire plant from seed every year. And perennial vines may grow at faster or slower rates. But many of those vines can outgrow the small spaces available in our gardens. Most hardy vines and climbers will have to be controlled by pruning, depending on its annual growth promotion. In some years, each vine must be controlled and kept in bounds. Pruning is a continuous process. Grapes can just get away from you in a few days. The same is true of Trumpet Vine and Engelmann Virginia Creeper. I have observed these vines growing more than a foot each week under favorable conditions. If you depend on trellises to hold up your vines, you must hold the vines to their supports with hand pruners. In severe cases, a hedge shear may accomplish the task very effectively. Watch for a variety of insects on vines. Most are similar to shrub pests and are controlled by the same chemical pesticides. A cover spray which is applied to the entire foliage is recommended every three weeks in summer, since insects hide and multiply behind the protective cover of the vine foliage.

Vines for Arbors and Pergolas

A cozy garden is a restful place to listen to the birds and watch a few cumulus clouds float by. But when the temperatures in summer exceed 85 degrees, we need shelter and protection. Arbors and pergolas are ideal places to seek comfort and protection when it is hot and dry. An amateur handy with carpenter's tools can create an arbor or pergola structure fit for a king. Designs for such projects are available from lumber dealers and in inexpensive Ortho and Sunset books. These structures should be situated where a view can be enjoyed or an attractive focal area of the garden can be observed. An arbor or pergola does not need to be secluded, just comfortable as a spot to seek rest, read a good book or listen to good music.

Vines are very helpful in achieving the needed privacy. A well-placed wooden structure may be entirely sheltered by vines in two years or less. If you use grapes, aim for density of cover and shade, not fruit production. But you may, of course, enjoy what the vines produce.

Climbing roses are attractive, but they do not produce the same density of cover as grape vines.

Clematis

Their flowers are lovely in June — then often sporadic during the rest of the summer. Clematis produces good foliage density and flowers, but it has to be pruned back frequently, to near the one-foot level, so it can develop new growth and cover each year.

Annual vines may grow very rapidly in May and June, but it will be August before they can screen out the hot sun overhead. Morning Glory and Scarlet Runner Bean are dependable, but they simply cannot compete with a good, solid perennial vine such as Concord grape, the most dependable cover for pergolas and arbors. If you are willing to twist soft shoots and branches frequently enough, you can also try Engelmann or St. Paul Virginia Creeper. But you cannot go on a two-week vacation and leave your vines in disarray. You will have to prune patiently when you return.

The permanence of evergreen vines such as English Ivy would be of great advantage in arbors and pergolas. But in our region, the winter sun is much too hot for them to sustain, causing constant annual defoliation and frequent die-back.

GROUND COVERS

In places where even a Kentucky bluegrass lawn is difficult to grow or maintain, you should consider using ground cover plants. These plants, if properly chosen and nurtured, can do precisely what the

name "ground cover" says — and with a minimum
of work on the gardener's part. They cannot,
however, fill every need. Ground covers should be
used only in limited spaces or special locations —
and not at the exclusion of turf grass. Most ground
covers can be severely damaged by active family
recreation. Many cannot even be walked on or tip-
toed through. But ground covers can frequently help
you in areas where outdoor activities can be controlled and where you need extra help.

The only ground cover plants on which active
recreation and family play can be sustained are Kentucky bluegrass and other turf grasses. Broadleafed
ground cover plants cannot withstand foot traffic.

Ground cover plants are useful in a variety of
ways. Some of these plants adapt easily to almost any
circumstance, such as where the soil is poor or in
isolated places that are dry and difficult to water sufficiently. Ground covers sometimes can spread
enough to conceal bare spots that were created by
traffic, drought or other causes. Some ground covers
succeed in heavy shade where Kentucky bluegrass
just gives up. Many ground covers have contrasting
colors and textures that add interest to gardens. In
addition, they can provide protection from erosion
caused by wind or water.

Ground covers initially cost 10 to 20 times as
much as a comparable amount of Kentucky bluegrass
per square foot. So you probably will cover only part
of the ground at first and wait for the plants to grow
and spread. Until the coverage of the intended area
is complete, you will have to pull weeds from the
bare spots and pick up the trash and debris that gets
caught in the spaces.

Ground covers are rarely sold in seed form. Most
often, ground covers are offered in packs of 48 or 64
small plants. The plants also can be purchased in
half-gallon or gallon containers, but they can
become very expensive unless you only need a few.

A few nurseries offer some ground covers field-
run. If you buy them in this form, you must divide
the fleece into smaller sections as you plant. Pray a
lot and water the plants at least twice daily until they
start rooting in their new location. When they are
rooted firmly enough to resist a slight tug, you can
reduce watering to a nominal frequency.

Choosing the Right Number of Plants

To cover a 500 square foot garden area with
ground cover junipers requires at least 20 one-gallon

plants or 12 five-gallon plants. In spite of this generous coverage, you still may have to wait four to seven years before the area is virtually covered.

This sounds discouraging, but species of *Juniperus horizontalis* are rarely sold at bargain prices. A nursery needs several years to produce a saleable plant — which increases the price.

To be successful with ground cover plants, you should keep in mind a few basic rules:

a. Ground covers must be tough plants that can compete well in their environment.

b. They should spread quickly. However, that is not always possible. Some are just too dainty for larger areas.

c. Ground covers should remain green or gray and reasonably attractive even when a period of drought is beginning to take its toll on other plants.

d. Ground covers should have few, if any, insect or disease problems and should look good when everything else around them is in temporary shock from unusual weather conditions.

e. Ground covers should spread their vines and broaden in size easily, even under trying environmental conditions.

f. They should survive winters easily without much help from you.

You may think I have just described a weed to you. Fortunately, ground covers are not weeds. But some can be if applied in the limited spaces.

Preparing the Soil for Ground Covers

Before you plant ground covers, you will probably have to improve your soil. Follow the basic guidelines outlined in Chapter 1. Most ground cover plants prefer a gritty soil with an abundance of organic matter. And they develop much faster if they are not handicapped by stagnating water or slow drainage.

Ground Covers for Hot, Dry, Sunny Areas

RECOMMENDED GROUND COVERS

Wooly Yarrow *(Achillea tomentosa)* — Gray foliage; spreads easily; gets 8 to 10 inches high; blooms in July.

Alyssum Goldentuft *(Alyssum saxatile)* — Yellow blooms in April or May. 8 to 10 inches high.

Alpine Rockcress *(Arabis alpina)* — White flowers in April; prefers rocky soils; six inches tall.

Wormwood "Silver Mound" *(Artemisia sp.)* — Silvery foliage; may get 12 inches tall.

Ground cover installation is a little more precise than laying sod. The plants are more expensive. They must be in straight rows at equal distance. Lay it out carefully before you start planting.

Tap container against a solid edge so soil ball drops out easily.

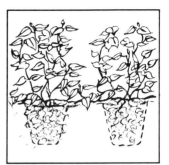

Remove plant carefully and plant at the same depth as in the pot.

Apply root stimulator and water frequently to get the plants started well.

Snow-in-Summer *(Cerastium tomentosum)* — 4 to 6 inches tall; white flowers in June.

Spurge *(Euphorbia sp.)* — Most yellow-flowered in spring; varies from 8 to 12 inches tall; must have well-drained soil.

Rock Soapwort *(Saponaria ocymoides)* — Pink flowers in May; 9 to 10 inches tall.

Wormwood "Silver Mound"

Snow-in-Summer

Dragonblood

Sedum

Stonecrops *(Sedum sp.)* — Most flower in May or June; vary from 1 to 15 inches high, depending on variety. Very tolerant of dry, poor soils. Useful varieties include Dragonblood, Hexagon, Oregon, Lydian, Orange, and Spanish.

Houseleeks *(Sempervivum sp.)* — Vary from 2 to 12 inches high; flower and bloom periods also variable; thrive in poor soils.

Ground Covers That Prefer Sun and Good Soils

Moss Sandwort *(Arenaria verna)* — Up to three inches high; whitish-purple flowers in May.

Common Thrift *(Armeria maritima)* — Foliage about four inches; flowers to 10 inches high; pink flowers in June.

Harebell *(Campanula carpatica)* — Blue-white flowers from June on throughout July; 8 to 12 inches tall; needs drainage.

Maiden Pink *(Dianthus deltoides)* — Red and white flowers in May; foliage 5 to 6 inches tall; slow to spread.

Cottage Pink *(Dianthus plumarius)* — Red, pink or white flowers in early June; foliage six inches tall; needs drainage.

Thrift

Dianthus

Dianthus

Wild Strawberry *(Fragaria sp.)* — One of the few ground covers that can be grown from seed; Alpine variety very hardy; fruit up to one inch.

Coralbells *(Heuchera sp.)* — Tufted mounds of almost round foliage with dainty, red flowers in June; foliage only three inches high.

Sweet Alyssum *(Lobularia sp.)* — An annual grown from seed; colors white, pink and purple; may get 5 to 6 inches high.

Moneywort *(Lysimachia sp.)* — Small, round leaves; about three inches high; bright yellow flowers in summer; keep soil moist.

Mint *(Mentha sp.)* — Some gardeners would not consider mint a ground cover; when it gets away, it becomes a weed. Some will vary from 6 to 10 inches high; very aromatic foliage.

Creeping Phlox *(Phlox subulata)* — Leaves stay

Coralbell

Alyssum

Alyssum

Pansies

evergreen in some winters; flowers very early in spring; pink, white and lavender colors; foliage 6 to 8 inches high.

Lavender Cotton *(Santolina sp.)* — Can be trimmed to short border; yellow flowers in June; does not like extreme cold; very drought resistant.

Thyme *(Thymus sp.)* — Needs watering in hot summer; several varieties useful, including Wooly, Lemon, Creeping Thyme and Mother-of-thyme.

Tufted Pansy *(Viola cornuta)* — Flowers from June to August in various colors; foliage 6 to 10 inches high; many hybrids available.

Ground Covers for Shaded Areas

Geneva Bugle *(Ajuga genevensis)* — Foliage 1 to 2 inches high; flowers blue in May or June; spreads well.

Carpet Bugle *(Ajuga metallica crispa)* — Foliage 1 to 2 inches high; blue flowers in late May or June.

Curly Bugle *(Ajuga reptans)* — Several varieties and leaf colors available; short foliage; blue flowers.

Lily-of-the-Valley *(Convallaria majalis)* — White, fragrant flowers in June; foliage up to six inches high; should be contained.

Plantain Lily *(Hosta sp.)* — Most grow foliage about 10 inches high; blooms in summer; prefers a rich soil; very hardy.

Golden Cinquefoil *(Potentilla aurea)* — Foliage to six inches high; golden flowers in early summer.

Spring Cinquefoil *(Potentilla verna)* — Foliage 3 to 6 inches high; yellow flowers in May to June.

Primrose *(Primula sp.)* — Needs rich soil; cannot take much sun; many hybrids and various

Ajuga

Hosta

Spring Cinquefoil

Primrose

elegant colors available; flowers in May; foliage up to six inches high.

Sweet Woodruff *(Galium odoratum)* — Prefers partial to full shade; tiny white flowers in June; leaves, up to eight inches high, have sweet-scented aroma; used for spicing white wines.

My favorite ground cover plant is *Potentilla verna* or Creeping Cinquefoil. It spreads well in a short time and is cost-effective if purchased in 64 packs for larger-area needs.

A variety of ground cover plants have different soil and exposure requirements. They vary all the way from hot, dry areas to full shade. Do not easily compromise on your selection.

Cotoneaster

Broadleafed Evergreen Ground Covers

Kinnikinnick *(Arctostaphylos uva-ursi)* — Mountain or foothill native; no winter sun; red berries; foliage six inches high; white flowers in June.

Rock Cotoneaster *(Cotoneaster horizontalis)* — May get too high, but can be kept to 12 to 18 inches by pruning; red berries in winter; semi-evergreen.

English Ivy *(Hedera helix)* — Has many different leaf cultivars in milder climates; we are happy to get it established in full shade; covers ground area quite well, and faster than some other ground covers.

Creeping Holly Grape *(Mahonia repens)* — 8 to 12 inches high; yellow flowers in May; blue fruit starts in June; needs a rich, organic soil and shelter.

Germander *(Teucrium sp.)* — Needs sun to partial shade; gray-green foliage, 12 to 16 inches high; blooms purple in late summer.

Periwinkle *(Vinca minor)* — Needs full shade; winter sun can burn foliage; blue flowers in early June; vines about six inches high; spreads quickly.

Periwinkle

Several aromatic or culinary herbs may also be used in limited ways as ground covers. Useful varieties include English lavender, chamomile, and spearmint.

Coniferous Evergreen Ground Covers

Juniper ground covers are valued for their low moisture needs and have become widely used to cover larger areas. They should have irrigation on a year round basis, twice a month spring, summer and fall and once a month during winter.

Groundhugging junipers offer some of the finest and most durable examples of ground covers. They are attractive 12 months each year and need

Juniper — Andorra   *Juniper — Wilton*

relatively little care. Some junipers grow much faster than others, but the slower ones often are the ones most worth waiting for.

The availability of these plants will depend on local demand and gardeners' experiences. This is where you will have to trust your nurseryman, because he should sell only those that have a good record in your locality.

Here are some recommended varieties:

Juniperus chinensis

Sargenti — 12 to 15 inches high; good soil.
San Jose — 12 inches high; sage green.
Gold Coast — 12 inches high; gold tips.

Juniperus horizontalis

Andorra — light green, turning plum in winter.
Bar Harbor — grey-blue, turning to silvery plum.
Blue Chip — silver-blue color.
Wilton Blue — slow-growing; one of the best.
Plumosa "Youngstown" — improved Andorra.
Prince of Wales — bright green; very low.
Hughes — silvery-blue; retains color well; up to 15 inches high.

Juniperus sabina

Arcadia — bright green; prefers full sun.

Rocky Mountain Tip:

Most evergreen ground cover plants are more expensive to begin with and take more years to cover than deciduous plants. But they are elegant, attractive and decorative for 12 months every year.

Broadmoor — soft green; very dense; 12 to 18 inches high.
Buffalo — bright green; spreads fast; 12 to 18 inches high.

Juniperus procumbens nana — To six inches high; good for rock gardens.

Using Mulches As Ground Covers

The use of mulches as ground cover has gained popularity steadily in recent years, especially where water is hard to get or expensive.

Many organic materials are suitable for mulching. The ones you choose can depend entirely on what you consider acceptable and attractive. I could not be persuaded that straw or coarsely shredded branches are attractive enough for me to use. But various commercial bark mulches or chunk bark are very attractive, neutral-colored organics that conserve moisture and prevent soil erosion. These materials and many others also work wonders against weeds.

Mulches used as ground covers can reduce soil temperature and in some instances act as a protective shelter. Sawdust, wood shavings, and chips also work well as ground covers. Some may be too bright in color to be fully appreciated, but what they can accomplish does not depend on color. Compost or leaf-mold is another organic material useful as ground cover. They may have to be replenished every two or three years, but when they are used as a ground cover, they enrich the soil and enhance the biological lives of useful micro-organisms. Even grass clippings can be used as a mulch-style ground cover. Bulk peat moss — if it is relatively inexpensive — can also furnish a superb mulch ground cover that gradually enriches your soil. Use one to two cubic yards per 1000 square feet or two to three balls of compressed packaged peat moss.

Using Inanimate Materials As Ground Covers

Another effective form of ground cover involves using certain manufactured materials, as well as inorganic objects found naturally all around us, such as gravel, small pebbles, granite, and crushed or lava rock commonly used in landscapes. These natural materials are heavy, and they collect heat. Their use should be restricted to service areas or small garden locations where maintenance of other ground covers would be difficult.

The use of plastic sheets under rock is a form of ground cover that has advantages as well as problems. Weed control and moisture control are easier, but the lack of moisture replenishment and air to the roots of the plants may be counterproductive. If black plastic is used, it should be cut into strips so water and air have access to the roots below. Some new fibrous plastics now being sold do not restrict air and moisture access to subsoils. These are sold under the trade names Marifi and Trevera.

Though it is expensive, a calcine clay material of glazed clay sold under the names Turface or Terragreen is an excellent ground cover material. It does not collect and absorb heat like most rock products. It also soaks up water, won't pack down solidly, is sterile, and is neutral in soil reaction.

Other related mined materials that are good for some garden uses are vermiculite and perlite. Vermiculite is composed of super-heated, exploded bits of mica. Perlite is a processed volcanic material that is very porous and light, but could easily act as a ground cover by itself. Mixed with other materials, such as peat moss or vermiculite, it is quite practical as a mulch-style ground cover.

You can walk on inanimates without compacting or damaging them. On live plants you may have to tiptoe very carefully.

Watering Vines, Climbers, and Ground Covers

WATERING

Native plants and ground covers can be watered according to need. Some desert or semi-desert plants are very moisture-efficient, because of their exceptionally large root systems. The number of plants that can be used from the native desert or plains flora are quite limited. Under summer heat they will develop more enjoyably if they are watered twice a month. In winter they also need occasional moisture. Mountain natives generally have a higher need for moisture as we try to duplicate the precipitation of their habitat.

Vines that are evergreen, such as English Ivy and Euonymus Wintercreeper, need some water on a year-round basis. Deciduous vines such as Virginia Creeper and grapes need very little water during the off-season, but at least weekly watering during spring and summer, and for fall foliage development. Clematis should not be allowed to get too dry even in winter. Some extra mulching will help.

FRUIT TREES AND OTHER FRUITING PLANTS

ALMOST every Western state has some commercial fruit production. Colorado has the Grand Junction-Delta-Paonia area for peaches, apricots, pears and sweet cherries. Utah also has fine peaches, sour cherries and apricots. New Mexico has some of the same, plus pecans if you go far enough south. Nevada could raise fruit in other places than their casinos (slots). Montana has some production. Idahoans also raise fruit. I recently saw a budding grape production enterprise near Caldwell.

GROWING YOUR OWN FRUIT

The facts are clear. You can raise some delicious homegrown fruit almost anywhere, if you can muster the necessary elements.

First, you need sunlight. As bright as it is in our Western region, that is a natural. Sometimes I wish we could have a lot more precipitation. But the sunshine is perfect.

Next, you need a decent soil. I don't mean all topsoil. Just a soil location that drains well and is a little better than a heavy gumbo clay.

Third, you need some means of irrigation. If you can afford it, a trickle system is ideal for fruit trees. I do it with Leaky Pipe, a piece of hose that oozes a little water for the trees and gets their roots wet without flooding. Watering also can be done with a little kitchen or bathtub waste. The tree roots don't mind a little detergent. In fact, it lets the water percolate easier.

Fourth, you also need some shelter. Severe, harsh winds really can damage the dormant buds of fruit trees. Some natural form of screening, such as a tall hedge or a group of junipers or pines, can help

When buying bare-rooted trees, use three simple checks to be sure you get a healthy plant:

Twigs should be turgid and bend readily, not dry and shrivelled.

Buds should be moist and green nearly ready to break.

When you scratch the trunk or branches, it should show green underneath.

you get that extra protection your trees need when it is very cold and nasty outside. In very frigid places, we often place fruit trees north of a home or garage, because it warms up more slowly there, and does not encourage blossoming too early. Apricot, peaches and sweet cherry blossoms are more likely to stay in the bud through some of the late winter chills. Most apples, pears, plums and sour cherries don't need the extra protection.

If you are lucky enough to have a large open area, you can have a fruit orchard. But don't feel bad if your garden has room for only one or two trees. Unless you have a dugout or a sound root cellar, where would you put and store all the apples, anyhow? Some of the time, our apple trees come up

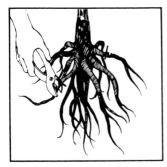

How to plant fruit trees: Before planting, broken roots or excessively long roots should be pruned back. (See also page 126.)

Dig a planting hole 50% wider and deeper to accommodate the tree's roots comfortably. Add organic matter like peat moss or bark mulch and mix with soil as the tree is planted.

Set the tree no deeper than it was at the nursery. With bare-rooted trees, observe where the soil mark is indicated. Containerized trees are planted at the same depth. Now plant and fill hole ¾ full.

> **Rocky Mountain Tip:**
> You don't need an orchard to enjoy fruit from your garden. Fruit trees are able to serve a dual purpose. They may act as a screen, produce fruit and provide some shade. They require little extra care.

with two or three bushels each. That's a lot of apple pies or baked apples or fritters. Our home is too warm for storing fruit. I put the apples in boxes and keep them in our garage. And then it gets so cold that the apples freeze. So we have to convert them all to sauce. I expect you share with me some of the trials of a city gardener. I hope you don't discourage easily, either.

Proper Location and Spacing

Fruit tree spacing naturally depends on the trees' respective sizes. Dwarf and semi-dwarf trees need less room than standard trees. And even some standard trees don't get as large in the West as they do in New York or Michigan. Pruning can do the rest to keep fruit trees in a manageable size and shape. My recommended spacing for fruit trees is approximately as follows:

Tree	Preferred Spacing
Apple — Standard	25-30 feet
Apple — Semi-dwarf (MM 109)	12-15 feet
Apple — dwarf (Malling IX)	5- 8 feet
Cherry Sour — Standard	12-15 feet
Cherry Sour — Dwarf	5- 8 feet
Peach — Standard	12-15 feet
Peach — Dwarf	5-10 feet
Pears — Standard	12-15 feet
Plum — Standard	12-15 feet

POLLINATION

Before you make a decision of what fruit tree or trees to plant, you must consider the pollination needs of various types and varieties. Not all fruit trees are self-fruitful. Some are, but others have special needs for pollination. Some are actually self-unfruitful. They may even be inter-sterile. Perhaps a few simple definitions of these terms will help you make sound decisions.

Pollination is the process by which male pollen is transferred to the stigma of the female flower and grows down to the ovary to fertililze it. Self-pollination is simple. Pollen from a single variety fertilizes the ovary of the same plant. Cross-pollination occurs when wind or insects transfer the pollen from one variety to the ovary of another.

Self-unfruitful — little fruit sets unless the blossoms are fertilized from another variety's pollen.

Inter-sterile — neither of two varieties will fertilize the other.

Here are the pollination requirements for popular fruit trees:

Apples — most apple trees produce better if they can be cross-pollinated by another variety in your yard or a nearby neighbor's garden. Actually, two neighbors could ensure success if they acted neighborly and planted two different apple varieties nearly at the same time.

Pears — need another variety for pollination. Most are self-unfruitful. Also, their nectar is less attractive to bees than the nectar of apples and cherries and such plants as tulips, lilacs and basket-of-gold. But having a beehive nearby can ensure success.

Sour Cherries — all sour cherries are self-fruitful.

Sweet Cherries — all commercial sweet cherry varieties are self-unfruitful and most are inter-sterile. Need pollinator trees.

Peaches, Apricots, Nectarines — most are self-fruitful except J.H. Hale, which is self-unfruitful and needs a pollinator.

Plums — Most European plums are self-fruitful. Plum trees of Japanese origin need a pollinator.

The honeybee is the most dependable pollinator. Wind cannot always be depended upon. In a backyard situation, it may be impractical to set up a beehive, but one certainly would ensure better pollination. Wild bees are helpful, but after a rough winter their numbers are down so much that relying upon them for pollination becomes a gamble. Perhaps I ought to point out that bees do not like windy, cool, or wet weather. Other flowering plants, such as crabapples or even weeds in bloom, are competitive for the attention of bees. Chemical sprays

Rocky Mountain Tip:

Pollination of fruit trees is necessary with some types to produce fruit. Most sour cherries and plums are self-pollinated. Almost all peaches except J.H. Hale are self-fruitful. Apples, pears, and sweet cherries must have pollination to set fruit.

must be avoided during the bloom cycle to avoid losses of bees. It takes a wild bee population almost all summer to restore its numbers after pesticide exposure.

The trees I have selected are applicable to general locations up to 6,000 feet.

Sour Cherries

These are among the most dependable fruit trees for your garden. If you have room for only one tree, this is the one. Sour cherries are very hardy, tolerate mediocre soil and produce a crop just about every year. You can harvest enough fruit from one tree (about 12 to 20 quarts) to have some delicious cherry pies or homemade cherry preserves. I recommend the following varieties for our Western territory:

Montmorency — The best pie and freezing cherry. Ripens around late June to mid-July. Excellent flavor. The robins like them, too. Tangy flavor.

Meteor — Dwarf, very hardy. Should be successful to elevations of 7,500 feet. Used for pies and preserves. Maximum height is 10 to 12 feet.

**THE BEST
FRUIT TREES
FOR ROCKY MOUNTAIN
GARDENERS**

Sour Cherries — Montmorency

North Star — Dwarf. Maximum height is eight feet. Hardy and productive. Fruit is standard size, often larger.

Suda — A Stark Brothers Morello-type cherry. Red juice. Excellent for preserves. Replaces the old English Morello, which is no longer traded.

Sweet Cherries

Kansas Sweet — Semi-dwarf. A little sweeter than Montmorency but not quite as dependable. It is self-pollinating, reaching a maximum of 10-14 feet. A little more tender than the sour cherries.

Stella — A newer variety available in standard and dwarf. The dwarf tree may not adapt as well. The standard trees should be desirable as they are not too large. The cherry is wine-red and self-pollinating. Tree will about equal the size of Montmorency, which is about 15-18 feet. Needs some protection.

Black Tartarian — A small, sweet cherry that is dark red and a good pollinator for Bing, Lambert, Napoleon and other sweet cherries.

Van — Also recommended as a good pollinator. Widely used by commercial growers.

The above-named standard sweet cherry varieties may only produce dependably in warm-winter localities, such as Paonia, Colorado, Salt Lake City, or St. George, Utah. The dwarf varieties are less hardy and often tender.

Apples

Apples can be depended on in most of the Rocky Mountains and Great Basin regions. Altitude is the only major factor that will limit production. Some early maturing varieties can be tried at elevations to 8,000 feet, but not many. There are so many old and new varieties of apples, however, that it is hard to make choices. Stark Brothers of Louisiana, Missouri, have developed many excellent patents that are worthy of consideration. I will enumerate some that I like. All apples need a nearby pollinator variety, and preferably also a beehive nearby.

Red Delicious — This apple is very popular. It is a good-tasting variety that stores well. Has very good resistance to bacterial blight (Fireblight). Many selections have been made on the basis of color. Some are red all over. Semi-dwarf varieties are a good choice for home gardeners. Matures (ripens) September 1-15.

Golden Delicious — More susceptible to Fireblight, but a very good, all-purpose apple. Spicy,

Question: I used Ortho Vegetable and Fruit Spray on my Delicious apple tree. I soaked the tree twice according to directions. At picking time 70% of the apples were wormy. Are there other more effective sprays?
Answer: The most important part of codling moth control is timing. The first cover spray is applied seven days after petal drop. The next cover spray is applied three weeks later and repeated every three weeks until early August. It may take four cover sprays. The best recommended chemicals are Diazinon and Sevin. Sevin also thins fruit set by about 25%.

Apples maturing

sweet flavor. Bears at 4 to 5 years of age. Good pollinator for other apples. Matures with Red Delicious.

Lodi — The best choice for mountain valleys to 8,000 feet. Very early maturing: at 5,000 to 6,000 feet, August 15; at 6,000 to 7,000 feet, September 1. Subject to Fireblight. Very cold-resistant. A green apple when mature. Good cooking and pie apple. Pollinates other early apples. Standard size tree is recommended in higher elevations over dwarf trees.

McIntosh — One of my preferred apples for eating out of hand. Matures before Delicious, about August 25 to September 5. A very juicy, crisp apple. Pollinates early varieties well. Dependable in cold places. Should be tried to elevations of 7,000 feet.

Winesap — Late maturing (mid-October). One of the best storage apples if you have a cold storage that won't freeze. Poor pollinator for other trees. Jon-A-Red or Golden Delicious will pollinate winesap. May ripen too late to protect from frost. Dwarf available as a spur-flowering tree. (Spurs are short twigs along main stems that can mature two to four apples each year.)

Jerseymac — Very early maturing (August). Tasty McIntosh cross. Where summers are hot, Jerseymac succeeds better than most varieties. Very cold-resistant.

Jonathan — A popular commercial variety. Late maturing, September 25 to October 10. Good flavor. Susceptible to Fireblight. A good pollinator for other mid- to late-season varieties.

Jon-A-Red — Improved variety that ripens earlier, September 10-20. Will be partly self-fruitful. Stores well.

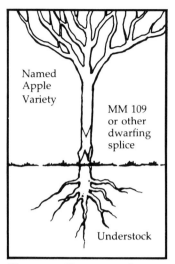

Upon a seedling rootstock a splice of dwarfing wood can be grafted between the root and the named apple variety. Standard roots adapt better to Western soils than dwarfing rootstocks or understocks.

Jon-A-Del or **Jonalicious** — Both are excellent crosses that provide a better, tastier fruit. Have some disease resistance (inherited from parent.) Ripens early October.

Liberty (Stark) — Very disease-resistant. McIntosh taste. Good general use apple. Very hardy. Suitable for mountain locations. Matures mid-September.

Prima (Stark) — Very resistant to Fireblight. Tart flavor. Keeps well. Ripens early September.

Priscilla (Stark) — Delicious cross with good blight resistance. Matures late September.

Chieftain — A good cross of Delicious and Jonathan. Good-tasting fruit at harvest. Stores well, also. Matures late September.

Red Baron — Very hardy, bred in Minnesota. General-use apple, crisp and juicy. Ripens September 10-25.

Haralson — A very hardy winter apple. Keeps well in storage. Crisp, red, flavored fruit. Matures September 1-15.

There are still others you may favor, such as Wealthy as a late-summer apple, Corland as a quality keeper, and Rome Beauty as a baking apple. But most of their individual qualities are represented in some of the newer crosses.

Dwarf and Semi-Dwarf Apples

Dwarf and semi-dwarf apples are becoming more and more popular. They can be maintained so much easier by the home gardener. The problem I see is that there is a wide variety of different dwarfing understocks which are used for top-working with a named apple variety. The Malling understocks in the trade are designated by the letter M and a Roman numeral from I to IX. Malling IX and VIII are still in popular use for dwarfing. Newer dwarfing stocks are the Malling-Mertens crosses with numericals from 100 up. MM 106 is a newer selection which roots much better and deeper than the Malling stocks. I have had several trees on this understock since 1970 without problems.

ROCKY MOUNTAIN TIP:

Many nurseries now produce spur-type apples. They set and mature fruit on short spurs making the apples easier to pick and often producing a better crop on a dwarf tree.

I hope more nursery producers and sellers will offer details on understock to their customers. At present, it is a guessing game since most nurseries don't even know what their dwarfing variety is.

Spur-Type Trees

An important discovery made by dedicated orchard experimenters is the spur-type tree. Stark Brothers Nursery was the first to discover these different fruit producers. The main difference is that a spur often produces several fruits, instead of just one as is ordinarily the case. Spur types are also generally semi-dwarf naturally. So the desired height is achieved with mechanical grafting. Other nurseries besides Stark now offer spur-type trees, but Stark's has the largest assortment by far. When a dwarf stem piece is inter-grafted — that is, used between a sound root and a spur — a double dwarf is produced. This has even greater home garden appeal, because a well-producing tree uses only a nominal amount of space in the garden.

Pears

If you want the enjoyable taste of fresh pears in your garden, you can plant one of the hardy pear varieties. Only a few of them are Fireblight-resistant, and these are the ones you should select from. Pear trees may become quite tall. So a semi-dwarf selection is easier to keep up with. All pear trees must be cross-pollinated with another pear of a different variety.

Bartlett — Most local suppliers feature this pear as the only choice. It is very susceptible to blight, but a good, sweet pear that matures in September.

Maxine — This older variety is fully resistant to Fireblight. It is still chosen for a fine flavor and mid-September maturity. Very cold-resistant.

Luscious — Very hardy and Fireblight-resistant. Quality dessert pear. Matures early September.

Moonglow — Juicy fruit that matures in late August. Resistant to Fireblight.

Starking Delicious — Hardy variety that matures mid-September. Extremely disease resistant.

Seckel — Small sugar pear. Should be picked mid-September. Will ripen in a week or more. Very Fireblight-resistant.

Tyson — Very early-maturing sugar pear. Small fruit with spicy flavor. High blight resistance.

Pear

Peach in bloom

Peaches

Most peach tree varieties are a bit fickle in our climates. The temperature tolerance for most is -10 degrees F. But a few have more hardiness. I will enumerate these first. Only J.H. Hale and Halberta need pollination from other varieties. Peaches grow faster than most other fruit trees, and therefore need to be trimmed more every winter.

Reliance — Available in dwarf and standard. Credited to sustain -25 degrees F. without loss. Reliance has medium-size, yellow-fleshed fruit. I recommend the standard size. (A standard size peach tree, properly pruned every year, rarely exceeds 12 feet in height.) Matures late August.

Polly — Very hardy, white-meated, freestone fruit. Matures early September.

Stark Frost King — This variety is promised to tolerate -20 degrees F. Very fine flavor for a hardy peach. Ripens in August.

Elberta — Large, delicious fruit with small, freestone pit. Ripens early to mid-September.

Redhaven — High production, with fruit of freestone quality. Fine-textured meat with delicious taste. Early September maturity. The most popular of all peach varieties in the Rocky Mountain region.

Plums and Prunes

Plums and prunes are a group of tree fruit much more cold tolerant than apricots. Yet they are often overlooked. I am sure you can get a fine crop of plums or prunes in most localities below 6,500 feet. All Japanese plums must have another Japanese variety for cross-pollination. Unless you really are determined to try some, however, I would rather sell you on varieties of American or European ancestry.

Marie Plum

Stanley — Very hardy, self-pollinating variety of freestone fruit. Ripens usually around mid-September. Can be picked green and matures indoors in a few days.

Stark Blue Ribbon — Self-pollinating. Handsome, large, blue fruit in September.

Monitor — Large, red-colored fruit. Very hardy variety from Iowa State University. Good yields in late August to early September.

Green Gage — Medium-sized green fruit at first — turns golden color at maturity and is self-pollinated. Hardy. Ripens September 10-20.

Waneta — This American plum is very hardy. It may be harder to find now. It produces a yellow-meated fruit of excellent flavor. Needs Toka or American plum as pollinator. Matures August 25 to September 10.

Ember — Yellow plum blushed red. Ripens in early September. Very hardy. Use Toka as pollinator.

Toka — Red fruit of very unusual flavor. Excellent pollinator for other hardy American plums. Ripens August 20-30.

Plums nearly ripe

Underwood — Red fruit ripens in August. Also very hardy. Toka is a good pollenizer.

Sapa — Dark-purple fruit, borne in clusters. Very hardy. Pollination from American plum and Toka. Matures August 20-30.

Apricots

These trees are borderline in the Rockies, because the weather so frequently interferes with the early bloom. If you have lots of room and a keen desire, you can try some of them. You may have luck in such locations as Albuquerque, Salt Lake City and St. George. I usually call them a nice shade tree with fruit every ten years. That may overstate the case, but in principle, I have observed apricots failing for close to 40 years.

Sungold and Moongold — Both are from the same Minnesota breeding and won't die, whether or not they produce fruit. If the weather has cooperated and allowed fruit production, the fruit will mature in late August — Sungold a few days later than Moongold, assuming, of course, that the weather has been cooperative and you did get fruit.

Apricot

Black Walnut

It's Worth Waiting For

Fruits from your own trees are worth waiting for. But for the very impatient home gardeners, we sometimes see offerings of larger trees, called semi-mature, which are supposed to produce fruit instantly. This is often a bit of an overstatement. By growing a tree in a nursery for four or five years and using a mechanical tree spade to move it, you can save a little time. But the root system still has to catch up with the top of the tree before miracles happen.

It is best to plant fruit trees that are at the 3 to 5 foot size. Most of the containerized stock at nurseries seldom is larger.

How soon you can expect edible results depends on several factors:

a. Climate — This we cannot change. We have to accept the good and the bad and like it. Drought and severe freezes can cost us time we did not anticipate to lose.

b. Location and soil — A more sheltered location will exclude winds and other stresses. This allows the tree to recover from shock more easily and grow more each year. The soil we can and should improve. A deep planting hole with lots of organic matter added to the soil helps the roots develop much faster.

c. Character of the tree — Some fruit trees just grow more rapidly than others. Dwarfs are slow-growing, but they often produce much earlier than standard trees. The following table can help you.

Time estimated from date of planting:

Type of Tree	Fruit — Years after Planting (2-3 year-old grafts)
Sour Cherry — Standard	3 years
Sour Cherry — Dwarf	2 to 3 years
Apple — Standard	4 to 8 years
Apple — Dwarf	2 to 3 years
Apple — Combination 4 in 1	3 years
Pear	4 years
Peach	3 years
Plum or Prune	4 years
Apricot	4 years

According to this schedule, there is little difference in how long it takes trees to bear fruit, except with apples. Apple varieties require a wide range of years before they begin fruiting. The more popular varieties, such as Red and Golden Delicious, take the longest time. There is little we can do about this. Some special effort like specialized pruning may shorten the waiting period perhaps by a year, but not much more. The best solution is to look at the tree's ornamental beauty for a few years before it begins to mature its delicious fruit. And when that time comes, you will be especially pleased with your tasty success and proud of your decision to plant it. I think most well-chosen fruit trees have more to offer in enjoyment than other ornamental trees. The taste and satisfaction provided by the fruit are pure joy and pride.

Fruit trees sometimes — fortunately not too often — fail to produce a crop for one or more years. There could be a number of reasons why this may happen. Most of them relate to climate, but some may be caused by our own omissions.

A tree that is not healthy in its general growth may fail to bear fruit until the obstacle is dealt with. Diseases may affect fruiting. Bacterial blight or scab may affect apples and pears. In rare cases it may also affect stone fruits and render their fruit worthless. If a disease occurs, we simply have to deal with it by the use of preventive or curative chemical treatments or prune to the extent that the tree may recover on its own.

Extremely cold winter weather — which I am glad to say is not an annual event — also can adversely affect fruiting of trees. Apple and pear trees rarely are injured unless the cold spell comes rather early or late in the season. Sour cherries are pretty durable, too, but sweet cherries, apricots, and peaches are easily damaged with few exceptions when temperatures fall below -10 degrees F.

When buds of fruit trees begin to swell near opening, a drop to 24 degrees may damage their fruiting ability. Fortunately, most fruit trees open their buds over a period of about two weeks. So even if some buds are frozen, others usually survive. Open blossoms are not likely to survive a temperature of 28 degrees F.

Question: Last year for the first time I had wormy cherries and wormy pears. I assume that if one would spray just before ripening most of this could be avoided. Please advise what kind of product I could use. Answer: The cherries have a fruit worm while pears have the codling moth larvae. Both can be controlled by Diazinon but the timing is different. On the pears you start spraying in late May and repeat every 2½ to 3 weeks until early August. The proper timing also helps for the cherries. First spray should be timed around late May and a second spray in mid-June.

Lack of sufficient cold weather could be a problem in a few sheltered places of the West. The fruit trees I have described must have a certain amount of chilling temperatures to induce dormancy. In most of our Western territory, we don't have to worry about that.

Inadequate light and exceptionally poor, rocky soil also may reduce fruiting expectations. Our light intensity in most instances exceeds the requirements. Soils simply have to be made a bit better than average by manual preparation to let a fruit tree grow and succeed. Also, very few trees will withstand a waterlogged situation. You can plant fruit trees near a leaching field (disposal area), but you will have problems in spring if the water table comes up too high for several weeks or months. Fruit trees must have good drainage.

Extreme root competition from an overly aggressive cottonwood or willow tree also may make it difficult for a fruit tree to produce and grow normally. I would hope you can avoid such a trauma.

Heavier-than-normal pruning of a thoroughly neglected tree (which no doubt you may have inherited) can affect normal fruiting for one or more years. No one can neglect a tree for 10 years and simply create order out of chaos in a single season. You have to have lots of heart to do what is needed.

> **Rocky Mountain Tip:**
>
> Failure to produce fruit on a mature and bearing tree can often be blamed on severe weather, insect damage, poor soils, extreme root competition, rabbit or rodent damage, or extremely large crops the previous year.

HOW TO PROTECT BLOSSOMS FROM SPRING FROST

I sometimes stand at the home office window and observe swirling snowflakes while our peach tree on the west side of the house is in full bloom. I cannot express the agony I feel when that happens. Or when hail begins to fall on the fruit. The helpless feeling is devastating. Someday, someone smarter than I am will invent a plastic umbrella that will activate automatically to protect the fruit trees from malice by the weather. Until then, we have to try other means.

There are a few time-tested but cumbersome ways to protect blossoms and fruit. One way is to cover the tree when weather like snow comes along later than expected. A comforter or something similar might help a lot. Of course, we have to erect additional supports also, because the weight of wet snow may be greater than the tree can support. This is most likely a fair solution if the tree is small. If it is larger than seven or eight feet, it would take a large comforter or plastic tent to cover it.

If the snow is light, we can use a garden hose and wash it off with a gentle stream of water. The big problem in the West really is not only the snow itself but the freeze that usually follows when the storm system has moved East and all we have left are dropping, chilling temperatures. A covering usually can be relied on for protection to about 28 or 27 degrees F. Temperatures much colder than that likely will make our efforts useless — unless the drop in degrees is only for a few hours.

A home gardener also may alleviate problems by placing a small kerosene space heater under the tree or a canopy. All we really need to create is a temperature change of around 10 degrees F. overnight. It may be worth the effort if you can do it.

There also is the old orchard practice of smudge pots. This was almost an annual practice in the Grand Junction area to protect a commercial peach and apricot crop. It usually resulted in some survival. Smudge-potting involved the burning of anything that produced heat and smoke. It largely has been countermanded by health officials because of the associated air pollution.

The use of radiant heat has been tried successfully. But the cost of electric power has risen so much in the Eighties that using radiant heat to protect blossoms must be an individual decision.

Rocky Mountain Tip:

Below freezing temperatures during the bloom could destroy a fine fruit crop in the making. It may pay to set up a kerosene lamp or heater under a tarp that covers the tree.

A large heat lamp may emanate enough heat to protect a tree if the tree also is covered. A constant light mist of water may provide enough protection if the temperature does not slip far below 30 degrees F.

All of these are hard decisions. I hope you will never have to make them.

Two Shoo-ins for Your Garden

GOOSEBERRIES AND CURRANTS

Surprise, surprise. May I present to you two of the most attractive, and effortless, fruits of a garden? These improved Rocky Mountain natives are naturals — and hardy up to 9,000 feet. The only reason gooseberries and currants lack popularity is because you hardly ever see them at the grocer's or at fruit stands. Most of the commercial production of gooseberries ends up in canned mixed-fruit cocktails, and currants turn into jelly and jams at Smucker's and other preserve-makers.

These attractive shrubs are so easy to grow and need practically no care at all. They can be used as a hedge or screen if you wish or planted as a mass in an assigned area of the garden. Ours have so naturalized that we have to fight back with shovels and pruners to keep them under control.

Our gooseberries are Pixwell, and they never fail to have a heavy crop. The care they receive is nominal. Every other year I literally throw a bushel or two of manure into the thicket, and that is all the nutrition they need. They get extra water from a little rose bed runoff, and the berries size beautifully. I pick about 15 to 20 quarts every year to keep our freezer full of the makings for gooseberry pies. What a delightful, old-fashioned flavor with my wife Naomi's best tender crust. That's what I call pure delight. We handle the project together. I pick the berries, and she nips them and freezes them. The rest is easy and enjoyable for me. The remaining gooseberries are for our birds and they love them,

Gooseberries

Currant

too. I have seen the bushes in full bloom in a snow
storm. The result was normal full production.
Nothing seems to hurt them.

Have you tasted fresh currants for breakfast lately, without sugar? You get the full flavor of these
berries, and they pucker your taste buds. Currants
are easy to grow, too. They will accept whatever soil
you can offer and make the best of it. Sorry, folks, in
Boise, Twin Falls, Pocatello and Idaho Falls. Currants
and gooseberries cannot be shipped to Idaho because
of an embargo due to White Pine Blister rust. But
elsewhere in our Western territory, both are legal,
though often hard to find. In the garden, space them
about four feet apart for gooseberries and three feet
for currants. Both color well in autumn. Not many
varieties are in commerce. But enjoy what you can.

Gooseberry Varieties:

Pixwell — A very hardy variety. Very tolerant
of poor soil. Spiny, but berries hang down from
branches, making them a little easier to pick. Yet I
have to give my hands a day's rest after each picking.
Color green, light pink. Maturity, mid-July. Bears
second year after planting.

Welcome — A new berry from the University of
Minnesota. Light green, turns pink when fully ripe
in mid-July. Has fewer thorns than Pixwell. Plants
bear second year.

Colossal — I cannot find a source of this berry
now. I have tasted it in Europe. Berries are the size of
a walnut. I have seen it catalogued in the United
States. Hope you can find it. You don't have to pick
so many to make a quart. Ripens early August.

Currant Varieties:

Red Lake — Berries are light-red at ripeness
(mid-July) in long clusters. Hardy like a native.

Wilder — Older variety that has remained
popular. Larger berries than most varieties. Extremely hardy and easy to pick in clusters. Matures
mid-July.

Improved Perfection — Large berries, very productive, excellent flavor. Ripens mid-July.

GRAPES

Though our hot summers and dry, sometimes miserable, winters are not the greatest for grapes, I consider them an easy crop for the garden. You really don't need excessive garden space for grapes. They often produce very well along east and west walls, fences and trellises. The main task grape vines require from you every year is pruning. They normally offer a very fine crop the third year after planting. From then on, the yearly return is almost automatic. And if you have little room for them, you can use the support of branches from a fruit tree to mature a crop.

Some varieties are suitable for wine-making, but most others are good just for eating or for juice, jams or jellies. They should be kept on the dry side during the bloom cycle, but after the berries have started to form, grapes need good moisture to size properly. If they get too much moisture, they produce excessive vine growth which you will have to prune sooner or later. Then, at maturity, they need to be dry again, so the taste or flavor is fruity. Most viniferous grapes from which wines are made need a longer season than we have to offer. They also have little chance in higher altitudes, because seasons are even shorter. I have produced fine crops of Concord grapes over the years. But I leave the making of wine to those who know how and have the environment and tools to succeed. I'd rather drink their wine than make my own vinegar. Many fine grape varieties are in the

Grapes

> **Rocky Mountain Tip:**
>
> Viniferous (wine-making) grapes require quite a long season to mature. For the home garden, some of the seedless varieties such as Himrod, Interlaken, Lakemont and Seedless Concord are a good bet.

trade now, and some are relatively new and superior.

If you have not started your grape culture yet, you must consider some basic requirements for success. You need a site with full sun exposure and good air circulation and a season of 140 days or more. Generally, we answer well to these demands. You also need a soil situation that neither is easily waterlogged nor shallow. This is a bit more difficult, but it can be met. You then only need to prune regularly, defend your crop against insects or birds, and have the patience to wait two or three years for the first crop to be harvested. But this is well worth it when the day of the first harvest arrives. What a joy it is to harvest your first crop from the vines. Arbors also can be cultivated with grapes. But here the cover and seclusion is more important than the grape harvest. We prune off only the excessive growth and accept what grape harvest we can collect with gratitude. Grapes may live for many years, but they transplant poorly after they are well established. It would be easier to plant a new grape vine than to depend on transplants.

The kinds of grapes that generally are most dependable in our Western region are:

Beta — A cross with the wild grape. Extremely hardy. Produces almost black fruit. Ripens late August. Very vigorous vine. Should be a good choice for arbors anywhere in our Western region.

Blue Boy — A Concord-type variety from Stark's. Productive and a nice, sweet, flavorful grape to eat out of hand. I like it very much. One plant produces about a bushel plus every September.

Buffalo — This New York State variety matures extra early, in mid-August. Blue-black in color. Produces very well. Accepts heat and occasional drought quite well.

Caco — Late-maturing, large red grape. Compact clusters to six inches long. Very fine table grape, but seeded. Starts to mature mid-September.

Concord — The most popular home garden variety. Succeeds everywhere and has fruit that

Grapes

matures in early September. Fruit is blue and has excellent flavor. Superior for jams and jellies.

Concord Seedless — Not quite as hardy as the seeded Concord, but matures August 20 to September 1. Because the fruit is seedless, it is a much better grape for the table. Clusters of fruit are smaller.

Himrod Seedless — A fairly new variety, larger than Thompson seedless, but with even better flavor. Very cold-resistant (minus 20 degrees F.) and also disease resistant. The best-eating white grape at this time. Ripens late August to early September.

Fredonia — An older grape quite hardy in our Western territory. Matures very early. Dark-blue color. May mature mid-August.

Interlaken Seedless — Another newer hybrid seedless variety. Color is whitish-green at maturity. Considered below-zero hardy. Mid-to-late-August maturity.

Lakemont Seedless — Not as hardy as Himrod but a good choice where it is not quite so cold. Matures early September.

Niagara — A good grape for fresh eating and a little wine-making. White to green when mature and

> **Rocky Mountain Tip:**
> Grapes should not be watered at flowering period.
> Grapes should be watered heavily when fruit in-
> ceases in size and should not be watered near maturi-
> ty to increase sugar content.

has a sweet taste and rich aroma. Ripens late August
to Labor Day.

Portland — The largest white grape. Very sweet,
spicy flavor. Matures in late August. A hardy vine
with a little shelter.

Suffolk Red Seedless — Currently the best
seedless variety to plant. It applies to every possible
use, namely juice, jellies, jams, pies and even for a little homemade wine. Matures September 1-10. Excellent hardiness.

BERRIES Raspberries

Raspberries are likely the most elegant and
flavorful fruit from our gardens. You know they are
quite hardy, because we find some growing wild all
over the mountains and the West. But the garden
varieties are infinitely better. Their taste is sweet,
and if you eat them off the bramble, they are excellent. Vanilla ice cream only makes them more tan-
talizing. Raspberries prefer a soil with sound
drainage. There are everbearing and single-crop
varieties. The single-crop kind are for the more difficult climates. But if you prepare your soil, you
should be able to grow everbearing varieties successfully. Actually, the name "everbearing" is a
misnomer. These plants produce a fall crop on new
canes the first year and a summer crop on the same
canes the following year. Then, after the summer
harvest, the canes are done and can be pruned. The
new growth then remains for the fall crop. Spring
pruning should be avoided unless dead tips are
trimmed away. Raspberries produce a nectar the bees
love. When they bloom, do not spray anything. If
you must, use Malathion late in the day after the bees
have returned to their hives. After bloom, raspberries need a lot of water to size the fruit. They accept
runoff water without complaint. You even can use
waste water.

Red varieties generally are the most reliable.
Black raspberries are somewhat less productive. Purple and gold raspberries depend a bit on good soil

and protection. The best varieties for Western gardens are as follows:

Red Raspberries

August Red — This variety matures its fruit on three-foot canes first in late August, with a second crop in early summer. Hardy and well-adapted to higher elevations.

Fall Red — Very fine, large berry. Produces late August to early September, again in early summer. Ideal for freezing, pies and jams. Very productive until hard frost.

Heritage — Very hardy. Produces early to mid-July in carryover canes and from mid-September on until frost in the fall. Canes grow up to five feet tall. No support is needed for Heritage.

Latham — The most popular single-crop variety. Used largely in commercial production. Hardier than most. A good variety for elevations up to 8,500 feet.

September — Vigorous and hardy canes grow to five feet. Fruit is matured in mid-September for a month or more and again early July. We had this berry in the garden for many years. Fruit sizes well and is delicious.

Raspberries

Black Raspberries

Black Hawk — A large, sweet, juicy berry. Matures from late July on for about two weeks. Adapted to hot and dry environment.

Cumberland — Used a good deal by commercial growers. Large-size berry. Matures mid-to-late July. Fruit is sweet and firm.

Gold Raspberries

Fall Gold — A large, golden fruit variety. Hardy and produces extra-large, tangy, sweet berries in July and again in September.

Forever Amber — A new golden variety. Tasty and sweet. Withstands severe temperatures. Produces early summer only.

Purple Raspberries

Amethyst — Produces very fine, large crops of purple berries. Has a distinct flavor and outyields most other varieties of raspberries. Try a few of these, and more if you like them.

Sodus — The color of this variety actually is purple-red. Very hardy even under extreme temperature changes. Adapts well to mediocre soils.

Strawberries

Strawberries

You'd better believe it: Strawberries need super soil. I have seen so many struggling strawberry beds, and they are mostly the fault of poor soil. Strawberries need everything the plants normally cannot find in our soils. They need a loose, viable (crumbly) soil about neutral or slightly acid with lots of humus, say five percent. A sandy soil actually is better than a clay soil. If you want to harvest luscious berries, you can. But not fresh out of the chute. It takes several years to improve the soil and you should use it for raising vegetables before the time is right to take the step to strawberries.

The popularity of strawberries is undeniable. All of us love to fancy ourselves walking into the home with three or four quarts of berries at the peak of sweetness and aroma. But it takes patience and restraint. Eventually, however, the light is green. I recommend raised beds for strawberries. Two or three levels of railroad ties make the drainage and aeration superb. Plants may be set about 15 to 18 inches apart in early spring. They should have weeks to root before the heat of summer is upon us. Strawberries are heavy feeders. If you want your entitlement of berries, you should apply about four pounds of a 8-12-4 or 4-12-4 or 6-10-4 commercial fertilizer per 100 square feet of beds.

Strawberries don't like root competition from trees, shrubs, or other pushy garden ornamentals. They also like full sun or an east exposure that is still bright in the afternoon. Any new planting needs help in establishment. You should handpick off all blossoms during the first year until mid-July. You will still get a good return during late summer and fall, but the plants won't suffer.

Strawberries are a terrestrial plant. Although you often see colorful pictures of climbing strawberries with beautiful berries, they look to me as if they are from a greenhouse or have been staged. Even barrels produce less strawberries than some pictures indicate. Not many plants grow up and down if they were created to grow horizontally. Some of the fancy five-foot pyramids or towers with berries all over them are not for hot, dry places like the West. I can go for three-tier square, round or oval beds that have 8 to 10 inches of soil on each level. I simply want to make it clear that not everything always works. If you want to gamble with a few plants, choose the ones where the odds are on your side. I gamble a little, too, but I first calculate my chances.

Strawberries in our region are subject to several insects and two difficult-to-control diseases: Red Stele and Root or Crown rot. They can be controlled only with the use of disease-resistant varieties. But if you notice a few plants that appear unhealthy, you must remove them quickly. Diseases spread from sick plants to healthy ones.

Winter mulching of strrawberries no longer is done with straw, as the name would suggest, but with fluffy materials that don't blow easily. The purpose of mulching is not to keep the soil warm. Rather, it is to keep the soil cold to prevent heaving of the plants, which damages their roots. You must wait until the ground freezes before you mulch. Use bark dust, leaves, Christmas tree boughs, evergreen prunings, or even grass clippings.

It takes about 25 plants per member of your household to have enough berries. My recommendations for the best varieties are these:

Cyclone — A single-crop variety for July production. Very productive. Very vigorous.

Fort Laramie — The best everbearing variety for cold hardiness and disease resistance. Has survived -30 degrees F. without mulching. Very vigorous and long production period.

Ogallala — A cross with wild fragaria of the Rockies, made by researchers Hildreth and Powers at the Cheyenne Horticultural Field Station in the 1940's. Has some of the inherited wild strawberry flavor and qualities. Fruiting is almost continuous from June 'til frost. Has to be used or frozen without delay. Very hardy; drought and disease-resistant.

Ozark Beauty — A very vigorous variety that produces lots of flowers and berries from July to October. A berry for all uses with excellent flavor but no disease-resistance claimed.

Quinault — An everbearing variety well suited for sheltered localities. Fruit is large but a little soft. Heavy producer in late summer.

Surecrop — June variety. A very good, all-purpose strawberry. Production is heavy in early July. Has good disease resistance.

Tioga — A California variety that is very tolerant of alkaline soil. Has some virus resistance where virus is a problem. Not as cold-tolerant as could be desired.

Blueberries

There are lots of blueberry lovers among us, but the plants don't tolerate our soils too well. Blueberries will grow only in acid soils. We can use a 50% mix with Canadian peat moss when we plant, then add some aluminum sulfate each year to maintain acidity.

Blueberries are not nearly as winter-hardy as most other small fruits. They need full sun, yet winter protection and shelter from harsh winds. They are at best a gamble in most of the Rocky Mountain areas and the Great Basin. And you need at least two varieties to get pollination for a crop.

The more popular varieties are:

Blueray — Early maturity. Large fruit.

Early Blue — Medium-size berry. Light blue at maturity. Ready in July.

Coville — Late maturity with very large berries. Tart until fully ripe.

HOW TO PRUNE GRAPES AND BERRIES

Whether the pruning of grapes is a science or an art has never been documented conclusively. Vine-growing as practiced by the ancient Egyptians is believed to have been at a very primitive level. Pruning was as yet unknown. In Greece, however, pruning seems to have reached an advanced stage of development. The Greeks about 200 B.C. credited the skill of pruning to an accident. They learned the art of pruning from a donkey, they claim. The donkey nibbled twigs and other portions from a grapevine, which then produced better results the following year than all other grapevines in the same vineyard.

The year's work in the vineyard still starts out with winter pruning. Exactly how a grapevine is pruned depends on the age of a plant, its vigor and health, plus the characteristics of a given variety. Pruning of fruit-bearing plants or vines is still a most important and responsible job. Its main purpose is to regulate the vine's performance and a proper balance between fruit production, quality and growth.

To simplify the program for home gardeners, I assume a basic concept of a grape plant and proceed with the technique accordingly. You may have neglected your grape plants; it has been demonstrated that the final results of such inaction generally are meager and unreliable. I propose a simple management of the grapes. This will produce for you measurable and dependable results and more grapes every year.

First, you must learn to differentiate between bull canes, fruiting canes and water sprouts. Bull canes are the long and thick ones. Water sprouts are the very thin canes of the shortest internodes. What remains in between are the fruiting canes or fruitwood.

Bull canes are the longest and heaviest canes the plant produces. Strangely enough, we don't keep these at all. They usually are budded five to six inches apart. Water sprouts are quite thin and often dried up and brittle by mid-winter. Buds are one and a half to two inches apart. They, too, are of little value. After pruning off both, you may still have too many fruiting canes on the vine or plant. Since we should not keep more than 80 buds total, we can split up what remains according to our own best judgement. I find 8 to 10 canes with 8 to 11 buds acceptable and excellent assurance for a good crop. This applies to Concord and Blue Boy grapes, as well as Niagara, Freedonia, Red Suffolk, Himrod or Interlaken. Viniferous (wine-producing) varieties are under test in Western states. We are looking for short-season varieties that have good wine-making qualities. In the vicinity of Boise, Idaho, some commercial vineyards now are in production.

Raspberries are easy to prune mostly because only minor tip pruning is involved, in April. The real fact is that everbearing raspberries need no major

Question: Will you please print instructions on pruning grape vines? We have them in an arbor.
Answer: For arbors the instructions are very simple. You only prune off what grows out of scope of the arbor. Fruit production is secondary to shade and comfort. For production only, prune first the spindly thin canes, then the thickest canes that have 4 to 6 inches between buds. That leaves fruiting canes only with distances of 2½ to 3½ inches between buds. You then keep only a maximum of 80 buds (10 canes) to obtain best fruiting.

pruning until July, after the summertime harvest of berries. They always produce first a fall crop and then the following year a summer crop on the same canes. After the summer harvest, we can prune off all but the current year's growth, which will fruit in the fall and again in the summer of the following year. Tip pruning of raspberry canes only involves the dry tips that show up due to cold weather or dehydration.

More important is the late-winter pruning of gooseberries and currants. These are without any doubt the hardiest fruits we can depend on annually. Neither cold winters nor late freezes seem to interfere with their fruiting. But gooseberries can grow so aggressively that they exceed their bounds with volunteer layers wherever a branch touches the soil. Without pruning, the bushes are apt to overproduce, and the size of the berries then will be small. Annual pruning will increase fruit size and quality.

Currants are equally hardy but not nearly so aggressive in growth. Moderate pruning or thinning will suffice without affecting yield noticeably.

HOW TO TRELLIS GRAPES

The subject of trellising grapes also deserves brief discussion. Since grapes produce tendrils for their own support, we must erect stakes or wires to which they can attach. Young plants usually are allowed to grow at their own volition during the first year in location. Then we must begin to choose during the late dormant season. Two popular methods are the vase-shaped system and the Four-Cane Kniffin system.

The vase system suggests selection of two healthy canes that can be supported on trellis or

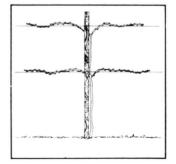

The Four-Cane Kniffin system of trellising grapes works well and allows good maintenance for years.

The Four-Cane Kniffin system in leaf.

wires growing upwards in a V-shape. From this structure, the remaining fruiting canes can be chosen each year for production of quality grapes.

The Four-Cane Kniffin system calls for a central stock usually supported on a stake from which four structural canes are selected. These four then are trained sideways on supporting wires for lateral growth. The stock and four laterals make up the basic structure of the plant from which the fruiting canes emerge. The 80-bud rule still applies and governs annual pruning for fruit production. Grape pruning should be done in February or March to avoid loss of sap. This also is known as bleeding.

HOW TO PRUNE FRUIT TREES

The annual pruning of fruit trees is a task we simply cannot omit if we have hopes for good production from our trees. What makes the task even more compelling are the prices we have paid recently for fresh and canned tree fruit. These are not likely to be reduced in the face of increased production, harvesting and marketing costs.

Fruit trees unfortunately have anything but a standard development of growth. For this reason, no two trees grow exactly in the same manner. Pruning therefore is intended to correct that part of natural growth that would produce a thicket of twigs and branches. Our main purposes for pruning are to reduce a tree's potential crop to a quantity it can size and mature, to clear out the inside structure by eliminating all new growth that tends to grow inward or straight upward; and to encourage spread of the tree canopy without excessive height. I have several apples, pears, and cherries in my back yard which I maintain below 15 feet in height. Anything taller than that could interfere with overhead wires and would be too tall for me to prune safely. Also, it is doubtful that my own spray equipment attached to the garden hose could reach high enough to do an adequate job of insect control.

If you prune every year, it should not be difficult to maintain the thinning out process along the major limbs and branches. Depending on the type of

---

Rocky Mountain Tip:

Pruning of apples and cherries depends mostly on thinning of newest growth and removal of twigs and branches that grow upward and to the inside of the tree.

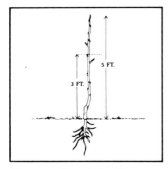

Prune sapling at planting.

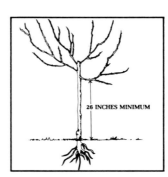

As the tree grows, prune to select the best scaffold limbs (the mainstay of the tree). The lowest branch should be 26 inches or more off the ground.

Fourth year — keep pruning out the twigs that grow upward and inward. Put a good spread on the tree but keep it low for easy maintenance and fruit picking.

tree, you should be pruning in the outer 12 to 18 inches where most of the twig growth occurs every year. This portion needs thinning from 30 to 50 percent. Peach trees need the most severe pruning, and plum trees often require the least. Apples, pears, and cherries are somewhat in between.

Apple and pear trees have a tendency to grow narrow and upright. With them we always must prune to the outside. Always make a pruning cut just above a bud on a twig that points to the outside. By doing this repeatedly for several years, you can create a much broader tree form. Remember also that 80 percent of tree fruit are produced in the outer 12 to 18 inches of a tree. With dwarf trees this is particularly important, because many of them mature at a spread of less than a fourth of a standard tree. But dwarf trees produce crops in fewer years after planting (two to four). Besides, who nowadays has the facility to store 15 to 20 bushels of apples from a standard tree?

Peaches must be pruned more than other trees because they usually grow more aggressively. In Western Colorado, fruit growers prune their trees every year as much as 65 percent. I am only suggesting eliminating about 40 to 50 percent of the new twigs in the outer reaches of the tree. Plums need less pruning because their growth is much slower. But cherry trees need a good pruning every year, because they have such a long season to grow after the fruit harvest. I prune my two cherry trees about 30 percent every year after thinning out on the inside. It takes a little more time to prune cherries,

> **Rocky Mountain Tip:**
> Peaches must have the most severe pruning of all tree fruit every year because they grow the most. Commercial orchardists prune them 65 to 70 percent every year. You will do well to follow this.

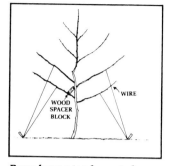

Pears have a tendency to be narrow and upright-growing trees. Pruning to the outside and use of spacer blocks or wire sometimes force the tree to grow more as we want it.

but a mid-winter pie will reward you handsomely for your pruning efforts.

On apple and pear trees, it is also important to prune away diseased twigs and branches. Pruning off diseased or dead limbs and branches counts against the total pruning effort. You simply prune less live wood after eliminating dead or damaged branches from your trees.

Grafting Fruit Trees: A Gamble

GRAFTING

Recently, after I suggested grafting as a possibility in developing fruit trees, I received a very interesting letter from a dedicated fruit hobbyist in the Longmont, Colorado area. He not only described his propagation very clearly but suggested that I cover this subject in greater detail.

Grafting offers one of the few opportunities for preserving older fruit varieties of merit that no longer are catalogued or produced in the nursery trade. I am not sure that it is purely quality we are seeking; nostalgia also plays at least a small part in many people's lives.

While I was deploring our dry climate and the effect on grafting, this amateur fruit gardener made a very intense study of the subject and developed some sound practices that enabled him to score 88-percent success in 1980 and 97 percent in 1981. He has worked on apples, pears, peaches, and apricots. The results with apples were the best.

Since there are literally hundreds of older, almost extinct apple varieties of merit, I want to pass on some of the most important points of his methods that have led to such a high degree of success. I am not suggesting that everyone suddenly take up grafting as a new garden hobby. But I would like to develop your thoughts on the subject for a future garden experience. There are even several smaller nurseries that specialize in the revival of old, nearly extinct apple varieties. Some are oversold already and are taking orders for future delivery. If you can obtain scion wood of an oldie such as Fameuse, Pippin, Yellow Parmaine or others, you might consider grafting.

The first thing in grafting is to understand the terms involved, such as stock, scion, matrix and cambium. Stock is the understock to which we graft. It has to be of the same genus as the scion, which is the desirable variety we wish to top-work to the stock. The place we prepare to receive the scion is the matrix. There are several types of grafts, but for starters I want to discuss only the cleft graft. If you are interested in others, I suggest you obtain one of several books on grafting. To accomplish the cleft, we cut with pruners a twig or branch at about ½ to ¾ inch in diameter and split with a knife down the branch to achieve the cleft about 1 to 1½ inches deep. Then we follow these very sound directions:

1. If you can obtain a good library book on grafting, look at the pictures carefully.

2. You need a very sharp knife with a good wide blade not only for the cleft but also to shape the scion.

3. Scion wood are tips of branches about 4 to 6 inches long taken from year-old wood of the desired variety. It should be collected when the tree is fully dormant (before March 31.) You may have to wrap and seal the scion wood by either applying raffia or grafting tape for several weeks in a vegetable crisper of your refrigerator until it is time to make the graft. You want to plan on doing the grafts about April 20 unless we have an extra early spring or a tree's buds are breaking earlier.

4. When ready to graft, cut the scion wood twigs to a sharp point at the bottom.

5. Now you have to learn about cambium. It is the cell-growth layer directly under the bark. It needs to fit in direct contact with the cambium of the stock plant. Where the two cambium layers touch, the scion and stock callus grow together. The faster, the better; otherwise, the matrix dehydrates before the two join.

6. Now we apply either paraffin wax or grafting wax to create a seal as airtight as possible over the cleft and the cambium juncture. You also can use Teflon plumbers' pipe thread sealing tape or electric tape, but these are inferior to wax. Incidentally, placing the cambium joint on the south side encourages faster callus, because it is warmer there every day.

7. Take off tape near the end of May. Grafting wax or paraffin will flake away as growth occurs. You can expect from 16 to 30 inches of scion growth the first year. Let only the top bud grow and break off the lower shoots and those especially on the stock below the matrix.

WATERING FRUIT TREES

The fruit gardens need timely irrigation. And the timing must coincide with each season's progress. There is little need for any water while cherries, peaches, plums, and apples are in bloom. In fact, heavy moisture at flowering will reduce fruit set. But a few weeks later, when fruit is becoming noticeable, the trees need a good, deep watering. Later on, within three weeks of maturity for cherries and apples, irrigate again. Peaches need a good water supply once they commence to size. A little shortage of water will hasten maturity.

Unless the surrounding soil is very dry, apples and plums can secure their water needs easily without excessive irrigations. With apples, you should stop watering about three to four weeks short of maturity.

Before bearing age, young trees should be watered every three weeks to ensure sound structural development of scaffold branches and limbs.

> **Rocky Mountain Tip:**
> Most fruit trees need little water until the fruit commences to size. Then one or more thorough irrigations are needed to obtain high-quality fruit.

Dwarf fruit trees on dwarfing understock must be given special watering care. Dwarf apples usually are on Malling or Malling-Merten roots that are not overly aggressive. Frequent watering, however, encourages good root anchorage in the garden. Dwarf cherries should have normal watering similar to standard cherries. Dwarf peaches are often on apricot roots. They also need frequent watering and winter watering in our dry region.

INSECT CONTROL

A Spray Schedule for Fruits

Everything that grows in our gardens has enemies that try to compete for our desired results. Wormy apples, for instance, are not very acceptable especially when currently available pesticides are safe and closely watched by the Environment Protection Agency or other responsible public organizations.

Apples and Pears:

Codling moth:
1st application:	7-10 days after petal drop
2nd application:	2 weeks later
3rd application:	2 weeks later
4th application:	2 weeks later but before August 10
5th application:	2 weeks later if needed

What to use:
Sevin 50% WP or slurry
(1½ tablespoon/gallon water)
Diazinon 25 EC
(1 tablespoon/gallon water)
Methoxychlor 50 EC
(1 tablespoon/gallon water)
Malathion 55% EC
(1 tablespoon/gallon water)

Use Sevin at least 2 days prior to harvest.

Use Diazinon at least 21 days prior to harvest.

Use Methoxychlor at least 7 days prior to harvest.

Use Malathion at least 3 days prior to harvest.

Mites can be a problem with apples and pears. Use Kelthane for mite control according to the label.

Peach and Plum Insects

These trees also have their specific problems. But they are not as common a threat. The peach crown borer is the most injurious larva attacking at the soil level where the bark is relatively soft. They bore their way into the hardwood, and damage the water conducting portion of each tree. In severe situations the tree may eventually die. Accepted control is during early July and early August by applying Diazinon 25 or Lindane at two tablespoons per gallon of water to the lower portion of the trunk, but not on foliage or developing fruit. All Purpose Fruit spray may be used instead of the above chemical.

It may also be necessary to spray mites with Kelthane in mid-June at two tablespoons per gallon of water.

Small Fruit Insects

Strawberries may have weevils, leaf hoppers, aphids, and slugs on occasion. Malathion 50 at one tablespoon per gallon of water is a safe and effective control for all of these except slugs. For slugs, liquid

Mesurol and Metaldehyde dust are reasonably effective. It also helps to water in the morning hours and spread bark dust on the ground between plants. Slugs have trouble negotiating such a surface.

Raspberry and Blackberry Insects

The raspberry cane borer is a hideous pest that is almost impossible to contain. It is found inside the canes that suddenly wilt. Orthene is not registered, nor are other systemics. The best answer is pruning away the wilting canes before the borers reach pupation on their way to maturity. If you use a systemic, you cannot use the berries during the same season for 30 days.

Gooseberry and Currant Insects

Both are known to be attacked by a fruit worm. Since the use of pesticides is obviously not practiced, the crop of berries can still be picked, but infected berries will float. After harvest of the berries, any pesticide use is proper. Since these plants bloom often before the last frost, no other controls are suggested.

Grape Insects

In all but commercial vineyards, insects are only an infrequent problem. Aphids and spider mites are controllable with Malathion and/or Diazinon at one tablespoon per gallon of water. Diazinon must not be used less than 20 days prior to harvest, Malathion not less than three days prior to harvest.

ANNUALS

ANNUAL flowers are the jewels of the garden. They live only one season, growing from seed to seed during that time. But from June until frost, they will reward you with continuous bloom. With their nearly unlimited range of colors and shades, they have a wonderful effect wherever you choose to plant them. And they are easy to grow. Annuals are so thankful for even a little care that they can reward you handsomely even if you are a novice gardener.

Annuals are particularly important in the Rocky Mountains and Great Western Basin regions because most of them are so durable. They withstand summer heat and often thrive in mediocre soil — two features we have in great abundance. An occasional high wind does not affect them severely, and hail does not wipe them out. Some can even survive a night or two of temperatures below freezing.

Each year, you will discover new and improved annuals to choose from, many with awards and international medals won in tough competition. Developments in the science of genetics in recent years have presented us not only with incredibly fine hybrids, but also with some triploids or mules that have three sets of inherited characteristics, and tetraploids that have four sets. But Rocky Mountain gardeners have many old favorites, also.

Rocky Mountain Tip:

Annuals are nearly instant success even for novice gardeners. They are easy to plant from seed or starts, accept mediocre mineral soil with ease, and remain rewarding and beautiful even in great heat.

Marigolds

Zinnias

Begonias

A Head Start

Some annuals can be grown easily from seed, and I will discuss these later. However, many annuals need a head start in a controlled facility such as a greenhouse. Your best bet is to buy these plants already growing in flats or small boxes. Commercial growers are equipped to provide the proper temperature, humidity, pest control, and fertilization to give these plants a good start. They also use dwarfing compounds to keep the little plants short and sturdy.

When you purchase bedding plants, you will find them in a variety of containers. For years, 12-pack plastic containers have been popular. Lately, however, 4-pack and 6-pack containers of plants have become prevalent. And 1-packs also are on the market, containing a single marigold, dianthus, celosia or other annual. These larger plants give the appearance that you have been growing them for quite a while. They are also more expensive. But for patio tubs or front door planters, they can create an impressive effect right from the start.

How to Harden Bedding Plants

Once you buy bedding plants, the process of hardening them — getting them used to the outside environment — is very important. Unless they have come from a supplier who had them outdoors, these little plant starts could have a rough time if you set them out the same day you buy them from a greenhouse or garden center.

No matter where the plants have come from, however, it is a good idea to harden them. At first, place the plant packs outside in the shade — weather permitting — during the daylight hours only. A few days later, if no freezing temperatures are predicted, you can leave them out overnight. Next, move them out of the shade long enough to catch the morning sun for a few days. Then expose them to full sun for a few days. Now they will be ready to plant in your garden.

BEDDING PLANTS

Annuals are sold in packets ranging from 4 to 12. Each plant is an individual cell to reduce root damage and transplanting shock.

Individually potted larger plants are more expensive but they are more impressive from the beginning.

Petunias

> **Rocky Mountain Tip:**
> As long as you remove the faded blooms on annual flowers they will continue to flower almost continuously. When petunias get stringy it's time to prune half of them for better fall performance.

Prepare the site before transplanting. First remove weeds and sod debris.

Spade or rototill some organic matter such as peat moss, manure or compost into soil.

Add superphosphate or bonemeal, 1 lb. for every 100 square feet.

Rake soil smooth prior to planting.

How to Transplant Bedding Plants

Before you remove the plants from their packs, be sure the site has been prepared. A well-structured soil that has been worked with a spade or tiller will give the little plants much better support than a raw-earth location.

Remove each plant from its plant pack. If two or more plants have grown together, their roots have become interlaced. Use a knife or spatula to cut the plants apart, or break the soil and pull them apart. Either way is damaging, but the separation has to be done. The plants in individual little plastic pockets will be easy to separate. But you must try to break the roots loose a little by squeezing the root ball. Now you are ready to plant.

To use the small plants for bedding, use small stakes or rocks to mark a pattern so the plants will be in straight lines and equal distances apart. For each plant, use a trowel to dig a small excavation about the size of the root ball or slightly deeper. Set the

Space your annuals out to be sure you have enough cover. If one or two plants short, just enlarge spacing a little.

Remove peat pots entirely. They don't seem to let roots grow through them too easily.

plant in it and press the soil down firmly over the roots. Your little plants are now launched in your garden.

You can help them avoid wilting or shock by adding a prepared mixture to the water that you will use to water your new transplants. Mix some root stimulator or Ortho Up-Start in a bucket or sprinkler can and add a tablespoon of Revive for each gallon you mix. Water the little plants thoroughly with the prepared mixture, and they will be straight and spiffy the next morning. Unless the weather is quite warm, the initial watering will be sufficient for several days. Then water as needed and feed monthly.

GOOD CHOICES FOR BEDDING PLANTS

Almost all experienced gardeners have favorite annuals. My bedding-plant choices are below, in alphabetical sequence. You'll notice that I prefer some over others for their colorful nature and ease of culture.

Ageratum

Sun to partial shade. Height 5 to 6 inches. This lovely border plant is very compact and works beautifully for informal edges around a flower bed. It also is excellent in mass plantings. Set plants 10 to 12 inches apart. Its hybrids are the most uniform and continue to bloom until frost; however, the first night with air temperatures of 31 degrees will turn

Question: We live in the mountains at 8,500 feet elevation. What are the safest annuals for us to use?
Answer: At your elevation you are likely to have some freezing nights even in June. The annuals that can take freezing nights to about 26 degrees F. are petunias, alyssum, snapdragons and asters. Most others could be damaged at 30 degrees even if covered.

Snapdragons

Ageratum

Ageratum — Blue Blazer

Alyssum

Question: We planted a border of white alyssum this year. It was beautiful. Will this border reseed by itself and how is it best handled? The dry plants are still in place.
Answer: Leave the old dry plants in place until cleanup time in April. Then just pull the plants, but leave the soil as is. By late April or early May you will notice thousands of seedlings. Water them along with the rest of your garden and give them a little plant food. They survive well.

ageratum brown. Colors: blue and white. The best varieties: Blue Blazer, Blue Danube, Blue Surf, Summer Snow and Spindrift.

Alyssum

Sun to light shade. Height up to 3 inches. This is an old favorite for borders, edges, patio tubs and boxes. Alyssum blooms early and continues without letup. Set plants 10 to 12 inches apart. Several colors are offered: white, rose and lavender. The best varieties include: Carpet of Snow, Rosie O'Day and Royal Carpet.

Aster

Sun to partial shade. Height 6 to 24 inches. Asters are dependable cutting flowers and very decorative. In the valleys of the Rocky Mountains,

Asters

> **Rocky Mountain Tip:**
> In mountain valleys among the best choices you can make are sweet peas, snapdragons and asters. With cool nights and sunny days, their colors are deep and rich and their flower stems sturdy and tall.

asters are an excellent late-summer annual. Dwarf varieties are especially desirable for the outside edging of a large flower bed. Set plants 12 to 15 inches apart. Some, such as Pot 'N Patio, grow only six inches high. But others, such as Powderpuffs, reach up to 24 inches. Colors: red, pink, purple, blue, rose and dark blue.

Begonia (fibrous rooted)

Sun or shade. (Tuberous Begonias are considered perennials and need full shade.) Height up to 10 inches. The variety of colors include white, rose, pink, salmon scarlet, and red. The proper distance between begonia plants is 8 to 12 inches. Begonias are also one of the best annuals to move indoors in autumn. With adequate light, they will bloom well.

Celosia

Sun. Height 6 to 20 inches. Set 8 to 10 inches apart. Celosia, a long-time favorite, comes in plumed and crested varieties. Colors: crimson, scarlet, pink, orange, gold. The best include All-America winners such as Fireglow and Apricot Brandy. Other attractive varieties: Red Velvet, Empress, Forest Fire and Golden Triumph. Celosia dries easily for winter bouquets.

Begonias

Celosia

Coleus

Question: Are Dahlias considerd annuals or perennials, and why?
Answer: Dahlias may be grown from seed, and in that case they are considered annuals. They have single anemone-type flowers or small doubles in many colors. Dahlias may also be grown from tender tubers, as perennials. These are the ones that produce the magnificent cactus, semi-cactus, and other formal and semi-formal blooms up to dinner plate size in a wide range of single and combination colors. Tubers must be dug after the first hard freeze and stored at 40 to 45 degrees in dug-outs, cellars, or unheated crawl spaces or basement rooms.

Dahlia

Coleus

Shade outside or good light indoors. Height up to 15 inches. Set 12 to 15 inches apart. It is a little unfair to call coleus a flower. It has flowers, but they are overshadowed by the plant's spectacular foliage. Wide variety of colors: light yellow to green, purple, dark red, medium red. Several series of coleus are particularly interesting: Fiji, Saber, Seven Dwarfs and Wizard.

Dahlia (annual)

Sun. Height 1 to 2 feet. Set 15 inches apart. Dwarf varieties can be used effectively in planter boxes and pots or as borders. Offered in shades of white, yellow, pink, rose, orange, red, and purple. Rigoletto, Redskin, and Sunburst are excellent series.

Dianthus

Sun. Height 7 to 12 inches. Set 10 inches apart. Dianthus plants are also known as Annual Pinks. They are attractive favorites for pots, edges, and bedding. Snowfire, Magic Charms, and Queen of Hearts are All-American varieties. All are hybrids and come in salmon-pink, white, coral, scarlet, and crimson.

Dianthus

Geraniums

Geranium

Sun or open shade. Height 10 to 18 inches. Geraniums have been favorites for years, and seed geraniums are becoming increasingly popular. A seed geranium grows into a small plant topped by neat umbels of flowers. But to start the seeds in time for summer blooming, you must plant them in January. Unless you have a greenhouse, you may need to purchase small plants for your garden. Set 10 to 12 inches apart. Geraniums prefer well-drained soil and monthly feeding. Move them indoors before cold weather, and they should last for years. Exquisite new colors and blends are available, and new ones are added each year. Outstanding choices include the Sprinter Hybrid series and such varieties as Bright Eyes (cherry-scarlet), Cherie (salmon-pink), Jackpot (scarlet-red), Showgirl (pink with white eye), and Red Elite (red).

Rocky Mountain Tip:

Among flowering plants in the garden, geraniums are the most popular for the move indoors before the cold weather sets in. Repot these plants in fresh potting soil and control all insects so they don't move piggyback into your home.

Heliotrope

Heliotrope

Sun. Height 18 to 20 inches. Set plants 12 to 15 inches apart. Heliotrope is not one of the more popular annuals, but its violet blossoms are very fragrant and have a spicy quality. Flowers can last up to three weeks. The plant needs good soil with good drainage.

Impatiens

To me, this is the Western region's brightest, most versatile flower for shady locations. I have impatiens every year on my patio and front porch. Several varieties work well. Super Elfin hybrids range from 6 to 12 inches high. Grande hybrids have two-inch flowers, and the plants range from 9 to 16 inches high. The Impatiens hybrids sometimes grow as tall as 24 inches. Blitz Hybrid, which is scarlet, is a variety of special merit. Other good choices: Shady Lady, Rosette Hybrid, Futura Hybrid and Zig-Zag

Impatiens

Hybrid. Colors: salmon scarlet, white, pink, fuchsia, and orange.

Lobelia

Sun, afternoon shade. Height up to 4 inches. Lobelia's dainty flowers are excellent for hanging baskets and patio tubs. They can also be planted in flowerbeds as borders. Most dwarf varieties of lobelia grow only four inches high and cascade beautifully. Some of the best choices: Bright Eyes (violet-blue), Crystal Palace (dark blue), Rosamond (rosy-red) and Sapphire (dark-blue with white eyes).

Petunia

Sun. Height 12-16 inches. Set 8 to 12 inches apart. Petunia's variety of colors and combinations easily make it the annual most widely used for bedding, window boxes, patio tubs and hanging baskets. They are brilliant in the foothills. The versatile Cascade series are lovely, large Grandiflora petunias with ruffled edges and solid colors ranging from dark blue to white. The Ultra series of Hybrid Grandiflora petunia offers seven different striking colors. Petunias include the Cloud series and the Joy series, which offer six or more colors. The Frost series are also quite attractive — they are solid colors with a white rim on the fringes of their petals.

Among the multi-color petunias, the Razzle-Dazzle Hybrids are a standout. Its flower has a white star against a field of red, deep rose, deep blue, and crimson. The petunias of the Plum series, meanwhile, have a veination of blue, purple and pink from the flower center.

Petunias

Many other Hybrid Multiflora varieties are available. The Bouquet series and the Delight series are two very popular double petunias. They have many petals with a confused center. There is no throat visible and these double petunias can give you many colors and blends.

Spectacular colors and wide choices are not the only reasons for petunia's popularity among Rocky Mountain gardeners. The plants are somewhat frost-hardy; they can withstand temperatures of 28 to 30 degrees with little risk. You can set the plants out before the last killing frost; May 1 in many places, May 25 in high mountainous areas. They will start to grow quickly. You probably will not start petunias from seed unless you have a greenhouse. Outdoors, the seeds are slow getting started. Beginners should probably choose started plants from a garden supplier.

Fertilize your petunias once a month and they will reward you with dozens of flowers. But watch for aphids. Spray with Malathion 50 or Orthene if necessary. Read the products' labels for proper dilution.

Phlox

Sun or partial shade. Height up to 7 inches. Set 8 to 12 inches apart. This small-flowered annual is a lovely little border plant. Phlox grows with great profusion and offers beautiful clusters of blooms, some star-shaped. Most phlox varieties grow only seven inches tall. My favorite is Twinkle, which has fringed, star-shaped flowers in many color combinations.

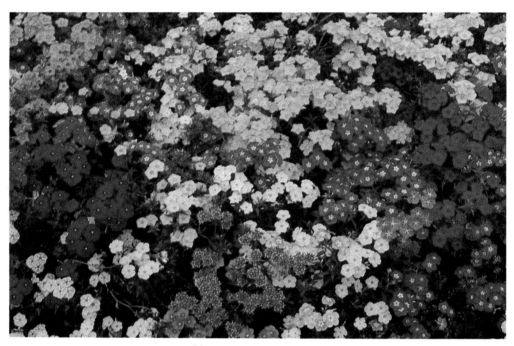

Phlox

Portulaca (Moss Rose)

Sun. Portulaca does not grow more than 6 inches tall and survives temperatures of 95 degrees in full sun. It has fleshy leaves and flowers in a variety of colors. Some are single, while others are fully double. Outdoors, it is better to use started plants rather than seeds. Hybrid Sunglo offers 10 colors and double flowers.

Salvia

Sun. Height 7 to 16 inches. Set 8 to 10 inches apart. Salvia is an excellent and durable bedding plant. Most varieties are fiery red. I have seen them used effectively in many superb public gardens, especially in the formal gardens of Versailles Palace in France. Variety names tell the story of salvia's usual color: Blaze of Fire, Hot Shot, Red Blazer, Pirate and St. John's Fire. Purple Blaze, however, lives up to its name. And certain salvias are blue and could perform as perennials in very warm, protected locations.

Snapdragon

Sun. Height up to 36 inches. Set 6 to 10 inches apart. Snapdragons are a colorful annual, and they

Salvia

Snapdragons

do well in the Rocky Mountains. Their flower spikes look beautiful in just about any garden. I have five favorite snapdragons. Madame Butterfly offers azalea-like flowers in many brilliant colors. The flowers of the Bright Butterflies series come in many clearer shades and colors. Little Darling grows only 12 inches tall but provides a variety of colors. And the Pixie mixture offers six colors of florets on spikes only 6 to 8 inches tall. All of these have been introduced by Glenn Goldsmith of Gilroy, California.

Other snapdragons that work well include: Burpee's Double Supreme hybrids, which grow 30 inches high; Bellflower hybrids, which grow 15 to 33 inches high; and Topper hybrids, which reach 36 inches.

Snapdragons can be planted with early petunias. Plants can be set out from the greenhouse in April and May. Snapdragons can stand a few cold nights with temperatures down to about 28 degrees. Sometimes, they reappear from last year's roots. But be wary of rust disease on second-year plants. You can recognize rust disease by the rust-colored spots or pustules on the underside of the foliage.

Verbena

Sun. Height up to 8 inches. Set 6 to 8 inches apart. This well-behaved bedding flower continues to produce flower clusters in many colors throughout the summer. I especially like verbena's compactness. Verbena Blaze (red) was an All-America winner in 1954 and is still an excellent choice. Springtime and Sparkle offer a wide range of colors. Another good choice is Amethyst, a 1969

Verbena

Vinca

award winner; however, it is sometimes difficult to find.

Vinca (Periwinkle)

Prefers shade, will tolerate some early or late sun. Height 10 inches. Set 8 to 12 inches apart. The star-shaped flowers of the periwinkle range from white to rose-red. Periwinkles are excellent for Rocky Mountain gardens because they tolerate many different situations, from hot and dry to shady and cool. The plants also show up well in patio tubs and planters. Vinca Polka Dot won an award in 1969 and remains a popular choice. Its flowers are white with cherry-red centers.

Viola

Partial to full shade. Height 6 to 8 inches. Set 8 to 10 inches apart. Violas, which are smaller than pansies, come in many colors: solid, bi-color, and picotees. A picotee is a flower which has one basic color with a margin of another color. Violas are beautiful bedding plants and are worth attempting both in mountain valleys and resort areas. I have seen lovely plantings of violas in Vail, Colorado, and other mountain villages.

Violas will bloom longer if they are protected from the full heat of summer and if faded flowers are picked before seed forms.

Violas

Zinnias

Zinnia

Sun. Set 6 to 10 inches apart. Zinnias are actually best grown from seed. But if the weather is uncooperative (hail the first week of June, for example), you can still enjoy zinnias by using bedding plants. In the Rocky Mountains' hot spots, where plants are sun-drenched day after day during the summer, zinnias are very special annuals. Excellent choices range from the 1984 award-winning Border Beauty Rose (20 inches) and Scarlet (22 inches), to Thumbelina, which grows only 6 inches high. Many zinnia varieties have won awards, including the classic Peter Pan Hybrid series developed by Colorado's Charles Weddle. Weddle has been awarded seven All-America medals for his introduction of eight colors, including Peter Pan Plum and Peter Pan Pink. As a flower-show judge, I have awarded many blue ribbons to Zinnia Envy, an apple-green zinnia of perfect form.

There are many, many zinnias to choose from that will do well in the Rocky Mountain regions. Zenith hybrids produce 5-6 inch, cactus-like, ruffled flowers at a height of 30 inches. Burpee's Big Tetra hybrids have stunning, dahlia-like blooms about 6

Rocky Mountain Tip:

Zinnias are highly susceptible to mildew. This disease simply ruins your whole display. Start spraying against mildew with Funginex or Benomyl before August 1, and repeat every 14 to 18 days until late September.

inches across. The bi-color Whirligig series (24 inches) offers scarlet, rose, or carmine flowers with white, gold, pink, or buff petal tips. Candy Cane produces 3-inch flowers of pink, cerise, and rose stripes in white. And some yellow blooms are striped or flecked orange-scarlet.

THE BEST ANNUALS TO GROW FROM SEED

Some annuals sprout more quickly and vigorously than others, and Rocky Mountain gardeners can grow them successfully from seed; however, finding the seeds may not always be easy. Greenhouses or garden centers may not stock the seeds of certain annuals because the varieties are not much in demand. Some annuals simply do not transplant as successfully as others, so they are best grown from seed. Some seeds, such as geraniums, grow so slowly that they must be started in a greenhouse in January if you want summer color. Many annuals, however, can be grown from seeds sown into the garden bed when the danger of cold nights is past. The following is a list of my favorites:

Alyssum

Alyssum is usually sold as a started bedding plant, but I mention it again here because its seeds will germinate outdoors in many Rocky Mountain-area localities, such as Denver, Salt Lake City, Billings, Great Falls, Santa Fe, Albuquerque, Grand Junction, Boise, Twin Falls, and Reno, before mid-April. You can grow alyssum as a border during summer and, once fall and winter return, leave the dead plants in place. Next April, you should find new alyssum seedlings growing near the dead plants. Then all you have to do is transplant any excess

Alyssum

seedlings to fill in any bare spots. If you are careful with your alyssum, you can continue having new plants year after year.

Bells of Ireland

These plants will reproduce from year to year, if you let them seed; however, the seeds are sometimes hard to find from commercial sources. Some seed houses, such as Rocky Mountain Seed Company in Denver, still catalog them. But Bells of Ireland are among the favorites of amateur flower arrangers, because they fit so easily into monochromatic designs. They are best started outdoors about a week before frost-free season.

Calendula (Pot Marigold)

Sun. This plant's flowers are prized for their bright yellows and oranges. Calendula is particularly well-suited for Rocky Mountain areas that stay on the cool side. Its seeds can be started outdoors about

Calendula

Marigolds

Cosmos

April 1-15. To ensure good flowering through August and into the fall, pick the blooms that fade. Calendulas grow into bushy plants up to 18 inches high.

Cosmos

Sun. Cosmos is a lovely border plant tall enough to make a cheerful backdrop for other annuals. It produces flowers from late June until frost. Variety Sunset is orange and an All-America gold medal winner. Variety Diablo is redder with semi-double flowers. For continued flowering, pick off the blooms that wilt.

Gaillardia

Sun. Gaillardia reaches about 24 inches high and produces blossoms from early July until frost. It also tolerates sandy soils better than many other annuals and seldom is set back by summer heat. Variety Gaiety has marigold-like or carnation-like blooms in rose, yellow, orange, maroon and bi-colors. For earlier flowers, Gaillardia can be started indoors from seed about March 20. It can be started outdoors May 10.

Gaillardia

Marigold

Sun. It can be started outdoors on a frost-free date week. This is one of the most popular annuals in the United States. In fact, the late David Burpee championed the marigold as America's national flower. It is native to North America. In the past 25 years, the marigold has become one of the most widely hybridized garden flowers. On the 50th anniversary of All-America flower selections, a hybrid marigold First Lady was selected by the judges as the #1 All-Time All-America flower.

French marigolds are the ones with the smallest flowers, and African marigolds produce the largest plants and blooms. Most hybrids strike a middle range, and you literally have hundreds of excellent choices.

Among the best for Rocky Mountain gardening are the following hybrids: Burpee's Lady, Climax, Galore, and Jubilee series. The Nugget series of Mule marigolds which do well in the Rockies are triploids — they have three sets of inherited features — and produce no seeds. Super Star Orange Hybrid (Burpee) is a tetraploid series of marigolds — they have four sets of inherited features and produce no seeds — and also do well in the Rockies.

Marigolds

Morning Glory

Morning Glory

This is the best and most dependable annual vine to use when covering a woven-wire fence. Morning Glory will also grow up poles and other supports, such as shrubs and remains of dead trees. Morning Glory does best in full sun, but will accept a bright location that is only partially exposed to the sun. Can be started outdoors May 1-10, 10 days later for 6,500-foot elevation; 20 days later for 7,500 feet. Scarlet O'Hara, an All-America winner of many years ago, is still available. It has crimson-carmine blossoms. Early Call Rose, an All-America award in 1970, has blossoms that are crimson-carmine with white throats. Early Call Blue's blossoms are violet-blue with a creamy throat. Heavenly Blue is another popular variety. It is a bright sky-blue color with a creamy throat.

Nasturtium

If you want an easy, fast-growing and colorful annual, try nasturtium. Its flowers are fragrant, and it thrives in an average-quality soil with good drainage. Nasturtium may succeed better than other annuals in a sandy or gravelly soil if you water them often and feed them once a month. This annual

Nasturtiums

comes in climbers as well as low-growers. The low-growing types are usually less than 12 inches high. Double Dwarf Jewel is a lovely, full-throated choice. It comes in golden yellow, mahogany, and orange-scarlet colors. Whirlybird blooms in mixed colors but is spurless. Semi-tall Double Gleam is a trailing type that will climb to three feet with support. Fordhook Favorites by Burpee may even climb six feet high on a trellis. A bonus of this annual is that nasturtium leaves can be used with other greens in salads.

Salpiglossis

Sun. This annual, which blooms in mid-summer, produces trumpet-shaped flowers on sturdy, uniform plants about 30 inches high. Color mixtures include gold, rose, red, crimson, and blue shades with contrasting veination. Salpiglossis can be started between April 25 and May 15 — 10 days later for 6,500 feet, and 20 days later for 7,500 feet.

Scabiosa (Pincushion Flower)

Sun. Here is an easy annual that is sure to produce results, and the flowers are excellent for arrangements and cutting. Start outdoors May 1-15. Dwarf Double comes in blue, white, lavendar, and rose colors on stems about 18 inches tall. Hardy and productive Giant Imperial produces 2-3 inch, fully double flowers in similar shades on stems that are 30 to 36 inches inch.

Sweet Pea

Few annuals or perennials can match the delicate fragrance of sweet peas. Sweet pea plants do

Sweet Peas

very well on trellises, fences or even netting support, and they can be sown quite early, usually in late March or when the soil thaws in the mountains. They are frost hardy when a sudden chill occurs, and thrive in mountain valleys.

In our region, sweet peas should be planted in a location facing east with the morning sun, so excessive afternoon heat will be avoided. One of the best climbing sweet peas, Burpee's Galaxy, comes in a wide range of colors. And some newer bush-type plants are useful in small spaces, such as Burpee's Patio (nine inches high) and Burpee's Bigora (15 inches high).

Tithonia

Sun. This daisy-like annual is also known as the Mexican sunflower and is excellent in hot, sunny locations. Variety Torch, a 1960 All-America selec-

Tithonia

tion, is fiery orange-red with flowers up to three inches across. Its blossoms grow on bushy, vigorous plants 4 to 6 feet high. Variety Sundance has stems three feet high and may prove more manageable.

Zinnias

For a colorful massed effect, zinnias are un-equaled. No other annual is more heat-tolerant or is available in a warmer range of colors. When it's time to select bedding plants like petunias and marigolds, it's also ideal timing for sowing zinnia seeds. Many of the newer varieties, especially some All-America award-winners, frequently cannot be bought as bedding plants. You must get the seed packets from a mail-order house, such as George W. Park in Greenwood, South Carolina, Burpee in Warminster, Pennsylvania, and others. The time to sow zinnia seed outdoors is about four to six days before your local average last freeze. Your zinnias from seed often out-produce those from bedding plants because zinnias are not the easiest to transplant. Excellent varieties are Big Top, Ruffles, and Zenith series, All-America Peter Pan, Border Beauty, and Fantastic Light Pink, all hybrids. One of my favorite zinnias that wins many county fair ribbons every year is apple-green Envy.

> **Rocky Mountain Tip:**
> While petunias are best planted from semi-mature starts, zinnias and marigolds can be grown from seed with ease. Plant seed about the time of your average frost-free date and your seedlings will come up in 7 to 10 days depending on how warm the soil is.

HOW TO START ANNUALS FROM SEED

A Small Miracle

I love to watch seeds develop into tiny plants. It is really a small miracle how a tiny seed can contain all the needed parts of a plant. Some flower seeds are smaller than specks of dust.

Starting your own annuals from seed can give your garden an important head start once the weather finally settles. There are some seeds that can be started in March that might not flower before August if you waited until May to sow them. You will be a happier gardener if your flowers bloom in June.

When you do start your own plants, be sure to involve the entire family, especially children and grandchildren. Show them what you have learned from other gardeners. Observing the growing process can be an adventure.

We have a tendency to grow more plants than we need. Give the extras to other family members and friends — they will appreciate your thoughtfulness, and their gardens will benefit.

To get annuals started indoors, you will need some containers and starter mix, as well as window space, good artificial lighting or a small greenhouse.

Containers

Almost any type of container two to three inches deep is suitable for starting seeds. Aluminum or plastic food containers work well and can be reused. Garden centers and greenhouses keep plastic starter trays in stock.

Starter Mix

Putting garden soil in containers is not a suitable way to start seeds. Starter mix must be sterile and very fluffy. You can buy planter soil, such as Jungle Growth, or commercial starter mix, such as Redi-Earth or Metro-mix. Or you can mix your own medium by using equal parts of perlite, vermiculite and peat moss.

Planting the Seeds

Fill your containers with starter mix and saturate the mix with water. If you have trouble getting it to absorb water, add a few drops of liquid detergent or Revive to the water. This increases the moisture intake into starter mixes and clay soils. Next, treat your seeds with Thiram or Captan seed protectant to guard against seedling blight or damping-off (a stem

Marigolds

Question: What success will I have growing some new seed geraniums? What is the germination period to flower?
Answer: Geraniums from seed is a slow process. According to best sources the seed should be sown by home gardeners in late December and early January to make good-sized plants for setting out by late May. If you have a small greenhouse you can start the seed in mid-January to early February for best results. Repot the plants twice before they go to the out-of-doors.

disease caused by fungal organisms). To do this, open the seed packet and add just enough protectant powder to cover the tip of a small pocketknife blade. Fold the packet closed and shake for about 20 seconds. Now, you are ready to sow.

Carefully place the seeds on the moist soil mixture and cover them with a quarter inch of the starter mix. Very tiny seeds, such as petunia, are not covered at all. Place each container in a clear plastic bag and put them in a warm place (70 to 75 degrees F.) until the first tiny seedlings emerge. Then move the containers to a cool, bright window where the temperature stays around 55 to 60 degrees. Here, the little plants will develop sound roots as they grow.

When the plants have developed their second sets of true leaves, you can plant them individually in peat pots or plastic cups. Be sure to use a good potting soil. The longer you keep the seedlings in their starter mix, the more you will need to add a little plant food to their water. Use Rapid-gro, Miracle-Gro, Peters, Hyponex or fish emulsion, and follow the product's directions.

GIVING ANNUALS THE RIGHT CARE

Annual flowers do not require a lot of attention. However, a few well-timed practices, such as watering, feeding, pinching, pruning, and seed removal, can noticeably improve their flowering quality.

Watering Annuals

Most annuals have rather shallow root systems, so they need water often to be succulent and attractive, especially in the summer heat.

I have a brick planter in the front of my house that I plant with red geraniums and white petunias. Even though it is really hot out there when the

FEEDING ANNUALS

Annuals like a boost with fertilizer every 30 days. 15-30-15 is a high phosphorus food that flowers love.

Coleus and foliage plants would do better with a 12-12-12 or similar.

Ageratum

temperature hits 90-plus degrees, the geraniums and petunias thrive there because I water them a little every morning. Take the water away from them and in five days the petunias have gone to "Plant Heaven," and in 7 to 10 days so have the geraniums.

Other annuals I keep in hanging baskets on our shaded patio also need water every day. These include ageratum, lobelia, impatiens and fibrous-rooted begonias. In sun-drenched flowerbeds, our petunias and other annuals need water about every three to four days in rich, organic soils. In sandy soils I would water them a little less every other day.

Pinching

Pinching — deliberately breaking off certain leaves, stems or blossoms — is a good way to encourage more flowers. Among annuals, pinching is

Impatiens in basket

especially useful with petunia plants when you are first planting them in your garden. Most often, the petunia plants you buy have a single stem, three to five inches high, with one or two flowers on top. You should pinch off these flowers — yes, it hurts to have to do that to plants you have just paid for. This initial pinch, however, promotes sideshoots and helps the plant grow bigger, and continuous flowering is delayed by only a few days.

Most flowering annuals should be pinched early in the growing season. Annuals I do not pinch are: alyssum, begonia, lobelia, nasturtium, portulaca, sweet pea, verbena and viola. These have bushy growth.

Pruning

Some annuals tend to bloom more attractively if they are pruned in mid-season. You can rejuvenate your petunias in August by pruning the tip of a new shoot (five to eight inches long) to three to five inches. This removes the unwanted seed that is maturing. Leave the other half of the plant as is until the pruned half blooms again. Then prune the second half of each plant. You should have lovely petunias through September and October.

Other annuals that can be improved with pruning are: impatiens, ageratum, fibrous-rooted begonia, coleus, nasturtium and verbena.

Seed Removal

Many annuals will not give you excellent, continuous flowering through the summer and fall unless you remove the seeds that appear. Before

Verbena

Double Petunias

seeds mature, remove them with scissors, pointed pruners, or a knife. These seeds cannot be replanted due to immaturity. Seed removal is almost mandatory with snapdragon, ageratum, aster, begonia, annual dahlia, dianthus, geranium, heliotrope, salvia, verbena, viola, and zinnia. Sweet pea also continues to bloom better if you do not let it set seed early.

Dianthus

The mature seed pods of sweet peas can be kept as a source of seeds for next year.

If coleus plants set flower spikes, they should be removed by breaking them off or cutting them off. They are not very attractive anyway. At flower shows, coleus with flower spikes are considered poor specimen entries — it is a sign that they have received too much light.

Annuals Get Some Bug Attacks Too

The only plants outdoors that do not attract any insects must be the plastic ones at the corner service station. All others are known to create some attention in the insect world.

Fortunately, since we don't usually eat flowers, all general purpose pesticides are safe to use. Aphids and mites are among the most common attackers. They can be easily handled with Malathion and Kelthane. Grasshoppers are a more deliberate menace because they feed on anything in their way. Again, Malathion is recommended. You can strengthen your defense by using Sevin-mol on border plants and shrubs.

I also consider whiteflies as a serious problem on impatiens, fuchsias and sometimes petunias. The best control now is Resmethrin.

There is also a nasty little worm that destroys the unopened buds of geraniums. This budworm seems to be difficult to fully anticipate. You can start spraying your Geraniums as soon as you set them outside, with Orthene or Meta-systox-R. When you get a head start by spraying every 14 days you can usually prevent all but the most nominal damage. Leafhoppers

Double Impatiens

Pink Geraniums

sometimes get on petunias and other annuals also. They usually yield easily to Malathion 50 if you use it on warmer days.

Millipedes, centipedes, sawbugs and slugs are not insects. Slugs are the more damaging among these. They should be controlled with Mesurol, or liquid and dust of Metaldehyde. Some gardeners lure them with flat dishes of stale beer. They drown in the beer. Not all are willing to die that way.

Annuals That Can Be Moved Indoors in Fall

MOVING ANNUALS INDOORS

If you have enough window space, fall's first killing frost need not be the end of your geraniums, begonias, coleus and other outdoor plants. A number of annuals can survive the move from garden to indoors. In a bright room or a sunny window, in fact, they often grow right through a Rocky Mountain winter and can be planted again next spring.

To succeed with annuals indoors, you must follow a sound cultural program and maintain a cool, bright home or apartment. Some plants are easy to handle, and others need special care or conditions that may be difficult to provide.

The annuals easiest to maintain indoors are: geranium, coleus, impatiens, fibrous-rooted begonia, and fuchsia. Among the most difficult are: ageratum, tuberous begonia, pelargonium and petunia.

How to Succeed with Annuals Indoors

Moving plants indoors should be a gradual process. Plants should be dug up carefully and replanted in plastic or clay flower pots or other containers with good drainage. The containers should not be too big;

a bit confining is better. You should use a good potting soil, not garden soil. Garden soil can get so firm that it is almost like concrete. I prefer Jungle Growth potting soil, and I follow up with Up-Start or root stimulator to get the fine hair roots growing quickly.

Prune the plants after you pot them. This will prevent excessive drying and help them survive the shock of moving indoors.

Geraniums are the annual most often moved indoors. After a few weeks, geranium plants will drop all the leaves they produced outdoors. But don't worry, they will soon form new leaves that are smaller, lighter green and on longer stems — leaves better suited to indoor light.

To keep geranium plants flowering indoors, place them in good light and in a place where the temperature stays at about 50 to 55 degrees. We usually keep our homes too warm for geraniums.

The Rocky Mountain region's climate is too dry to handle geranium plants the way that is the custom in the eastern United States. There, gardeners hang the plants upside-down in frost-free garages or basements until the next growing season. However, if you are short on window space, you can envelop the roots of geranium plants with wet sphagnum moss, prune the plants and place them in plastic bags. Kept in nominal light, the geraniums should survive until late January. But then you must pot them. They will not last until spring in plastic. Another storage method that works well for many geranium lovers is to dig up the plants and replace some of the soil with wet sphagnum peat moss. Then wrap the plants fairly tightly in newsprint and place

Question: My husband is an excellent carpenter. He would like to build some window boxes and patio tubs. Which type of wood is most desirable for these purposes?
Answer: The wood that is considered most moisture tolerant is redwood. If you can find some good dimensional lumber for the boxes, redwood is the most ideal choice, followed by red cedar. The latter is much harder to find.

Geraniums

the rolls in large, double-thickness grocery bags. Store the sacks in a cool basement or frost-free crawl space until late March. Then place the dry plants in buckets of water for three weeks and pot in rich, organic potting soil to get them going again.

Indoor Light

If you have more plants than windows, you can use electric lights. In a basement room, fluorescent fixtures work better than incandescent bulbs because fluorescents put out more infrared and ultraviolet rays which plants need. In order to survive, most plants will need 8 to 10 hours of artificial light; for better blooms, allow 15 to 16 hours. Coleus thrives indoors. Fuchsia needs the best light of a north-facing window, and even there, it may not flower well unless helped along nightly by two to three hours of light from a 40-watt fluorescent tube.

Indoor Pests

Before bringing plants indoors, be sure they have no live insects or mites. If you find live pests on plants, take the plants back outside and use a good systemic spray such as Orthene or Meta-Systox-R, then keep them in the garage overnight. White flies are especially a menace in the house or apartment and can be very tough to control, even with Resmethrin.

How to Root Annuals Indoors with Cuttings

Another way to keep annuals going through winter is to take three-inch cuttings in the fall and root them indoors. This propagation technique works well with coleus, fuchsia, geranium and pelargonium. The best medium to begin with is a mix of equal parts by volume of vermiculite and perlite. But commercially prepared starter mixes are also good. Rich potting soil can be used, but it is not sterile. Coleus can be started well in water. Dip the cuttings in a rooting medium such as Rootone or Hormex before potting in regular potting soil. Water and enclose the containers in clear plastic bags to reduce moisture loss. Check the soil periodically and water when dry. Keep the containers out of direct sun but on a warm, bright windowsill. When the cuttings are well-rooted, take the plastic bags off.

Geraniums

Indoors or out, annuals are a treat for the Rocky Mountain gardener.

PERENNIALS

PERENNIAL flowers differ from annuals in that they do not complete their cycle in a single growing season. Perennials constitute a more permanent improvement of the garden and require a better soil situation than annuals. They grow for at least two years or more. For the sake of keeping them properly classified I divide perennials into three classes:

1. **Herbaceous perennials** — Plants that come up from the same roots every year, then, at the end of the season, die down to the ground, leaving only dry stalks that must be cleaned up late in winter. Most perennials belong to this classification. Chrysantheum is one of them.

2. **Woody perennials** — Plants that normally maintain a certain basic structure above the ground from which they bud and develop every year. Roses and tree peonies belong to this group.

3. **Bulbs, roots, etc.** — Bulbs are modified stems from which the foliage and flowers emerge every year. Much of each bulb is a storage facility like a fleshy root, such as an iris rhizome, a begonia tuber, or a Dahlia root.

For simplification, I also would add biennials to the perennial group, although biennials usually complete their growth cycle in two years. Foxglove is a biennial.

Perennials have need of a better quality and well-drained soil as their roots continue to develop more every year. Some perennials require full sun, some need partial shade, and a few thrive only in full shade. They also have need for an additional cultural program besides pinching, pruning, and seed removal: They need disbudding. The word clearly suggests what is done. Many perennials, including peonies and roses, develop a flower terminal with more than one bud. The more buds they develop, the smaller each resulting flower. All the available energy is channeled to many blooms. If, however, we remove — by manual action — all but one bud on a stem, this will allow all the energy made by the leaves on this stem or shoot to be directed toward a single remaining bud. The result often is a flower two or three times the size of several smaller blooms. If you want as many flowers as you can get, you naturally will settle for smaller blooms. But if you are grooming your blooms for an entry at the local county fair or flower show, then you want to come up with the showiest bloom — even though extra size counts very little. I am an exhibitor, too. When I make an exhibit entry, I want to be proud of it. I want it to be the best. Standard chrysanthemums are grown disbudded and often under shade cloth, which helps them to bud earlier. You ought to see what extra effort proud amateur gardeners go to get these beautiful (what we call "football") mums.

Rocky Mountain Tip:

Perennial flowers are more demanding than annuals. They need a much better, deeper soil, better drainage, and a location where they may remain undisturbed from 3 to 10 years. Many of them accept partial or full shade. Others love the full sun.

If you have a large enough garden, you may want to set aside a very visible portion for a perennial bed. But if your garden is small, you may want to select from the all-season bloom list presented below. Pick those that mature at a preferred time and spot them where they can provide color and interest for your garden. A now-dated concept in landscaping declared it unsuitable to place flowers in the front of a home, referred to as the public or street area. Flowers were to be kept hidden from all but those lucky enough to be living or entertained in the private area or back yard. We are more permissive nowadays. At my home, there are always roses in front — in bloom or with a promise.

The perennial bed should be as far as possible from large trees and certainly not heavily shaded. Perennials are touchy when it comes to root competi-

Where tulips, daffodils and summer flowering bulbs are to be planted, some soil improvement with peat moss is worthwhile. Also, bulb food, bonemeal, or superphosphate can be added at depth of planting to help bulbs along to good flowering.

tion. Even the least aggressive evergreens want to compete with roses and other perennials for food and water. If the drainage is less than acceptable, you may want to consider raised beds. They are work to install, but the results are worth the effort.

If you are in a wind-exposed situation, there are a few extra virtues by which to select perennials. The ones you choose should grow close to the ground, and not very tall, like delphiniums and lilies. They should have a sturdy growth development. They also should have small rather than large leaves. Small-leaved plants recover better and more quickly from the small incidents of hail. You also should choose perennials that have a quality of drought resistance. We don't live in a rain-forest eco-system. We must learn to accept our limitations gracefully and make the best of what we have. Finally, our perennials must be able to grow in alkaline soils. Not many Westerners have the luxury of an acid soil. It is too cumbersome to acidify a larger flower bed with continuous applications of acid peat since the chemicals, such as aluminum sulfate, iron sulfate, and sulfur, must be used with caution and in relatively small amounts.

Although a few foolhardy crocus and daffodils sometimes flower in March, I will start my flowering schedule with April.

April — crocus, daffodils, tulip species (Kaufmannia, Greigii), snowdrops, grape hyacinths, creeping phlox *(subulata)*.

May — tulips, hyacinths, daffodils, violas, pansies, lily of the valley, bleeding heart, forget-me-not (Mysotis), primrose, pinks, Sweet William, alyssum (Basket-of-Gold), candytuft (Iberis).

June — iris, Oriental poppies, roses, daylilies, columbine, peonies, delphinium, lupines, coralbells, plantain lilies, Madonna lilies.

July — phlox, gladioli, lilies, Shasta daisies, Tritoma, Achillea, gaillardia, foxglove.

August — dahlias, cannas, lycoris, Gloriosa daisies, gayfeather, coreopsis, gladioli.

September-October — chrysanthemums, Michaelmas daisies, gladioli, delphinium (second flowering).

PERENNIALS FOR ROCKY MOUNTAIN GARDENERS

Perennials A to Z . . . and How to Care for Them

Most perennials with the exception of spring flowering bulbs should be planted in April or May, unless otherwise noted.

A

Amaryllis, hardy *(Lycoris)* — Full sun is a prime need. The foliage greens in April and May, and dies down when the hot weather starts. Then, after many weeks — suddenly in August to September — the leafless stems (scapes) shoot out of the ground like asparagus. At the top, about 10 to 12 inches high, are four to eight lovely lily flowers. Group planting is encouraged. Plant hardy bulbs in October. Lavender in color.

Amaryllis

Basket-of-Gold

B

Basket-of-Gold *(Alyssum)* — Prefers a sunny ledge; blooms very showy gold in early May. Plant in spring of previous year and let plants develop. Six-packs available at greenhouses. Water once or twice during dormant season. Blooms about 10 to 12 inches high.

Begonia, tuberous *(Begonia)* — Grown from bulbs each year in rich soil (half compost). Bulbs must be protected over winter in a non-freezing storage area. Fascinating flowers in white, pink, red, orange, and yellow. Some tuberous begonias are suitable for hanging baskets. Must be grown in full shade. Stems are very fragile, need shelter. (Fibrous rooted begonias are annuals; see page 253.)

Bleeding Heart

Cannas

Bleeding Heart *(Dicentra)* — Lovely pink to red flowers along the top of a stem in late May to early June. Plant a small starter from a greenhouse in April or May. Bloom from second year on. Prefers partial shade, grows to about 18 inches in height. There is a new white variety called Pantaloons, by Wayside Gardens. They also feature a hybrid Luxuriant that repeats if faded flowers are picked.

C

Canna *(Canna)* — Planted in early May or 10 days before frost-free season, blooms from midsummer on from roots that must either be mulched six inches deep or dug in October after the first frost. The roots may be stored in root cellars with dahlias. The roots should be dug after the foliage has frozen. Foliage is then pruned, roots should cure for two weeks in the house and then can be inserted in vermiculite or peat moss in a place where temperature remains above 40 degrees F. Add a little moisture to the mulch when dry to prevent dehydration of the roots. Some cannas grow to five feet and more every summer. Some varieties have green foliage, others have red. Canna is the only relative of the banana we can grow in the West. Dwarf Pfitzer varieties will flower at 30 to 36 inches. Excellent tall varieties are City of Portland (pink), Red King Humbert (orangered), and The President (red). Need full sun and rich soil. Roots are planted 24-30 inches apart.

Chrysanthemums *(Chrysanthemum)* — The fall season would be very void of color and excitement without mums. They love the full sun. Propagations are made in early spring from clumps that send out new starts. Outer portions are the youngest and best for separations and an increase in the number of plants. Mums should be pinched twice to obtain a bushy plant. Cushion mums make colorful mounds of hundreds of small flowers and start as early as August. Flowers are often brilliant up to a month. Larger flowered varieties should be selected by hardiness. Florists' plants often perform poorly outdoors and could be a disappointment. Many varieties of mums offered by Western and Rocky Mountain nurseries were originated at the Cheyenne Horticultural Field Station and the University of Nebraska (North Platte) by the late Glen Viehmeyer.

Chrysanthemums

Chrysanthemum flower forms are made up of two different parts, namely ray florets and disc florets. The elongated florets are the ray florets; the short, tufted at the center, are the disc florets. These flower forms generally are:

1. Anemone — one or more rows of ray florets on the outside. Center is made up of disc florets.
2. Decorative — ray florets are long and usually wide. Disc florets are not visible. Most mums look like this.
3. Incurve — flowers are larger. Ray florets curve up and in toward the center of the bloom.
4. Pompom — Smaller, rounded blooms with flat or quilled ray florets.
5. Single — resemble a Shasta daisy. Single outer row of ray florets with a large center of disc florets.
6. Spider — Ray florets are rolled and elongated, sometimes up to three inches long. Spoons are similar. They are fuller and stiffer. Some have a spoon at the outer edge of the ray florets.

The first pinch is made when new chrysanthemum shoots are 6 to 7 inches high. (A pinch is the removal of upper-third of stem and foliage.) The pinchings may be rooted and more plants gained by this practice. Try to pinch again about three weeks later.

If you want very large blooms, you can try to raise standard mums. For this purpose, disbudding is step one. Normally, the central bud is protected, but if it has been damaged, a side bud will perform equally well. Standard mum blooms usually are grown under shade cloth and are supported by twine or string both lengthwise and sideways. I believe this is something best learned from an experienced grower.

Question: My chrysanthemum plant grew exceptionally large this year but had only a few straggly flowers to show for all my efforts and care. What can I do next year to have better results?
Answer: It would be well to remember that chrysanthemum pot plants have neither the hardiness nor the desirable growth properties for what we need outdoors in this region. Most greenhouse growers who produce pot chrysanthemums for the florist trade use varieties to respond mostly to light manipulation for desired flowering. The outdoor chrysanthemums that are hardy do not need the desirable features of a greenhouse flowering plant. To obtain better denseness for your plant next year you must also pinch your plants. This is accomplished by breaking or cutting off the upper 3-4 inches when the plant is 8-10 inches high. When sideshoots develop the pinching process is repeated again to further reduce the plant's height in favor of more flowering shoots.

Columbine

Chrysanthemums are photosensitive plants. They set buds only when daylight becomes short enough to trigger this action. Varieties vary in their photosensitivity. Greenhouse pot plants usually are too late for a Western garden.

Columbine *(Aquilegia)* — Colorado state flower. Needs partial to full shade (Colorado Blue), but McKana's hybrids do well even in the sun. Plants have decorative foliage and prefer good drainage. Flowers are dainty, and most of them have spurs. Spring Song strains have almost double flowers. Colors are red, blue and yellow. Seed should be sown in late September. Greenhouses offer started plants in six-packs.

Coralbells *(Heuchera)* — An excellent ground cover perennial with lovely 18-inch stems of dainty blooms. Native to North America. Leaves are round

Coralbell

Coreopsis

to scalloped. Attractive to hummingbirds. Accepts sun to full shade. Needs a well-drained humus soil. Seeds should be planted within 30 days of maturity in the wild or outdoors. This is usually in early fall. Several varieties are available in orange-coral; some are white (June Bride, Wayside); and some have a range from white to coral-red (Bessingham Hybrids, Wayside).

Coreopsis *(Coreopsis)* — By any other name this is one of the easiest perennials to grow. It tolerates full or half-day sun and almost any type of soil except concrete. It is very floriferous and stays that way from July until frost. Sunburst has a double ring of petals on the outside, making it appear like a golden daisy. Variety Sunray is very double but still shows its pistillate centers. Variety Gold Pink is a dwarf. A relatively new variety called Zagreb has fern-like foliage and naturally forms a mound of green with golden flowers. All coreopsis are highly tolerant to heat and drought, and most bugs find them distasteful. I could rate it among the ten best perennials in the West.

Crocus *(Crocus)* — This modest little vane of the early spring seems to multiply and repeat well if we don't accidentally mow its foliage off prematurely. Crocuses are fall-planted. They like sun when blooming, but the foliage hangs on longer if it is shaded in May and June. Colors are white, yellow, lavender and blends.

Crocus

Daffodils

D

Daffodils *(Narcissus)* — In the 1960s, most bulb dealers stocked a choice of, at best, ten varieties of daffodils in September. Lately, the number of offered kinds has increased remarkably. I still think King Alfred (yellow), Mount Hood (white), Mrs. R. O. Backhouse (shell pink trumpet on ivory perianth) and Spellbinder (sulfur lemon) are the best all around. There are hundreds of other varieties that you can choose from at your dealer or from mail-order catalogues. I do not favor ordering directly from Holland; you will get better bulbs from your local retailer at a very competitive price. There are all sorts of pitfalls in shipping across the Atlantic. In Holland, there is always a great temptation to order direct; however, I try to discourage this. Much of the local supply in Holland is leftovers. The American garden trade orders a year in advance, and it orders every year. That is why it has only the best.

Besides the large trumpet daffodils, some daffodils also are flowered with smaller "cups" and minute "eyes." Many now are confused doubles like the Twinks. Some are multiple-flowered. They have two or more flowers for each stalk. Silver Chimes is lovely, as are Geranium and Enriched. Please plant daffodil bulbs eight inches deep. They will naturalize and grow into drifts if they hang on to their foliage into July each year.

Dahlia *(Dahlia)* — Dahlias are one of the showiest of garden flowers. You may have to be patient in our regions until July before they really dazzle. The colors and blends are endless, and the

Dahlia

flower types are from round to cactus form. In the years I have judged dahlias at state fairs, I have seen some blooms exceeding dinner-plate size. There are pompoms, colarettes, decoratives, semicactus, cactus and ball types. Some are in solid colors: others are exciting blends. But for display in a vase or in the garden, the cactus form of dahlias are my preference. Small dahlias usually are on 24 to 30 inch plants. The large flowers are on three to five foot plants. Dahlia tubers must be dug and stored to be safe year to year. This is a process similar to Cannas. Don't forget them outside in November. (See also, page 255.)

Daylily *(Hemerocallis)* — What used to be referred to as a lemon lily has become one of the most exciting lilies in the garden trade. The new hybrids come in colors a far cry from the roadside wildlings I saw in the Central states. Not only have the flowers become lovelier and larger, but flowering periods now extend from June until September. The flower petals overlap generously and, in many varieties, are gently ruffled on the outer margins. It would be difficult to single out favorites. Some catalogues offer breeder's mixtures where you can buy three or four for the price of one choice variety. The only thing that leaves me unimpressed is the foliage of daylilies. It's hard to landscape around it. Full sun to partial shade is their preferred range of habitat. They naturalize well in perennial borders or grouped by themselves.

Question: How deep and how far apart should Dahlias be planted?
Answer: Dahlias should be planted 5 to 6 inches deep and at least 24 to 30 inches apart. I would establish a solid wooden stake at planting time. The plants get heavy and need support against the wind.

Question: My daylilies bloom beautifully but the ends of the leaves turn ugly brown. How can I prevent this?
Answer: The brown ends are caused by soil alkalinity or salts. Hold back on fertilizer but be generous with granular sulfur which will help to take care of your problem gradually.

Daylily

Delphinium

Delphinium

Delphinium *(Delphinium)* — This elegant hybrid of the larkspur family has become one of the most spectacular garden perennials. The flower spikes are of regal appearance. Delphiniums require an abundance of plant nutrients and a well-drained soil. Roots should be planted in April-May — sometimes in the fall. If planted in the fall, be sure to keep the soil moist. Light shade to full sun is a requirement. They are very sturdy plants where nights are cool, such as in lower mountain valleys. Delphiniums need staking, especially where gusts of wind could arise. Colors range from white to pastel blue to royal blue, lavender, and purple. Pacific Giant varieties have florets up to three inches. A light winter mulch is appreciated. Do not let plants get too dry.

Sweet William

Carnations, Pinks, Sweet William *(Dianthus)* — Since they all are members of the same genus, I will discuss them together. They are perennially dependable for lovely, fragrant flowers. Their foliage is bluish-green. Some pinks are in mixed colors and with attractive markings on the petals. Grenadin mixed colors are lovely for bouquets and arrangements. Sweet William actually is a biennial and has numerous flowers in a single stem. All Sweet Williams prefer a sandy or gritty soil with very good drainage. Carnations are very hardy and should be welcome in mountain locations. They all fit well into rock gardens and near ledges in the garden.

F

Forget-Me-Nots

Forget-Me-Nots *(Myosotis)* — This little shade-loving plant would love to be near a running stream or brook, perhaps even a small waterfall. It likes humidity. Available in medium and light blue. I have even seen it in pink. Some are good as ground covers; others grow to six inches high. They should be planted when small plants are available — usually April or May.

Foxglove *(Digitalis)* — Prefers a moist, well-drained soil in partial shade. Three-foot spikes with bell-shaped flowers come white to shell pink to deep rose in color, and some are dotted with darker colors. Variety Foxy was awarded an All-America Award in 1967 for often flowering the first year.

G

Foxglove

Gayfeather *(Liatris)* — A native of North America that produces tall spikes of white, lavender, and purple flowers. Grows 24 to 36 inches high. Can be used for backdrop. Plants need to be 15 to 18 inches apart. Prefers partial sun but not too demanding about soil.

Gladiolus *(Gladiolus)* — The spikes yield a bounty of beautiful florets. Glads are grown from corms, a solid bulb. Because they are not winter-hardy, they must be dug in the fall, dried for a few weeks, cleaned and stored over winter in a dry, cool place. Discarded hosiery filled with bulbs hangs easily from a nail or hook. Sizes of florets and spikes vary with variety and series classification.

The National Gladiolus Society has made All America selections each year for a long time. I

Gayfeather

Gladiolus

Gladiolus

remember one old variety, Spic "N" Span, that was perennially hard to beat at flower shows. Now it is nearly forgotten, because so many amateurs have created new varieties. The miniatures have become popular because they fit well into small gardens. Glads should be planted several times, at two week intervals from early May until mid-June. That extends their flowering in the garden. These bloom spikes have no fragrance. But their colors and blends are endless and exciting.

Gloriosa Daisy *(Rudbeckia)* — Daisy-like yellow to gold flowers with mahogany markings. Very tolerant of drought, heat and poor soil, but loves the sun. Some are single, and some are semi-double flowers. Greenhouse growers usually offer small plants in packs in April and May.

Grape Hyacinths *(Muscari)* — These fall-planted perennial bulbs are very dependable. In partial shade, the foliage remains green well into summer. Multiplication of bulbs is endless. In some instances, they may have to be contained. Blue and white flowers grow to six inches high.

Hollyhocks *(Althaea)* — The most exciting powder puff forms of these flowers are well worth planting in the garden. Most older varieties are not, because they are coarse and mostly tall and unattractive. Hollyhocks are a biennial that sometimes forget what they are and come up again. The many colors range from white to dark red, with shades of pink. Fringed doubles are lovely.

Hyacinths *(Hyacinthus)* — Of all the flowers of early spring, these are my favorites. I love fragrance in flowers, and hyacinths really have it. They should

Gloriosa Daisy

Hyacinths

Hyacinths

be planted in October to November, using an average flowerbed soil. In most years, I force several pots into bloom in the home. We have an old spare refrigerator in the garage that comes in handy. In October, I pot three to four bulbs per clay pot. I water them well and place them in the refrigerator at about 39 degrees (normal temperature) for 10 to 12 weeks, and water as needed. In that time, they root in the soil. Eventually the buds swell. When buds become large and yellow, I take one pot at a time for a few days into the basement. That allows the bud to stretch a bit. Now the pots go on the brightest, coolest window, where the flowers develop in two more weeks. The fragrance of one pot permeates the whole home living area. It is elegant. Varieties I like best for forcing are: Jan Bos — red; L'Innocence — white; Pink Pearl — pink; and King of the Blues — blue.

Outdoors, hyacinths last for several years longer if their locale is shaded after flowering by planting in a shaded location. That allows the foliage to remain green longer and ensures good reflowering for years. In the sun, hyacinth's leaves mature too soon, and bulbs get smaller and soon are lost. Plant bulbs eight inches deep. The recommended depth of six inches is not deep enough to obtain the finest bloom spikes.

I

Iris *(Iris)* — A popular late May to early June flowering durable perennial. The American Iris Society awards the Dykes Medal every year for the

Iris

Iris

Question: When and how much can I cut Iris back? The leaves are so tall.
Answer: It is not necessary to cut back Iris foliage in summer. Many home gardeners will do so to give other plants in a perennial border adequate light. You can cut the foliage back about 50 percent, anytime after bloom.

best new variety. Many amateurs are hybridizing bearded iris. The number of new names each year is astounding. Iris prefer sun or at least partial sun. Iris flowers have two sets of petals. The petals that reach up are called standard and those that fall down are called falls. New color combinations, and blends have been more and more outstanding.

Since iris multiply naturally and very prolifically, many collectors trade newer introductions. If you have an iris fancier nearby, get acquainted with her or him; you may reap some benefits from such a neighbor. Hybrid bearded iris grow from rhizomes. These roots must be divided every two to four years. Use a complete plant food with high phosphorus — a formula such as 8-12-4 — when you replant the iris. The best time for divisions is July to August. Cut the foliage back to half when you separate.

Dutch Iris

You don't need beginner's luck with iris. They almost grow by themselves. They prefer a good soil but will still succeed in mediocre clay soils. Alkalinity does not seem to bother them much.

Dutch iris are bulbs we plant in October for late spring flowers. They are more limited in colors, having only blues, yellows, purples, whites, and some blended colors. They range from 18 to 24 inches in height and prefer a sunny exposure and good drainage.

L

Lavender Cotton *(Santolina)* — This perennial's grey-green foliage actually is more decorative than its yellow flowers. Lavender Cotton is heat and drought resistant; very adapted to the West. It prefers a soil with good drainage. Available in silver and green. Averages about 12 to 15 inches high. Can be trimmed. Planted in April to May.

Lily *(Lillium)* — Lilies are exciting flowers in our garden. When they are in bloom, the fragrance from them on the patio is exquisite. Jan de Graaf is likely the most successful and widely-known breeder of fine hybrid lilies. There are fine Asiatic lilies including Mid-Century hybrids, Enchantment, Firecracker and Scarlet Emperor, just to mention a few. Then there are the Aurelian hybrids, including some of my favorites, such as Black Dragon, which is extra fragrant, and Pink Perfection, an Olympic hybrid. Then there is the fragrant Easter lily or Madonna lily *(L. candidum)*, which can be planted outdoors and may reflower in your garden if Easter

Lily

is early enough. It is hardy and will bloom in June and thereafter. Lilies prefer a well-improved soil with good drainage. There are really too many lilies to mention, but they are all glorious garden subjects. The tall lilies need some shelter from wind, and some support. All lilies should be planted in November. Because this is late for many gardeners, the trade keeps bulbs in cold storage and offers them for sale in March and April. You may plant them either way.

Lupine *(Lupinus)* — A semi-shaded spot or morning sun is ideal for this pea family flower arranged in large numbers on tall spikes in the garden in blue, white, yellow, salmon, purple, pink and red. Lupines flower in June. They will grow quite well in alkaline soils if they have drainage. Maximum height of the plant and flowers is 36 inches. Russell's Lupines are really beautiful.

Lupine

O

Oriental Poppy *(Papaver)* — If you need a splash of vivid colors in your garden, Oriental poppies are for you. They usually come into peak bloom in late May or early June. Their brilliance shines in many colors, including orange, red, pink, white, rose, and orange with a white center (China Boy, Wayside). The plants grow about two and a half feet tall, with flowers to three feet. The plants are best divided every few years when the tops die down in August or September. Oriental poppies prefer a rich, well-drained soil. They like to be fed with 8-12-4 fertilizer in early summer.

Question: My Oriental Poppies have finished blooming and are seeded now. Does it pay to save the seed?

Answer: If you want to raise Oriental Poppies from seed you can save the seed after the capsules have turned completely dry. Then sow the seed in October and keep moisture in that bed almost all winter long, weather permitting. If you don't want the seed, cut the seed pods off before the energy of the plant is wasted.

Oriental Poppy

Pansies

P

Pansy *(Viola)* — Although a perennial, the pansy is often treated as an annual and behaves that way if its seed heads are not picked off. Some of the finest are Swiss Giants and Majestic Giants (AAS in 1966). There are also newer varieties such as Mammoth Giants and Vikings. Colors range from white to blue, including purple, yellow, rose, and scarlet. Many have mixed colors. Pansies prefer to be shaded from the heat of the sun, but with enough watering and a sandy soil, they will withstand sun. Often, they make it through the winter as they should. They are lovely in the spring garden.

Peony *(Paeonia)* — To fully appreciate what a wide range of peonies are now offered, you must

Peonies

Peonies

Phlox

Question: My phlox has been in full bloom for a month. It is beautiful except for the leaves. They are covered with a white spotting. How can I deal with this problem?
Answer: What you have reference to is Downy Mildew. It occurs on quite a few perennials but most severely on phlox. Some varieties are more resistant to the disease than others. I have had good results with Funginex if I start early enough to apply the spray. Watch your phlox next year and when you see the first spots on the lower leaves it's time to start spraying with Funginex. Repeat every 3 weeks or after a heavy rain.

consult the catalogues of peonies specialists or Wayside Gardens. Although Felix Crousse, Festima Maxina, Sarah Bernhardt, and Monsieur Jules Elie are the popular standbys, they don't hold a candle to the likes of Bonanza, Do Tell, Sword Dance, and Lotus Queen. Add to this Estate peonies and hybrid peonies such as First Lady, Raspberry Sundae, and Pink Lemonade, and you have difficult choices to make. Planting time for peonies is September, although roots are often chilled for April planting. One of the most important points in planting peonies is to plant them very shallow in well-improved garden soil with adequate drainage. Planting them too deep is one of the major reasons why they don't bloom. Peonies also should generally remain without cultural disturbance for 7 to 10 years. They don't like competition from tree roots, which, in a small garden, is hard to avoid. Properly disbudded, peonies are one of the most magnificent flowers of the spring garden. Try them and you'll love them.

Phlox *(Phlox)* — Phlox are so easy to grow, and come in many colors, including lavender, white, pink and rose, and darker red centers. They practically take care of themselves, except for mildew. Downy mildew can now be controlled with Funginex and/or Benomyl. The secret is not to wait too long. Once mildew gets a head start, it is hard to control. Mark June 15 on your calendar as the date for a first application and follow up every 15 to 20 days. Phlox grow 24 to 42 inches high and reflower through summer into fall if you prune off the faded flowers. Average garden soil is acceptable. They even have a fragrance you might like.

Another phlox is well adapted for your garden: phlox *subulata* or creeping phlox. It blooms very early, usually in April, in lavender, pink and white. It is lovely on edges, in ledges and rock gardens. It grows about 6 to 8 inches high. It likes good drainage and gritty soil.

Plantain Lily *(Hosta)* — If you use this plant as a ground cover in full shade, you will be happier than if you expect magnificent flowers. I would honestly consider the bloom secondary. Some hostas have variegated leaf form adding extra interest. This plant prefers a moist, organic soil. It is also heavily attacked by slugs, which you can spray against with Metaldehyde or Mesurol. Most hostas grow about 15 to 18 inches high, but they don't spread very much. Flower stems have small, white, or lavender-colored flowers in early summer.

Primrose *(Primula)* — The foliage rosettes of primrose provide one of the neatest ground covers you can select. Plants produce as many as 15 to 20 flowers to a single stem. Some varieties available now have flowers that measure an inch to an inch-and-a-half individually. Almost unbelievable colors exist, from white to dark blue, with all the various shades of pink, blue, and red in between. Primroses prefer a moist situation with excellent drainage. They are lovely in April and May when the flowers first appear. Watch for slugs — they like primroses, too.

R

Rose *(Rosa)* — This very popular flower is discussed later in this chapter, under a separate heading.

S

Shasta Daisy *(Chrysanthemum)* — Yes, believe it or not, this flower is in the genus Chrysanthemum, although neither its foliage nor flowering habit is remotely similar to a mum. The Shasta daisy is the product of a cross made in the late 19th century by Luther Burbank, the wizard of the plantsmen. It is not sensitive to the length of daylight. It is a very lovely, highly dependable garden flower and easy to grow. Best started from greenhouse six-packs in April and May, Shasta daisies may reach flowering the first summer. A well-drained average garden soil is desired. Many flower forms are offered by

Shasta Daisies

Tritoma

nurserymen. Alaska is a single with yellow centers. Marconi is a frilly white double. Moonlight, Majestic, Polaris, Wirral's Pride and Cobhan Gold (yellowish) are other offerings. These range from 18 to 20 inches. Little Princess and Little Miss Muffet will only grow 12 inches high with smaller flowers.

T

Tritoma or Red Hot Poker *(Kniphofia)* — Tritoma's foliage could be compared to that of a yucca; however, the flowers remind me of a fireworks rocket going off. For this reason, I like to call it "the flower of Independence Day." The bloom is very striking in red, yellow, and white. Adapts almost anywhere. Insects find it undigestible. Can stand lots of heat and drought. Good garden soil is needed.

Tulips *(Tulipa)* — These occupy first rank in popularity among all spring-flowering bulbs, and should be planted in October/November. There is an almost unlimited choice of types, magnificent colors and exciting varieties. Among the earliest to bloom in your garden are the Kaufmanniana and Greigii hybrids. Many of these are only 10 inches high. These are followed very soon by the Forsteriana hybrids that include the Emperors in several colors, especially the striking Red Emperor. Then come more early tulips, including Early Doubles that range from 10 to 20 inches high. Next come the Darwins, such as President Eisenhower, President Kennedy, and Gudoshnik. The mid-season group includes the Cottage tulips, the Triumphs, and some with fringed petals. The lily-flowered tulips then

Question: I have several tulips that did not bloom this spring. When should I dig them and replant them for next year?
Answer: You should allow the foliage of the tulips to remain green as long as possible. When the leaves turn brown the bulbs are mature. You can then dig them anytime before the first of September. Replant only the larger bulbs about 7 to 8 inches deep in October. Also use a marker to spot the bulbs later when you want to dig them up.

Tulips

mature in mid-May. The Rembrandts and Parrot tulips are among the last to bloom. In each classification there are endless selections. Buy your tulips from a local dealer if you can. He likely has the best sizes at a good price. If you are not near a dealer, some mail-order houses have catalogues with many proven choices. I do not advise sending our dollars directly to Holland. Support your local establishments if you can. And please plant your bulbs at least eight inches deep. The literature says six inches. In full sun or sandy soils, go 10 inches deep. The deeper the bulbs (up to a 12-inch limit), the longer they will produce. With shallow plantings, tulips last only two to three years. Do not injure or mow the foliage before it matures. That also could cause an early demise of your bulb investment.

Tulips

Yarrow

Y

Yarrow *(Achillea)* — One of the hardiest perennials known and needs a fair to good soil. Can be a weed in the lawn that is hard to control. Elegant, feathery foliage is topped by colorful inflorescences. Tolerates heat, severe cold, drought, and even some abuse. Even a hailstorm rarely bothers it. Plant from six-packs in April. Divide every three years in March or October. The Pearl and Angel's Breath are white. Coronation Gold and Moonshine are yellow to gold. Red Beauty is dark pink. Flowers cut at full opening can be dried easily for winter bouquets and arrangements.

The Best Perennials for Shade

A shady garden spot is a restful place. And it can be a growing place. Many more perennials than annuals are shade-orientated. You may not really need them all. But as trees and shrub masses get larger and more massive, they shade more of your garden against the singeing heat of the sun. The following perennials previously discussed in this chapter are excellent flowering plants for partial to full shade:

Foxglove

Bleeding Heart	Pansy
Coral Bells	Plantain Lily
Forget-Me-Not	Primrose
Foxglove	

Other Spring and Summer Flowering Bulbs

Pansies

Among spring-flowering bulbs, there are several that the garden trade designates as minor bulbs. Yet they are completely hardy, very durable,

Allium Giganteum

Fritillaria

and particularly suitable in rock gardens and narrow ledges. All of them are very suitable and lovely for planting in mountain communities. Let me briefly describe them for you:

Allium *(Allium)* — As the name promises, these are fancy onions. The most attractive is the Giganteum from the Himalayas. It produces a colossal, lavender-colored ball of hundreds of flowers. Golden Garlic (Moly luteum) flowers in golden umbels in June. *Roseum Grandiflorum* is a pink variety with a mauve tinge on a handsome stem. Plant the *A. giganteum* bulbs in October/November eight inches deep, the others five to six inches.

Fritillaria *(Fritillaria)* — Also called Crown Imperial, this truly unusual spring flower should be planted in October/November. Varieties *Imperialis Aurora* and *Lutea Maxima* produce pendant flowers in red and yellow respectively. The flowers are attractive, but from the bulbs and plants a skunk-like odor emanates that is less than desirable. Another variety, *F. persica adiyaman,* has dark plum bells. All perform well in part-shade borders and rock gardens.

Glory-of-the-Snow *(Chionodoxa)* — These are among the earliest spring flowers. They create patches of brilliant blue when the snow melts away. These hardy plants are most effective when planted in drifts or groups. The bulbs should be planted about three inches deep in October or November.

Squills *(Scilla)* — Plant bulbs 3 to 4 inches deep in drifts and masses, in October/November. Flowers appear in lovely blue. Siberica Spring Beauty has sterile blooms that last for a week or longer. *Scilla companulata* blooms in June in white, pink and blue.

They must be shaded, or they will not last but a few years.

Snowdrops *(Galanthus)* — In a warm winter, you may see Snowdrops in the garden in January of February. The graceful flowers are white. Should be planted four inches deep, in October/November. Plant where the soil is shaded.

Snowflakes *(Leucojum)* — The flowers are little white bells in graceful spikes. Flowering time is early May. Plant bulbs in October/November 3 to 4 inches deep in a shaded location.

Tuberous Begonias *(Begonia)* — If properly stored, tubers will produce positively spectacular flowers. When you pot the bulbs in March or April, the concave side should be up and the round side down in very rich soil. Potted plants should be transplanted to the outdoors in late May. I use half Canadian peat and half compost soil. Must be grown in absolute shade and in sheltered spots. Watch for holes in the leaves suggesting slugs. Several flower types exist in a range of colors. Hanging basket varieties are lovely, but a challenge. They don't like dry air and wind. Mine do best on our north-facing patio.

Begonias

Century II

Queen of the Garden

Prized for their delightful fragrance, roses have been the favorites of all garden flowers for centuries, possibly since the ancient history of mankind. The earliest origin of roses was found to have occurred 60 million years ago in Central Asia, spreading from there all over the Northern Hemisphere. In the Northwestern United States and near Divide, Colorado, fossils of roses estimated to be 35 million years old have been found. History is full of references to roses. In ancient Rome and Greece, the flower was associated with love, with womanly perfection and with deities (goddesses).

Roses have also become a symbol in many other ways. They have influenced fashions, artists, and interior design. They became the most popular flower adorning china, silver, and wall decor. They have appeared on coins, stamps, currency, and on coats of arms. The District of Columbia and four states have elected the rose to be their official flower.

Modern roses have come a long way since ancient days. The greatest development of the rose has occurred since the 1930's. Numerous hybridizers have made controlled crosses that combined many good rose features in some of the newest award-winning patents. One of the great introductions from the House of Meilland in France was the Peace rose. It won an All-America Selection award in 1946 and, since then, has become the most popular rose of all times. Many excellent newer roses have since been introduced. I will share with you my choices of the best roses in commerce now for each popular classification.

THE ROSE (ROSA)

Bob Hope

For the purpose of classification in the trade, roses are listed by types, patent numbers, and names. The most popular roses today are hybrid tea roses. They represent about 65 to 70 percent of annual sales in the United States. Next popular are Floribunda roses. They are cross hybrids of polyanthas and hybrid teas and combine some of the best qualities of tea roses, but are smaller in size of bloom. They usually have several buds for each terminal stem and may form candelabras once a year on which they could have as many as 20 blooms. Some years ago, hybridizers came up with some in-between seedling plants that had multiple flowers but were larger plants, often as large as hybrid tea roses. This new class became the Grandiflora class of roses. Climbers also are sold as hybrid tea climbers and as hardy climbers. The hardy ones are generally more suitable for our Rocky Mountain and Great Basin regions. Hybrid tea climbers bloom well in some years after a relatively mild winter. After severe cold, they often fail to produce enough flowers. The summer production of flowers develops mostly on carryover canes from the previous year. In severely cold winters, these climbers die nearly to the ground. In sheltered localities, it is a good gamble to plant some. I have a few in my garden. I enjoy their flowers and do not grieve when extreme cold causes them to fail in some years. In recent years, miniature roses — also called minis — have gained support. They are much smaller plants that produce beautiful blooms a fraction the size of other roses. For a gardener with very limited space, they allow the planting of many more plants than Floribundas or larger roses.

Another type of rose widely planted in California is the tree-rose. A variety is grafted on top of a standard ranging from 30 to 48 inches high. The losses of these roses in our harsh winter climate, according to my observation, are too substantial. I therefore cannot recommend such an investment (about $20 per plant) unless you have greenhouse space for wintering these beautiful plants.

The Best Hybrid Tea Roses

As I see it — and mostly from personal observation and experience — this is the list:

Bewitched — medium pink, very lovely pink on a tall plant.

Century II — pink, improved Charlotte Armstrong.

Bewitched

Chicago Peace — pink blend, still among the best.

Chrysler Imperial — red, I have won Queen of the Show with it.

Double Delight — red with whitish center.

First Prize — pink blend, a beautiful flower.

Garden Party — near white, the first great Peace hybrid.

Granada — red blend, very fragrant, many blooms.

King's Ransom — dark yellow, still the best yellow rose.

Lady X — mauve, always tallest in our garden blooms well.

Miss All American Beauty — medium pink, blooms well.

Mister Lincoln — dark red, the highest-rated red rose.

Mojave — orange blend, does not rate high now, but very lovely.

Paradise — mauve with red margins, lovely, fragrant.

Pascali — white, the best white rose, lovely form.

Peace — yellow blend, terrific blooms; still among the best.

Royal Highness — light pink, excellent form, lovely.

Sweet Surrender — pink, superb rose fragrance.

Paradise

King's Ransom

Tropicana

Tiffany — pink blend; an oldie, but what quality.

Tropicana — orange red, one of the best of all times.

If you had room for only six roses, I would narrow the list to Chicago Peace, King's Ransom, Mister Lincoln, Pascali, Peace and Tropicana. But that would be a hard choice for everybody to accept. Choose what you really like and enjoy them.

The Best Grandiflora Roses

Arizona — orange blend, in my garden, better than its rating.

Bing Crosby — orange blend, lovely, fragrant rose.

Camelot — medium pink, a beautiful color.

Olé — orange red, a real brilliant color for boutonnieres.

Pink Parfait — pink blend, our bush opens hundreds of flowers.

Queen Elizabeth — pink, class likely was created for her.

Sonia — pink blend, could be large enough as Hybrid Tea.

The Best Floribunda Roses

The best Floribunda roses are those that seem to repeat well year after year:

Betty Prior — medium pink, very productive, semi-double.

Europeana — dark red, repeats well, excellent color, double.

First Edition — orange blend, highly rated.

Bing Crosby

Ginger

Gene Boerner — medium pink, lovely but hard to find.

Ginger — orange red, for many years in front of our home.

Iceberg — white, very high rating for a white rose.

Ivory Fashion — my choice for a white floribunda.

Little Darling — yellow blend, highest-rated.

Sea Pearl — pink blend, lovely but hard to find.

Sunfire — orange red, the color sells it.

Sunsprite — dark yellow with three-inch flowers.

The Best Climbing Roses

The hardy climbers that I can recommend with confidence are:

Blaze or Improved Blaze — brilliant scarlet-red flowers averaging two to three inches, in profusion in June and repeating in smaller numbers throughout the season.

New Dawn — very hardy, light pink, flowers borne more intermittently, prefers an east exposure.

Old Fashioned All American Beauty — one of the most lavish displays of pink color in June. I had one years ago. Since then, it has become almost extinct. I discovered a new source at the High Country Rosarium, 1717 Downing St., Denver, CO 80218. Write them for a catalogue.

Paul's Scarlet — very similar to Blaze but does not repeat quite as much.

Question: Will I have trouble growing climbing roses in Denver?
Answer: If you choose the right varieties of climbing roses you should be very successful. The most hardy varieties of roses are Blaze, Paul's Scarlet and New Dawn. These will thrive for many years on fences or trellises. The Climbing Hybrid tea roses are a bit of a problem in the Denver area. In very sheltered locations they make it through a normal winter in good enough condition to flower the following year. If Hybrid tea climbers survive their canes from one year to the next, they are likely to bloom well that year.

Miniature Roses

The Best Miniature Roses

Miniature roses, according to reliable accounts, had their origin with a small, potted *Rosa rouletti* from a small village in Switzerland, where a single plant in Monsieur Roulet's possession in 1917 had been a family heirloom for around 150 years. The little plant was hardy, and its flowers were described as the size of a Swiss five-centime coin, a little smaller than a dime. Since 1920, mini roses have been developed with much personal support of Robert Pyle of the nursery firm of Conard-Pyle, whose roses are referred to as Star roses. Mr. Pyle engaged two breeders, Jan de Vink in Holland and Pedro Dot in Spain, to hybridize miniature roses. Jan de Vink's Tom Thumb was the first mini to be patented in 1936, and Baby Gold Star followed in 1940. Since then, mini roses have enjoyed explosive popularity. The plants can be easily propagated from stem cutting during the summer. Most amateurs find the protection of a glass (Mason) jar over the cutting helpful to obtain rooting and development.

To take a slip or stem cutting, remove a faded bloom and about 2 to 3 inches of green stem. Trim off the lowest leaf, dip the cut end in Rootone F or Hormex, and insert the lower half of the cutting in garden soil. Water well and place the jar over the cutting. In about six weeks, you will notice new growth. Eight weeks after starting the cutting, you should be able to remove the jar. You may keep the new plants or give them to friends. But any sale (of patented plant material) is prohibited by law, unless you have special arrangements with the patent's owner.

There are now hundreds of minis in commerce and new ones appearing every year. These are some of the best:

Baby Katie — pink blend.
Cuddles — deep pink.
Dreamglo — red blend.
Heidi — medium pink.
Magic Carousel — white edged with red, and one of my favorites.
Mark One — coral orange.
Pacesetter — white.
Peaches 'N Cream — pink blend.
Poker Chip — red with yellow reverse.
Puppy Love — orange blend.
Rise 'N Shine — yellow.
Starina — orange red.
Top Secret — medium red.
Toy Clown — red blend.

How to Select Good Rose Plants

Roses in commerce are graded under a grading system that is generally adhered to by all nursery organizations that sell plants at wholesale and retail. The top grade is the #1 grade. It requires that such a plant must have a sound root system and three well-spaced, vigorous canes. It must be free of diseases and insects. The #1½ grade is very similar to number one, except that the plants need to have only two strong, well-spaced canes, or three canes with slight root system damage. Many #1½ roses are potted and sold growing in containers. The lowest rose grade is #2. It usually is a weaker plant with either substantial root damage or only a single strong — or several weaker — canes. A #2 rose is a poor investment even though it may be lower in cost. I hope you buy your roses to last for many years of enjoyment. The extra dollar you spend will be long forgotten in ten years.

Marina

Rocky Mountain Tip:

The most successful rose plants are #1 roses that are bare-rooted and unwaxed. West Coast mail order houses will ship them if they are not locally available. Second best are container-grown plants.

French Lace

There are also culls. These are the plants left lying in the field when the graders get done. They often belong to the farmer who cared for the plants in the field. Cull roses usually are sold in dozens by mail-order houses for a relatively low price. But they are generally poor quality. A backyard is not a place for a collection of low-grade rejects. It is a place of rest, enjoyment, and achievement. It takes much time and labor to produce a fine garden rose.

How Roses are Sold

Roses are sold by various suppliers (1) growing in containers, (2) bare-rooted and unwaxed, and (3) packaged with or without a wax coating over the green stems or canes.

If you are a novice and have a good source of container-grown roses nearby, you can safely go that route. All you have to do is plant the rose carefully without disturbing the soil ball.

Bare-rooted, unwaxed roses are my preference. You can plant these roses from the beginning and care for them along the way. They must be planted dormant in April.

Packaged waxed roses also must be planted in April. My concern with them is root damage. A plant's roots are forced into a narrow tube package, to which shavings (or shingle-toe) is added. The wax is supposed to protect the rose from drying in commerce. But the wax will not easily flake off. If the waxed cane is exposed to strong Western sun of high intensity, the cane will turn black as the wax melts. Many rose plants are lost that way every year.

Packaged roses without wax may be found. The retail dealers don't like these because they dry out too fast and incur losses that must be replaced. But they are safer than waxed roses.

How to Plant Roses

A ten-dollar rose plant deserves a ten-dollar planting hole. Dig a hole 18 inches deep and at least 15 inches wide. Save the top three inches of soil in a separate pile. That good soil is needed later in the bottom of the hole. After digging the planting hole, you must test the drainage. Fill the hole with water to the rim in late afternoon. If, at breakfast time, the water has drained away, all is well. If 2 or 3 inches of water remain, you can dig a little deeper and add 2 to 3 inches of sand and gravel in the bottom of the hole for drainage. But if there remains enough water to take a foot bath in, you must look for a spot with bet-

Oregold

ter drainage. After arrival of mail order or locally purchased plants, their roots should be soaked in a bucket of water or a tub for at least 24 to 48 hours.

If you are unable due to weather to plant within three days, you must heel the plants in, outdoors. Dig a trench 12 inches deep and place the dormant plants on a slant. Then throw a shovel full of soil over the roots and add the next plant until they are all heeled in. Cover portions of the canes with excess soil and then water. Canned or potted roses may be cared for in their containers until planting.

After testing the drainage, mix two 2-pound coffee cans full of dry Canadian peat moss and a handful of Superphosphate or bone meal with some of the top soil and build a cone-shaped mound in the bottom of the hole. Next, remove the rose plant from the bucket and prepare to prune. Even though the plants are pre-pruned, they need some more work. Side branches that tend to grow inward should be trimmed. Also, if the green canes are over eight inches tall above the bud union (the thickened portion on top of the shank from which canes extend), they should be pruned back to above an outside bud. To stimulate new root development it is also recommended to re-trim the ends of the roots just a half inch. All broken roots also are removed at the break. Now you are ready for planting.

Test the level of the bud union to the soil level. If the bud union is level with the bed, you may fit and plant the roots erect over the soil cone. If the bud union is too deep, add more top soil to the cone. If the bud union extends above the soil level in the bed, you must lower the mound to continue to plant.

Add soil and peat moss to the hole until it is about three-fourths filled. Then, from an open-ended garden hose, add water to the hole until it is filled to the rim. Let the water percolate down. Now add some root stimulator or Ortho Up-start to a bucket of water and pour this over the remaining depression. The soil will already have settled some, and the bud union eventually will end up about two inches below the garden soil level. That is extra protection for severe freezes that could kill the improved rose variety that was budded onto the under stock (usually Dr. Huey or *R. rugosa*). Now finish up by mounding the excess soil over the canes. That protects them against unfavorable weather and slows bud growth while roots are developing. The mound gradually can be removed by June 1 on unwaxed roses. Waxed canes benefit by leaving the mound intact for the larger portion of the first growing season in the garden. It may appear a little odd, but it is safer to keep the mounds in place.

Caring for Roses Through the Seasons

Question: What do you recommend for feeding roses? Last year I used Miracle-Gro. Do you think they need some bonemeal? What are the best sprays or systemics?
Answer: There is nothing wrong with Miracle-Gro. Bonemeal is heavy on phosphorus so you also will need some more nitrogen with it. Systemics added to fertilizers like in Ortho and Fertilome are well-balanced foods for roses that seem to work well against most insects. At least that has been my experience in the past.

In the first year after planting new roses, you should not expect a big production of blooms. It takes time for the roots to restructure contact in their new soil environment. Water the plants about every 10 to 14 days, depending on temperatures and precipitation. I use two 100-foot lengths of Leaky Pipe in the rose garden. It oozes the water out slowly but restores soil moisture thoroughly. Do not feed new roses more than once during their initial year. The phosphate is already in the soil. A half cup of

Brandy

10-20-10 or 8-12-4 would do well for new roses, applied in late June or early July.

Established garden roses should have three feedings each year. The first can be applied in May, the second after the first flowering cycle, and the third in late July to mid-August. Roses should not be fed any later, because they may not harden for winter well with too much plant food. In the second and third feeding, you may use a prepared fertilizer-systemic insect control combination to obtain control of aphids, mites, and other chewing insects.

The use of protective (or preventive) fungicides is also very helpful to prevent spread of three common rose diseases: mildew, blackspot and rust. Although these may not occur at the same time, it is wise to use the best available broad-spectrum disease control, Funginex. It is the only fungicide that controls all three diseases if used exactly as directed on the label. Benomyl will control powdery mildew and partially blackspot, but it will not work against rust. Ferbam is generally a sound rust control. If you can obtain Funginex, you should use it beginning late June and every two to three weeks until mid-September. From the standpoint of safety to bees and other useful insects, Funginex is of practically no concern. Also, for additional insect control needs, Malathion 50 at one tablespoon per gallon of water and/or Orthene at two tablespoons per gallon of water can be sprayed during late evening hours after bees have returned to their hives. Late-hour spraying also avoids foliage burn to tender leaves.

> **Rocky Mountain Tip:**
> Fungus diseases such as powdery mildew, rust, and blackspot are not uncommon in rose gardens. Some varieties are more susceptible than others. You can prevent these diseases by timely spraying with Funginex or Benomyl, systemic fungicides.

Cultural pruning after each bloom cycle assures — with most garden roses — good repeat flowering through the summer. The best way to activate new growth is by pruning just above a five-leaflet leaf. On vigorous plants, we can make the pruning cut above the second five-leaflet leaf counting down from the faded bloom. Spindly growth is unlikely to produce good flowers and should also be pruned.

Late-winter pruning should reduce the overall

Daffodils

size of the over-wintering rose canes to about 8 to 12 inches. After severe winters, they may need pruning to near the soil. Floribunda roses usually need less pruning. Just a thinning of thin stems normally is adequate unless the growth was unusually vigorous the previous year. Hardy climbing roses need not be pruned until after the major June bloom cycle. Climbing hybrid tea roses must be pruned according to the damage done each winter. On climbers, we prune back the most vigorous canes to about four feet. Excellent summer bloom production is the special reward for conscientious pruning. Mini roses are not much in need of pruning. Only exceptionally long stems should be pared.

CARING FOR PERENNIALS

Watering Perennials

Most garden perennials are rooted much deeper than annuals, so watering is needed less frequently. Spring bulbs such as tulips and daffodils need water most as they stretch to bloom. Also, they need watering occasionally during a dry winter. Peonies require most of their water from the time they are budded until full bloom. Delphiniums and lupines should have most of their water as the flowering spikes or stalks develop and again in late summer for a second bloom. Lilies and hemerocallis need watering weekly until after bloom has ended, then only when the other garden plants are watered. Dahlias and cannas need watering every two to three days until frost. Chrysanthemums perform well with moderate watering, except more water is needed when their flowers open in August and September. Roses should be watered deeply every two weeks with a real soaking — their roots are 15 inches down or deeper. Most other perennials will thrive with good watering every five days except in sandy soil where watering a little less every three days is adequate. Perennial beds and roses do respond well to winter watering on a monthly basis unless the ground freezes. I use two 100-foot lengths of Leaky Pipe hose to water my roses. The water oozes out in droplets and overnight the entire rose garden gets a very good drink. Leaky Pipe hose is traded under several names. It is made from recycled automobile tires.

Tulips

How to Control Insects and Diseases on Perennials

Like most other garden plants except weeds, perennials are generous hosts to an assortment of garden insects and diseases.

Rose — Fashion

Insects can be classified as sucking and chewing types. Sucking insects pierce through the plant's epidermis and suck plant juices. They include aphids, thrips, scales, leafhoppers, and mites. Controls for sucking insects include Malathion, Orthene, Di-Syston, and Meta-systox-R. Mites also can be controlled with Kelthane.

Chewing insects make up the remainder. They include grasshoppers, plant bugs, caterpillars, leafrollers, leafbeetles, borers, and saw flies. Few of these are specific. Many are referred to as general feeder insects. Controls for chewing insects include Sevin, Diazinon, Methoxychlor, Cygon, and Orthene. Since the time of the insect attack varies throughout the season, it is recommended that label directions and instructions be followed carefully. If and when you must spray, please proceed only if there is no wind and no rain expected within the next four to six hours. Commercial sticker/spreaders also should be used to obtain the best adhesion of the sprayed chemical to the treated plants. If in doubt, consult with local agricultural authorities.

There are numerous ways to obtain good controls of insects on perennials with non-toxic programs. Bacillus thuringensis has been successfully demonstrated to control the worms or caterpillars of lepidopterous (butterfly) insects. Just a hard water spray can interfere with mites, but this also may damage foliage and flowers. Safer's insecticidal soap works quite well for some gardeners when they need a quick, non-toxic control remedy. But most of the non-toxic chemicals have not worked well in all situations. New control methods are under trial, but it takes time and much investment of money to obtain acceptable results.

Fortunately, in our region, diseases on ornamental plants and flowers are nominal. Powdery and downy mildew may be controlled with Funginex, Benomyl and Acti-dione. Blackspot and rust control for roses already has been discussed. Bacterial blight of apples, pears, hawthorn, and crabapples fortunately does not affect perennial flowers. Rust may be an occasional problem. Funginex, Ferbam, or Captan are accepted controls. Virus diseases are not a large problem overall and hardly so with perennial flowers.

VEGETABLE GARDENING

VEGETABLES grow best in full sun. If you must make a choice of morning or afternoon sun, choose a bed in a noon to late afternoon location for tomatoes, squash, cucumbers, beans, melons, peppers and eggplant. These crops thrive in heat. The morning sun, on the other hand, is most helpful for leafy vegetables, root crops, peas, onions and perhaps sweet corn.

Maintaining excellent tilth and soil texture is simple if you apply organic matter in late fall and again in late March. Turn it under with a spading fork or till it under with a Rototiller. The best organic materials include poultry waste, steer manure, compost, and leaves or leafmold. My tomato patch gets this treatment every year. I use three bags of any of these for about 60 square feet. I know that sounds like a lot, but it makes a big difference in growth and yield of my plants.

If you have had problems with grubs or slugs, an application of sulfur will discourage them temporarily. Disease organisms also have a way of surviving in our garden soils, most often on debris that accumulates during the growing and harvesting seasons. Sulfur is a valuable sanitation aid to reduce the potential carryover of some disease sources from year to year.

Soil preparation with organic materials also improves drainage, moisture retention, and aeration of our soils. Some vegetable crops, such as celery, and strawberries need a more porous soil quality than many others. That brings me to the subject of raised beds. If you enjoy growing some of your own vegetables without putting a strain on your back — you can.

A vegetable garden

Growing Vegetables in Raised Beds

Many good all-purpose vegetable fertilizers are sold at garden outlets. For vegetables that are expected to fruit like tomatoes or peppers we need an 8-12-4 or similar analysis. For green vegetables like lettuce, spinach, rhubarb, etc. we need a 10-5-5 or similar analysis.

Raised beds are a new trend in gardening. They produce earlier, better and without the bending or stooping you may otherwise have to do. And they offer considerable advantages, particularly in higher mountain localities. They warm up much more readily in the spring, they drain much better, and they guarantee good soil aeration. Raised beds also are neater in appearance and easier to weed.

Raised beds may appeal to anyone, not just the elderly or handicapped. We don't have to punish our physical well-being by overdoing anything. Raised beds are a little extra work initially, but they pay off for you in a short time.

There are now several methods recommended for constructing raised beds. The best is a wooden frame built from redwood (which does not decay very fast). Let's say you want a garden 8 feet by 12 feet, about 100 square feet. Two sections 4 feet by 12 feet are easier to manage. Leave only a foot between them, so the space your raised bed occupies will not be too large or in anyone's way. Designs and ideas on how to build raised beds can be found in several garden construction books, such as Ortho's *Garden Construction Know-How.* One of the easiest ways to construct raised beds is with used railroad ties. These need to be bolted down and fastened at the ends. A raised-bed height of 8 or 12 inches is not much, but it helps the veggies and strawberries grow faster, because the soil warms up so much sooner and drains so much better.

A dedicated gardener I once knew called her raised beds her "arthritic garden." It was fashioned from cinder blocks bound together by mortar. If you don't need too large a bed or have room for several, a large, old truck tire or tractor tire will allow you to raise several kinds of vegetables in a relatively compact area.

The soil on these raised beds should be fluffy, organic, and one that warms up early. Strips of black plastic can be used to further warm up the soil mix, which should contain about 30 percent lightweight materials, such as vermiculite, perlite, or bark dust.

A large planter box about 12 to 20 inches high can be placed on a sunny patio to raise vegetables or kitchen herbs.

There is another way of creating a raised bed. It involves digging a 12-inch-wide walk (8 inches deep) between two flower or vegetable beds, with the soil placed on top. Then the walk is filled during the season with organic wastes, and at the end of the growing season, another 12-inch-wide walk is dug on the outside, covering the previous walk with the soil from the new walk. This sounds like a simple, practical idea that requires no construction; however, don't forget that your vegetable garden will be two feet wider each year.

Question: What is the difference between buying seeds in a store or ordering them out of a catalogue? Answer: There is no difference. Often you can get more of the newer varieties out of a catalogue. The seed racks don't have the latest until the seed supply has increased several years after introduction.

How Big Should Your Garden Be?

GARDEN SIZE

If you are an experienced gardener, you can determine from successes of the past how much garden is right for you. You will have learned how much weeding, hoeing, cultivating, or watering you must do to have a neat garden — one that you are proud of and that produces well.

A novice, however, is likely to attempt a little too much at first. My experience — after helping kids, adults, 4-H leaders and members, and even Boy Scouts in getting started for many years — is that if I cut their intent in half, their interest will not vanish too quickly. For a novice, a garden 8 by 8 or 10 by 10 is quite enough. You can always increase your plantings next time if you feel you can handle more.

One good garden size is 20 by 30 feet. Some crops take a lot more space than others. Many gardeners or beginning gardeners I have counseled love asparagus, which does well in alkaline clay soil. But those gardeners often are ready to eat those fat, white-to-green stalks even before they get the roots planted. And when I tell them that it takes at least two years to get good production, their faces drop noticeably. Finally, when I mention that it takes at least 10 plants per family member and preferably 15 plants, they think I am a little overzealous. How hard it is to learn some things.

If you are a very ambitious gardener who intends to raise all the veggies for a family of four, then we are talking in the range of 1,500 square feet of garden. That's more like 30 by 50 feet or 25 by 60 feet. A garden that big makes one early to bed and early to rise, because you cannot work well or for very long in the heat of each day.

A vegetable garden also can be created in small planters and tubs on the patio or balcony, or in hanging baskets. I admit this is a tiny attempt, indeed. But it works with a little patience and effort and helps add ambiance. Crops that are well suited for container gardening are radishes early, followed by tomatoes or cucumbers, such as Patio or Spacemaster. You also can grow several kitchen herbs, chives, or green onions in patio tubs or containers. And leaf lettuce or spinach is certainly worth several pickings. We don't need a lot of garden to prove the gardener in us.

Rocky Mountain Tip:

If you live in a townhouse or otherwise have very little space for vegetables you can get good results from patio tubs, whiskey barrels, and other planters. Some vegetables grow well on a patio or a balcony. Some don't adjust as easily.

Many elderly or handicapped gardeners start out with tubs and eventually may take a small lot in a neighborhood community garden. Children's gardens should be very small at the outset, until the excitement urges the kids on and on. And Mom and Pop, please don't put the kids' garden patch behind the scenes somewhere. They must be right in front so everyone can admire their efforts and give them encouragement. I have judged and encouraged a lot of 4-H gardens. And when it came to rewards, we recognized every effort, no matter how small. I have never forgotten the encouragement I received, as a kid gardener, from strangers.

Community Gardens

Community gardens are especially inviting for those who have little space to garden at home. People of all ages can participate in community gardening.

In many towns and cities vacant land has been

set aside to afford flower and vegetable raising as a form of recreation. National organizations like Gardens-For-All have been actively involved in creating such opportunities for children and the elderly. In Denver, Salt Lake City, Albuquerque, and many other cities of the West, and their suburbs, private and public organizations have supplied access to water and have prepared the soil in advance so private citizens and youngsters can become active gardeners. In some locations, volunteer instructors have given valuable assistance to help these gardeners experience success in their endeavor. In many instances, major seed companies and garden centers have donated seed and plants to make many dreams come true. Community gardens produce excellent crops, and are a healthy activity and a new skill for gardeners.

Choices for Rocky Mountain Gardeners

THE BEST VEGETABLES TO GROW

Most people are tempted to grow many different vegetables. But before you make your choices, there are several important assessments you must honestly make. They are the size of your garden, the amount of energy you can depend on (or family assistance you can be sure of), and what you really like to eat.

I recommend that you start modestly and increase your program as you learn.

How much of your garden gets at least six to eight hours of sun each day can limit your plans. Actually the longer you improve the soil, the better organized your garden becomes. Then it is proper to enlarge a garden, because you will have learned good timing, and you can use your spare moments wisely. A novice gardener really needs a guiding hand to learn some of the tricks.

The amount of energy you — and perhaps other members of the household — can produce counts very realistically toward deciding what and how many vegetables to plant. You may have other endeavors, such as flowers and fruits, that take time and special care. Enjoy what you are doing; don't allow yourself to become a slave of your garden. That also means don't be too soft on yourself. A small garden that is well tended and weed-free will encourage you. A weedy patch may produce vegetables, but you won't be proud of it, and you won't show it off.

> **Rocky Mountain Tip:**
> Enjoy your garden and the work in it, but not to the point of exhaustion or slavery. Gardening is good for you. Keep it that way.

Be sure not to over-exert yourself. You should know your own limitations — if your heart is not what it used to be, you can follow a schedule of 10 minutes of work, then 20 minutes of rest. You will get much more done when you work on this basis.

There is really no benefit from excessive physical work. I cannot count fatigue as a sound objective. I have been a heart patient for years. I enjoy gardening on a little more leisurely basis now. But the achievement of the fresh, red tomatoes, the ripe cherries and apples, the peaches when the weather allows it, the raspberries, gooseberries, and grapes are well worth my time. And they all generate a little self-esteem.

The real test, however, is what you like to eat and what your family will enjoy. These crops are the ones you want to raise. You can be generous with your friends and neighbors if you have excesses. But don't belittle your effort by begging someone to eat what you raised but really don't like.

While I am writing about what is best for you to grow, I will divide the more popular vegetables into categories and let you choose yourself. Some choices even can be double-cropped. But it is your garden, and you should decide.

Early Vegetables

These can be planted or sown before the last killing frost. But to sow the seeds in our Western

Peas

Broccoli

region much before April Fool's Day is risky, because the soil generally does not warm up quickly enough to help seed germination. Good early crops are:

Beets	Peas
Carrots	Radishes
Celery	Spinach
Leaf Lettuce	Swiss Chard
Onions (seed or sets)	Turnips
Broccoli	Brussels Sprouts
Cabbage	Cauliflower

Late-Planted Crops

These can be grown either from seed or started plants. But they need a warming soil even more than the early crops. I must admit that I rarely plant my tomatoes before June 10 in Denver. If I lived on the east side of town, I would plant about 10 to 14 days earlier. The most successful late crops are:

Bush Beans	Green Pepper
Pole Beans	Pumpkin
Sweet Corn	Squash
Eggplant	Tomatoes

Sweet Corn

Second-Crop Gardening

If you want to garden with zest and vigor, you can use the same space twice. Some second-crop vegetables, such as late-planted broccoli, yield well into October in a warm, sheltered spot. Other good second crops are leaf lettuce, spinach, and radishes. A second sowing of beets and turnips may be delightful for your October table. A late planting of onion sets will supply you with fresh onions for your salads as long as they last.

What you can get late from your garden is often

Zucchini

the finest of the season. When old mean winter is blowing down our necks, you might like to beat him out of something that others find hard to get. The joy of success and the taste of it is worth it.

Vegetables That Are Harder to Grow

Some of the more difficult crops, because of our generally shorter seasons, are Celeriac and various kinds of melons. These will be discussed later in more detail.

There are also several perennial vegetables that may be very desirable, if you can dedicate enough space to them. They are:

Asparagus	Jerusalem Artichoke
Horseradish	Rhubarb

FROST-FREE DATES

When Is It Really Safe to Plant?

Deciding when it is safe to plant is one concern you will have to determine on your own, since conditions can vary greatly in different parts of the Rocky Mountain region. In some years due to the weather, a growing season in any locality of the West may be 20 percent shorter or longer than average. You can even reach for a Farmer's Almanac and obtain weather data from it that won't be realized. But we are not the only ones who are victimized by unreliable weather. In 1984, for instance, I saw a lot of badly damaged palms along the Gulf Coast. And I was assured by locals that this had been caused by a very severe winter, the most severe in over 20 years.

Without attempting to fix any blame for bad weather, it would appear only practical to curtail weather risks by conservative assessment of average frost-free dates. Extra shelter may be useful, but gambling on the weather is with only fair odds. My tomatoes may be outdoors earlier than June 10, but the extra warming of the soil in two weeks also makes the plant grow so much better. In fact, I suspect they catch up with earlier transplants in less than 30 days.

Learn not to trust the weather more every year. Sooner or later, you'll pay a sad price for it.

What to Grow in the Mountains

What vegetables you can grow in the Rockies depends to a large degree on shelter and elevation. At up to 6,500 feet elevation, you can grow almost any vegetable that is successful in the plains — unless your frost-free season is less than 100 days.

From 6,500 feet to 7,500 feet, you most likely are

Early planted tomatoes can be wrapped with quilts or old comforters. It's work. I'd rather dig up the plant for a few days, pot it and move it into the garage until the weather warms up again.

Peas on the vine

better off sticking to vegetables that can stand cold nights.

Above 7,500 feet, you generally are limited to the crops listed below, unless you have a plastic tent or some other means of controlling temperatures. Cold frames equipped with heating cables will let you start many plants earlier than outdoors. But you need shelter also because soils warm up quite slowly.

These vegetables are hardier:

Beets	Broccoli	Brussels Sprouts
Carrots	Cabbage	Cauliflower
Leaf Lettuce	Peas	Radishes
Onions	Swiss Chard	Turnips
Kohlrabi	Horseradish	Rhubarb

America's Most Popular Vegetable

TOMATOES

Tomatoes are America's most popular vegetable or fruit. Nearly 75 percent of all gardeners raise some type of tomato.

Tomatoes are a native of the Americas, although they are now widely grown in most parts of the civilized world. Recently, on a trip to Christchurch, New Zealand, I found Sweet 100's in private gardens. Some short-season varieties are grown in Alaska.

Rocky Mountain Tip:

Tomatoes need a warm well-drained organically enriched soil. They thrive in heat of the Western sun. They root deeply and start to fruit as soon as nights remain above 54 degrees. Some are early, some are late. All are delicious to eat.

Tomatoes

Hotcaps and walls-of-water retain daytime sun's warmth and shelter plants from cool and freezing nighttime hours early in the season.

In the Rocky Mountain and Great Basin regions, tomatoes are highly successful, because high light intensity and warm sun create an environment they prefer.

The plants can be grown in the home beginning in March and set outside two months later, after a determined hardening-off process. The hardening-off process allows the plants to get used to outdoor temperatures and conditions little by little, until they can be left on a patio overnight in temperatures above 35 degrees. Tomatoes also can be purchased growing in six-packs or in individual containers for transplanting in May. Some growers like to place their plants outdoors early under hot-caps (a cone-shaped protective cap that keeps temperature warmer at night) or behind so-called walls-of-water, which are clear plastic enclosures of the plant — outside walls are filled with water. This protects the tomato plant against cold weather damage.

We cannot change the soil temperature very fast, which affects only root development. It is altogether safer to let the garden soil warm up before setting plants in it.

Tomatoes need a well-drained soil that is crumbly and rich with humus. I usually turn several bushels of compost, leafmold and manure under in my tomato bed to enrich the soil. If you miss only one year of enriching the soil, your results will fall off noticeably.

I let my tomato plants remain on the shaded patio until early June. It makes the roots pot bound in small plastic containers. But when I set the plants in the garden, the new freedom of the roots makes them feel so much better.

There are several valid techniques in setting out tomato plants. I dig to a depth of 10 inches, place some superphosphate or bonemeal in the planting hole and remove the lower leaves before planting. Each leaf axil under soil will develop more roots. Some gardeners lay the stems horizontally below the soil. Either method is acceptable. Used automobile tires make good raised beds for tomatoes — if you have enough room for tires.

You can train your plants in several ways. I use metal stakes called Tomato Towers to support my plants. I also use some round and square wire baskets and let the plants climb on them. These reuseable wire forms work well to support the plants and also conserve space.

You also can speed maturity of your tomatoes by using solar energy. Black plastic, laid in strips over the soil, will keep the soil warmer and allow collected solar energy to keep the area warmer into the night. Tomatoes usually set fruit two weeks earlier with this treatment. You also can collect flat, three-pound pebbles along a mountain stream and carry them home. Then you apply black spray paint to each rock and lay them under the plants above the soil in threes and fours. They, too, collect radiant heat and emit it at night, making the plants set fruit earlier. Most tomato plants do not set fruit (pollinate successfully), however, until night temperatures remain above 55 degrees.

> **Rocky Mountain Tip:**
> In mountain valleys it is quite a challenge to raise tomatoes, because the nights are so cool. A small plastic cover over a frame may give your plants a better fruit set and improve their performance. In Great Britain, almost everybody does it.

After planting, I apply Ortho Up-Start or any other root stimulator to shelter the plants from shock. Do not expose plants to the hot sun suddenly.

This may cause sunburn that damages the foliage of the transplants.

Tomatoes also may be grown in hanging baskets on a patio or balcony. Certain cascading varieties, such as Burpee's Basket King and Park's Goldie Hybrid, are suitable for this culture. Water these plants daily, especially in warm weather. Fertilize monthly with an 8-12-4 or 6-10-4 fertilizer.

The major tomato diseases are Fusarium and Verticillium blight, which are that most often cause premature loss of plants. However, these are not the only diseases, nearly 40 tomato disorders are known in the United States. Fortunately, our dry climate makes many of them of no consequence in the Rockies. Also, nematodes (microscopic soil worms) are only a rare problem in the West.

The Best Tomatoes for Your Garden

In recent years, many new hybrid tomato varieties have been introduced with the designation VFN or VFFNT behind their names. These letters mean that they are resistant to Verticillium and Fusarium blights or Verticillium Fusarium (Strain 1 and 2) nematodes and tobacco mosaic diseases.

Some of the most highly disease-resistant tomato varieties, and their times from planting to maturity, are:

Tomatoes

Freedom — 75 days
Celebrity — 70 days
Gurney Girl — 75 days
Park's Extra Early — 52 days
Big Pick — 65 days
Park's Whopper — 70 days

A large number of tomatoes are rated VF or VFN and include these resistant varieties:

Pole King — 75 days
Better Boy Hybrid — 75 days
Rushmore Hybrid — 66 days
Beef Eater Hybrid — 85 days
Early Cascade — 52 days
Floramerica — 70 days
Terrific — 70 days
Small Fry Hybrid — 65 days
Toy Boy Hybrid — 55 days
Burpee's Super Steak — 80 days
Burpee's Early Pick Hybrid — 62 days
Beefmaster Hybrid — 80 days

There are still other fine tomato varieties that I am very fond of. These include:

Early Girl — 54 days

Spring Giant Hybrid — 68 days
Sweet 100 — 70 days
Fantastic Hybrid — 65 to 70 days

There literally are dozens more varieties, depending on who is selling the most seed in your locality. Some of the older, open-pollinated, non-hybrid tomato varieties are not quite comparable to the newer hybrids, especially since they are not disease-resistant. If you cannot obtain a satisfactory choice locally, the major mail-order houses will certainly be happy to supply you with their best.

One little but important reminder: We know that tomatoes also attract a variety of insects. Among the most feared is the tomato hornworm, an ugly critter that can reach three or more inches in length and devour a lot of a plant in a day. I dust my tomatoes from the day I set them in the garden with a tomato dust. Another feared tomato pest is whiteflies. They are, at best, difficult to control. In our current arsenal of chemicals, Resmethrin is a good control for whiteflies. The flies also succumb to a surprise attack with Malathion 50.

Many tomatoes are over-watered. Under fair soil conditions, they should do well with a deep irrigation about every 10 to 12 days. In containers, they need some watering every day. A black spot opposite the stem is known as blossom end rot, a non-pathogenic disorder caused by over-watering or irregular watering. To correct the problem, try to avoid over-watering or irregular watering.

You also can prune off flowers forming after October 10. They probably won't make anything worthwhile during the current season.

Not all vegetables are uniquely successful or easy to grow under all conditions. But I will point out those that are suitable for higher elevations outdoors. I am reminded of a very ingenious setup near Frisco, Colorado, at an elevation of about 9,500 feet. Some resourceful young people put up a very crude set of posts and rolled a heavy-duty piece of clear plastic over the top and down the sides. They raised the plastic by rolling it up on warm mornings. Then they rolled the sides down at sundown. It was amazing to me that inside this "tent" they actually raised excellent tomatoes and few summer squash, along with a lot of leafy and root vegetables. Sure, it was a little extra work. But it demonstrated ingenuity and a will to succeed. If you are up in a mountain valley, you might want to try this yourself. Most native

Question: For the past two growing seasons I have had serious problems with whiteflies on my tomatoes and other plants. I have tried several products without success. Is there any way to control this pest?
Answer: Whiteflies are our most serious garden pest problem. They have become more numerous every year. It is possible to hurt them if you spray daily with Malathion 50. It may take seven or more warm days of spraying. And you must sneak up on them, surprise them. Then they cannot fly away before you hit them with the spray. Resmethrin may also work well against whiteflies.

VEGETABLES FROM A TO Z

Asparagus foliage

lumber sawmills should be able to supply your needs.

A

Jerusalem Artichoke — The roots or tubers of this delicious weed are crunchy when eaten raw or grated in salads. Tubers are planted in May, six inches deep, preferably in a waste area. If you can leave them there and dig only what you need, you have a perennial supply. The plants are like sunflowers and a bit unruly. But the taste pays for it all.

Asparagus — This is one of my favorite vegetables. I like it best cold after marinating the cooked spears in a vinegar and oil dressing for several hours. You can complete this symphony of five-star taste by sprinkling chopped chives over the salad. The really big problem in growing asparagus is that it takes 10 plants or more per family member. You have to have an extra 250 square feet of space for 40 plants. Do not attempt to harvest any asparagus spears until the second year from plants or the fourth year from seed. To plant, you must dig a trench 12 to 15 inches wide and eight inches deep. Spread the roots out radially and cover with about three inches of soil until tiny shoots appear. Add two more inches of soil, until the trench has been refilled. Water thoroughly once a week. If you purchase roots, soak them in a bucket of water for 48 hours before planting.

Question: I have an asparagus bed heavily overgrown with a grass called quackgrass. Is there a weed killer that will work without making the asparagus inedible or killing them?
Answer: You will notice that the quackgrass emerges long before the asparagus spears come out of the soil. As soon as the grass is eight inches tall, spray it with Round Up contained in Ortho Kleen Up. The chemical translocation to the roots will not affect the asparagus until they grow above the soil. The chemical will not affect the wholesomeness of your asparagus spears later.

B

Bush Snap Beans — Plant seed after frost danger is over and soil has warmed well. Use Captan as a seed protectant against diseases. Make a furrow 2½ inches wide and insert the seed about three inches apart. You can plant another row about four weeks later to amplify your supply of snap beans. Among green stringless beans are excellent varieties, such as Burpee's Tenderpod (50 days) and Greensleeves (56 days). Topcrop is another excellent producer (49 days). Gold Crop waxbean (54 days) is among the best. For raising beans on poles, consider Kentucky Wonder, available in both green and wax. Blue Lake pole bean also has about a 60-day maturity time. If you have enough garden space, you also can raise pinto and red kidney beans. They are a commercial crop in various portions of the region.

> **Rocky Mountain Tip:**
> Beans are relatively easy to raise, can be picked more than once, and are simply delicious. Watch for bean beetles. They are the only insect that damages the bean crop.

Beets — Beets are very hardy and easy to grow. They grow better in sandy soils. In clay soils, some humus must be turned under to keep the soil of good quality, texture, and drainage. Sow seed about a half inch deep in rows and thin to two inches after seedlings have established well. The best trick to avoid a lot of thinning is to mix beet and radish seed and plant them together in the same row. Since radishes

Beet foliage

Beans

mature in 30 days, beets have more room to develop in about 60 days. Water every 5-7 days. Harvest when beet roots are two inches in diameter.

Thinning yields tender greens, if you like them. After being introduced to Silver Beet tops from Australia during World War II, I have lost my enthusiasm for them. They were tougher than New Zealand spinach. Little Bull is a gourmet baby beet and very tender (56 days). Detroit Dark Red is still the most widely used variety. Red Ace is a 53-day hybrid that has fewer zones in the root.

Broccoli

Broccoli — Where the nights are cool, especially in mountain valleys, broccoli produces an abundance of delicious and tender sprouts. Plant moderately deeper than in the seedling flat. Broccoli should be watered every 5-8 days. Our daughter has grown some in her garden near Eagle, Colorado, and when they get tired of broccoli, I get the last sack full of sprouts. They are tender and tasty, actually much better than commercially grown sprouts. Harvest when the flowers are evident. Three good varieties are Bonanza Hybrid, Green Goliath, and Green Cornet Hybrid. All mature in about 55 days.

Brussels Sprouts — This crop is best started in early summer and takes about 90 days to mature. Water every 5-8 days; better when the nights get cooler in October. Jade Cross E Hybrid is among the best for home gardens. This is another crop that does well in the mountain valleys up to 9,500 feet.

C

Cabbage

Cabbage — This is a fine crop if you have the patience and the space. I have raised a few heads and I am sure home-grown cabbage is extra sweet and flavorful. You have to fight the cabbage worms all the way to get acceptable heads. If you are limited in space, go for crops that you can harvest more than once. Once planted, water every 4-6 days — harvest when heads are well-formed and solid. Excellent varieties are All America winners Emerald Cross Hybrid (63 days), Savoy Ace Hybrid (85 days), Ruby Ball Hybrid (red 68 days), and Savoy King Hybrid (90 days). The shorter-maturity plants can be set out in partial shade as a second crop in July, after the peas have finished.

Carrots — A good crop for every garden. You can grow a lot of carrots, and you will love them fresh out of the ground. Sow two or three seed packets 10 days apart. Water intermittently, and then

Carrots

harvest when carrot roots are 3 inches or longer. Pull test carrots to determine progress. What you don't use by October, you can mulch with compost 10 inches deep and dig up during winter. Since few gardeners have really deep soils, you will do best with Danvers Half Long and Nantes Half Long. Treat carrot seed with Thiram or Captan to avoid failures common in cool, wet weather during spring.

Question: We have a problem growing carrots. For several years they have been infested with maggots and then they become woody and stunted. How can we control these pests?
Answer: Treat your soil with Diazinon. You can use the 5% granules or Diazinon garden dust before sowing the seed or a side dressing or drench on either side of the row of carrots after the seedlings have merged. Repeat the side dressing after 3 weeks.

    Cantaloupes — Melons need great warmth and a long season. Once planted, water frequently — every 3-4 days. That is why they grow so well commercially in the Arkansas Valley of Colorado near Rocky Ford. Harvest when netting turns flat and melon appears orange. Many newer hybrids promise mature melons in 75 to 85 days. I always wonder if they meant from bloom? If you have extra space, try cantaloupes where the summer is very warm and

Cantaloupe

nights are not too cool. I have noticed a lot of cantaloupe plantings with small fruit. The leaves don't taste very good. And maturity depends on warmth. If you are in a community where cantaloupes succeed, the word will soon get around to you.

Cauliflower — The best way to try this member of the cabbage family is to secure plants and place them in rows 1½ to two feet apart in morning sun and afternoon shade. Water every 3-5 days. You have to pull the outer jacket leaves together to encourage the flower head to grow and remain white. Variety Purple Head is much easier to grow. It matures purple, not white, and is very tender. Snow Crown Hybrid and Snow King Hybrid are All America winners. A good crop for the higher elevations and mountain valleys.

Celeriac or Root Celery — This is not a popular crop but is very delicious. I like it pressure-cooked for about eight minutes, then peeled and sliced ⅜ inch thick, and marinated in vinegar and oil or Italian dressing. To grow celeriac takes super soil, and it should be watered every 2-3 days. Will mature in 130 days or more. You may need more than a learner's permit to succeed.

Celery — It takes extra care and room to raise good celery. It is a crop for professional growers. Celery should be watered every 3-5 days and takes 120 or more days to mature. Then the blanching is a special process. Burpee offers Tendercrisp (105 days) and Golden Self-Blanching (115 days). If you can purchase a ten-pack of small plants, you can experiment with them. If you succeed, you can expand the following year.

Swiss Chard

Swiss Chard — Between pickings of spinach, chard is a good summer green that produces abundantly. Should be watered every 3-5 days. Harvest before the leaves exceed 10 inches. It is as good a source of vitamin A and C as spinach. Watch out for slugs. They like chard, too. Sawdust over the soil near chard is a fair discouragement. Excellent in mountain valleys.

Sweet Corn — If your garden is 10 by 20, you can have at least one or two rows of this delicious crop. Homegrown sweet corn is worth the extra effort. I remember with joy the corn feasts with horticulturists George and Sue Kelly when they lived in the Denver area. In recent years, a most dramatic improvement has been made with sweet corn. It is known as the E.H. factor (Everlasting Heritage). Earliglow E.H. matures in 75 days. Kandy Korn E.H.

Sweet Corn

takes 90 days to be ready to pick. These lasting-sugar-content genetic hybrids are worthy of consideration. Most of the seed now is used by commercial growers. The corn remains sweet up to eight days from picking. Give your sweet corn a real shot of nitrogen fertilizer around July 4th. Most lawn fertilizers will do. If you want an earlier-maturing variety, I recommend Early Sunglow (62 days) and Gold Rush Hybrid (63 days). Silver Queen E.H. is a white variety that matures in 87 days. White Sunglow matures in 65 days.

> **Rocky Mountain Tip:**
>
> When you select sweet corn seed for your garden, look for the varieties with the designation E.H. They are super sweets. Eventually more varieties of this type will become available in the seed trade. Watch for them.

Cucumber — The burpless hybrids have moved out in front in popularity. Many new varieties are gynoecious (female flowers only). It takes a male pollinator variety to produce cucumbers. Make sure the male seed are included in the seed packet . . . and please, plant all the seed. You can guess what happens when the male seed remains in the packet.

Cucumbers need a well-drained, rich soil. It pays to plant a shovel full of manure six inches under the seed in a hill. When in production, cucumbers need watering more frequently than other vine and summer crops. So they should be in the lower area of the garden to prevent over-irrigation of tomatoes or pep-

Cucumbers

Question: What is the secret for getting cucumbers to produce? These plants came up from 12 seeds, were full of blossoms, but produced only two useable cucumbers? Can you help me out?
Answer: I believe there are two possible reasons for your evidently poor crop. The first is that the variety you planted likely was a hybrid. Some of these have only female flowers. The seed companies usually include a male pollinator variety in such a packet. Possibly none of the male seeds grew or none were sown. Anyhow in the future, plant the whole packet. The second possible cause for lack of fruiting is cool nights in June and July. Some cucumber blossoms don't set in temperatures below 55 degrees F.

pers. Pick the fruits before they exceed six inches. When cucumbers mature, the plant stops producing. Some varieties, such as Saladin, can be picked early for pickles or grown a little longer for salad slicers.

> **Rocky Mountain Tip:**
>
> If cucumbers taste bitter it is undoubtedly due to irregular irrigation. Cukes must have plenty of water. Plant them as far away as you can from tomatoes and peppers. Cucumbers develop quickly. In only a few days you can pick a 6-inch fruit from a small start.

Several newer varieties are called bush cucumbers. They produce full-sized cukes on a very small vine suitable for patio tubs and hanging baskets. The burpless hybrids such as Sweet Success and Sweet Slice mature in 58 to 62 days. Pot Luck can be grown in an even smaller pot in 53 days. Plant three seeds to a hill and keep only the best two. Enjoy cucumbers fresh off the vine in salads, dips, or as pickles.

E

Eggplant — I like fried eggplant, but it does not grow as easily for me as tomatoes. Beauty Hybrid is two weeks earlier than Black Beauty and matures in about 67 days. Water eggplant every 3-6 days, depending on the soil. Most oval-shaped varieties have similar maturities. The long, slender Ichiban Hybrids are a week earlier yet. I just don't like the name eggplant. The French call them aubergines, which sounds much better.

G

Garlic — This pungent member of the *Allium* genus is highly rated for select culinary uses. It grows from cloves (bulb sections) planted in April. Matures in about 100 days. Harvest the bulbs in the fall, store some for culture next year, and enjoy the rest with selected foods. Garlic should be treated like an onion.

H

Horseradish — Roots initially are spring-planted and should be watered weekly. When you harvest in late fall, return the upper portion of the root to the soil for next year's crop. The remainder is yours to transfer into horseradish sauce. A good, well-drained soil is a basic requirement.

K

Kohlrabi — This interesting plant produces a large, turnip-like bulb above the ground on its stem. Kohlrabi is available in green and purple and should be watered every 3-5 days. It matures in about 55 to 60 days and can be eaten raw or cooked. I prefer them cooked and sliced in a creamy sauce. Grand Duke Hybrid was an All America winner.

L

Lettuce — No matter how tiny your garden is, you have enough space for a row of lettuce. There are the looseheads, the crip heads, the cos or Romaine,

Question: When and how do you plant garlic seed? I have a sackful to plant.
Answer: Garlic seed is planted the same way as onion seed in early spring. About April 1 to 10 is fine. Plant the seed about a half inch deep in a furrow. The rest will take care of itself.

Garlic

Kohlrabi   *Leaf Lettuce*

and the butterhead lettuce. To make a salad really colorful, grow some Ruby, which is intensely shaded red. Salad Bowl is another loosehead that won All America awards. The butterhead or Bibb lettuce has a different texture I like. You can sow seed when soils warm to 52 degrees or higher. Don't cover the seed. They need light for germination. Water lettuce every 3-5 days. You can pick leaf lettuce several times. You can even raise lettuce in tubs on a patio or a balcony. Lettuce is a superb crop in mountain valleys.

O

Onion — If you like to flavor your food or have fresh green onions at your table, this is a good crop, since it does not require much care or attention. Onions are very easy to grow from seed, from sets or from small plants. From seed, it takes at least a part of your season to obtain green onions and may take up to 120 days with excellent, well-drained soil to make two-to three-inch bulbs. From sets you can serve green onions or scallions at your table in about four weeks. Onion plants are certain to produce excellent onions for winter storage in all locales, except in the higher mountain areas. Onion sets work well in planters and tubs on a balcony or patio. I stick the bulbs (sets) in the ground between tomato plants and, presto, in four weeks I have a tasty harvest. I then push another set in the same spot and 30 days later I have another table serving. This works well through the season. Some organic gardeners might have you believe that the onion's pungent fragrance drives bugs away. That may be partly true, but it

Onions

Rocky Mountain Tip:

Onions grow best in a light gritty soil. From sets it is easy to produce a 3 to 4 inch onion in a normal summer. When you dig your crop let them dry for a few days in the sun. They will store longer and better in a root cellar. You can also freeze a bunch for later uses.

doesn't work against onion maggots that devour the lower end of onions below the soil. Diazinon works well against the maggots, but you have to apply it before you plant. When you notice the damage, it is already too late.

Some of the best onions for the garden are Yellow Sweet Spanish, White Sweet Spanish Grano types, and Crystal Wax, which are milder than most. In mid-September, you can walk down the tops, which allows the bulbs to mature. When you dig the bulbs, leave them lying on top of the soil for a few days to dry. You can store some of your onions if you have a cool dugout (38 to 40 degrees) or a protected crawl space below your home where it won't freeze. Otherwise, you can peel the onions and freeze them until you are able to use your harvest. Try not to store your crop too long. It eventually may deteriorate. Commercial onion growers have developed controlled storage to a fine science. You cannot duplicate this easily.

P

Parsnips — If you like to use these at the table and space is no problem, Hollow Crown parsnips do well in a rich, well-prepared soil. Water parsnips every 3-5 days. Parsnips are very similar to carrots, only they need a deeper soil quality. Frost will not damage parsnips. You can harvest them all winter long if you cover the row with enough compost or mulch to keep the soil from freezing. Parsnips take a long season. They should be thinned to four inches to develop freely.

Peas — Peas are a very good garden vegetable. However, I would not recommend raising pod peas, because the frozen product you can buy at your market is excellent in quality, and you don't have to pick and husk them. What I would like you to try, if you have not already, are the edible-pod peas.

I first tasted Sugar Snap in 1977 in Boise, Idaho, when they had not even been named yet. Then, in

Peas

1978, they were awarded the rare All American Gold Medal Award, because they were the greatest breakthrough in vegetable breeding in 25 years or more. This variety and some others that have come out since then are so delectable raw off the vine that they are used more often in dips. The shell or husk is sweet and edible like the peas inside. A newer variety is called Sugar Ann, and it does not have to be trellised three feet like Sugar Snap. Burpee also lists Sugar Bun (56 days) and Sweet Snap (64 days). Have fun and enjoy this good munching from the garden.

Sweet Peppers (and hot peppers, too) — Sweet pepper I like, but hot peppers don't go well with my European-bred digestive system. I remember the first Jalapeño pepper I ate in Roswell, New Mexico — it was also the last. Sweet peppers are a very good crop

Parsley and Peppers

for our Western region. They like lots of hot sun to grow and need water every 5-8 days. Incidentally, the color red or yellow does not mean hot. Some green-podded varieties, such as Hungarian Wax, Long Red Cayenne, and Jalapeño, are the hot items. Bell Boy is a hybrid that does well and produces a smaller pepper with blocky fruit and thick walls. Gypsy Hybrid, also an All America winner, is a pointed pepper where growing seasons are short. It is a very compact plant.

Potatoes — Although potatoes are grown commercially in most of the states, they are not one of the easiest vegetables under general, small-garden conditions. The problem is irrigation. If you have enough space to devote to this crop, you should use an early maturing variety such as Norgold or Norland, or even the ancient Bliss Triumph.

Pumpkin

You can plant as the soil warms, generally after April 15 except in high altitude areas where planting should be delayed until May 1. Water potatoes every 7-8 days. Dust your potatoes along with the tomatoes for insect protection. Potatoes from seed are a novelty item. I have not tried them myself, but reports I have gathered have not given me a very positive feeling. Most gardeners who tried them went back to planting Norlands from seed pieces.

Pumpkins — Here is another crop that needs lots of room to grow in. A small field is not too large. But pumpkins are fun for kids and grandchildren when Halloween rolls around. Big Max takes at least 120 days. Some of these weigh up to 100 pounds — for lots of pumpkin pies. Spirit Hybrid is an All America winner that takes only about 25 square feet per plant. Fruit weighs up to 10 pounds.

If you leave the handle on when you harvest pumpkins, you can store them dry and without freezing for months. Lady Godiva Pumpkin has hull-less seed that needs no shelling after roasting.

R

Radishes — You either like radishes, or you don't. I love them from the French Breakfast types (who could eat them for breakfast unless you drink beer with them) to the Munich beer radishes and the Daikon radish. If you have very friable, well-drained soil and can irrigate them often, you have a good chance to succeed with radishes. Cherry Belle, an All America winner years ago, is still rated well. The Easter Egg Hybrids come in a range of colors.

Radishes

Question: Why can't I ever grow a decent second crop of radishes? I have planted them at all times of the month, light and dark of the moon, early and late. They always grow luxuriant tops and hard bitter little roots. What am I doing wrong? I would like to have a continuous crop all summer long.

Answer: I presume your problem is a common one. We all would like to achieve but our soils and our climate are against us. First, most of our soils are not like those of truck farmers along the Platte and Clear Creek rivers. They have good river soil. Second, our summer temperatures are too warm for radishes. 90 to 95 degrees F. makes several vegetable crops turn unacceptable. If you lived somewhere where the summer highs are in the 70's you would have better success with radishes but few tomatoes, summer squash, or cucumbers. The best suggestion I can give you is to plant radishes in summer shade. And water them a little every day.

Rhubarb

Question: My rhubarb leaves get red spots on them and then turn brown. It does not seem to kill the plant. Is this a disease and if so what should I use to combat it?
Answer: Leaf blights are not uncommon with a number of garden plants. They are caused by fungus organisms. I suggest use of Captan or Zineb fungicides next summer before the red spots appear. It will still allow use of the stalks for kitchen use and enjoyment in pies and preserves.

The ground needs to warm up before radishes will grow well.

Rhubarb — To be sure, this is another garden perennial that you may or may not like as a family. Some families may be divided over rhubarb. It needs good space without root competition but a little out of the way, because we don't plant it often. It takes two to three years to grow it from seed. Most localities offer grown roots for planting. Water rhubarb every 10-14 days. Valentine has deep-red stalks, while Victoria is green-shaded red. Both varieties are popular and tasty and combine well in preserves.

S

Spinach — America and Melody Hybrid are All America award winners. Both yield well — usually three crops if you pick leaves only. Water spinach every 3-5 days; harvest when leaves are 1½ to 2 inches across. Melody Hybrid is resistant to mildew and mosaic, not a big problem in the West. It is a good home garden crop, because it adds to salads when you need it, early and late in the season. The biggest insect problem: leafminers. These are hard to control once they work inside the leaves (between the epidermis walls).

Squash — Until the present time, we had two distinct types, summer and winter squash. Now this has become muddled by new varieties that can be cooked like summer squash or baked fully matured like winter squash. Squash should be watered every 3-4 days. My preference is for the cylindrical zucchini types.

Spinach

Summer squash are very productive when they start. The more you pick them, the more they produce. There are many to choose from. Almost every seed company has developed its own zucchini types. Among the best are Ambassador Hybrid and Gold Rush, All America Winners. Numerous other summer squash may be interesting. Peter Pan is a scalloped squash, and Gourmet Globe is a round zucchini. You also can select the older yellow crookneck and straight types, but their quality is much inferior to the hybrid zucchinis.

Winter squash range in size from the acorn type to the giant Hubbards. Best tasting to my palate are Sweet Mama Hybrid, an improved Buttercup type. Butternut Waltham is another small winter squash of excellent flavor. I don't see many listings of seed for

Question: I have planted spaghetti squash. I don't know how it will look when it is ready to pick. It is a light green now, almost white. How large and what color will it be at maturity?
Answer: The fruit matures about 10 inches long and 9-11 inches in circumference. It will then be tan in color with a little pink overtone. It stores well for a while like a Winter squash.

Summer Squash

Winter Squash

Buttercup Squash

Banana anymore, but the Hubbards are excellent with turkey and beef roast dinners.

Jersey Golden Acorn is one of the new types that can be enjoyed as summer squash and later matured as winter squash. Overgrown summer squash can be oven-broiled with meat and cheese inside, after seeds are removed. What a deightful taste.

T

Turnips — This root vegetable finds a place in many gardens. Sow seeds in early April — water every 3-5 days and harvest when roots are 2-2½ inches in diameter. I don't exalt over turnips, but my wife loves them raw or cooked. Tokyo Cross Hybrid is an All America winner that is of better quality than Purple Top White Globe. Flea beetles are often a problem on turnips. Diazinon will control them.

W

Watermelon — Watermelon is grown from seeds, in early to mid-May. Water every 5-7 days. The problems in growing watermelon are the same as with cantaloupe. Much depends on your growing season and warm nights. I have tried New Hampshire Midget and some of the other small melons. There are many seeds between just a few bites. I like to suggest Sugar Baby. It is extra sweet when ripe. Super Sweet Seedless Hybrid and Triple Sweet Seedless Hybrid must be pollinated by Sugar Baby to produce. Try some for fun if your garden space permits.

WAYS TO WATER VEGETABLES

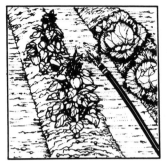

Run hose slowly with a bubbler in furrows or basins, saturating root zone around plants. Stop when saturation is reached.

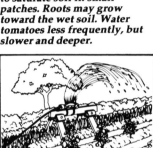

Use drip, or trickle, irrigation to saturate soil in small patches. Roots may grow toward the wet soil. Water tomatoes less frequently, but slower and deeper.

Fill one-gallon nursery cans sunk in ground and let the water ooze into the ground.

Use overhead irrigation only when absolutely essential. This may promote diseases.

Vegetable Maturity   WHEN TO HARVEST

Although many vegetables are harvested premature for commercial shipment we should harvest at peak of maturity from the garden.

Tomatoes should be picked only when they are fully ripe and brilliant red or yellow in color. The warmth of the sun makes them taste extra good.

Beans must be picked when the pods are smooth and snap readily and before the seed inside become noticeable on the outside.

Beets, turnips and carrots should be crisp but not woody. 2½-inch beets and turnips are usually tender. Carrots should have a small core and break readily. Radishes should be picked when they are fully round, about 1½ inches or less in diameter.

Summer squash are best small. Zucchini should only be 6 to 8 inches long. Scallop should only be 2 to 3 inches wide. Winter squash, large or small, must have a skin firm to nail pressure. The same is true for pumpkins.

Sweet corn must be plump with juicy kernels and a light yellow color, except for Country Gentlemen, which is always white at maturity.

Green peppers should be well developed and have thick walls when they are ready for picking. Chili peppers and jalapeños usually do not have as thick a wall.

Cucumbers should be picked when they are 6 to 8 inches long and fairly slender. The larger the seed the less edible they become. Pickles must be picked when firm and 2 and 4 inches long for best pickling.

CONTAINER GARDENING

Growing Vegetables on the Patio

If you live in an apartment or a townhouse and have little or no suitable garden area, you can grow vegetables on a patio or a balcony. You might even try it in window boxes. The only basic requirement for container gardening is that there is adequate light. This can be part sun, and it could be light shade. I have even observed some mirror-like contraptions to increase light on a patio.

Containers you may use can vary from very attractive to unattractive but useful. Redwood tubs and planters are neat and useable for many years. Eventually, they may be stained to keep up their attractive appearance. Much less costly, and frequently a disposable item, are large nursery containers made from compressed cardboard or papier-maché. You get only one season's use out of them, but if they were free, you haven't lost much when their bottoms disintegrate.

Ceramic tubs or large pots are very useful, and if you are careful, they may serve you for years. I have some old clay containers that I bought many years ago in Laguna Beach, California. I still have them and use them occasionally. South of the border, Mexican craftsmen make very large clay containers that are useful. But you have to be careful, because they are not fired too long and are quite soft. All these ceramic pots must have adequate drainage holes. Large plastic buckets can also be useful. Although their appearance is not the greatest, they still perform the task.

Soils you use must be light and fluffy. Mixes of vermiculite, perlite, peat moss, ground bark, and even Terragreen are useful since they drain easily and provide superb aeration. Some commercially sold composts, leafmolds and Jungle Growth potting soil are excellent organics that do not create undesirable odors but still support the growing plants well. Light watering is needed daily in summer, as dehydration is one of the basic problems of pot culture.

The light requirements are very simple. Partial shade to bright full shade are the best. The light quality should be excellent, but direct sun may be a liability.

> **Rocky Mountain Tip:**
>
> If you live in a mountain community like Avon, Colorado, or Snowbird, Utah or Taos, New Mexico, you may want to be safe by planting your tomatoes in tubs or containers, so you can carry them inside on cooler nights. This is not against the rules.

The crops you can raise in containers are limited mostly to those that grow and produce above the ground. Tomatoes are number one. They succeed most often, and a proud gardener can have a little celebration with each harvested fruit. I have also grown onion sets successfully in a bucket. Even radishes may work if it does not get too hot. Leaf lettuce and spinach are easy and should be tried. Pot Luck cucumbers will produce two to six fruits on a single vine. And if you like fresh carrots, try the tiny Little Fingers baby carrots. Chives, parsley, and other kitchen herbs do very well in patio containers as well.

Growing Your Own Herbs   HERBS

Many good books have been written in recent years about herbs. Some herbs are easy to grow in our Western regions; others are more difficult. Among the most popular, some are annuals, some are biennials, and the rest are perennials. In the days before biochemistry was an everyday term, many herbs were used for medicinal purposes. They did not do much to improve the flavor of your food, but they lessened pain, and aided in healing many human ailments.

There has been a decided re-emphasis of these plant-orientated medications. Not everything we have created synthetically has all the same qualities of natural healing herbs. As a youngster, I remember, when a chemist paid me for collecting camomile and plantains. That was some of the earliest money I earned with horticultural plants.

> **Rocky Mountain Tip:**
> You don't need to be a herbalist to grow some parsley and chives to spice up or decorate your table. Chives really add zest to your salads and even egg omelets. Parsley can be very decorative on meat dishes and cold plates as garnish. Both are very easy to raise.

I like to classify herbs according to ease of culture. This group is quite easy and a good start for novices:

Sweet Basil	Lavender
Dill	Mint
Caraway	Sage
Parsley	Chives

The herbs that may suggest gardening experience are mostly perennials. I classify them as more difficult:

Sweet Marjoram	Shallots
Oregano	Taragon
Rosemary	Thyme

Most herbs should be watered every 3-5 days and fertilized monthly. After that, they should do well on their own.

Sweet Basil — Variety Opal is purple in color, but has the same qualities of flavoring as the green variety. It has a clove-like taste and makes a very attractive border.

Dill — A useful herb when you want to make pickles. If it gets away from you, it can turn into a weed. It is usually dried before pickling use.

Parsley — Several different types are available. Some have curled leaves. Some are larger, others smaller. Parsley is used in soups, sauces, meats, and as a garnish. If it is really fresh, I like to nibble it.

Caraway — We use caraway seed to flavor breads, cakes, cookies, and potato salad. It also flavors potatoes and cabbage well when boiled. Caraway is very easily grown. It has white flowers.

Chives — These are among my favorites. We gather what is left in the garden every year before severe cold and chop and freeze. I love chives on scrambled eggs with diced Swiss cheese. Have you ever eaten a chives sandwich? Country rye bread and butter covered with chopped chives. Try it. Chives are as easy to grow as grass.

Lavender — The scents and fragrances of

Sweet Basil

Dill

Parsley

Chives

Lavender

Sweet Marjoram

Sage

Tarragon

Thyme

Oregano

Mint

lavender are used in dried flowers, in the linen, or undergarment drawers. Lavender is easily grown in borders. Even the foliage is sweetly scented.

Sweet Marjoram — Fresh or dried leaves are used to season a variety of different foods. I like it best in German sausages. It also adds flavor in homemade salad dressings. You can grow seedlings in a sunny window and transfer them outdoors when the weather has settled.

Oregano — Used mostly with Italian pasta. Not as easy to grow as some other herbs. Used widely on pizza. Some garden suppliers sell small starts, which may be easier for you than from seed.

Mint — An excellent flavorful herb for teas, juleps, iced beverages, but a real tough weed when it gets out of hand. I have seen it go under sidewalks, patios, and even driveways. You must confine it or it is too late. Needless to say mints are easy to grow.

Rosemary — Prefers an alkaline soil but needs good soil moisture drainage. Seeds germinate very reluctantly, so give it time and patience. Prefers shelter. Dried leaves can be used in soups, stews, and gravies. Flavors chicken well.

Sage — This is almost a weed in the Western areas. Foliage is greyish in color. Very pungent; used in soups, salads, and on game fowl.

Shallots — If you are a weekend gourmet, you cannot go without shallots. Often you only rub the bulbs against a pot or pan to obtain a mild suggestion. They are not hard to grow. They are hard to carry over, outdoors, or in storage. I get only a few new plants every year.

Tarragon — If you need a sweet-scented aroma, tarragon can supply it. Plants will get quite large if you can keep them through dry winters. Tarragon is used with other herbs in a large array of foods.

Thyme — Can be grown for a variety of uses, such as ground cover, between flag stones, and in rock gardens. Thyme is very aromatic. It is used in gravies, clam chowder, and with stews and poultry. A lovely, well-behaved plant.

Vegetable Garden Bugs, Diseases and Controls

INSECTS AND DISEASES

It is indeed unfortunate that insects compete with us for a bountiful harvest. I am not ready to haul out the control artillery every time I see a certain garden insect. However, you will soon learn how incredible their potential to increase is. Some — aphids, for instance — may have as many as 10 to 12 generations in a single year. There are some insects that damage a very specific crop. Others are not as great a concern. Grasshoppers are general feeders that take on anything tasty in their path.

> **Rocky Mountain Tip:**
>
> One of the easiest ways to deter tomato horn-worms and other insects is to dust your vegetable plants repeatedly with a good garden dust. These dusts often combine a fungicide and two or more insecticides. Dusts are quite safe and do not affect edibility of the vegetables at harvest.

There are some cultural ways in which we can make inroads against insects. It is a sound practice to turn under or compost vegetable residues when they occur at harvest time. Weed control also seems to deter insects to other, less cultivated garden areas. Also, you must remember the predatory insects in the garden that help us keep the culprits in check. We must try to protect them and use chemical sprays only when they are recommended and at rates that are safe under normal use.

It is important to read the label each time you prepare to use a garden pesticide. These labels were written and printed at great expense to protect you and your environment. If in doubt, check with a professional county extension agent who has been trained to advise you. Do not apply pesticides to plants close to harvest. Do not store any diluted sprays in unmarked containers. It is absolutely safe to use them up, then double-rinse the equipment,

Duster — infrequently used, although I dust my tomatoes. Most other pesticides are applied in liquid form.

Trigger sprayer — easy to use for small spray jobs in the garden, especially for spot insect or weed controls.

and store it in a dry place until you need to use it again. There are some important rules relating to chemical pesticides. It may be well for you to memorize these:

1. Read the label and understand it. If a waiting period is suggested, follow it carefully. Make certain that the dilution rates are fully understood.

2. Select the chemical pesticides that lists control of the insect on the label so you can count on control. If it rains, wait until foliage is dry before spraying.

3. Apply any pesticide at the suggested timing. If it instructs you to wait 12 to 14 days between applications, do not double up. Also, the insect damage may be more severe if you fail to control an insect at its juvenile stages.

4. When you spray, apply a sticker-spreader with the pesticide. That will improve the adhesive qualities of your spray and assure better control. If you are dusting, try to cover as much of the foliage as possible.

5. Certain fungicides are compatible with insecticides and may be applied at the same time. Many vegetable sprays contain both if they are general-purpose types.

Certain non-toxic pesticides can be used in the garden. Preparations of Bacillus thuringensis, such as in Thuricide, work well on worms of moths and butterflies.

Vegetable diseases generally are uncommon in

Shaker — often used for bait application against slugs or grasshoppers and for spot weed control.

Hose-end sprayer — simple and easy to use. Just follow the markers on the jar and fill with water to the level of gallons you are preparing.

Compression sprayer — the plastic cones don't rust or corrode. The pump may need new rubber inserts after a year or two of use. They are quite accurate.

our hot, dry regions. Tomato diseases were of concern but have been avoided largely by introducing disease-resistant hybrids. Sulfur is an excellent disease deterrent. In some instances, Captan and Zineb are recommended. I believe, however, that incidence of plant diseases are more an exception than a rule.

The most common vegetable insects and their controls are:

Aphid

Cabbage Looper

Cutworm

Grasshopper

Spider Mite

Squash Bug

Whitefly

TYPE	VEGETABLE AFFECTED	CONTROLS
Aphids	cabbage, cucumbers, melons, potatoes, peas, beans, beets and tomatoes	Malathion, Diazinon
Blister beetles	tomatoes, potatoes, beans	Diazinon
Mexican bean beetle	beans	Sevin
Cabbage worms	cabbage, cauliflower, broccoli	Diazinon Rotenone
Corn ear worm	sweet corn	Sevin
Cucumber beetles	cucumbers, melons, squash and pumpkins	Malathion, Sevin, Rotenone
Cutworms	all crops	Diazinon
Flea beetle	radish, potatoes, turnips and cabbage	Sevin, Rotenone
Grasshoppers	all vegetable plants	Malathion, Diazinon
Colorado potato beetle	potatoes and tomatoes	Sevin, Rotenone
Psyllids	tomatoes and potatoes	Sevin, Malathion
Red spider mites	beans, melons and cucumbers	Kelthane, Malathion
Squash bug	squash, melons and pumpkins	Sevin
Tomato hornworm	tomatoes	Sevin
Tomato fruitworm	tomatoes	Sevin
Whiteflies	tomatoes	Malathion, Resmethrin

INDOOR PLANTS

EVERYONE should experience the joy of indoor gardening. Start out with houseplants that respond readily to nominal care and have a good survival rate. Beginners find a good deal of joy with the following plants:

1. **Pothos** — Appears like a small-leafed philodendron and responds with good growth, with minimal care.
2. **Philodendron** — The small heart-shaped leaf variety is easily grown and will sustain with irregular care for a period of time.
3. **Chinese Evergreen** — This plant develops many new leaves with adequate light and minimal care.
4. **Syngonium** — Needs only mediocre light and care.
5. **Sansevieria** — Although progress may be slow, this plant develops many new leaves readily.
6. **Swedish Ivy** — With relatively good light, this plant develops many scalloped leaves and tendrils.
7. **Chlorophytum** — The green variety is easier than variegated types. Will flower soon and make new offsets.

GARDENING INDOORS WITH TROPICAL PLANTS

Growing tropical plants indoors has gained great popularity in recent years. Many people, including young people, who do not have much outdoor garden space have developed a keen interest in growing greenery for decoration and enjoyment. One measure of this added interest is the fact that the variety of plants offered for indoor gardening has tripled in a short time. Not only have homes and

Chlorophytum

Rocky Mountain Tip:

Indoor gardening is a fun activity for children. One of the first things they need to learn is that daily watering is detrimental to houseplants. Let them feel the soil and learn when it is dry enough to water again. Also teach children to go easy with the use of fertilizers. They don't help a sick plant get well — they help a growing plant grow better.

apartments seen a substantial greening, but office buildings, shopping center malls, and many public facilities also have benefited from "plantscaping," a new business opportunity for recent horticulture graduates.

Since most of us live in traditional homes, not greenhouses, the light and other environmental factors we can provide for a tropical plant are limited. We may easily forget that tropical plants can trace their origins most often to sub-tropical habitats or the rain forests of the tropics. So the conditions we present to our houseplants may be quite different from their needs or native surroundings.

LIGHT

Sufficient Light for Your Plants

Before you select plants for your home, you must determine if the amount of light you can give them compares with the light they would get in the tropics. You can give tropical plants too much light or not enough light, and this often accounts for some of the failures you have with indoor plants. Once you know how much light you have to work with, you can make plant selections that will ensure success.

There are differences between your home and the tropics. The most important one is that the length of daylight in our region varies seasonally much more than in the tropics. Our shortest daytimes in the Rocky Mountains last a little more than nine hours. In the tropics, the shortest daytimes are about 12 hours. Our longest days are about 15 hours, nearly the same as in the tropics. But even then, for plants indoors near a window, you have to deduct at least 30 minutes from the mornings and late afternoons to be realistic about the light level. A plant that can get by with twelve hours of light will not do much with only eight hours. And therein lies the problem. Even next to a south-facing window, you cannot get enough plant activity in eight hours when twelve are needed. So we simply must make

Weeping Fig

choices, and know the limits under which we can operate, even with supplementations of artificial light.

Using Window Light

One of the superior lighting situations for plants in a home is a window with southern exposure. Western exposure is nearly as good, and east comes in third best. But there are not many types of plants that can stand the intensity of our Rocky Mountain area sun at elevations of 4,000 to 10,000 feet. So we must modify the rays of the sun with thin, veiled curtains, or a glass window covering that eliminates much of the glare or light intensity. Some plants, such as cacti and certain succulents, can sustain our strong sun in winter. But they are exceptions, not the rule. There is evidence that a veiled curtain on a south window actually increases the area of light adequacy. It extends the light several feet into a room, thereby increasing the number of plants that may benefit near a south window. Other factors also influence light quality. Light-colored walls in a room increase the light available to plants. Reflection of the sun off a wall opposite a window also increases the light quality in a room. Naturally, any light that can enter a plant room through a skylight, a greenhouse-like attachment, or an atrium also will help.

Pothos

In an average home, you can be successful with many plants. But you will have to use the trial-and-error method over a period of 6 to 12 months to determine which plants are right for your setting. If a plant starts to drop leaf after leaf from the start, it is obviously a poor choice. If a plant gets new leaves that are smaller and longer-stemmed, the problem is a shortage of light. You may be able to correct the situation by using a 40-watt fluorescent tube for three to four hours each night, especially from November to March.

Philodendron

It may be helpful to place marginal plants in the shade outdoors from late May through September. Often, these plants will sulk a little when you bring them back indoors, but they will benefit from their accumulated summer reserves, since they have had the advantage of being in the semi-tropics (your covered patio) for the summer. I have found this evident with many plants that, by necessity, spend October through May in my basement, under purely artificial light. In fact, one of my tables is in such poor light that the 40-odd geraniums just barely survive

Syngonium

until I can place them outdoors again for their deserved respite.

Using Artificial Light

Most homes are not constructed so that they naturally provide enough light for houseplants. This is no one's fault. After all, we expect privacy in our homes that cannot be achieved with walls or panels of glass.

Plants outdoors in the full sun may receive as much as 10,000 foot-candles of light during a bright summer day. Yet, in an average home, one has less than 60 foot-candles the moment we walk away from a window. Most commercial and amateur greenhouses have an average of 1,000 foot-candles of light, which is considerably more than in the living or dining room.

Scientific tests indicate that African violets grow best at 500 to 600 foot-candles. A 40-watt, standard, cool-white fluorescent lamp, 12 inches above the foliage, will provide that amount of light if it is burned for 16 hours a day. Do not keep lights burning 24 hours a day. This may have an adverse effect on some plants. In poorly lighted rooms, we can supplement the natural light with three to four hours of spotlighting. In the evening, spotlights should be placed 3-4 feet away from the plant. This would just about make up the difference and make it possible to grow the plants satisfactorily. The majority of houseplants do well with 12 to 16 hours of artificial light each day. Plants have a tendency to grow unevenly unless they are turned frequently. Turning them will ensure that all sides obtain equal light exposure.

Rocky Mountain Tip:

Most tropical plants and cacti cannot tell the difference between sunlight and artificial light. The only thing that counts is the length of the photoperiod (light period) so the plant has enough light for its manufacture of carbohydrates every day. In short day periods the growth falls off.

Lighting Trays and Cases

Fluorescent tubes are now available in various lengths and strengths. A pair of four-foot, 40-watt tubes spaced about 12 inches apart will provide light for a growing area about 30 inches wide on a table or

Indoor fluorescent light

tray. Wooden or metal plant cases may be prepared from a number of materials. They can be arranged to contain as many as four separate trays and the distance between trays can be regulated from 12 to 18 inches, depending upon the type of plants to be grown and the normal height that they are expected to attain. The quality of construction and finish depends on where the case is to be placed in the house. If placed in a visible area, the product should be sufficiently attractive so it will be a decorative asset and will not detract from the home decor. A portion of a shelf may even be enclosed with glass or plastic, making it possible to grow orchids in the living room area. Houseplants need both blue (ultraviolet) and red light to grow properly. The soft white tubes or bulbs can supply the needed red, while the daylight fluorescents can supply the blue, especially if they are used in combination or pairs.

Special Fluorescent Plant Lights

American manufacturers of electrical equipment and light bulbs have produced a new type of fluorescent tube. Two of the product names are "Gro-Lux," and "Plant-Gro." These tubes were designed especially for the purpose of growing houseplants in poorly lighted portions of the home. These fluorescent tubes combine all the light frequencies and color qualities to satisfy the needs of houseplants. The tubes may be arranged in pairs, threes, and fours, depending on the size of the area to be illuminated. While they appear to be a fine step in the right direction, and make it possible for many amateur gardeners to enjoy a wider assortment of houseplants, they are not the final answer to this craft of light engineering. Undoubtedly, competitive products will be improved over the years to eventually give us a potential of growing anything we wish under average conditions in our homes. The arrival of more usable bulbs in shorter lengths will bring the enjoyment of fine indoor plants to a good many additional gardeners.

It will be well to remember that a houseplant which is artificially lighted will normally require a little more moisture and fertilizer than plants that don't require as much light. The light needs of all plants, especially flowering plants, should be tested in each instance by varying the length of exposure and the distance from the bulb or tube to the foliage. If manual control of lights for houseplants is impractical, a timer switch can be wired into the lighting system. It will automatically control the length of exposure.

Spotlighting of plants in living rooms, halls, and floor planters may be desirable for special effect or decorative purposes. It is essential that the spotlight not be placed too close to the plants, as this may lead to foliage burns which could disfigure the plant and cause permanent damage.

WATERING   How to Water Properly

Question: Are houseplant care gadgets, such as moisture and pH meters or soil test kits, worth buying?
Answer: Some are very helpful and worthwhile; others are just toys. The Plant Moisture Monitor is very useful to me. Larger plants may appear to be dry at the soil surface but have much moisture six inches below. This monitor will tell you precisely when it is time to water. It helps to avoid overwatering, which is a common practice. The purpose of pH monitors is to tell us when the build-up of soluble salts in our pot plants is too high. But if you repot these plants in fresh potting soil once every year or every other year, you will automatically be reducing the pH. Soil test kits at best are unreliable. The test results are variable. You would be wiser to invest the money in fresh potting soil.

Next to improper lighting, improper watering is the second important cause of problems in houseplant culture. Most home gardeners use the "by guess and by gosh" method of watering.

For most of your plants, if you have a well-drained pot or container, the excess water runs out before it can do any harm. But pots that are not drained at all (many of the 12-inch-deep and larger pots) can become waterlogged without your suspecting it, because the surface soil may look or feel dry. One safe way to determine when to water — or not water — is to use a Plant Moisture Monitor (PMM), a $13 gadget made by an electronics firm in Boulder, Colorado. Powered by a nine-volt battery, this electronic tool has two metal prongs that are pushed into the soil. The moisture content of the soil determines the electrical resistance between the two prongs, and the level of moisture is recorded with a colored light. Green means adequate moisture, yellow is the caution signal, and red indicates things are very dry. I sometimes find myself wanting to water, but the green light on my PMM says no.

Large containers that are poorly drained also may benefit if you apply a product such as Oxygen Plus, and you can use the same soil in the pot a good deal longer. Oxygen Plus and similar products contain a base of hydrogen peroxide, which aerates the soil in the lower part of the container.

The condition of your water can also make a difference in plant care. I prefer to run tap water into gallon jugs and place them in our basement for a few days. This adjusts the water temperature to about 60 degrees and allows some of the chemical additives, such as chlorine, to escape. Other water that can be used beneficially for watering indoor plants is bathtub water, laundry water (without chlorine bleaches), collected rain water, and any water previously used in the kitchen (to wash salads and fruits, for example).

Fresh tap water should not be used on houseplants, because it is too cold. And any water that has been treated by chemical softeners usually contains a high level of harmful sodium salts.

Where water supplies are alkaline, a whitish deposit eventually may form on top of the soil. It looks worse than it is. You can easily deal with this problem by removing such alkali deposits with a spoon or spatula. Then just replace with fresh soil of equal depth.

Temperature and Humidity

Besides light and water, several other factors have a direct influence on how well plants grow indoors. One factor is temperature. Most indoor plants tolerate normal fluctuations or changes in temperature from daytime to night. Many homes become quite warm on a normal summer day. But with the proper use of openings, they can be cooled off at night into the upper sixties and low seventies. Depending on their origin, the plants will either feel comfortable — or less so. Plants native to a dry desert, such as certain cacti, accept warm temperatures with low humidity. But plants that originated in a rain forest of an Amazon jungle or on a tropical rain forest island may feel very unappreciated in a home with temperatures of 90-plus degrees and 15 percent humidity.

It is difficult to discuss temperature without discussing humidity, too. These two environmental factors are closely allied. For instance, I have discovered that, at a temperature of 55 degrees, a

HELPING PLANTS ADAPT

houseplant may not feel a 25 percent humidity as severely as it would if the temperature was 75 to 80 degrees. I have also found that lower humidity levels are more readily tolerated by green-foliage plants than by flowering plants. African violets and other Gesneriads are quite particular about this. Other plants, such as pot chrysanthemums, are less noticeably affected. A flowering Easter Lily or Poinsettia will have its flowers much longer if it is kept at 55 to 60 degrees rather than 68 to 70, which, for most people, is normal room temperature. But if the humidity were higher in our homes, we would be less comfortable at higher temperatures. Plants, however, react in the reverse manner. Lower night temperatures not only prolong flower life but allow plants to make a physiological recovery, increase turgidity (the absorption and holding of moisture in the tissue of a plant), and increase bloom color. Outdoors, out of the direct sun, houseplants can tolerate temperatures in the nineties as long as they have water and are allowed to cool off during the night.

Rocky Mountain Tip:

In my experiences with indoor plants I have found that there is a direct relationship between temperature and humidity. Lack of adequate humidity at a comfortable room temperature (68-70 degrees) is much more a problem than at 55 degrees. It appears that at the lower temperatures many plants seem to accept lower humidity easier.

In the average home where humidity is quite low, you should select indoor plants that are known to tolerate this condition. The only alternative is to influence humidity by other means. Gardenias, for instance, should have their pots partially submerged in bowls with standing water. The humidity that is created by evaporation helps the plant to flower successfully. Without this "foot bath," gardenias often bud, but then drop the buds before they can open. Another way to increase humidity around plants is to place the pots on pebble trays that have a constant shallow water level. Plants that are placed together in a small living room area also assist each other by moisture evaporation. They generally like each other's company.

It is also possible to attach a mechanical humidifier to the heating or ventilating system of a home. This should be designed and installation supervised by a competent individual or engineer.

Ventilation

Ventilation is easily overlooked when working with indoor plants. Most of them, particularly flowering plants in bloom, are very sensitive to drafts or heat from registers of a heating system. Forced air has a drying effect on the atmosphere inside a home, while hot water and radiant heat have less influence. Most houseplants are sensitive to natural or blended gases. Some refuse to bloom, while others drop their flower buds before they can open. A sudden turn to yellow foliage on a previously healthy plant could signal a gas leak in the home that needs to be discovered and repaired.

> **Rocky Mountain Tip:**
> Most flowering plants like African Violets and Begonias are very sensitive to drafts. Other foliage plants are less prone to be injured by unexpected air movements or chills unless the situation is quite severe. Freezing temperatures are harmful.

Choosing the Right Soil Mix

POTTING SOIL

Since tropical houseplants usually originated in a rain forest environment, they need a rich potting soil. These soils must have several physical properties that are important to plants. Among these are good structure and cohesion-adequate porosity (the pores that absorb and hold the water) and favorable composition. In addition, soils must have good drainage and aeration, sufficient humus content and microorganisms to break the humus down, proper pH or soil reaction (acid, alkaline or neutral), and quickly usable fertility. The soil pH is a logarithm expression of alkalinity (7.1 to 8.8) or acidity (6.9 down to 3.5), with neutral at 7.0.

Soils can be a composite of organic and mineral ingredients. Organic materials should be partially decomposed, such as peat moss, animal waste, compost, leafmold, earthworm castings, and bark mulch. Mineral-origin materials include clean sand, garden loam, vermiculite (mica), perlite, and Terragreen (expanded clay). The ratios of these materials in a soil mix could vary according to the type of plant for which a soil mix is selected or prepared. Unless you have a lot of these ingredients on hand, there is no advantage to mixing and preparing the soil yourself as you might have done some years ago. Today, the garden industry offers almost all kinds of soil with the features you need. For example, some soil mixes used for plant propagation and for cacti and succulents contain no actual soil at all. Examples are Promix or Metromix. Soils such as Jungle Growth contain a high amount of organic matter. It is very fluffy and supports almost all flowering house plants, with the exception of African violets and orchids. I have used it with great success on foliage plants and have not found it excessively organic. It is widely available and can be asked for by name. Worm castings are useful if mixed with other soils or used as an enrichment at the top of the soil in a pot that does not need complete repotting.

I should also note here that certain organic and inorganic market preparations such as Oxygen-Plus, similar peroxide base products, and Restore, can be applied to larger containers to aerate and/or decay excess organic waste accumulations. This simply bypasses the need for soil replacement, which can be difficult with a large house-plant.

Some succulents such as Jades need a fairly rich organic soil in spite of their fleshy-leaf nature. They are not from a desert and don't like to be potted like a desert plant.

Soils for orchids need fir bark or Osmunda fiber if plastic or clay pots are used. The container must be large enough so new growth is an inch or more inside the rim of the container. Broken clay pieces or Turface chunks are used in the bottom inch of the container.

Indoor hanging baskets must have a highly organic soil makeup to hold moisture, plus a reservoir to hold excess moisture. A plastic liner can be adapted for this purpose. Because dry atmospheric conditions are normal, frequent light watering is suggested to maintain healthy, attractive hanging baskets. The frequency of watering depends largely on prevalent room temperatures.

HOUSEPLANT CONTAINERS

Choosing the Right Pot

Today's marketplace has so many different houseplant containers that no single dealer can offer them all. Plastic containers have been most widely used. They are not ornate, but work well in transferring a plant from the growers to the distributors to garden centers and eventually to your home. Clay pots may be better than plastic, since they allow for some breathing. However, their weight and fragile condition makes shipping more of a risk. Containers may also be made from fiberglass, wood, aluminum, copper, brass, and many other materials. Most noted in recent years are the plant pots that contain a reservoir of extra moisture. They require water replenishment only once a month under average conditions.

Glazed flowerpots frequently are more ornate but have no drainage holes. Ceramic potters don't normally consider this important. You can create a little reserve drainage by placing 1½ inches of sand or gravel in the bottom below the potting mix. Or you can establish a plant in a plastic container, then simply put it inside the more decorative pot.

It's Worth the Effort

Growing houseplants from seed may be a slow process, but it is more fun than always purchasing small plants as a start. It takes patience in some instances, because some seeds are more than reluctant to sprout. But your reward is so worthwhile, and you'll be very proud of your achievement.

To prepare for this project, you need starter mixes and proper containers. Although you can sterilize good garden soil, you will be disappointed with the resulting soil texture. It will be too firm. What you need is a fluffy propagating soil mix, which can be purchased from a garden supplier. Such starter mixes are blends of vermiculite, perlite, fine sphagnum moss and fine bark dust from redwoods. You may want to add some of the time-tested starter mixes, such as Pro-mix, Jiffy Mix, and Readi-Earth. Practically all of these are sterile, requiring no special treatment to control seedling blight (Rhizoctonia) or small bugs such as gnats. The only minor problem with these prepared starter mixes is that they contain no plant food. To compensate, use a small addition of Rapid-gro or Miracle-gro with the water as soon as the plantlets begin to develop good growth. The seeds usually contain enough stored food to get the little plants started. Before sowing, you must moisten the starter mix thoroughly, since a short period of drought can be deadly to seedlings. Tepid water with a little detergent added will speed up the moistening process.

Seed sowing depends on the size of the seed. Some seeds are very large (avocado or coconut) while

GROWING HOUSEPLANTS FROM SEED

others are not much bigger than a speck of dust (Saintpaulia or African violet). Large seed should be covered by enough soil mix (once to twice the width of the seed). Simply poke the seed into the moist soil mixture to the desired depth. Small seeds should be spread over the moistened soil-mix surface.

For plants of tropical or subtropical origin, the temperature for germination is somewhere between 68 and 85 degrees F., depending on their native habitat.

For germinating containers, you can use clean, empty, plastic cottage cheese containers or the lower three inches of a plastic bottle. To control moisture after sowing, put the container in a plastic bag or place a piece of glass over the starter mix. When seedlings germinate, you must hasten to remove the glass and open the plastic cover to allow minimal air circulation. The plastic can be removed soon after germination is complete and the first cotyledons or leaves are visible. You can also use a glass jar, place it lengthwise, and fill it with a fourth of starter mix. Puncture some ventilation holes in the lid before you close the jar.

Avocados can be grown indoors. Two varieties are the Florida avocado with the round, larger seed; and the California avocado, which has a smaller, more pointed pit. I have started avocado seed in several media including water, a wet towel and starter mix. When you start them in water, you need to place three or four toothpicks into the seed so you can support the seed in a glass jar with only the lower half submerged in water. Planting them in a large pot (five to six inches), with starter mix and potting soil in equal parts, is the easiest method. They may take longer to sprout, but eventually they will succeed. Before planting, remove the outer thin skin from the avocado pit. Plant the flat part of the pit down. Leave the tip of the seed exposed, because avocado plants need light as soon as they sprout.

Avocado seeds may take as long as 15 to 16 weeks to grow. Much depends on the fruit's maturity when it was picked. The more mature the fruit was at picking time, the faster the visible germination. But as much of the crop is picked immature for shipping, the seed may take a while to actually grow. The five-to-six-inch container is large enough to accommodate the extensive root growth of the plant. Avocados perform better if they are not transplanted too often. They can be placed outdoors in full shade during the summer. They may develop into a good-

Avocado

sized plant if you are lucky. But if they don't, you need not grieve. You got the seed for free. You can always start another. Have fun with your avocados. They are a free challenge from nature.

The geranium, also known as Pelargonium, is an excellent indoor plant to start from seed. Since the Carefree series won All-America Selection some years ago, many newer hybrids have been added to the list. You should start your seed soon after Christmas to enjoy some blooms indoors before you set the plants into containers or the garden for the summer. It takes about five weeks to sprout geranium seed. It takes another 12 to 15 weeks to get them to flowering size. Give your geranium seedlings as much light as possible. Under artificial light, they need 15 to 16 hours per day. Keep soil moist for germination.

Citrus is another interesting group of seeds to grow, including Calamondin oranges, grapefruit, lemon and lime. You can start these as soon as you take the seeds from the fruit. They take about 15 days or more to sprout and usually more than one year to reach flowering size, unless you have a greenhouse or a conservatory. Don't expect quality fruit from them, but they are very neat green foliage house plants. Wash the seed in tepid water and blot dry between towels, then plant without delay.

Date seeds also respond quite easily if the dates are fresh when you eat them. They are treated much like citrus. For proper germination, the soil mix should be moist, but not saturated.

One of the more interesting seed I have tried is from Clivia (Kafirlily). It is best started in the spring. The temperature needs to be 72 to 75 degrees. In six to seven years, this handsome foliage plant (very similar to Amaryllis) will have a flower stalk with up to 14 blooms every year. Mine usually blooms in early summer. Young plants need two to four hours of sun, but 15 to 16 hours of fluorescent light. Needs average potting soil, likes to be root bound.

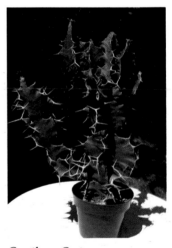

Cowthorn Cactus

Other good projects are African violets, Begonias, Columnea, asparagus fern, Cyclamen and cacti. Have fun — and patience.

Ways to Grow New Plants

VEGETATIVE PROPAGATION

Almost every gardener who devotes some time to houseplants is also an enthusiastic plant propagator. After all, one way to impress one's friends and relations is to bring them a start of something that is already a proven success in your home. Propagation of indoor plants takes patience and know-how.

We propagate plants not only because we want to, but because they need it. After several years, plants in a home become overgrown, even unsightly. They may have only a little green at the top, but otherwise look quite barren. Such plants also may be quite unresponsive to every attempt we make to improve their appearance. They may have become physically damaged by mechanical equipment, by excessive direct sun or by an unfortunate placement in a traffic-sensitive area.

Another very good reason for vegetative reproduction is that a plant may be a mutation. Mutants rarely grow from seed, but a vegetative increase may be 100 percent successful. And plant propagation increases one's holdings and opens an opportunity for trade, exchange or plant giving. Whatever the reason, it is a fascinating hobby.

There are numerous ways for vegetative propagation; however, not all work well in every case. Slips or cuttings of softwood (new growth on plant that later turns to hardwood) are popular. Geraniums, ivies, philodendrons, pothos, Swedish ivy, Wandering Jew and many others are most often propagated in this manner. The important requirement is that the portion to be rooted must have two to three true leaves and must be soft or succulent enough to root easily. Rooting can be promoted with indolebutyric compounds such as Rootone or Hormex. Best temperature for rooting is about 75 to 80 degrees F.

Split-leaf Philodendron

A few indoor plants can also be propagated by division of roots, especially if several shoots exist. A division can be made for each emerging shoot. Immediate repotting is recommended for separated roots, followed by moisture saturation to overcome shock. Sansevieria and Aglaonema are good plants for the root division method.

Leaf cuttings are a popular way to grow new indoor plants. African violets are usually increased in this manner, and will work better in a rich soil rather than in water. Also, most Crassulas or Jade plants propagate easily from leaf sections. A single leaf will do quite well. Most sectionalized cacti, such as Opuntias, root easily if the lower end of a top section is placed in good potting soil. It is advisable to let the point where we break off the cutting "suberize" or dry for a few days before potting it for the rooting process.

Jade

Stem cuttings are not as popular as leaf cuttings, but they are easy. They may take longer than other means of vegetative propagation. Good examples for stem cuttings are Ti plants and Dieffenbachia. We take an old stem of Dieffenbachia and cut it into 2½-inch lengths. The lower end, after drying, is inserted into good house plant soil. In a few weeks after rooting, a small shoot will emerge from near the top and small leaves soon will unfold.

Air layering of a rubber tree is very similar, except that the rooting is achieved while the top portion of the plant is still attached to the mother plant. A cut is made two-thirds of the way into the stem. Rooting hormone is applied to the cut and a toothpick inserted to keep the cut portion separate. Very moist sphagnum moss is then wrapped around the cut area, and plastic is wrapped air-tight around the sphagnum. Soon, roots will fill the moist sphagnum moss.

Offsets also work easily for plant increase. Such plants as Bryophyllum, Chlorophytum or Piggyback plants may have many offsets that are either partly rooted or otherwise easily induced to develop a root system. One of these plants may reproduce several times each year, resulting in a large number of offsets.

One of the newest, most scientific means of plant reproduction is by slivers of clonal meristem tissue. These are always genetically pure and identical to the parent used in reproduction. This relatively novel process should become more popular in the next century.

Rocky Mountain Tip:

Making softwood cuttings or slips is the most popular method of plant propagation. And it is normally very successful. The top three inches of any shoot usually root quite easily in propagating mix or even in water. But you must add a teaspoon of vinegar to a pint of water to hold down little fungi that may rot the cuttings in the water.

POTTING AND REPOTTING HOUSEPLANTS

When cuttings and seedling plants are rooted sufficiently to be on their own in regular potting soil, 2½ to 3-inch pots generally are popular for their initial potting. It is not advisable to overpot a plant simply to avoid having to transplant it more often. "Overpotting" is when a small plant is planted in an oversized pot.

The first step in potting is to cover the drainage hole with a piece of broken clay, then follow with about a half-inch of good potting soil. Now hold the little plant between two fingers of your left hand (if you are right-handed) and add more potting soil while your thumb and ring finger hold the pot. When enough soil has been added to nearly fill the pot, press down with your two fingers that held the plant. Compact the soil and roots slightly, making sure the potting soil is the same depth on the little plant as the rooting medium it was in. Now begin watering by submerging the pot in a container so water can saturate the soil and roots by way of the drainage hole.

Most actively growing houseplants need repotting from time to time. There are some plants that grow very slowly and may not need repotting for several years. And some plants actually suffer until they become potbound. Some common plant examples that prefer to be potbound are Clivia, Chlorophytum, Jade and numerous cacti. A telltale sign for repotting is when lower leaves one by one mature and fall off. It is relatively simple to turn the pot upside down and knock the container loose against a sink or table top. The roots will indicate if the pot has indeed become too small.

When repotting appears needed, it should be done as soon as possible. January and February are good months for this task, but anytime is proper if it will allow the plant to continue or resume healthy growth. Have everything you need ready before you knock the old soil away from the roots of the transplant: A small trowel, a dibble stick (6 to 10-inch round or square piece of wood to depress soil), the larger-sized container, fresh potting soil and a pair of shears or pruners to prune the roots a little if necessary. The actual process of repotting is quite similar to potting seedling plants. You don't have to be as gingerly with more mature plants. Cover the drainage hole with a piece of broken clay pot and

Rocky Mountain Tip:

Any indoor plant that has grown nearly 50% also needs that much more root system to remain normal and healthy. This root system needs a larger container and fresh, rich soil. Most potting soils become overused and stale as well as compacted and salty after a time.

add some potting soil. Now insert the plant, holding it with one hand while adding soil to fill the pot held in the other. In the end, compress the soil at the outside with the dibble stick so it is moderately firmed. If a plant has grown too tall, you may pinch out the top at this time. Watering should be done from a pan from below, through the drainage hole. Leave the repotted plant in this moisture medium for the first 48 hours.

Feeding Indoor Plants

FERTILIZING

Like most other plants, your houseplants need a little fertilizer containing three major plant food elements: nitrogen (N); phosphoric acid (P); and potassium (K). A multitude of brand names are available in the retail trade. According to law, the analysis of fertilizer is expressed in three figures on the label, such as Rapid-gro 23-19-17 or Miracle-gro 15-30-15 or Schultz 10-15-10. Use any of these according to the label instructions and dilute them in water. They are too concentrated for any other use. For acid-loving plants such as azaleas, we need a higher nitrogen analysis, such as Acid-gro 30-12-11 or Mir-acid 30-10-10. The latter also contains small amounts of minor and trace elements such as iron, zinc, copper and boron.

The frequency of fertilizer applications depends on how much growth you want and need, on the time of the year, and on the health condition of the plant. Please do not assume that a plant that gradually has achieved less than attractive appearance needs only a shot of plant food to get well. A patient in a hospital cannot be cured by a good meal alone — and neither can a plant. Nutrients help a plant grow normally and maintain its attractive appearance. But when the environment causes a plant to fail, the cause of the problem must be determined before it can be corrected.

Although most plant food labels for houseplants don't mention it, I recommend that you abstain from feeding them during the months of low light and rest period, December through February. Otherwise, a monthly feeding should keep them well nourished and happy. Excessive applications of houseplant foods or nutrients turn to salts in the soil and could be more harmful than good.

Organic nutrients may also be given to houseplants, although it has not been shown that they are more beneficial than granular or liquid inorganic nutrients. Fish emulsion, bloodmeal or bonemeal are usable, but could create odor problems indoors.

Above all, try to be reasonable and use good common sense when applying houseplant fertilizers.

That brings me to the interesting subject of talking to plants. If you want to, you can — anytime you feel like it. Some folks enjoy it and think it stimulates plants to grow. Music has also been said to help plants to grow. According to the American Academy of Sciences, no evidence has ever been produced to prove or disprove this theory. It is a fact that plants grow near noisy industrial plants and international airports. I guess this proves that sounds do not hurt plants, although it is hard to tell if sounds help them.

> **Rocky Mountain Tip:**
> There are a host of different houseplant foods or fertilizers marketed under various brand names. Most are enough alike so it makes very little difference what product you use. The plants simply cannot tell the difference. They value your care. Organic fish emulsion is no better than any other food. It may just be more expensive.

PINCHING, TRAINING AND SHAPING

Promoting Orderly Growth

Pinching may be unpopular with many home gardeners who like to observe or even brag a little about the maximal growth of a houseplant. Pinching is just a control over a plant that is expected to occupy a designated space or area but which, for reasons we sometimes fail to understand, does the unexpected. Such excessive growth can be curtailed by pinching. All we really attempt is to encourage the plant to make new growth in a more orderly fashion. I presume ivies and philodendrons need such pinching most often. On occasion, a whole branch or twig of a plant needs to be removed for the sake of neat appearance. I call this pruning. Disbudding would only relate to flowering plants. But it is rarely needed, because most faithful indoor gardeners are proud enough when one of their plant friends decides to bloom. They don't want to disturb the plant or in any way control the flowering. I know I would not disbud except perhaps on a gardenia that may set as many as three or four buds in the same terminal. Then, reduction in numbers will improve flowering.

Some plants, such as twining ivies, philoden-

Hoya

drons, pothos and others, may benefit from being trained to a small support or trellis. Some Hoyas and Syngonium also need a little help with a pole to achieve better light exposure.

> **Rocky Mountain Tip:**
>
> Washing and cleaning larger houseplant foliage from time to time will remove dust or accumulated grease deposits. The best way is with a mild detergent solution and a soft rag or a sponge.

Plan Ahead

Have you given any thought about vacations and how they may affect your houseplants? Well, in most cases, you can make advance preparations for them. In fact, an absence of a week or ten days might even be a relief for them.

Your indoor plants can easily be prepared for your ten-day vacation. Some plants don't need any help at all. These include all cacti, most succulents, the Jade plants, Chlorophytums and Sansevierias. African violets are much thirstier and need special help. Many growers use wicked containers, with the wick drawing moisture constantly from a reservoir below. You can also place your African violets individually in plastic bags, add an inch of water to the soil, let the remains drain into the bag to be used later, and place them in the same spot as before. Do not close the bags at the top. For those that are slightly overpotted, add extra water in a saucer and fill it to the rim after the soil in the containers has been saturated with water. You even can add a small amount of peat moss at the soil surface. This, too, will prevent moisture loss from the soil and will keep the plant moist a few days longer. If these plants get a little dry before you return, don't fret over that. Even in the tropics, they must go through dry periods and they do it ever so well. You can also place a very large plant which is in a slightly undersized container in a water bucket and add enough water to last for two weeks. Placing plants in slightly subdued light also helps them overcome drought a little better.

Avoid the use of plant foods on your houseplants before you depart. You can feed them normally upon your return. You can also use large plastic bags or trash bags and set them up for several plants. Fold them back to the top of the plant pots, so

VACATION PLANT CARE

Schefflera

you do not exclude normal light. Don't depend on electricity. Power outages are often caused by high demands in hot weather or by thunderstorms. Inspect your houseplants carefully for insect problems, especially those that are placed together in a large trash bag. Where plants are close, they can have quite a multiplication of insects in two weeks. Spray against houseplant pests before you depart, and inspect for culprits again carefully after your return.

For longer periods, a friend, housesitter or neighbor surely can be trusted with the watering of your indoor plants on a reciprocal basis. You do it for them, and they do it for you. It works very well for many gardeners.

DISH GARDENS

A dish garden is an arrangement of different plants, generally in a bowl-like container with three to four inches of good, well-drained soil. One common mistake in the construction of dish gardens is that they are made too shallow, which makes it difficult for them to hold enough soil for the plants. Lack of soil causes early root competition, allowing the most vigorous to continue at the expense of the less aggressive ones. Therefore, dish gardens must be adequate in width and depth.

Another common error with dish gardens is combining plants in a single container which do not have similar temperature, soil, light and moisture requirements. Anytime we water such a dish garden, we are bound to overwater some plants and underwater others. Plants which have the most interesting leaf surface textures and forms often are not usable because of differences in basic cultural needs.

Taking Care of a Dish Garden

Though plants in dish gardens may fit together culturally, they still may differ in their basic growing patterns. We can control this to a degree by timely pruning and pinching. We also can, in time, remove a single plant from the combination and replace it with a similar plant, only smaller in size, without completely rebuilding the dish garden. Omission of fertilizer applications will also slow up certain plants and allow others to catch up with them. The type of soil used in a dish garden depends on the plants used as well as drainage. If the drainage is shallow, the soil must be fairly coarse and have a one-inch base of gravel or crushed rock underneath.

The dish garden should be strategically placed

so that plants within it obtain enough daily light ex-posure to prevent spindly growth. A window pane must not be more than eight inches above the rim of the container. Consider the dish garden location before purchasing plants. A thorough evaluation of the cultural conditions in the selected spot will determine the plants that will succeed in the dish garden.

How to Arrange Plants in a Dish Garden

The arrangement of plants within a dish garden is very important. The same principles that apply to artistic floral arrangements are also followed in the composition of dish gardens. There must be a focal point that draws to the eye, such as notable color, form, or leaf surface. Other supporting plants should be relative to each other in proper scale, placement, and visual weight. The surface texture, density, and shape of foliage are also important considerations in order to obtain a pleasing end product. The plants must also be relative in size or scale with the container of the dish garden. Very tall plants do not look natural in a very low bowl, while very short plants do not appear well arranged in a rather large planter. The use of small stones, sticks, or cones often enhances a dish garden's appearance.

Plants Suitable for Dish Gardens

Plants in dish gardens should not grow too fast, so you won't have to prune or replace them often. Examples of plants suitable for dish gardens: Pep-peromias, Aluminum plant, Sansevieria hahnii, dwarf ivies, Aglaonema, Pothos, Cryptanthus, Tolmiea (Piggyback plant) and any combination of cacti and/or succulents.

TERRARIUMS

A terrarium is a dish garden which uses a container such as a glass bowl, aquarium, or similar enclosed glass container. Most terrariums are open at the top, though this is not absolutely essential. A Wardian case is a similar structure, which contains some means of maintaining humidity and temperature, which is not done with terrariums.

Large brandy snifters have become popular for the arrangement of house plants. They are decorative and of a distinct advantage when placed on circular tables, where a round container is much more natural than a square-shaped one. The space that is available for planting in a brandy snifter is very limited and utmost care must be used in plant selection. You should choose small plants that are slow growing.

Terrariums are most adaptable to those types of houseplants that love a warm, humid situation and often cannot be grown in a dish garden or in an ordinary dwelling. Cacti and succulents are not thought to be good plant subjects for terrariums because of the high moisture condition that generally prevails. Covering the terrarium would also cause so much condensation on the sidewalls of the container that it is simply not suggested.

Planting the Terrarium

To plant a terrarium, you need a few special hand tools, such as tweezers and a dibble. The construction of the terrarium is slow and tedious. Apply a one-inch layer of gravel or crushed clay pieces at the bottom of the container. A one-inch layer of sharp sand should follow, then a porous, but rich, potting soil mixture is added about one and a half inches deep. The potting mixture is temporarily placed in a mound to one side and used as each plant subject is placed in its new spot. Each plant must be small enough to remain within an inch or so of the top rim of the container but must be well past the seedling stage, because there is no room for plant babies in such an arrangement. The tweezers then are used to place each plant carefully in the sand. Provide enough potting soil mix to cover up the root system. A teaspoon eases the soil handling job. The use of peatmoss is sometimes suggested but not really necessary because the humidity and moisture in the container are usually sufficiently high. Some terrariums are electrically heated — thus, especially suited for plant and seed propagation. They are sold as miniature greenhouses. Small artistic figurines are sometimes added to a terrarium to create additional interest and attraction.

Taking Care of a Terrarium

The proper location of a terrarium is out of the direct sun but in very good light. Watering must be done sparingly and only when the soil is notably dry. The best way to determine the watering need is by digging into the soil with a spoon. If the soil appears dry, apply some water and check again in a few hours. Soon you will be able to tell the normal water needs of a terrarium simply by observing the soil color. The easiest way to ruin a terrarium is to keep the soil continuously wet. Standing water in a terrarium is fair assurance that the plants will not survive long. Normal houseplants are not able to grow in waterlogged conditions. Keep removing any dead leaves that naturally may appear. Also, any plant that reaches above the rim of the container has grown out of scale of the entire plant arrangement and either must be severly pruned or removed and replaced with a new, smaller or scaled plant specimen. Fertilization sould be administered only occasionally, whenever the general appearance of the plants indicate that a supplemental feeding is needed.

Plants Suitable for Terrariums

Terrariums are more difficult to control than dish gardens. Examples of good terrarium plants: Flame violet, African violet, Maidenhair fern, Baby's Tears, Croton, and mosses.

Controlling House Plant Pests

INSECTS

Houseplant pests usually are introduced from the outside, rather than invading the home by themselves. Any plant that is added to your collection should, therefore, be isolated for about 30 days and again carefully inspected for any symptoms that could indicate an infestation.

Most houseplant insects are sucking insects. A number of houseplant pests may occur, but most of them can be controlled with modern insecticides. If a plant of little individual value is badly infested with a certain insect, it should be discarded without delay. This will prevent further spread of the insect to other, more valuable plants. Also, the use of sterilized soil usually helps prevent infestations of springtails and earthworms. These pests are no great problem but are somewhat annoying.

Insect buildups can also be prevented by periodically washing the foliage of all houseplants. Use a mild detergent solution prepared in a bucket or tub so the foliages of entire plants may be submerged in the soapy water for about 30 seconds. While this does not prevent infestation, it discourages insect buildup on plants.

Another effective method of controlling insects on houseplants is with an insecticide dip. Prepare the dip according to directions. Usually a tablespoon of 50 percent Malathion for each gallon of liquid will give good results. Simply dip the foliage of each plant into the solution for about 30 seconds. Rubber gloves should be worn for your own protection. A cardboard disc, held over the rim of the pot, will prevent soil from falling out of the container when it is turned upside down.

Handpicking a few insects when they first get stared is a good stopgap — if it works. Usually it does not serve for very long, and sterner measures soon must be undertaken. Alcohol may be used on a toothpick, match, swab, or a commercial cotton applicator tip for the removal of aphids or mealy bugs.

The following insects are the ones most commonly found on houseplants:

Aphids: Softbodied, sucking insects 1/16 to 1/8 inch long. They usually feed on newest growth and tender flowerbuds. Vary greatly in color. Both winged and wingless forms are found. Aphids excrete a sticky, honeydew that makes foliage appear shiny. Malathion and pyrethrum sprays or dips are good control. Orthene spray protects the plants.

Mites: both the red spider mites and the cyclamen mites can be found feeding on houseplants. They are so tiny that they are difficult to notice with the naked eye. Red mite-infested leaves take on a speckled grey-green appearance. Cyclamen mites cause deformed or stunted new growth. Best control for both is a dip of Kelthane or Malathion. Kelthane is the more effective chemical.

Mealybugs: Softbodied insects that appear as though they were dusted with flour because of their wax covering. They suck plant juices from stems and leaves. The best control is Malathion and Resmethrin.

Scales: Small, stationary insects that suck plant juices from either leaves or stems. They vary from 1/16 to 1/4 inch in size. Colors range from white to black. some are softshelled, others hardshelled. Add 1/2 teaspoon of household detergent to two teaspoons of 50 percent Malathion in a gallon of water and dip or spray for control. Orthene is also effective.

Sowbugs: Sowbugs have oval, grey to brown-segmented, shell-like bodies. When disturbed, they roll into a ball. They are more active at night, as they feed on decaying organic matter and small roots of houseplants. Control can be achieved with Diazinon.

Whiteflies: These also are sucking insects that feed mostly on the underside of leaves. Adults are 1/16 inch long and winged. Infested leaves become pale, turn yellow, and drop off. Honeydew is excreted over surfaces where both adults and young feed. Dipping or spraying with Malathion or

Rotenone solution is recommended. Resmethrin is also effective.

Springtails and Gnats: Use a chemical pest-strip with Vapona (DDVP). Plants may also be sprayed with hand or pressure sprayers, but this should be avoided inside the home. A garage is satisfactory or, weather permitting, the outdoors which is even safer. Aerosols are sold under many commercial labels. They generally are considered reliable but must be held at least 18 inches from the plant to avoid freezing damage from the spray mist.

Controlling Houseplant Diseases

DISEASES

Houseplant diseases are difficult to control, but fortunately, they are rare. The outbreak of any houseplant disease generally indicates irregular environmental conditions.

Here are the most common diseases and ways to control them:

Mildew: This fungus looks like a white powder on the surface of leaves and flowerbuds. It is encouraged when plants have been kept too wet, when they are too crowded, when there is insufficient ventilation, and also, when plants are kept in too dry an atmosphere. Control may be achieved by correcting faulty growing conditions and by dips or sprays using Funginex or Benomyl.

Stem rot or Root rot: This decay of stems or roots is often caused from overwatering or poorly drained conditions that may exist in a container which has no drainage hole at the bottom. It is best to discard plants that display this type of disease symptom. Control is not easy but may be tried with sulfur or Funginex.

Botrytis blight: This fungus disease causes a brownish-grey mold — first spotting, then later rotting the leaves. Often, excessively high humidity encourages this condition. It also affects stems at later stages. Funginex may be tried to control botrytis blight.

Discoloration of foliage: This hardly could be considered a disease condition, although the symptoms are frequently similar to fungus diseases or insect damage they are easily mistaken for them. Foliage discoloration may be due to internal (systemic) or external causes. Frequently, insufficient light or inadequate humidity are causes for this type of problem. Internal causes may include improper fertilization, wrong soil reaction, or irregular soil moisture conditions. When tips of leaves discolor, it is most often due to drafts, dry atmospheric surroundings, or inadequate light. An affected plant should be moved to different areas in the home to determine, by trial and error, which location is most favorable. Diseased portions or tips of leaves are unsightly and can be removed with scissors.

> **Rocky Mountain Tip:**
>
> One of the most common houseplant pests is annoying but harmless. It is generally known as a fungus gnat. They often enter a home with a new bag of potting soil or a new plant. A plastic pest strip set up near the suspected plants will eliminate most of these little pests in 36 hours. Repeat after two weeks.

THE 15 BEST HOUSEPLANTS

Sansevieria

Syngonium

My Favorite Selections

I really don't understand why all "best" lists have to be on the basis of ten. By describing my 15 top choices for you, I can make more gardeners happy and present a better selection for all.

My selections are made on the basis of how well I can grow that plant under my own mediocre conditions in our own home — how well it responds to nominal light and what care the plant needs on a year-around basis. Soil and water needs are also considered, along with growth habit and appearance over several years. Many of my plants have decorative qualities, but that should not be a prime consideration.

1. **Sansevieria** — there is no question that the Sansevieria or Snake plant is the most durable of all houseplants. I think it is the only one that can be grown in a closet. If you give it too much light, it turns yellow. Two sizes (tall and squatty) and several interesting leaf variegations are available. It needs little water and light and only moderate warmth and low humidity.

2. **Syngonium or Nephthytis** — This one is also called Arrowleaf plant because of the shape of its leaves. It is my top choice for the office desks which are not next to a window. It needs only minimal light and humidity, moderate warmth and watering.

3. **Philodendron** — The Philodendron family deserves special mention. The size of their

Philodendron

Jade

Rubber Plant

leaves vary from the small-leafed climbing Philodendron scandens to larger leaves of Philodendron cordatum. All are decorative and easy to care for. All need moderate light and temperature and medium humidity, but they can be kept fairly moist. They should be repotted every 12 months in good organic soil.

4. **Jades** — The Jades or Rubber plants are tough succulents from South Africa that thrive in full sun. They prefer a well-drained, sandy soil with rich organic matter mixed in. This plant should be kept moist during the growing period from April to July. Overwatering is not beneficial. Mature plants should be kept in the same container to restrict growth.

Pothos

5. **Pothos** — Pothos or Devil's Ivy is often mistaken for Philodendron. It is popular for its green and variegated foliage. It is a plant that grows well in mediocre light, low humidity and moderate warmth. It should be kept moist, not wet. It can go for a week or more without watering.

6. **African Violets** — African violets or Saintpaulias are the only good flowering plants among my top 15. Violets can be grown under fluorescent light, but prefer a cool north window. Repotting every six months is essential. Soil should never be dry, but humidity is not very essential.

7. **Dieffenbachia** — Also called Dumbcanes, dieffenbachias are huge, large-leafed plants.

Dieffenbachia

Chlorophytum

Norfolk Island Pine

Many varieties have spectacular leaf variegations. Avoid cold water and keep the plant warm in winter. It prefers moderate humidity and moist soil. Keep pot well drained.

8. **Chlorophytum or Airplane Plant** — This one makes spectacular offsets that propagate very easily. Variegated forms need much more light than the green variety. A cool room of low humidity and fair light are all it needs. Keep soil moist but not too wet.

9. **Norfolk Island Pine or Araucaria** — This is our indoor Christmas tree. With fair light, low temperature around 55 degrees F., and some humidity, it benefits from good periodic watering. It loves a shady patio in the summer.

10. **Cacti** — Cacti of all forms and descriptions are the most underrated houseplants for sunny windows. They don't grow very fast, but they don't mind months of neglect. Many mamillarias will bloom better if you don't water them in winter. Otherwise, keep them warm and bright.

11. **Grape Ivy** — Grape ivy or Cissus needs fair light, medium warmth, not much humidity, but moist soil. You can take cuttings in late summer to make more plants.

12. **Swedish Ivy** — Swedish ivy or Plactranthus and I became acquainted at a cousin's garden in Laguna Beach many years ago when not a single book on houseplants even listed it. Today, it is our best hanging basket vine. It tolerates heat, dry air and mediocre light. What more can you ask of a plant? Propagate clippings in the spring

Cactus garden

Hoya

Clivia

Dracaena

and late summer to keep it from growing too long.

13. **Clivia or Kafir Lily** — This was my grandmother's parlor plant, and it was of mammoth proportions. If kept dry and unattended in winter, it will bloom for three weeks in late spring or early summer. I like it better than Amaryllis. Moderate temperature, fair light and low humidity suffice.

14. **Dracaena** — Dracaenas in several variegated forms are good, faithful indoor plants. Mediocre light and humidity should be supplemented by warm temperature and moist soil. Dracaena marginata is the most popular of the lot.

15. **Wax Plant** — The Wax plant or Hoya also survives in semi-darkness and low humidity, but it should be kept moist and warm. Our wax plant in the living room never blooms. Given a sunny window, it will bloom handsomely. My Hoya bella in our hanging basket blooms on the patio all summer long.

There you have my top 15. Enjoy as many as you can.

AFRICAN VIOLETS

The African violet or Saintpaulia was discovered in the wilds of East Africa in 1894 and came to the United States via Europe. But until the 1930's, it gained no particular interest. Since then, the momentum has increased at such a pace that today the African violet is claimed to be the most popular houseplant in the United States. It is a pot plant of great versatility, adapting to almost any home situation where adequate light can be found.

Even though early crosses and hybrids resulted from a few dedicated Saintpaulia breeders, the names of some of the great early varieties can still be found in literature and in local and regional garden shows. Among these are Blue Boy, Amethyst, Horseman, Double Blue Boy, Neptune, Du Pont, Lavender Pink, Blue Girl and Pink Beauty.

Crosses, observed mutations and variegations of foliage have since taken over, and a great multitude of leaf forms, leaf patterns and flower forms have been created and have become popular. Colors now range from deep blue-violet to the palest blues, from deep purple to the palest lavender, from deep red violet to lavender pink and from bright red to the palest pink, with white as the purest.

Some African violet growers claim they obtain flowers all the time. Others like to state their problems as they are. Some larger flowered varieties, such as the Du Ponts, do not flower as profusely as many others. As a nationally accredited Master Judge, I must always consider the floriferousness or the number of flowers present for maximum score. About 30 to 35 per plant would in many instances warrant a near-perfect score. But the foliage or leaf pattern, its uniformity and perfection in the arrangement, easily determines who the top growers are.

Adequate light is one of the basic requirements for African violets. In our region, the intensity of summer sunlight must be diffused by veiled curtains to prevent damage to plants. East and west windows are preferable, as long as there are no outside shadows that compete with our normal light source.

African violets like to be warm. Up to 72 degrees in the daytime and 62 to 65 at night are excellent ranges. Violets don't like heat; if it gets to the high eighties or nineties, African violets sulk.

African violets prefer a good constant but moderate supply of water. Many commercial growers have them on wicks all the time. The wicks draw up moisture to the soil and roots from a reservoir below. Saucer watering also is generally accepted if the use of wicks is impractical. Water should be of room temperature and may have a nutrient solution added. Once in a while, violets should be watered from the top to wash away excess salts that may occur from bottom or wick watering.

Clean foliage is essential to obtain maximum carbohydrate-energy production by plants. When cleaning is needed (about twice a month), you can wash off the dust and grime with a kitchen sink shower. You can cover up the soil with plastic so it does not become unduly saturated.

Humidity is a factor we cannot solve easily. African violets love a 60 to 75 percent humidity. Our ability to match this is low. If you have enough plants near one another, they may help bring the humidity up a little higher. Keeping the temperature slightly lower also may be helpful in equalling the normal humidity needs of plants.

Unless you have a lot of violets, you can use prepared African violet soil mixes. If you have many, you may want to mix your own soil. This should contain equal parts of peat moss or leafmold and rich potting soil plus half a part by volume of vermiculite and/or clean sand. Some old animal manure may be used as part of the peatmoss or leafmold part. The pH should be between 6.5 and 7.5

African violets accept any fertilizer that is relatively high in phosphoric acid and has less nitrogen and potash. Prepared foods such as Rapid-gro, Miracle-gro, Hyponex, Peters, Black Magic and many others are suitable. Some growers like to use a mild solution of nutrients all the time; others believe nutrients should be provided twice a month. I suggest you experiment a little and settle with whatever produces reliable results.

When you pot or repot African violets, don't be too generous. They bloom much more readily if the

"shoe fits tight." For this reason it may be necessary to replace the soil more often than with most other houseplants.

For home enjoyment, it does not really matter if your violets are single-crown or have multiple crowns. But if you intend to enter your lovely plants at the local flower show, they must be single-crown or may face elimination by the judges.

Although African violets may have some rare special problems, most of their insect and disease control is covered adequately in this chapter.

African violets have some fancy Gesneriad relatives. Many aficionados of violets enjoy growing some of the others, also. Sinningia and Rechsteineria are tuberous rooted — or fleshy-stem rooted and both require a little more light than other violets. But otherwise the culture is about the same. Episceas are also popular. Their foliage is very attractive, ranging from shades of green to copper and brown. They, too, respond well to identical care of African violets. Columneas are also quite popular. Many cascade beautifully and have lovely flowers. There are several other Gesneriads available, but their distribution is a bit more limited. They are all a challenge for indoor gardeners who have fair to good light. Your thumb will turn a little greener when you try them.

Index